and insider tips

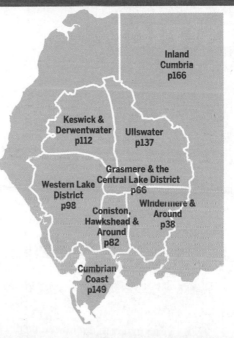

Inland
Cumbria
p166

Keswick &
Derwentwater
p112

Ullswater
p137

Grasmere & the
Central Lake District
p66

Western Lake
District
p98

Windermere &
Around
p38

Coniston,
Hawkshead &
Around
p82

Cumbrian
Coast
p149

VITAL PRACTICAL INFORMATION TO
HELP YOU HAVE A SMOOTH TRIP

Glossary

THIS EDITION WRITTEN AND RESEARCHED BY

Oliver Berry   APR   2012

welcome to The Lake District

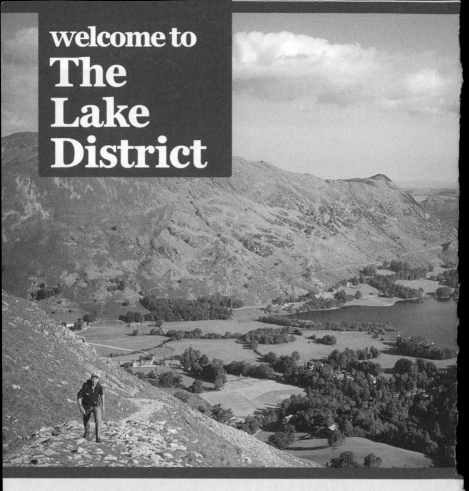

The Home of British Hiking

To appreciate the grandeur of the views, you need to get out on the fells. Hikers have been coming to the Lake District ever since the early days of Victorian tourism, and walking on the fells remains an essential part of the Lakeland experience. If there's one man whose spirit looms largest over the history of hiking in the Lake District, it's Alfred Wainwright: a passionate hill walker, painstaking cartographer and gifted writer, whose original Pictorial Guides are still the preferred choice of many walkers, despite the fact that they're getting on for six decades old.

Land of History

Though modern Cumbria is a relatively young county, formed in 1974 from the old districts of Cumberland and Westmorland, its history stretches back into Britain's ancient past. Stone Age tribes, pagan druids, Viking settlers and generations of hill farmers have all left their own mark on the landscape, and for much of the Middle Ages this was a region plagued by conflict, ominously dubbed 'The Debatable Lands'. From ancient stone circles to lavish stately homes, it's a place where history often seems to be written right into the landscape.

For lovers of the great outdoors, nowhere in Britain can compare to the Lake District. It's home to some of the nation's most breathtaking natural landscapes, as well as its most beloved national park.

(left) View over Lake Ullswater
(below) Traditional pub in Cumbria

Food & Ale

Eating out in the Lake District is always a treat, whether it's settling in for a pint at a country inn, popping in for tea and cake at a village cafe or dressing up for dinner at a Michelin-starred hotel. The food here is full of heart and soul, and if you're searching for the stickiest toffee pudding, the crumbliest gingerbread, the hoppiest ales and the richest Sunday roast, you won't find anywhere to beat it in Britain.

Grandstand Views

'No part of the country is more distinguished by its sublimity,' mused the grand old bard of the lakes, William Wordsworth, and two centuries on his words still ring true. Britain's largest national park is a place where you can almost hear the creak and grumble of Mother Nature's cogs at work, with a parade of panoramic landscapes that never fail to fire the imagination: wild hilltops, rugged valleys, misty tarns, emerald fields and shafts of sunlight breaking through the cloud. The Lake District has always been a place of inspiration and escape, and it's high time you found out why.

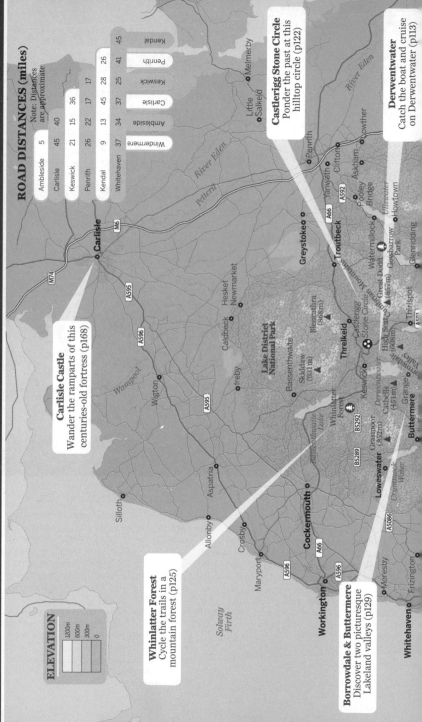

ELEVATION
- 1200m
- 600m
- 300m
- 0

ROAD DISTANCES (miles)
Note: Distances are approximate

	Windermere	Ambleside	Carlisle	Keswick	Penrith	Kendal
Ambleside	5					
Carlisle	45	40				
Keswick	21	15	36			
Penrith	26	22	17	17		
Kendal	9	13	45	28	26	
Whitehaven	37	34	37	25	41	45

Carlisle Castle
Wander the ramparts of this centuries-old fortress (p168)

Whinlatter Forest
Cycle the trails in a mountain forest (p125)

Borrowdale & Buttermere
Discover two picturesque Lakeland valleys (p129)

Castlerigg Stone Circle
Ponder the past at this hilltop circle (p122)

Derwentwater
Catch the boat and cruise on Derwentwater (p113)

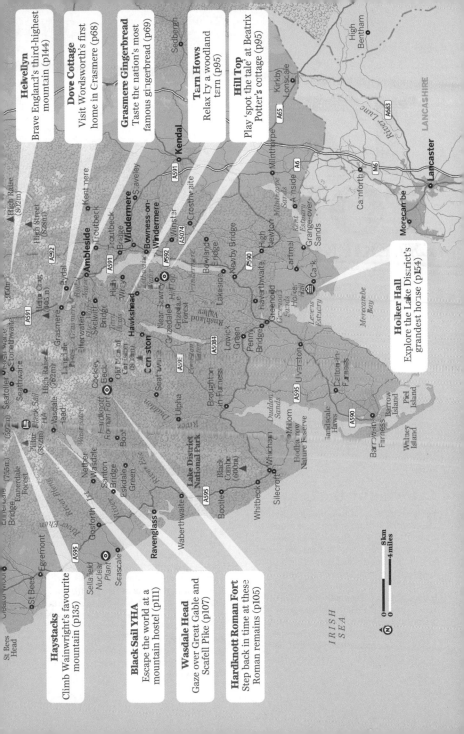

Helvellyn
Brave England's third-highest mountain (p144)

Dove Cottage
Visit Wordsworth's first home in Grasmere (p68)

Grasmere Gingerbread
Taste the nation's most famous gingerbread (p69)

Tarn Hows
Relax by a woodland tarn (p95)

Hill Top
Play 'spot the tale' at Beatrix Potter's cottage (p95)

Holker Hall
Explore the Lake District's grandest house (p154)

Haystacks
Climb Wainwright's favourite mountain (p135)

Black Sail YHA
Escape the world at a mountain hostel (p111)

Wasdale Head
Gaze over Great Gable and Scafell Pike (p107)

Hardknott Roman Fort
Step back in time at these Roman remains (p105)

IRISH SEA

LANCASHIRE

17 TOP EXPERIENCES

Cruising on the Lakes

1 You couldn't come to the Lake District and not venture out on at least one of its namesake lakes. Cruising has been a popular pastime since the mid-19th century, and stately boats still putter out across several lakes, including Windermere, Coniston and Ullswater. For scenery, though, it's tough to top Derwentwater (p113). Studded by wooded islands and fringed by fells, it was one of Beatrix Potter's favourite lakes, and seen from the deck of the Keswick Launch on a crisp autumn evening, it's easy to understand why.

Climbing Helvellyn via Striding Edge

2 The ascent of Striding Edge to the summit of Helvellyn (p144) is renowned as one of the most thrilling fell walks in the Lake District, and rightly so. It's a classic, halfway between a challenging hike and a full-blown mountain scramble: from Glenridding or Patterdale, the route climbs up along a classic knife-edge arête, formed eons ago by a long-disappeared glacier. There are dizzying drops to either side, but the views are mind-bogglingly grand – and they get even better as you make your descent along Swirral Edge.

Castlerigg Stone Circle

3 Those ancient Britons certainly knew a good building site when they saw one. Avebury and Stonehenge might steal the limelight, but this hilltop circle (p122) near Keswick beats them hands-down when it comes to location. Nestled on a high plateau, ringed by a natural amphitheatre of mountains, it has the most impressive setting of any of Britain's ancient monuments. Although the circle's exact purpose remains unclear, it just goes to show that location, location, location was just as important in Neolithic Britain as it is today.

Dove Cottage & Rydal Mount

4 Wordsworth's home at Dove Cottage (p68) has become a mecca for the Romantic movement, but the poet actually spent most of his life at Rydal Mount (p74). Both houses are open to the public, and allow a fascinating glimpse into the private life of one of England's greatest poets. The houses are littered with fascinating artefacts – look out for William's picnic box, spectacles and ice-skates as you wander round – and don't miss the chance to sit in the summer house where he liked to read his latest verse aloud.

Whinlatter Forest

5 England's only mountain forest (p125) covers the hilltops to the west of Keswick, 790m above sea level. Created by the Forestry Commission in an attempt to make up for timber shortages following WWI, the forest has since become one of Cumbria's most popular woodlands, with mountain-bike trails, a tree-top assault course and forest walks to explore. It's also become an important habitat for the endangered red squirrel – you can watch live video feeds from squirrel nests in the Whinlatter visitor centre.

Hardknott Roman Fort

6 The Roman fort of Mediobogdum (p105) guarded the vital supply route from the Cumbrian coast to the forts along Hadrian's Wall. Perched on one of Lakeland's highest passes, surrounded by empty hilltops stretching to every horizon, it must have been one of the loneliest postings in the Roman Empire – especially since most of the conscripts came from the Dalmatian Coast, now in present-day Croatia. Not much of the fort remains, but you can still make out its essential layout, and the views to the coast are wonderful.

Wasdale Head

7 It's official: Wasdale Head (p107) is the nation's favourite view (or at least it was according to a recent TV poll). Popularity contests aside, it's hard to better Wasdale in terms of scenic drama. Gouged out by glaciers, the valley is surrounded by a parade of some of England's highest summits, including the daddy of them all, Scafell Pike. It's also one of the few places where it's genuinely possible to appreciate the majesty of the Lakeland landscape without actually having to slog your way to a summit. Wasdale Head Inn, at the head of Wasdale

ASHLEY COOPER/ALAMY ©

Carlisle Castle

8 Carlisle's rust-coloured castle (p168) bears the scars of several centuries of conflict, a reminder of the troubled days when Scotland and England were still arch enemies and marauding bands of Border Reivers regularly plundered the frontier. Clambering along the battlements is a great way to cast your mind back into the city's war-torn past. Look out for the castle dungeons and the infamous Licking Stone, supposedly worn smooth by parched defenders during one of the castle's many sieges.

Traditional Inns

9 There's nothing like warming your toes in front of a flickering fire, pint of ale in hand, and you'll find the Lake District has some of the cosiest inns anywhere in England (p207). In days gone by they would have provided welcome refuges for hill farmers and coach travellers, but these days they're more likely to be frequented by hikers and bikers. While some have gone down the gastropub route, the best have remained true to their roots: slate floor, crackling hearth, wonky beams, real ale and all.
The Kings Arms, Hawkshead

Borrowdale & Buttermere

10 The neighbouring valleys of Borrowdale and Buttermere (p129) are for many people the loveliest of the Lake District's dales. From Keswick, the valley of Borrowdale rolls past a patchwork of green fields and drystone walls all the way to Honister Pass, before tumbling down the other side towards the gleaming lakes of Crummock Water and Buttermere. These twin valleys are equally beloved by hikers and sightseers, and on quiet autumn evenings feel a world away from the hustle and bustle of the outside world.

Tarn Hows

11 Mother Nature's done a grand job of creating the scenery in this corner of Britain, but occasionally it doesn't hurt to give her a helping hand. Tarn Hows (p95) looks like a postcard that's come to life: a just-so combination of quiet tarn and sun-dappled woodland, perfectly framed by the surrounding hills. In fact, if it looks a little too good to be true, that's because it is: it's actually a superb example of the art of Victorian landscape gardening, created by local landowner James Garth Marshall in 1862.

Hill Top

12 The fairy-tale farmhouse of Hill Top (p95) is a must-see for any Potterite. It was purchased by Beatrix Potter in 1906, funded by the proceeds of her first book, and was used regularly as an artistic retreat until she finally moved for good to nearby Castle Farm in 1913. The house inspired many of her best-known tales, and fans will spot numerous elements from her books – most notably in the kitchen garden, where you half expect the fluffy tail of Benjamin Bunny to pop out at any minute.

11

12

The Summit of Haystacks

13 Alfred Wainwright fell head over heels for the Lake District while walking on Orrest Head in 1930, and his seven Pictorial Guides to the Lakeland Fells remain the guidebooks of choice for many walkers. He died in 1991, and his ashes were scattered at the top of his favourite mountain, Haystacks (p134). It's become a point of pilgrimage for people wishing to pay their respects to Wainwright – or AW, as he's affectionately known to his readers.

View from the top of Haystacks

Scenic Railways

14 A century ago the countryside would have echoed with the sound of chuffing steam engines, transporting timber, minerals, slate and iron from the Lakeland mines to England's rapidly expanding industrial cities. Several of these railways have been saved for prosperity, including the Ravenglass and Eskdale Railway on the Cumbrian Coast, and the Lakeside and Haverthwaite Steam Railway near Windermere. But for true connoisseurs, there's only one train trip that fits the bill, and that's the Settle–Carlisle line (p172), which clatters for 72 exhilarating miles across England's northern counties.

The maze sculpture in Holker Hall gardens

Sarah Nelson's Gingerbread Shop

Staying at Black Sail YHA

15 The YHA owns some magnificent properties in the Lake District. Black Sail (p111) is one of the humblest: a former shepherd's bothy with just a couple of rooms, a minuscule kitchen and facilities that would make most prison blocks look luxurious. But it's not the trappings that sell this hostel, it's the setting: lost among the high hills to the east of Ennerdale, where there are no roads, no telephones and no traffic to break the silence, and the only light pollution comes from the stars overhead.

Holker Hall

16 Few stately homes in Cumbria can match the pomp and ceremony of Holker Hall (p154). It's a marvel of Victorian ostentation, rebuilt in lavish fashion after a fire in 1871. The grand rooms are brimming with Chippendale furniture, priceless porcelain and oil paintings, but for many visitors it's the landscaped estate that steals the show. Keep your eyes peeled for fallow deer grazing on the lawns, and a gigantic lime tree that's said to be the biggest in England.

Grasmere Gingerbread

17 Halfway between a crumbly biscuit and a gooey cake, the homemade gingerbread sold at Sarah Nelson's famous shop in Grasmere (p69) is still made to the same secret recipe laid down by its founder over 150 years ago. It's a must if you're a fan of all things sweet and sinful, but it's certainly not the only treat on offer in the Lake District — sticky toffee pudding, Cumberland Rum Nicky and of course Kendal mintcake are just a few of the other things with which to indulge your sweet tooth.

need to know

Currency
» Pounds sterling (£)

Language
» English

When to Go

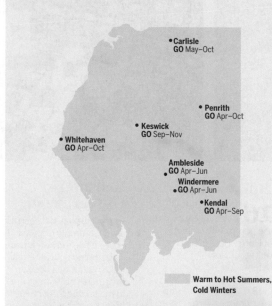

Carlisle
GO May–Oct

Penrith
GO Apr–Oct

Keswick
GO Sep–Nov

Whitehaven
GO Apr–Oct

Ambleside
GO Apr–Jun

Windermere
GO Apr–Jun

Kendal
GO Apr–Sep

Warm to Hot Summers, Cold Winters

High Season
» July and August are the busiest months in the national park.

» Half-terms and school holidays (especially Easter and Christmas) are also very busy.

» Accommodation prices are at their highest and traffic jams are common.

Shoulder Season
» Crowds thin out substantially in spring and autumn.

» Off-season deals are often available at B&Bs and hotels.

» Weather is often settled but beware of sudden downpours.

» Autumn colours transform woodlands.

Low Season
» Many attractions and activities close in January and February.

» Snow usually covers the high fells between November and March.

» Winter temperatures can reach several degrees below freezing.

Your Daily Budget

Budget Under
£60
» Dorm room in a hostel £15–20

» Self-catering from supermarkets £15

» Getting around by bus £5

» Hiking on the fells £0

Midrange
£60–150
» Double room in a B&B £70–100

» Mid range meals in pubs and cafes £15–20

» Petrol for the car £10

» Admissions and tickets £10

Top End Over
£150
» Room in a luxury hotel £150–200

» Three-course dinner with wine £40–60

» Guided minibus tour £50

Money

» ATMs available in main towns, but scarce elsewhere. Credit cards accepted (not American Express). Some B&Bs, restaurants and campsites only accept cash.

Visas

» Generally not required for travellers from most Western nations

Mobile phones

» Reception erratic outside main towns. Useful in emergencies, if there's a signal. Don't use your phone's maps when hiking – take a real map!

Transport

» Driving on the left, steering wheel on the right. Regular buses between towns, patchy in rural areas. Trains to Kendal, Windermere, Carlisle and Cumbrian Coast.

Websites

» **Go Lakes** (www.golakes.co.uk) Comprehensive information from the official tourist board.

» **Lake District National Park Authority** (www.lakedistrict.gov.uk) Background info on environment, activities and general news in the national park.

» **Lonely Planet** (www.lonelyplanet.com) Destination information, hotel bookings and more.

» **National Trust Lake District** (www.nationaltrust.org.uk/lakedistrict) Information on all the NT's properties and campsites.

Exchange Rates

Australia	A$1	£0.63
Canada	C$1	£0.61
Eurozone	€1	£0.87
Japan	¥100	£0.78
New Zealand	NZ$1	£0.50
USA	US$1	£0.61

For current exchange rates see www.xe.com.

Important Numbers

Brockhole Visitor Centre	☑015394-40001
Windermere Tourist Information Centre	☑015394-46499
Lake District Weatherline	☑0844 846 2444
Emergencies (ambulance, police, fire and mountain rescue)	☑999

Arriving

» **By Road**
The M6 motorway runs close to Kendal, Penrith and Carlisle.

» **Windermere Train Station**
Last stop on the branch railway from Kendal and Oxenholme. Frequent buses from Windermere to towns, including Ambleside and Coniston.

» **Carlisle Train Station**
Served by mainline trains north to Scotland and south to London Euston. Regional buses run from Carlisle bus station to the Lake District.

Driving in the Lake District

Driving in the Lake District is the most convenient way to get around, but you'll need to be prepared for traffic jams in summer, school holidays and around bank holidays.

With the exception of major roads (such as the A591 from Kendal to Windermere, the A66 from Penrith to Keswick and the A595 from Carlisle towards Cockermouth), most of the Lake District's roads are narrow, windy and often hilly. GPS is useful for getting to main towns, but can be counterproductive in rural areas, often directing you down minor roads and farm tracks. In the countryside, single-lane roads with passing places are common, so you'll need to be prepared to stop and let traffic pass, or reverse to the nearest layby.

Look out for disc parking zones on the streets of towns such as Windermere, Kendal, Penrith and Ambleside.

if you like...

Fell Walking

Fell walking isn't just a pastime in the Lake District, it's a passion. Peak-baggers devote their lives to ticking off each and every one of the Lakeland fells, often doing them more than once simply for the fun of it.

Helm Crag Wainwright called this the best-known hill in the country, and it's certainly a beauty (p72)

Catbells A Keswick classic, suitable for any age, any ability and any time of year (p117)

Langdale Pikes They're not the highest, but you'll struggle to find a more spectacular set of fells (p80)

Scafell Pike England's highest mountain is the one everyone wants on their summit list (p108)

Skiddaw This massive lump of granite dominates the skyline to the north of Keswick (p119)

The Old Man of Coniston There are endless ways to the top, but the views are always awe-inspiring (p89)

Getting Active

Fell walking certainly isn't the only way to get out and about in the great outdoors. Whether it's scrambling up a ghyll, larking about in the trees or biking down a forest trail, there are plenty of ways to get your pulse racing.

Kayak on Derwentwater Explore this island-studded lake under your own paddle power (p118 & p131)

Go Ape in Grizedale This treetop adventure course is one of two in the Lake District (p94)

Whinlatter Forest Park Bike trails criss-cross amongst the conifers at this mountain forest near Keswick (p125)

Honister Slate Mine Descend into the darkness on a guided tour into one of Borrowdale's oldest slate mines (p133)

Kankku 4x4 Charge across the Lakeland countryside in a souped-up 4x4 (p45)

Ghyll Scrambling This popular sport combines elements of climbing, diving, scrambling and wild swimming into one (p28)

Literary Landmarks

Literature and the Lake District go hand in hand, whether that means following in the footsteps of the Romantic poets or spotting locations from the books of Beatrix Potter.

Dove Cottage Wordsworth's most famous residence in Grasmere was also his smallest (p68)

Rydal Mount Just up the road from Dove Cottage, but altogether grander (p74)

Hill Top Beatrix Potter created some of her most famous characters at this cottage in Near Sawrey (p95)

Bank Ground Farm Arthur Ransome used this farmhouse overlooking Coniston Water as the model for Holly Howe Farm (p87)

Wordsworth House See where young William grew up in Cockermouth (p127)

Greta Hall Stay in the Keswick mansion once occupied by Samuel Taylor Coleridge (p120)

Kendal Museum Visit the museum where the famous fell walker and guidebook writer Alfred Wainwright served as honorary curator (p182)

» Levens Hall, with its topiary gardens, Kendal (p187)

Quiet Spots

There's no getting around it – crowds can be a problem in the Lakes, but with a bit of planning there are still plenty of quiet spots where you'll be able to take Wordsworth's advice and wander lonely as a cloud.

Watendlath Once the day-trippers have left for home, you should have this beautiful tarn to yourself (p132)

Lorton This little lake is well off the beaten track, so often stays pin-drop quiet (p126)

Duddon Valley Very few people ever take the time to explore this remote valley between Cockley Bridge and Ulpha (p105)

Ennerdale A pioneering project to return this isolated valley to its wild origins is well under way (p110)

Cumbrian Coast It might not be the Côte d'Azur, but Cumbria's coastline has charms of its own (p149)

Historic Houses

History often seems to follow you at every turn in the Lake District, and visiting one of the region's many stately homes is a great way to get a new perspective on the past. Take your time and, if possible, a guided tour.

Blackwell Admire the architecture of one of England's finest Arts and Crafts houses (p52)

Brantwood The Victorian art critic and philosopher John Ruskin designed this lakeside home from scratch (p84)

Levens Hall This Elizabethan manor was built around a fortified pele tower (p187)

Mirehouse This mansion, on the shores of Bassenthwaite, has been graced by a host of literary visitors (p123)

Dalemain Georgian on the outside, but with an architectural heritage stretching back to the Middle Ages (p139)

Holker Hall Glorious stately home surrounded by acres of private parkland (p154)

Food & Drink

Whether it's in a cosy country pub, a quiet village cafe or a Michelin-starred restaurant, there are endless ways to sample the Lake District's culinary credentials.

L'Enclume The Lake District has its fair share of big-name chefs, but none can match the imagination of Michelin-starred wunderkind Simon Rogan (p153)

Grasmere gingerbread The recipe for this trademark sweet treat is well over 150 years old, but it still tastes as good as ever (p69)

Drunken Duck The original Lake District gastropub, and still one of the region's finest places to wine and dine (p93)

Hawkshead Brewery Now based in Staveley, this award-winning brewery makes some of the region's top real ales (p55)

Cartmel Village Shop You'll see sticky toffee pudding on nearly every menu, but for the real thing there's only one address that'll do (p153)

Watermill Take a tour of this organic bakery, then pick up freshly baked cakes, breads and pastries (p178)

month by month

February

Winter hits the Lake District hard, with chilly temperatures and a carpet of snow that often persists on the fell-tops until March.

Dalemain Marmalade Festival

Dalemain House holds its annual jam-making jamboree in late February (www.marmaladefestival .com), with categories for Seville orange, citrus and chunky.

May

Spring is in the air, and with it come warmer temperatures and sunnier skies. Beware of sudden spring showers on the fells.

Keswick Jazz Festival

Keswick's five-day jazz fest (www.keswickjazzfestival .co.uk) attracts top names from the British, European and world jazz circuits. It's held at various venues around town. See p118.

Keswick Mountain Festival

One of the Lake District's top outdoors events (p118; www.keswickmountain festival.co.uk), with celebrity hikers, bikers and climbers congregating in Keswick in late May for the four-day festival.

Brathay Windermere Marathon

Iron-lunged competitors cover 26.2 miles around Lake Windermere in mid-May (p45; www.brathay windermeremarathon.org .uk). Hardcore runners can sign up for the Brathay 10 in 10, which involves 10 marathons in 10 days.

Fred Whitton Challenge

This gruelling event (www .fredwhittonchallenge.org .uk) entails a 112-mile slog over the Lake District's six highest road passes – on a bike. It's named after a former secretary of the Lakes Road Club, who died of cancer in 1998.

Holker Hall Garden Festival

Local food, horticultural displays and colourful blooms fill the grounds of Holker Hall. It runs for three days; local gardeners compete with special show gardens.

June

June is a great month to visit the Lake District, with fairly settled weather and the hectic summer season still a long way away.

Keswick Beer Festival

Can't tell your Ram Tam from your Cheeky Pheasant? Don't fret – Keswick's annual ale-fest (p118; www.keswickbeer festival.co.uk) is a great place to get a taste for the warm stuff.

Boot Beer Festival

Boot's pubs have their own ale-fest (www.bootbeer.co .uk) in mid-June. It's on a smaller scale than the one in Keswick, but at least you won't have to queue so long for a pint.

Coniston Walking Festival

One of the biggest and best-known walking

festivals (p87) in the Lake District, with lots of scheduled walks and guided hikes.

July

The balmy days of summer host lots of events, although the British weather doesn't always play ball. Bring a raincoat and a brolly just in case.

Ambleside Rushbearing

Rushes and wreaths are carried with pomp and ceremony around Ambleside to St Mary's Church. Held on the first Saturday in July.

Coniston Water Festival

Sailing, windsurfing, stone skimming and general larking about on the lake of Coniston Water. Held in early July (p87; www .conistonwaterfestival.co.uk).

Cumberland County Show

Cumbria's largest agricultural show (www .cumberlandshow.co.uk) features Cumbrian wrestling, dressage displays, prize bulls and sheepdog displays.

Windermere Air Festival

Fighter jets, bombers, stunt planes and parachutists take to the skies above Windermere in the region's largest air show (p45; www .windermereairshow.co.uk).

August

You never quite know what you'll get in August: clear blue skies if you're lucky, black storm clouds if you're not. Come prepared for both.

Lake District Summer Music Festival

This classical-music festival (www.ldsm.org.uk) runs for two weeks in early August and brings big-name classical performers to theatres, cafes and village halls.

Borrowdale Fell Race

One of the fell-racing classics, involving 6500ft of ascent and 17 miles of fells. Hundreds of runners set out from the Scafell Hotel, but not many make it to the end.

Kendal Mintfest

Kendal's annual carnival (p184; www .mintfest.org) contains street performers, musicians and plenty of odd costumes descending on the Auld Grey Town. Held on the August bank holiday.

Grasmere Sports & Show

Fell runners hit trails, hounds sniff scents, and wrestlers wear long johns at this traditional sports day (p74; www.grasmeresports andshow.co.uk). Held over the August bank holiday.

September

The first crisp nights of autumn arrive in the Lakes in September, and the woodland puts on a spectacular display of autumnal colours.

Great North Swim

The waters of Windermere are transformed into a gigantic swimming pool for this long-distance swim (p45; www.great swim.org). It may be September, but the water's still ice-cold.

Kendal Torchlight Carnival

Kendal's answer to the Notting Hill Carnival: daft costumes, street processions and decorated floats galore. Held in mid-September (www .kendaltorchlightcarnival .co.uk).

Westmorland County Show

Every year Westmorland puts its sheep and cattle on show near Kendal on the second Thursday in September (www.west morlandshow.co.uk).

Borrowdale Show

Hounds trail, fell runners race, shepherds shear and sheepdogs strut their stuff at Rosthwaite in Borrowdale. Held in mid-September (www .borrowdaleshow.org.uk).

Egremont Crab Fair & Sports

See the nation's most-flexible faces pull their ugliest expressions at this historic gurning competition (www .egremontcrabfair.co.uk). Held in mid-September.

October

October's weather see-saws between sudden sun and heavy cloud, but it's usually pleasant enough to hike on the fells until late into the month.

Taste District

Gourmet gala celebrating Cumbria's best beer brewers, chutney bottlers, sausage stuffers and bread kneaders, held at Rheged, near Penrith. Held in early October (www .golakes.co.uk/do/food-and -drink).

Ullswater Walking Festival

Organised hikes around Helvellyn, Fairfield, Gowbarrow, and the other summits around Ullswater. Held in late September and early October.

November

Winter's well on its way by November: the days are chilly, the nights are chillier and the fells may even have received their first dusting of snow.

(Above) Runners in the Windermere Marathon setting off from Brathay, Ambleside
(Below) Lantern festival procession at the Christmas lights switch-on in Ambleside

Kendal Mountain Festival

The best new films and documentaries from the adrenaline-fuelled world of adventure sports. Held in mid-November (p184; www.mountainfest.co.uk).

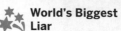 ### World's Biggest Liar

Hear improbable tales of flatulent sheep and giant turnips at the Santon Bridge Inn's fib-telling contest (p106; www.santonbridge inn.com/liar). Held in mid-November.

 ### Ulverston Dickensian Festival

Meet Bob Cratchits, Ebenezer Scrooges and Oliver Twists on the streets of Ulverston in this Christmassy procession at the end of November.

itineraries

Whether you've got six days or 60, these itineraries provide a starting point for the trip of a lifetime. Want more inspiration? Head online to lonelyplanet .com/thorntree to chat with other travellers.

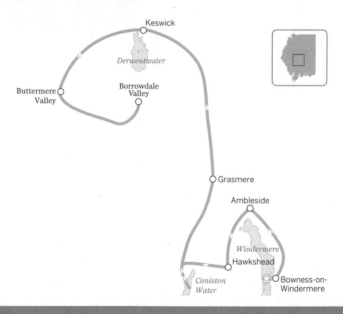

10 Days
Lakeland Classics

> Kick-start this trip with a cruise from the jetties at **Bowness-on-Windermere** and a stroll around its bustling streets. On day two head along the lakeshore to **Ambleside**, a lively market town where you can shop till you drop, dine till you whine and walk to your heart's content. From here, take a scenic spin south for a circuit of the picture-perfect village of **Hawkshead** and the grand lake of **Coniston Water**, where you can take your pick from two different cruise boats (one solar-powered, the other a converted steam yacht). Then it's time to head north to **Grasmere**, the heart of Wordsworth country: don't miss the poet's former homes at Dove Cottage and Rydal Mount, tied together with an afternoon exploring the excellent Wordsworth Museum. From Grasmere, drive north to **Keswick**, another lovely Lakeland town where you should spend at least a couple of days cruising the lake and hiking the fells: perhaps Catbells if you're a beginner, or Skiddaw if you're more experienced. Finish up with a tour around the gorgeous valleys of **Buttermere** and **Borrowdale**, interspersed with an underground tour of the old Honister Slate Mine.

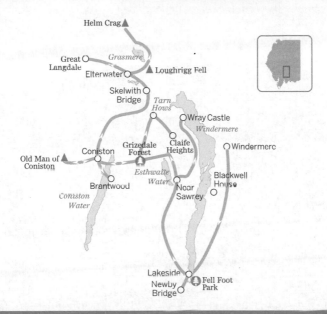

10 Days
Central Circuit

The centre of the national park is where you'll find many of its most fascinating sights. Begin with a couple of days exploring the area around **Windermere**. There are lots of family-friendly attractions around **Lakeside** and **Newby Bridge**, including the Lakes Aquarium, the Lakeside & Haverthwaite Railway and the relocated Lakeland Motor Museum. If the sights are too busy, refuge is never far away: you could explore **Blackwell House**, one of Britain's finest Arts and Crafts mansions, or take a peaceful walk around **Fell Foot Park**, a lakeside estate owned by the National Trust.

Next, travel round to the east side of the lake to Beatrix Potter's storybook cottage at Hill Top in **Near Sawrey**, followed by lunch at the Tower Bank Arms and an afternoon wandering the landscaped grounds of **Wray Castle**.

From here, head over to **Coniston**. Spend the morning cruising across the lake for a visit to John Ruskin's wonderful house at **Brantwood**. Have lunch at the homely Jumping Jenny cafe, then spend the afternoon slogging to the top of the area's most iconic peak, the **Old Man of Coniston**.

Devote the next day to exploring the treetop assault course and woodland trails in **Grizedale Forest**. Follow this up with a day wandering around the renowned beauty spots of **Tarn Hows** and **Claife Heights** – ideally including a slap-up lunch at the Drunken Duck Inn, one of the Lake District's most renowned gastropubs.

Spend the next day exploring the beautiful valley of **Great Langdale**, famous for its scenic hikes and country inns. The classic trek takes you along the string of summits known as the Langdale Pikes, followed by post-hike drinks in the hugger-mugger hiker's bar of the Old Dungeon Ghyll Hotel. If time allows, it's well worth detouring through the quaint hamlets of **Elterwater** and **Skelwith Bridge**, where the walks are gentler but the pubs are just as cosy. Don't miss a stroll to the waterfalls of Skelwith and Colwith Force.

Complete the journey with a day exploring a few of the central fells: the lofty viewpoints of **Loughrigg** and **Helm Crag** near Grasmere provide some of the most memorable vistas anywhere in the national park, not to mention a suitably scenic end to the trip.

ALAN NOVELLI/GETTY IMAGES ©

» (above) View across Little Langdale valley
» (left) First light at Brougham Castle, near Penrith

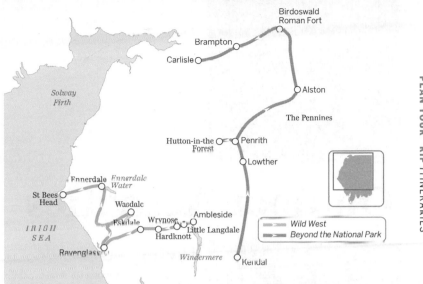

Wild West
Beyond the National Park

One Week
Beyond the National Park

> Some people never take the time to explore outside the park boundaries, but they're missing out on a whole chunk of Cumbria. This journey explores some of the county's inland attractions, beginning in the stout grey town of **Kendal**, which makes an ideal base for exploring the surrounding sights, such as the country house of Levens Hall and the superb farm shop at Low Sizergh Barn. From here, it's a trip up the A6 to see the renovations in progress at **Lowther**, currently the focus of a £9 million restoration project. Make time for a wander around nearby **Penrith** and the stately halls and lavish gardens of **Hutton-in-the-Forest**. Then it's time for a memorable road trip along the A686 into the bleak beauty of the **Pennines**, where you can spend a day riding the rails with the South Tynedale Railway from the terminus town of **Alston**. From here, it's a long loop north to Gilsland and the nearby Roman fort of **Birdoswald**, followed by a drive west along the course of Hadrian's Wall to **Brampton**. Complete the trip with a day or two in Cumbria's capital city, **Carlisle**, where you should definitely factor in time for visits to the castle, the cathedral and the Tullie House Museum.

Five Days
The Wild West

> This trip searches out the Lake District's wildest views. Begin in **Ambleside**, and head into the valley of **Little Langdale**, which marks the start-point for one of Britain's most breathtaking roads: the humpbacked drive up and over the passes of **Wrynose** and **Hardknott**, where the gradients sometimes reach 1 in 3 and the passing places are few and far between. Once you've crossed the passes, drop down into the lovely valley of **Eskdale** and its comforting country pubs, and continue west to the quiet coastal town of **Ravenglass**, where you can visit the ruins of a Roman bathhouse and hop aboard a historic railway. Travel north for scenic detours into the spectacularly wild valley of **Wasdale**, framed by several of England's highest peaks, and the nearby valley of **Ennerdale**, which is currently the focus of a project to return the landscape to its once-wild state. Finish up with a journey to Cumbria's most westerly point at **St Bees Head**, which is also home to one of northern England's largest seabird colonies. The cliff tops feel fantastically wild, and there's nowhere better in Cumbria to watch the sun set.

Outdoor Activities

Best Short Hikes

Helm Crag One of Wainwright's long-standing favourites, near Grasmere.
The Old Man of Coniston Short and steep, but worth the effort for the Coniston views.
Loughrigg Fell Little fell with a wraparound panorama across the central lakes.

Best Long-Distance Trail

Coast-to-Coast Wainwright-devised route covering 190 miles between St Bees Head and Robin Hood's Bay.
Cumbria Way 90 miles between Ulverston and Carlisle, with nonstop scenery en route.

Best Places for Biking

Grizedale Forest Family-friendly trails and outdoor sculptures.
Whinlatter Forest Two challenging routes for experienced bikers.

Best Thrills

Via Ferrata Brave the UK's only Via Ferrata near Honister.
Treetop assault course Clamber through the trees of Grizedale and Whinlatter.
Bushcraft Brush up on your fire-lighting near Esthwaite Water.
Off-road driving Drive an all-terrain 4x4 with Kankku, based in Windermere.

Hiking

If there's one activity that sums up the spirit of the Lake District, it's hiking. There are walks to suit every age and ability, ranging from valley rambles to full-blown multipeak circuits (dubbed 'horseshoes' or 'rounds' in this part of the world).

» For general advice on walking in the Lake District, contact the **Lake District National Park Association** (☎01539-724555; www.lake-district.gov.uk), which organises an excellent program of guided walks and rangers' talks.

» We've included a selection of walks for each region throughout this guidebook, ranging from easy to challenging. Major walking festivals are held in Ullswater, Ulverston, Coniston, Keswick and several other towns.

Hiking & Activity Guides

If you want to extend your hill-walking skills, many local companies provide courses in map reading, navigation, compass skills and mountain survival. You could also consider taking the **British Hill-Walking Leadership Certificate** (www.bhlc.org.uk), a tailored course run over three weekends throughout the year, which covers everything you need to know about walking safely in the fells. Official BHLC courses are run by **Summitreks** (www.summitreks.co.uk). Other recommended guiding companies:

» Carolclimb (p107)
» Distant Horizons (p139)
» Glenridding Guides (p143)

» (above) A mountain biker descends a trail into Patterdale
» (left) Crossing Stockley Bridge on the way to Scafell Pike

» Mike Wood Mountain (p117)

» River Deep Mountain High (p157)

» Treks and Trails (p184)

Long-Distance Routes

In addition to the standard fell walks, which can mostly be comfortably completed in less than a day, there are a number of long-distance routes you could consider if you're looking for a more epic challenge.

» The classic route is the **Coast-to-Coast Walk** (www.coast2coast.co.uk), stretching for 190 miles from St Bees Head on the Cumbrian Coast to Robin Hood's Bay, near Whitby on the coast of North Yorkshire. It was devised by none other than Alfred Wainwright himself.

» You'll need anything from a week to a month to complete most of the routes, but following a short section can be a great way to explore the Lakeland landscape and get off the beaten track.

» For baggage transport services, see p221.

Hiking Equipment

☐ Topographical map (Ordnance Survey or Harvey's)

☐ Compass

☐ At least 2L of water per person

☐ Spare padded socks

☐ Layered clothing (base, mid-layer and fleece)

☐ Breathable jacket (Gore-Tex or equivalent)

☐ Waterproof trousers

☐ Food, trail snacks and energy bars

☐ First-aid kit and sunscreen

☐ Mobile phone

☐ GPS unit (optional but useful)

☐ Gaiters (especially on muddy trails)

Cycling

If you like to do your sightseeing from the saddle, the Lake District is a great place to explore by bike. Check out **Cycling in Cumbria** (www.cyclingincumbria.co.uk). Also see p223 for more information.

» There are good bike-hire shops in Keswick, Ambleside, Windermere, Ulverston and Kendal, as well as at Grizedale and Whinlatter Forests.

» Grizedale Forest is one of the best places for off-road biking in the Lake District, with a network of trails specifically designed for cyclists.

THE WAINWRIGHTS

Alfred Wainwright listed 214 official fells at more than 1000ft in his *Pictorial Guides*, and for dedicated hikers in the Lake District, it's a lifelong achievement to stand atop the summit of every last one of the 'Wainwrights'. Once finished, walkers will have covered a distance of around 391 miles and around 121,900ft of ascent.

They can also register their success with the **Wainwright Society** (www.wainwright.org.uk), which holds a record of all its members who have completed the 214-fell circuit.

» Whinlatter Forest has three challenging routes designed for experienced mountain bikers.

» Most visitor centres can provide route suggestions and trail leaflets covering the best places to cycle in the local area.

» For long-distance routes, see p220.

Climbing & Scrambling

The Lake District's peaks and cliffs are an irresistible magnet for rock climbers, and there are few more spectacular places to test your mountaineering mettle.

» Classic ascents up Dow Crag, Gimmer, Esk Buttress or Broad Stand have been a proving ground for many of the UK's top climbers (notably Sir Chris Bonington). For climbing advice, contact the **British Mountaineering Council** (☎0870 010 4878; www.thebmc.co.uk) or the **Fell & Rock Climbing Club** (www.frcc.co.uk), which publishes the definitive guidebook series covering Lakeland climbs.

» Scrambling is a less extreme version of the sport which involves clambering up scree slopes, gullies and the like – it's halfway between challenging hiking and full-blown rock climbing. The spin-off sport of ghyll-scrambling is similar, but as it mostly takes place in river canyons, ravines and waterfalls, you're likely to get wet.

» Most activity centres and providers offer introductory sessions in rock climbing and scrambling. There are climbing walls in Kendal and Keswick where you can hone your skills before tackling a real rock face.

» (above) Fell runners on the climb to Fairfield
» (left) A climber in the Lake District.

SAFE HIKING

Though they're comparatively small in world terms, the Lakeland fells can still be dangerous if you're not properly prepared. Once you get off the beaten track, trails are often rough, exposed and indistinct, signposts are few and far between, and the weather can change without warning.

» Research your route well in advance, and choose one that's within your abilities. 'Cragfast' hikers are one of the most common call-outs for the mountain rescue teams.

» Always carry a proper map and compass, and know how to use them. A day spent brushing up your navigational skills with a local walking company might be a worth-while investment.

» Wear proper hiking boots (ideally with high sides to help avoid sprained ankles).

» On the day of your walk, let someone know your intended route and estimated time of return. Check the weather forecast before you set out and ask around for advice about any new hazards that may have cropped up along the route.

» Carry a mobile phone in case of emergencies.

Fishing

The Lake District contains some excellent fishing, whether it's for rainbow and brown trout at Esthwaite Water or for pike, perch and Arctic char at Windermere. You'll need a valid rod licence, available from the **Environment Agency** (☑08708 506 506; www.environment-agency.gov.uk), local tourist offices and some post offices. **Lake District Fishing** (www.lakedistrictfishing.net) is a good resource for angling-related info.

» Not all lakes are open to fishing and some operate catch-and-release policies, so make sure you know what the score is before you cast a line.

» Live bait is prohibited in many lakes as it increases the risk of disease and pest species.

Activity Centres

If you're not sure which sport you'd like to try, it's well worth heading for one of the Lake District's excellent activity centres. Most will allow you to pick your own activities and build up a tailored itinerary: you can just stick to one sport, or create your own multi day adventure. Some also offer residential courses, including meals and accommodation.

» Holmescales (p184)

» Newlands Adventure Centre (p118)

» Rookin House (p143)

» Outward Bound (p102)

Horse Riding

Trotting through the fells is a wonderful way of seeing the national park, and there are many places which can put you in the saddle.

» The best places to learn the ropes (or reins) are Rookin House Equestrian Centre near Ullswater and Bradley's Riding Centre near Ennerdale.

» Pony treks are also available from several farms and campsites, including Park Foot Camping near Ullswater, and Bowkerstead Farm near Grizedale.

» You can also trot along the sands of the Cumbrian Coast with the Murthwaite Green Trekking Centre, near Silecroft.

Water Sports

The Lake District is an excellent place to get out on the water. Vintage cruise boats travel out across many lakes, including Windermere, Ullswater, Derwentwater and Coniston Water, and most lakes have marinas and water sports centres where you can hire kayaks, canoes and row boats.

» Speeds are restricted to a maximum of 10mph on most of the lakes, so waterskiing and power-boating are pretty much off-limits.

» Some lakes (such as Haweswater and Thirlmere) are off-limits to bathers since they're used as water reservoirs.

» Swimming is only allowed in certain areas of the other lakes, and the water remains icy-cold for much of the year. Contact the National Parks Association (NPA) or the local tourist office before diving in.

Travel with Children

Best Regions for Kids

Windermere & Around

The most family-oriented corner of the lakes, home to the main visitor centre, lots of child-friendly restaurants and B&Bs, and plenty of attractions to keep enquiring young minds engaged.

Grasmere & the Central Lake District

Spectacular scenery, great walking, gingerbread from Sarah Nelson's shop and an unforgettable storytelling session by the UK's Storytelling Laureate.

Cumbrian Coast

Beaches and coast paths for walking, animal parks and aquariums for sightseeing, stately homes for wandering and sticky toffee pudding from the Cartmel Village Shop.

Inland Cumbria

Historic Cumbria: castles, ruins and landmark buildings aplenty, from the imposing fortress of Carlisle Castle to the ruins of Birdoswald Fort.

Keswick & Derwentwater

Activity central: delve into the depths of a disused mine at Honister, swing from the trees in Whinlatter and kayak across Derwentwater.

The Lake District for Kids

Inevitably, it's the outdoor pursuits that are going to be the real attraction for kids. Wildlife walks, boating, cycling and horse riding are all popular family pastimes, and most activity providers are well set up for dealing with kids.

Sights & Attractions

» Children qualify for discounted entry to nearly all sights and attractions (generally around half the adult price).

» Discounted family tickets are often available, which usually include entry for two adults and either two or three children.

» The Brockhole Visitor Centre (p45) has programs of events for kids, such as guided walks with National Park Authority (NPA) staff and outdoor activity days.

Accommodation

Call ahead to make sure kids are welcome at B&Bs and hotels.

Most hotels and B&Bs have a few family rooms, usually with a double bed, and bunks or singles, sometimes in an adjoining room. Reserve well in advance.

Most hostels will rent out their four- or six-bed dorms to families.

Renting a cottage or holiday home is the other option. There's a huge selection, but research carefully, as many places are inconvenient for supermarkets, shops and attractions.

Eating

Nearly all cafes and restaurants will happily accommodate children, although some of the more expensive establishments may not accept them under a certain age.

Rules on pubs and children vary. Most pubs accept kids during the day, but some won't accept them during evening hours. Ask behind the bar before you sit down.

Travel

The Lake District is small, so travel times are short. Child fares are available on nearly all public transport; children normally pay half the adult fare, and children under five often travel free. Family tickets can offer great value, especially if you're purchasing a day pass or rover ticket.

If you're driving:

» Children aged up to 12, or less than 135cm in height, must use a child restraint or child seat.

» Children aged 12 and 13 can use adult seat belts.

» Drivers are responsible for ensuring that under 14s are appropriately restrained.

Toilets

» Toilets are scarce beyond the main towns, and standards of hygiene and cleanliness can leave a lot to be desired in some public conveniences.

» Most sights and attractions (as well as all major supermarkets) have child-friendly loos.

» Nappies are available at chemists and supermarkets.

Children's Highlights

Outdoor Pursuits

» **La'al Ratty** The whole family will love riding this antique railway, which chunters from the Cumbrian Coast into the Eskdale Valley.

» **Go Ape** There are two treetop assault courses: one at Whinlatter Forest, the other at Grizedale.

» **Cycling in Grizedale Forest** Miles and miles of mountain-bike trails to explore in Grizedale.

» **Horse riding** Trot along the sands around Millom and Haverigg with the Murthwaite Green Trekking Centre.

» **Canoeing** Hire a canoe and head for one of Derwentwater's wooded islands.

Houses, Castles & Museums

» **Carlisle Castle** Walk along the battlements of this magnificent fortress in Carlisle, one of the best-preserved castles in the north of England.

TOP WALKS FOR KIDS

» Catbells (p117)
» Helm Crag (p72)
» Orrest Head (p43)
» Gummer's How (p43)
» Old Man of Coniston (p89)
» Loughrigg Fell (p71)

» **Hill Top** Visit the house where Beatrix Potter dreamt up her tales of mischievous squirrels and bunny rabbits.

» **Muncaster Castle** Spot the spooks at this centuries-old castle.

» **Keswick Museum** You can see everything from a mummified cat to a cobra's skin at this wonderfully quirky museum.

Animals & Wildlife

» **South Lakes Wild Animal Park** The region's largest wildlife park is home to giraffes, gibbons, lions, lemurs and much more.

» **Lakes Aquarium** The highlight at this aquarium near Windermere is the underwater tunnel where you can watch diving ducks and arctic char.

» **Trotters World of Animals** Kids are encouraged to get heads-on with the animals at this fun little zoo near Bassenthwaite.

» **Muncaster Owl Centre** Eagle owls, tawny owls, barn owls, pygmy owls – you name the owl, chances are Muncaster will have it.

» **Walby Farm Park** Pet lambs, pigs, ponies, goats and reindeer, then pedal a go-cart or ride the barrel train.

» **Bassenthwaite ospreys** Head for a bird hide and scan the skies above Bassenthwaite for ospreys.

» **Red squirrels** Spot red squirrels in the woodlands around Whinlatter, Derwentwater, Thirlmere and Lowther Park.

Rainy Day Activities

» **Rheged Cinema** If the weather's lousy, the big-screen 3D cinemas at Rheged are a great option.

» **Lakeland Motor Museum** View an amazing collection of classic cars near Newby Bridge.

» **World of Beatrix Potter** The tales of Benjamin Bunny, Jemima Puddleduck and Jeremy Fisher come to life at this fun attraction in Bowness.

» **The Beacon** Whitehaven's sea-going heritage takes centre stage in this engaging multimedia museum.

regions at a glance

The Lake District may be comparatively little compared to some of the UK's other national parks, but it packs a huge amount into a tiny space. Each corner of Lakeland has its own special sights and charms, but there are some things that are common to all: glorious countryside, fantastic walking and, of course, a nonstop parade of panoramic views.

The central lakes around Windermere, Grasmere and Coniston make the most useful bases, with most of the other key areas just a short drive or bus ride away. Outside the national park, Whitehaven is handiest for venturing up and down the Cumbrian Coast, while Carlisle or Penrith are ideal launch pads for exploring inland Cumbria.

Windermere & Around

Boating ✓✓
Children ✓✓✓
Food & Drink ✓✓

Cruising on the Lake
Windermere is England's largest lake, stretching for 10.5 stunning miles from end to end. It's a wonderful place to explore by boat – either on a scheduled cruise or under your own steam.

Kids' Activities
There's a wealth of things for children to see and do around Windermere, from climbing aboard a vintage steam railway to visiting one of the region's best aquariums.

Country Hotels
If you've always wanted to splash out on a luxury weekend in the country, Windermere is the place to do it. There are many lovely hotels dotted around the countryside, including a few with Michelin-starred restaurants.

p38

Grasmere & the Central Lake District

Culture ✓✓
Hiking ✓✓✓
Scenery ✓✓✓

Romantic Connections
Grasmere has a rich Romantic history thanks to William Wordsworth, who lived most of his adult life at Dove Cottage and Rydal Mount. You can tour both houses and also visit the village's excellent literature museum.

Fell Walking
If you're in the Lakes to stretch your legs, you'll struggle to find anywhere more impressive than Great Langdale – especially the classic hike over the humpbacked chain of summits known as the Langdale Pikes.

Rollercoaster Drives
Little Langdale marks the start for the amazing drive across two of England's highest road passes, Wrynose and Hardknott.

p66

Coniston, Hawkshead & Around

Culture ✓✓
Cycling ✓✓
Boating ✓✓✓

Literary Heritage
Three famous English writers have close connections with this corner of the Lakes: Arthur Ransome, John Ruskin and Beatrix Potter, who penned some of her best-loved tales at Hill Top in Near Sawrey.

Mountain Biking
A network of bike trails wind their way among the pines and conifers of Grizedale Forest. On your way round, look out for outdoor sculptures hidden among the trees.

Lake Launches
Coniston Water has a choice of two cruises: the steam yacht *Gondola,* lovingly restored to its Victorian splendour by the National Trust, or the Coniston Launches, recently converted to run on solar power.

p82

Western Lake District

Hiking ✓✓✓
Scenery ✓✓✓
Beer ✓✓✓

Wild Views
Few places feel as thrillingly wild as Wasdale Head, hemmed in by some of the nation's highest peaks. Many stay snowcapped well into spring, including the loftiest summit of all – Scafell Pike.

All Aboard
The toy-train choo-choos of the Ravenglass and Eskdale Railway have been puffing up the picturesque Eskdale Valley for well over a century.

Traditional Inns
There's nothing better for the post-hike aches than a pint of ale, and there are some super pubs to discover around Eskdale and Wasdale. Boot's inns hold their own beer festival, and the Wasdale Head Inn has its own microbrewery.

p98

Keswick & Derwentwater

Wildlife ✓✓✓
Activities ✓✓✓
Scenery ✓✓✓

Unusual Wildlife
Two of England's rarest wild residents can be seen near Keswick. You can spot red squirrels among the treetops in Whinlatter Forest, while Bassenthwaite is home to some of England's rare breeding ospreys.

Great Outdoors
Whether it's canoeing across Derwentwater, delving the murky depths of Honister Slate Mine or slogging to the top of Skiddaw, there are countless ways to get active around Keswick.

Postcard Valleys
The neighbouring valleys of Borrowdale and Buttermere sum up everything that's green and pleasant about the Lakeland landscape. Take the time to explore nearby Lorton and Loweswater too.

p112

Ullswater

Hiking ✓✓
Boating ✓✓
Scenery ✓✓

Hiking Helvellyn
If you really want to test your hiking mettle, the route to the top of Helvellyn via Striding and Swirral Edges is hard to better. If you prefer to hike solo, there are plenty of other summits nearby with far fewer crowds.

Ullswater 'Steamers'
The vintage boats plying the waters of Ullswater are no longer steam-powered, but they still boast their original chimney stacks and traditional green-and-red livery.

Lofty Drives
The spectacular road over Kirkstone Pass commands mind-bogglingly fine views across Ullswater and the surrounding fells – but your brakes will need to be in good working order.

p137

Cumbrian Coast

History ✓✓
Food ✓✓
Solitude ✓

Great Estates

The coast is home to two glorious country houses. Go ghost-spotting at Muncaster Castle, then explore the rolling grounds and architectural splendour of Holker Hall.

Food & Drink

The little village of Cartmel is the HQ of one of England's most creative chefs, Simon Rogan, but if you fancy something more down-to-earth, there are some great cafes and restaurants to discover in Grange-over-Sands, Ulverston and Whitehaven.

Coast Walks

Crowds are thin on the ground along the coast, so you'll be able to explore the blustery headlands and bird reserves in relative peace and quiet.

p149

Inland Cumbria

History ✓✓
Heritage ✓✓
Scenery ✓✓

Frontier Country

The troubled border between England and Scotland has long been a source of conflict. Gazing out from the ramparts of Carlisle Castle or the ruins of Birdoswald Fort, you'll feel like you've been transported to another age.

Historic Towns

Wander through several centuries of history in the Auld Grey Town of Kendal, the medieval market town of Penrith and Cumbria's capital city, Carlisle.

Scenic Railways

Carlisle marks the terminus for one of England's greatest train rides, the historic Settle-Carlisle Railway, which clatters though 73 stunning miles of the Yorkshire Dales, North Pennines and Cumbria.

p166

> **Every listing is recommended by our authors, and their favourite places are listed first**

> **Look out for these icons:**

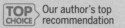 Our author's top recommendation

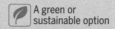 A green or sustainable option

 No payment required

On the Road

Windermere & Around

Best Places to Eat

» Punch Bowl Inn (p54)
» Brown Horse (p54)
» Jerichos (p47)
» Holbeck Ghyll (p48)
» Glass House (p63)

Best Places to Stay

» Boundary (p45)
» Gilpin Lodge (p48)
» Knoll (p53)
» Randy Pike (p60)
» Lakes Lodge (p62)

Why Go?

In terms of stateliness and stature, nowhere can match Lake Windermere, England's largest lake, which runs for a grand 10.5 miles from Newby Bridge to Ambleside. In his 1810 *Guide to the Lakes,* Wordsworth mused on 'the splendour, the stillness and the solemnity' of Windermere's waters, and it's surely no coincidence that it was here, gazing across the point-to-point panorama from Orrest Head, that Alfred Wainwright began his 13-year odyssey to chart all the Lakeland fells.

These days, stillness and solemnity might not be the first things that spring to mind in relation to Windermere. The nation's largest lake is also by far its busiest, and in summer the quayside crowds around Bowness can be oppressive. But tranquillity is never too far away: Windermere's west side is usually much quieter than its eastern shoreline, and you can always escape the madding crowd by simply hopping on a cruise boat or hiking up a nearby hilltop.

When to Go

Windermere and Ambleside are major tourist hotspots, so expect big crowds and traffic jams during holiday seasons. Things get extra busy around major events such as the Windermere Marathon (mid-May), the rushbearing procession in Ambleside and the Windermere Air Festival (both late July). Late autumn is a superb time to visit: the forests around the lake assume myriad autumnal hues, and the cruise boats, restaurants and attractions are much quieter than in the main holiday season. Some B&Bs and businesses close down altogether during the quietest winter months.

WINDERMERE TOWN & BOWNESS-ON-WINDERMERE

POP 8432

The largest natural body of water in England, Windermere has been a tourist magnet ever since the first steam trains chugged into town in 1847, and it still exerts an irresistible pull. It's a place where tradition and mass-market tourism meet head on: Victorian villas and slate-fronted hotels line up in ordered ranks along the streets of Windermere town, a mile uphill from the lakeshore, while down by the Bowness shoreline, cruise barges and row boats bob alongside the bustling piers. It's brash, busy and the summertime crowds can certainly take the shine off things, but Windermere is still an essential stop.

The train and bus stations, as well as the main tourist office and supermarket, are all in Windermere town. Most hotels and B&Bs are dotted around Lake Rd, which leads for a mile downhill towards Bowness and the lakeshore.

History

Prior to the 19th century, the area around present-day Windermere was little more than a collection of cottages making up the tiny farming hamlet of Birthwaite, but this sleepy settlement was changed beyond recognition when the decision was made in the 1840s to extend the west-coast railway towards Windermere in an effort to open up the Lakes to tourism from northern England's rapidly expanding industrial cities.

The plan met passionate opposition from many residents (some of whom were forcefully required to sell parts of their land to the railway company), not to mention a collection of local worthies including the newly appointed Poet Laureate, William Wordsworth, who wrote a series of stinging letters in opposition to the plan to the Board of Trade, the House of Commons and various influential newspaper editors. Wordsworth even found time to pen an anti-railway sonnet, published in the *Morning Post* in 1844.

Despite the opposition, the plan received royal assent in 1845. The original intent had been to run the tracks to the lakeshore, but due to the expense and technical difficulty presented by the gradient between Birthwaite and Bowness, the plan was changed to terminate the line near Birthwaite at a new station renamed Windermere.

The railway was completed in 1847, just two years after receiving its royal assent. In its inaugural year the railway carried more than 120,000 visitors into Windermere, heralding the arrival of mass tourism in the Lake District.

◎ Sights

Windermere is the largest lake in the national park, encompassing an area of 5.7 sq miles between Ambleside in the north and Newby Bridge in the south, with a maximum width of around a mile across. The lake is fed from the rivers Brathay and Rothay to the north, outflowing to the south into the River Leven. The deepest section of water lies near its northern end, where the lake bed is around 220m below the surface. Windermere supports a rich variety of underwater life, particularly pike, perch and a unique species of Arctic char, trapped here when the glaciers retreated at the end of the last ice age. It's also home to the largest population of goldeneye ducks in the Lake District. The name of the lake derives from Old Norse *Vinandr mere*, meaning 'Vinandr's lake'.

Windermere's shoreline is owned by a combination of private landholders, the national park and the National Trust (which owns the southern end around Fell Foot Park, and much of the western side), but the lake bed (and effectively the lake itself) is commonly owned by the people of Windermere as a result of the generosity of local philanthropist Henry Leigh Groves, who donated the sum of £6000 in 1938 to purchase the lake on behalf of residents. Since then the South Lakeland District Council has acted as landlord on their behalf, administering and maintaining its moorings and jetties.

Bizarrely, Lake Windermere is still officially a designated public highway (effectively the same as a road or motorway), a hangover from the 19th century when the lake served as a thoroughfare for barges ferrying coal, lumber, copper and slate between the local mines and the railway.

Windermere's Islands ISLANDS

There are officially 18 islands on Windermere, although some of the smaller ones amount to little more than a cluster of stones, foliage and shrubs (tiny **Maiden Holme**, the lake's smallest island, consists of just a single tree).

Largest of all is **Belle Isle** (Map p46), a densely wooded island of around 40 acres

Windermere Highlights

1 Take a **cruise** across the waters of Windermere and the wooded island of Belle Isle (p42)

2 Admire the Arts and Crafts elegance of **Blackwell House** (p52)

3 Ride the antique steam trains of the **Lakeside and Haverthwaite Railway** (p53)

4 Have afternoon tea in the grounds of **Fell Foot Park** (p52)

5 Get an eagle's-eye view of Windermere from the summit of **Gummer's How** (p43)

0 ___ 1.4 km
0 ___ 1 miles

To Kirkstone Pass (0.3mi); Ullswater (7.5mi)

River Kent

To Kendal (3mi)

6 Hawkshead Brewery

Staveley

Maggs Howe

Kentmere

Ings

The Dales Way

Gilpin Lodge

A591

A592

Windermere

Orrest Head

Holehird

Holbeck Ghyll

Troutbeck Bridge

Townend

Troutbeck

Queen's Head

Mortal Man

Wansfell Pike (487m)

Wansfell

Stock Ghyll

Trout Beck

The Struggle

High Sweden Bridge

Low Sweden Bridge

Loughrigg Fell (335m)

Rydal

Rydal Mount

Rydal Hall

Rydal Water

Grasmere Lake

River Rothay

Ambleside

A593

A591

River Brathay

Skelwith Bridge

Skelwith Force

Elterwater

Skelghyll Wood

Jenkin's Crag

Ambleside YHA

Stagshaw Gardens

Samling

Low Wood

Watersports Centre

Windermere YHA

Brockhole National Park Visitor Centre

Belle Grange Bay

Windermere

Wray Castle

High Wray

8 Low Wray Campsite

Randy Pike

Latterbarrow (245m)

Chaife Heights

B5286

B5285

Hawkshead

Grizedale Forest

Esthwaite Water

B5285

1 Windermere Lake Cruises

Bowness-on-Windermere

Windermere Ferry

Belle Isle

Brant Fell

⑥ Visit the vats at one of the Lake District's top beer-makers, **Hawkshead Brewery** (p55)

⑦ Leave the crowds well behind in the quiet **Winster Valley** (p54)

⑧ Spend the night in a traditional tipi at **Low Wray campsite** (p62)

ALL ABOARD!

The first passenger vessel launched on Windermere (or any English lake, for that matter) was the paddle steamer *Lady of the Lake*, built by Richard Ashburner of Greenodd for the Windermere Steam Yacht Co. The ship measured 80ft from bow to stern, carried up to 200 passengers and was luxuriously furnished with all the creature comforts expected by her well-to-do clientele, including a 1st-class saloon furnished with carpets, mirrors and cushioned seats.

All the great and the good of fashionable Lakeland society arrived to celebrate the ship's launch in 1845 (with the notable exception of William Wordsworth, who passionately opposed the idea of introducing pleasure vessels onto any of the lakes, and flatly refused to participate in the launch ceremony). To the sound of polite applause from the jetties and assorted parps, toots and cymbal clashes from the onboard brass band (borrowed for the occasion from the Kendal Cavalry), the ship set off on its maiden voyage from Newby Bridge to Ambleside; she continued in service for the next 20 years before finally being decommissioned in 1865.

opposite Cockshott Point. The island was originally home to a Roman villa occupied by the commander of the Roman garrison stationed nearby; during the Civil War it was occupied by the aristocratic Phillipson family, who were staunch supporters of the Royalist cause (legend has it that the island was shelled by Parliamentarian artillery from nearby Cockshott Point).

Then known as Long Holme, the island was purchased by Nottingham merchant Thomas English in 1774, who constructed the island's distinctive Italianate roundhouse and classical portico at a cost of around £6000 (Wordsworth subsequently lambasted it as a glorified 'pepper pot'). In 1781 English sold the island at a considerable loss to local mine owner (and MP for Carlisle) John Christian Curwen, who embellished the landscaped grounds, planted an arboretum of rare trees, and renamed the island 'Belle Isle' in honour of his wife (and cousin) Isabella. The island is still privately owned and is the only one inhabited year-round; it's off-limits to the public.

Other islands include the twin **Lilies of the Valley** (East and West), named after the blossoms that once grew here; **Crowe Holme**, which once served as a kennel for the hunting dogs of the Windermere Harriers; and **Lady Holme** (owned by the National Trust), which was formerly occupied by priests who lodged their brood of chickens on nearby **Hen Holme**, now a starting point for summer yacht races on Windermere.

The wooded island of **Thompson Holme** (known locally as Tommy Holme) has recently become a kind of miniature nature reserve, with a series of nesting boxes and conservation programs designed to study the local wildlife, while **Silver Holme** is rumoured to have been the inspiration for 'Cormorant Island' in Arthur Ransome's *Swallows and Amazons*. Holme, incidentally, derives from another Norse word meaning island.

Windermere Lake Cruises BOAT TOUR

(Map p46; www.windermere-lakecruises.co.uk) The first passenger ferry was launched on Windermere in 1845, and the tradition is still going strong. The lake's main cruise company runs a fleet of modern and vintage vessels: its oldest boat, *Tern*, was built in the 1890s, while *Swan* and *Teal* were both built in the 1930s.

There are several routes to choose from; on all cruises, you can jump off at one of the ferry landings (Waterhead/Ambleside, Wray Castle, Brockhole, Bowness, Ferry House and Lakeside), walk to the next landing and catch the next boat back.

A Freedom of the Lake ticket allows a day's unlimited travel and costs £17.25/8.65/47 per adult/child/family. Discounts are available before 11.30am on Fridays, and dogs travel free.

The **Blue Cruise** (adult/child £6.20/3.10) is a circular cruise around Windermere's shoreline and islands; it departs from Bowness with an optional stop at Ferry House. The **Green Cruise** (adult/child £7/3.50) is a 45-minute cruise from Waterhead/ Ambleside via Wray Castle and Brockhole Visitor Centre. The north-lake **Red Cruise** (adult/5-15yr £8.25/4.50) goes from Bowness to Ambleside, while the south-lake **Yellow**

Cruise (adult/5-15yr £9.80/5.90) goes from Bowness to Lakeside, stopping at the Lakes Aquarium.

The **Bowness to Ferry House** (adult/5-15yr £2.50/1.50) service links up with the Cross-Lakes Experience (p224) to Hill Top and Hawkshead.

Cockshott Point VIEWPOINT
(Map p46 This grassy headland offers one of the best views across to Belle Isle and makes a welcome escape from the busy quays of Bowness. The public footpath starts on Glebe Rd, winding through patches of woodland and pastureland along the lake's northeastern edge, offering wonderful views of the lake and islands. The path emerges at the southern end of Braithwaite Fold, near the Windermere Ferry.

World of Beatrix Potter CHILDREN'S ATTRACTION
(Map p46; www.hop-skip-jump.com; adult/child £6.75/3.50; ◷10am-5.30pm Apr-Sep, to 4.30pm Oct-Mar) This Beatrix Potter theme-land is a must for Tiggywinkle fans. It brings to life various scenes from the author's books (including Jemima Puddleduck's glade, Jeremy Fisher's Pond, Peter Rabbit's garden and Mr McGregor's greenhouse). The displays are obviously aimed at children, although don't be surprised if you see

plenty of starry-eyed adults wandering around too – the attraction is particularly popular with Japanese tourists. There's a well-stocked giftshop stuffed with cuddly Squirrel Nutkins and fluffy Benjamin Bunnies, and the Tailor of Gloucester tearoom makes a cute place for afternoon tea. Queues can be long, so arrive early.

Windermere Steamboat Museum MUSEUM
(www.steamboat.co.uk; Rayrigg Rd) This lakeside museum on Rayrigg Rd owns one of the nation's finest collections of steamboats, yachts and other lake vessels, but it's been closed for several years for redevelopment. Things finally look like they might be kicking into gear: the museum recently received a grant of £494,000 from the Heritage Lottery Fund towards its £7.1m redevelopment bid, and is currently seeking match funding. Check the website for the latest news.

🏃 Activities

Orrest Head HIKING
The most popular walk near Windermere is the bracing hour's stroll up to Orrest Head (784ft), famous for its 360-degree panorama encompassing Windermere, the Langdale Pikes and the Troutbeck Valley. It's also the first fell ever climbed by Alfred Wainwright; the great man reached the summit during a short holiday in 1930, sparking a life-long love affair with the Lakeland Fells.

The trail starts opposite Windermere Train Station near the Windermere Hotel.

Brant Fell HIKING
There's another wonderful outlook from the summit of Brant Fell (629ft). The trail starts near the end of Brantfell Rd, winding up the public path past Brantfell Farm before linking up with the Dales Way. It's an hour's stroll of about 2.5 miles there and back from Bowness, or you can follow the Dales Way north towards Windermere if you prefer (an extra 3 miles/two hours).

Gummer's How HIKING
It might be little compared to some of the better-known hills, but Gummer's How (1053ft) still packs a mightily impressive view that encompasses practically the whole of Windermere, stretching west all the way to the Coniston and Furness fells. It's a quick return walk of just over a mile; allow 1½ hours there and back.

ⓘ WINDERMERE COMBINATION TICKETS

If you're visiting several of Windermere's attractions, including the Lakes Aquarium, the Lakeside and Haverthwaite Railway and the Motor Museum, it works out much cheaper to buy a combination ticket. Prices here are for cruises from Bowness, but you can also buy combo tickets from Ambleside.

Boat & Train (adult/5-15yr/family £14.50/8.00/40) Cruise from Bowness and catch the train from Lakeside.

Boat & Aquarium (adult/5-15yr/family £16.25/9.35/48.30) Bowness–Lakeside cruise plus entry to Lakes Aquarium.

Boat & Motor Museum (adult/5-15yr/family £14.50/9.00/40.90) Bowness–Lakeside cruise and admission to the Motor Museum.

Boat, Motor Museum & Train (adult/5-15yr/family £20.10/11.80/55.90)

WINDERMERE & AROUND WINDERMERE TOWN & BOWNESS-ON-WINDERMERE

Windermere Town

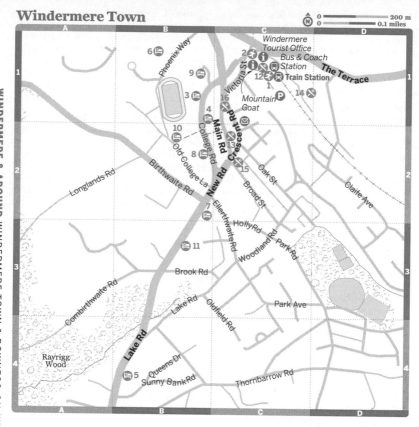

The fell looms up from the southeastern side of the lake. Drive south from Bowness on the A592, and look for a sharp uphill turn signed to Kendal just after the turning to Fell Foot Park. Park at the small Gummer's How Forestry Commission car park (marked on some maps as 'Astley's Plantation'), cross the road and follow the well-maintained path up to the summit. An ice-cream van often parks in the lay-by on summer afternoons, so you can reward yourself on the way back.

Boat Hire
BOATING
(Map p46; summer ☎015394-88178, 015394-40347; ◷9am-5pm Apr-Oct; winter ☎015394-43360; ◷Sat & Sun only) Traditional row boats and motor launches can be hired from the rental kiosk on Bowness promenade. Row boats cost £12 for up to two adults. Open-top motor boats cost £18 per hour for two adults, closed-cabins cost £22.

Controversially there's now a 10mph speed limit on Windermere (dropping to 6mph in the busier areas), which came into force in 2000 – a bone of some contention among local power boaters and waterskiers, who are now effectively banned from all of the major lakes inside the national park.

Windermere Canoe & Kayak
CANOEING
(Map p46; ☎015394-44451; www.windermere canoekayak.com; Ferry Nab Rd; ◷9am-5pm) This canoe company is based on Ferry Nab Rd near the Windermere Ferry, and hires out 'sit on tops' (single £20/30 per half-/full day, double £25/35) and canoes for more experienced users (from £30/40). Bikes can be hired for £20 per day.

Country Lanes
CYCLING
(Map p44; ☎015394-44544; www.countrylanes lakedistrict.co.uk; ◷9am-5pm) This bike-hire company is located beside the train station in Windermere (its Lakeside outlet was closed at the time of writing due to low visitor numbers). Daily rates are £19/12 for

Windermere Town

Activities

Sleeping

Eating

an adult/child front-suspension bike and £32 for full-suspension, and include bike, helmet, map and lock. Reservations can be made online.

Kankku OFF-ROAD DRIVING
(☎015394-47414; www.kankku.co.uk; Victoria St) If you've always been desperate to bring out your inner Jeremy Clarkson, then the petrol-fuelled adventures offered by this Windermere-based company might be just the ticket. Trips are run in various remote locations around the Lake District, and range from vertebrae-jangling expeditions in a 4x4 to introductory sessions with the company's new rally team.

Prices for 4x4 trips start at £39 per person, or £149 per vehicle. Rally trips cost from £250 for a full day.

 Festivals & Events

Brathay Windermere Marathon MARATHON
(www.brathaywindermeremarathon.org.uk) Steely legged racers take on the gruelling marathon around the shores of Windermere in late May.

Windermere Air Festival AIR SHOW
(www.windermereairshow.co.uk) The Lake District's largest air show brings aerial displays to the skies above the lake in late July. There is nearly always a gravity-defying display by the Red Arrows aerobatic team.

Great North Swim SWIMMING
(www.greatswim.org) Wild swimming is one thing, but you have to be pretty committed to take part in this mass outdoor swim in mid-June. Still, the event sees an amazing 10,000 swimmers take to Windermere's waters for ½-mile, 1-mile and 2-mile swims.

Sleeping

WINDERMERE TOWN

Windermere has more accommodation per square foot than practically anywhere else in the Lakes. Lake Rd, New Rd and the surrounding streets are chock-a-block with B&Bs and guesthouses, but it's worth booking well ahead for the best places.

Prices skyrocket in summer, and don't be too taken in by the 'boutique' tag – many of Windermere's B&Bs have developed ideas that are well and truly above their station.

TOP CHOICE Boundary GUESTHOUSE ££
(Map p44; ☎015394-48978; www.boundaryonline.com; Lake Rd d £100-160; [P][☎]) This is one place

i BROCKHOLE VISITOR CENTRE

If you're a first-timer to the Lakes, the national park's main visitor centre at **Brockhole** (☎015394-46601; www.lake-district.gov.uk) should definitely be your first port of call. It's housed in a fine mansion built in 1895 for the Mancunian silk merchant William Henry Aldolphus Gaddum, but has served as a visitor centre since 1969. There are informative displays on the geology, environment and history of the national park, as well as a kids' playground and lakeside gardens designed by Thomas Mawson (see p52). Staff can help plan sights and activities and also run regular guided walks and talks; check the website for the latest events.

The visitor centre is 3 miles from Windermere on the A591. Entrance is free, but the large car park is pay-and-display (£2.20/4/6 for two hours/four hours/all day). Windermere Lake Cruises and Buses 555 and 599 all make stops at Brockhole.

Bowness-on-Windermere

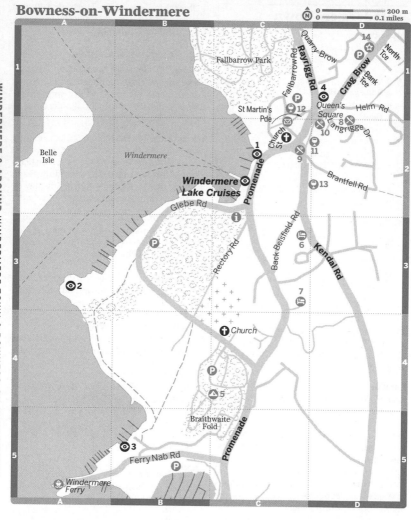

that lives up to its boutique pretensions: it's one of the most stylish little guesthouses in Windermere. Neutral palettes and minimal clutter define the rooms, all of which are named after prominent cricketers: ask for Fry, with its freestanding mirror and double aspect windows, or Hobbs, with its flashy shower and contemporary four-poster. Some rooms have baths in the bedrooms, which might not be to everyone's taste. Downstairs you'll find a chic lounge stocked with leather sofas, a woodburner and old copies of Wisden's to browse before a slap-up breakfast of Manx kippers, American pancakes and meats from Sillfield Farm. Really rather good.

Wheatlands Lodge GUESTHOUSE ££
(Map p44; ☎015394-43789; www.wheatlands lodge-windermere.co.uk; Old College Lane; d £80-170; 🅿🛜) In a town that's literally wall-to-wall B&Bs, the Wheatlands manages to poke its head above the crowd. It's in a tucked-away cul-de-sac just off Lake Rd, and the rooms are elegant without being over the top: they're smart and spacious, and boast slate-floored bathrooms with a choice of walk-in showers or free-standing Jacuzzi tubs.

Bowness-on-Windermere

◎ **Top Sights**
Windermere Lake Cruises C7

◎ **Sights**
1 Boat Hire C2
2 Cockshott Point A3
3 Windermere Canoe & Kayak B5
4 World of Beatrix Potter D1

⬛ **Sleeping**
5 Braithwaite Fold C4
6 Cranleigh C3
7 Lingwood Lodge......................C3

✕ **Eating**
8 Angel Inn D2
9 Jackson's C2
10 Postilion D2

🍷 **Drinking**
11 Bodega Bar & Tapas..............D2
12 Hole in t' Wall C1
13 Royal Oak D2

🎭 **Entertainment**
Old Laundry Theatre ....(see 4)
14 Royalty Cinema D1

Applegarth Hotel
HOTEL ££

(Map p44; ☎015394-43206; www.lakesapplegarth.co.uk; College Rd; s £62-67, d £130-206; 🅿🖥) This stately mansion at the top end of town was built by 19th-century industrialist John Riggs. Some rooms retain a Victorian vibe (four-poster beds, floral fabrics, bay windows) while others have been given a glam makeover (designer prints, mood lighting, plasma TVs). The lobby still boasts its original stained glass and wood panelling, and the downstairs restaurant, JR's, has views across Elleray Gardens.

Jerichos
HOTEL ££

(Map p44; ☎015394-42522; www.jerichos.co.uk; College Rd; s £45-55, d £80-105; 🖥) The main reason to visit Jerichos (formerly the Waverley Hotel) is to treat yourself to supper at the excellent restaurant, but if you feel like staying overnight you'll find small but contemporary rooms upstairs, all with en suites, pattern-print wallpaper and Lakeland prints on the walls. Some (such as 1 and 11) are shoebox-small; ask for 2 or 4 for more space.

Windermere Suites
GUESTHOUSE £££

(Map p44; ☎01539-444739; www.windermeresuites.co.uk; New Rd; d £140-280; 🅿🖥) Newly renovated by the owners of the Howbeck, the main selling point for the rooms here are their sheer size. They're simply huge; all are named after different Lakeland locations, but share the same penchant for white walls, gloss-wood floors, boutique wallpapers and enormous TVs. In fact, it might be too much for some, and it is on the pricey side.

Hideaway
GUESTHOUSE ££

(Map p44; ☎015394-43070; www.thehideawayatwindermere.co.uk; Phoenix Way; £80-170; 🅿🖥) Victorian features rub shoulders with a style-mag refit at this plush if pricey B&B. The cheaper rooms are cheap but bland; plump instead for the 'Super Comfy' or 'Ultimate Comfy' doubles, with spa baths and luxury furnishings. The best is the split-level number 12, with a spiral staircase down to the bathroom.

Archway
B&B £

(Map p44; ☎015394-45613; www.the-archway.com; 13 College Rd; d £50-55) There's nothing fancy about this traditional terraced B&B, but it makes a strangely reassuring change after the designer arms race that seems to be at work in many of the town's B&Bs. Rooms are small, although some boast distant views of the Langdale Pikes, and breakfast is almost comically generous.

Howbeck
GUESTHOUSE ££

(Map p44; ☎015394-44739; www.howbeck.co.uk; New Rd; d £100-160; 🅿🖥) Not quite as spangly as its sister business, Windermere Suites, but still an upmarket choice. Ten rooms, all crisply finished in up-to-date fabrics: a bit more cash buys extra spoils (plusher beds, fruit and sherry), but you won't completely escape the road noise.

Firgarth
B&B ££

(☎015394-46974; Ambleside Rd; www.guesthouseinwindermere.co.uk; s £38-55, d £70-100; 🅿) If you're doing Windermere on a budget, you could do much worse than this B&B on the main road from Windermere to Ambleside. The corridors are a shade shabby, but the rooms are pleasantly done in creams and yellows, and owners Colin and Pam are fantastically friendly. Definitely ask for a room away from the road if you're a light sleeper.

Lake District Backpackers Lodge
HOSTEL ££

(Map p44; ☎015394-46374; www.lakedistrictbackpackers.co.uk; High St; dm £14.50-16.50; 🖳) The only hostel in Windermere itself is a real let-down, with cramped dorms, basic kitchen facilities and alarmingly outdated furnishings, although it's handy for the station.

BOWNESS-ON-WINDERMERE

Number 80 Bed then Breakfast
B&B ££

(☑015394-43584; www.number80bed.co.uk; 80 Craig Walk; d £80-90) This four-room establishment is everything a modern B&B should be, and for once in Bowness you won't have to pay through the nose for the privilege of staying here. It's refreshingly unpretentious: rooms are smart and minimal, with mini-fridges to chill your wine and the odd flashy fabric to liven things up. Bathrooms sparkle, and breakfast is a classic choice of cooked, continental or veggie. And with rates as cheap as this, it's an absolute steal.

Cranleigh
HOTEL ££

(Map p46; ☑015394-43293; www.thecranleigh .com; Kendal Rd; d £115-169, ste £269; P🕾) No expense has been spared at this fancy pad just off the Bowness waterfront. The rooms each have their own individual quirks, but for an utter spoil the Sanctuary bungalow is the one to go for, with its remote-controlled fire, 8ft headboard and a glass bath that's straight out of Blade Runner. The rest of the rooms are less stellar, but offer better value.

Lingwood Lodge
B&B ££

(Map p46; ☑015394-44680; www.lingwoodlodge .co.uk; Birkett Hill; s £55, d £80-122; P🕾) Simple if unstarry, the six rooms at this detached modern house are pleasantly understated in creams and whites, with pine-effect furniture and pocket-sized digital TVs. There's ample parking and free wi-fi, and Bowness is walking distance.

Braithwaite Fold
CARAVANS £

(Map p46; ☑01539-442177; adult £5, child £2.50, sites £7.60; ⊙mid-Mar-Nov) Caravan-only site near the marina.

AROUND TOWN

There are some seriously upmarket country hotels around Windermere, but none of them come cheap.

Gilpin Lodge
LUXURY HOTEL £££

(Map p40; ☑015394-88818; www.gilpinlodge .co.uk; Crook Rd; r £230-380, lake house £410-450; P🕾) This luxurious country-house hotel pulls out all the stops. The feel is classic and rather formal, but it's far from snooty. Rooms are spacious and supremely stylish, all with fine views, Molton Brown bathstuffs and upmarket furniture. If your budget will stretch, the lovely lake-house suites boast cedarwood hot tubs and glass-fronted lounges overlooking private gardens. Rates include a gourmet five-course dinner. The hotel even has its own llama paddock.

Holbeck Ghyll
LUXURY HOTEL £££

(Map p40; ☑015394-34743; www.holbeckghyll .com; r incl dinner £245-399; P🕾) Another gloriously grand old dame, formerly a hunting lodge owned in the 19th century by Lord Lonsdale. The ivy-clad house still boasts much of its original Arts and Crafts character, including stained glass and mahogany panelling; for something more modern, ask for one of the detached suites near the main house. Rooms overlook sweeping grounds, and rates include four courses at the much-vaunted (and Michelin-starred) restaurant, renowned for serving some of the finest Anglo-French food anywhere in the Lakes.

Linthwaite House
LUXURY HOTEL £££

(Map p41; ☑015394-88600; www.linthwaite .com; Crook Rd; r £189-322, ste £308-531; P🕾) Another plush country retreat occupying a superb spot perched above Windermere, surrounded by private woodland walks, a croquet lawn, a private tarn and 14 acres of grounds. Rooms are sleek, chic and soothingly beige, with minimal decorative fuss (though they're small considering the price).

Samling
LUXURY HOTEL £££

(Map p40; ☑015394-31922; www.thesamling hotel.co.uk; Dove Nest; r weekdays £200-490, weekends £230-520; P🕾) If money's no object, this getaway (now owned by the von Essen group) is the choice for style gurus and sojourning celebs. Ten rustic-chic rooms and self-contained cottages drip with designer trappings: split-level mezzanines and slate bathrooms in some, claw-foot tubs, rain showers and private lounges in others. It's reached via its own private drive 3 miles north of Windermere.

Park Cliffe
CAMPGROUND £

(Map p41; ☑015395-31344; www.parkcliffe.co.uk; Birks Rd; site for 2 adults incl car & tent £20-28, caravans incl 2 people & car £25-29) Award-winning 10-hectare campsite between Windermere and Newby Bridge along the A592, with a choice of camping fields (Fell Side for lake views, Ghyll Side for power hook-ups, Moor How for caravanners), and facilities including a grocery shop, laundrette and cafe. Timber camping pods are also available for £40 to £45. You can have your own private bathroom for £14.

✖ Eating

Several of Windermere's best restaurants are located in luxury hotels such as Miller Howe and Holbeck Ghyll, both of which boast a Michelin star. They're usually open to outside diners, although preference is given to guests first.

TOP CHOICE Jerichos BRITISH ££££
(Map p44; ☎015394-42522; www.jerichos.co.uk; College Rd; mains £15.25 25; ☺dinner Fri-Wed) Windermere's long-standing fine-diner has occupied several locations round town over the years, but it's now firmly established as this sophisticated restaurant-with-rooms on College Rd. The menu is overseen by owner-proprietor Chris Blaydes, who cut his teeth under celeb chef John Tovey at the Miller Howe. Lakeland produce married with European flavours makes for a rich and rewarding experience, and the dining room oozes elegance with its tall sash windows, lustrous wood floors and velvety curtains.

Postilion FRENCH, EUROPEAN ££
(Map p46; ☎015394-45852; www.postilion restaurant.co.uk; Ash St; mains £12-16, set menu £18.95; ☺lunch & dinner) For nigh on 16 years the Postilion has been serving up some of Bowness' best food, and it's still going strong. It's tucked away off Ash St and looks unexciting from the outside, but inside it's all stripped beams, leather sofas and shiny woods. The menu mainly sticks to brasserie standards with a French influence: chicken breast with mushrooms and pancetta, perhaps, or lamb with mint and blackcurrant jus. The set menu is a bargain; book ahead.

Francine's BISTRO ££
(Map p44; ☎015394-44088; 27 Main Rd; lunch 2-/3-course menu £10.95/13.95, dinner mains £9.95-14.95; ☺lunch Tue-Sun, dinner Wed-Sat) You'll often find as many locals as tourists in this snug bistro (always a good sign), and it's run with homely efficiency by a husband-and-wife team. Dinky square tables and jugs of flowers conjure a French-bistro vibe, and the menu's a similarly continental affair: duck leg confit, rich pasta, sea bream and spicy bowls of mussels, followed perhaps with *sachertorte* or crème brûlée.

Angel Inn PUB ££
(Map p46; www.the-angelinn.com; Helm Rd; lunch mains £4.95-12, dinner mains £13-??) This handsome pub is perched on a grassy knoll just behind the Bowness lakeshore. The food is classic gastropub – venison and cranberry bangers, beer-battered coley – and the interior is slick and urban, with stripped wood floors and leather sofas. The grassy terrace with its shady parasols unsurprisingly gets busy on sunny days.

Jackson's BISTRO ££
(Map p46; ☎015394-46264; St Martin's Sq; mains £9.95-16, 3-course menu £15.95; ☺dinner Mon-Sat) Straightforward restaurant that concentrates on straightforward food – pan-fried fish, steaks, chicken, risottos – served among pine tables and potted plants. Don't expect anything earth-moving; do expect hearty food served in cosy surroundings.

Lazy Daisy's Lakeland Kitchen CAFE £
(Map p44; 31-33 Crescent Rd; lunch £3.50-9.95, dinner £8.75-11.95; ☺breakfast, lunch & dinner Mon-Sat) Hearty comfort food is the order of the day at this teensy country cafe at the top end of Windermere: steaming sausage served on a giant Yorkshire pud, or steak-and-Guinness pie dished up with lashings of gravy. Haute cuisine it ain't, but sometimes honest grub is all you're after.

Lighthouse CAFE ££
(Map p44; Main Rd; mains £8-20) Buzzy cafe-bar at the top of Windermere, ideal for pastries, coffee or a quick lunchtime snack. Plate-glass windows keep things light inside; opt for a street-side table if the outlook is sunny.

Booth's SUPERMARKET £
(Map p44; ☺8am-8pm Mon-Sat, 10am-4pm Sun) The main supermarket in Windermere, next to the station.

Lakeland CAFE £
(Alexandra Buildings; ☺8am-7pm Mon-Fri, 9am-6pm Sat, 11-5pm Sun) Flagship store for the kitchen-goods chain, with a pleasant cafe on the first floor.

🍷 Drinking

Bodega Bar & Tapas BAR
(Map p46; Ash St; tapas £2-8; ☺noon-midnight) Down margaritas and munch on tapas at this Hispanic bar just off the main Bowness drag.

Hole in t' Wall   PUB
(Map p46; Fallbarrow Rd) Lots of local ales are on tap at this venerable boozer (built in 1612), with the all-essential flagstones and fireplaces, plus a patio where you can watch the Bowness crowds buzz by.

Royal Oak   PUB
(Map p46; Brantfell Rd) Old-fashioned pub with a good selection of Lakeland ales (including Coniston Bluebird and Hawkshead Bitter).

☆ Entertainment
Apart from the town pubs and the theatre, Windermere is a bit short on things to do after dark.

Old Laundry Theatre   THEATRE
(Map p46; www.oldlaundrytheatre.co.uk; Crag Brow) This small provincial theatre hosts live entertainment, touring theatre and dance productions.

Royalty Cinema   CINEMA
(Map p46; ☏015394-43364; Lake Rd; adult £5-6, child £4.50-5) The town's cinema dates back to 1926 and is an endearingly old-fashioned affair (complete with velour curtains across the screen and a choice of circle or stalls). It's a short walk uphill from Bowness, and mainly screens mainstream releases.

ℹ Information
Branches of Barclays, HSBC, Natwest and Santander are on the main street in Windermere.

Internet Access
Elephant & Camel Café (4 Windermere Bank, Lake Rd; per 20min £1; ⊙10am-6pm Mon-Sat)
Library (Broad St; per ½hr £1; ⊙9.30am-5pm Mon, Tue, Thu & Fri, 10am-1pm Sat)

HAVE YOUR SAY

Found a fantastic restaurant that you're longing to share with the world? Disagree with our recommendations? Or just want to talk about your most recent trip?

Whatever your reason, head to lonely planet.com, where you can post a review, ask or answer a question on the Thorntree forum, comment on a blog, or share your photos and tips on Groups. Or you can simply spend time chatting with like-minded travellers. So go on, have your say.

Tourist Information
Bowness Tourist Office (Map p46; ☏015394-42895; bownesstic@lake-district.gov.uk; Glebe Rd; ⊙9.30am-5.30pm Easter-Oct, 10am-4.30pm Nov-Mar) Near the boat jetties.
Mountain Goat (Map p44; ☏015394-45161; www.mountain-goat.com; Victoria St) Runs minibus tours and the Cross-Lakes Experience (p224).
Windermere Tourist Office (Map p44; ☏015394-46499; windermeretic@south lakeland.gov.uk; Victoria St; ⊙9am-5.30pm Apr-Oct, shorter hr in winter) Opposite Natwest bank. Offers accommodation booking service (£3) and internet access (15 minutes per £1).

ℹ Getting There & Around
See p224 for details of the Cross-Lakes Experience.

Boat
Windermere Ferry (cars & caravans £4.30, motorbike £1.60, bicycle £1, pedestrian 50p; ⊙6.50am-9.50pm Mon-Sat, 9.10am-9.50pm Sun Mar-Oct, last ferry leaves 8.50pm in winter) Quaint car ferry which runs between Ferry Nab (just south of Bowness) and Ferry House (on the lake's west side). There's one roughly every 20 minutes, but queues can be horrendous in summer. The service often doesn't run during bad weather.

Bus
Most of the main bus routes around the Lake District run through either Windermere, Bowness or both. For National Express coaches and trains to Windermere Station, see p221.
Local buses:
555/556 Lakeslink Tracks the east side of the lake to Brockhole Visitor Centre (seven minutes, at least hourly), Ambleside (15 minutes) and Grasmere (30 minutes). Travels to Kendal (30 minutes) in the opposite direction.
505 Coniston Rambler To Coniston (50 minutes, eight daily Monday to Saturday, six on Sunday in summer, reduced service in winter) via Brockhole, Ambleside and Hawkshead.
599 Lakes Rider Runs from Kendal and Staveley to Windermere Station (three times per hour Monday to Saturday in summer, reduced service in winter), then continues to Bowness, Troutbeck Bridge, Brockhole, Waterhead, Ambleside, Rydal Mount, Dove Cottage and Grasmere.

Taxi
Bowness Taxis (☏015394-46664)
Lakes Taxis (☏015394-46777)
Windermere Taxi Services (☏015394-45282)

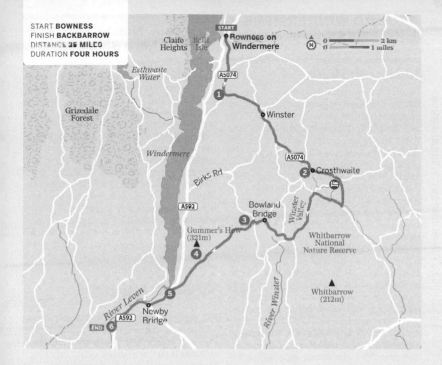

START
**Bowness on
Windermere**

A5074

❶

● Winster

A5074

❷ ● Crosthwaite

A592

**Bowland
Bridge**

❸

Gummer's How
(321m)

❹

Winster Valley

Whitbarrow
National
Nature Reserve

River Winster

Whitbarrow
(212m)

River Leven

❺

Newby
Bridge

A592

END ❻

Claife
Heights

Belle
Isle

Esthwaite
Water

Grizedale
Forest

Windermere

Birks Rd

A592

0   2 km
0   1 miles

Driving Tour
East Windermere

❯ This picturesque drive takes in the quiet countryside to the east of Windermere and includes some fantastic stops for food en route.

Take the A592 south from Bowness, then turn right onto the A5074 to reach ❶ **Blackwell House**, one of England's most elegant Arts and Crafts houses, created in 1900 by designer Mackay Hugh Baillie Scott for a wealthy brewer. If the weather's fine, the gardens make a great spot for elevenses, with panoramic views across Windermere towards Claife Heights.

Continue along the A5074 for around 3 miles, and turn left towards Crosthwaite, where a slap-up lunch awaits at the award-winning ❷ **Punch Bowl Inn**, run by the same people behind the much-vaunted Drunken Duck Inn near Hawkshead.

Once you've filled up on food, drive back to the A5074 and look out for the minor road signed towards Bowland Bridge. The road dips into the Winster Valley before weaving up the side of Strawberry Bank; as you climb the hill,

you'll pass the ❸ **Mason's Arms**, a favourite drinking hole for children's writer Arthur Ransome, who lived nearby in the 1920s.

At the top of the hill, the road levels out into Forestry Commission woodland before dropping downhill towards the lake. From the small car park at Astley's Plantation, it's a half-hour hike to the summit of ❹ **Gummer's How**, offering one of the best viewpoints over Windermere. Look out for cruise boats beetling across the lake and steam-plumes from the Lakeside and Haverthwaite Railway.

Continue downhill to the junction with the A592 and turn left. You'll see the entrance to the landscaped grounds of ❺ **Fell Foot Park** soon afterwards. The park is ideal for strolling and boating, or you could just tuck into afternoon tea at the boathouse cafe.

Last stop on the tour is the newly relocated ❻ **Lakeland Motor Museum** in Backbarrow, famous for its world-renowned collection of antique automobiles. From here, it's a 7-mile drive back to Bowness along the A592.

AROUND WINDERMERE & BOWNESS

Blackwell House

Located 1.5 miles south of Bowness on the B5360, **Blackwell House** (www.blackwell.org .uk; adult/child £7/4, garden only £4; ⊙10.30am-5pm Apr-Oct, to 4pm Nov-Mar) is one of the finest surviving examples of the Arts and Crafts movement. Inspired by the aesthetic principles of John Ruskin and William Morris, this 19th-century movement was a direct reaction against the machine-driven mentality of the Industrial Revolution, placing emphasis on simple architecture, high-quality craftsmanship and natural light.

The house was built in 1900 for brewing magnate Sir Edward Holt. Designed by Mackay Hugh Baillie Scott, the house bears all the hallmarks of classic Arts and Crafts design: light, airy rooms; a serene, symmetrical layout; and design motifs inspired by natural forms. Most importantly of all, nearly everything in the house was created by hand by local craftsmen; championing and protecting traditional skills was a key element of the Arts and Crafts ethos.

Wandering the hallways today, it's hard to believe that just over a decade ago the house was effectively derelict following stints as a boarding house for wartime evacuees and a girl's prep school. After a long campaign to raise funds to restore the house to its former glory, the property was purchased by English Nature in 1997 and completely renovated thanks to the Heritage Lottery Fund. It was finally reopened to the public in 2001.

The Great Hall is the house's most impressive room, deliberately built to echo the atmosphere of a medieval hall (complete with delft-tiled inglenook fireplace, minstrel's gallery and oak panelling). Another notable room is the White Drawing Room, which is flooded with light through floor-to-ceiling windows, and makes a stark contrast to the stern, masculine feel of the rest of the house. Upstairs, most of the bedrooms have been converted into exhibition spaces, although a few have been refurbished in period style.

Outside, the delightful grounds were laid out by renowned landscaper Thomas Mawson, who also designed gardens at Holker Hall, Holehird, Rydal Hall and Brockhole.

Lakeside, Newby Bridge & the Southern Shore

South of Bowness, the narrow A592 runs for 8 miles along the lake's eastern edge, ducking and veering through beech and oak woodland, while affording fleeting glimpses of Windermere's silvery surface and the eastern shore.

In the 19th century, this section of the lake was where many nouveau-riche industrialists decided to build their own lakeside mansions. Most have now been converted into expensive hotels, including **Storrs Hall** (www.elh.co.uk/hotels/storrshall), which was once owned by John Bolton, who made his fortune from the Liverpool slave trade and became famous for his lavish parties, attended by literary luminaries including Sir Walter Scott and William Wordsworth.

⊙ Sights & Activities

Fell Foot Park   GARDENS
(NT; admission free, parking charges apply for non-NT members; ⊙9am-5pm) This grand 18-acre sweep of manicured lawns and landscaped grounds is all that remains of a manor house that was demolished in around 1910 by its last owner, Oswald Henley, who intended to build a new mansion on the site but never quite got around to it. The site remained in ruins until it was acquired by the National Trust following WWII.

While the house may be gone, the gardens still make a glorious spot for a stroll, especially during the annual displays of daffodils and rhododendrons. From April to October, row boats can be hired from the estate's boathouses, where you'll also find a National Trust tearoom selling sandwiches, cream teas and cakes.

Lakes Aquarium   AQUARIUM
(www.lakesaquarium.co.uk; Lakeside, Newby Bridge; adult/3-15yr £9.15/6.10, see p43 for combination tickets; ⊙9am-6pm Apr-Oct, to 5pm Nov-Mar) Next to the station platform at Lakeside, the Lakes Aquarium explores a variety of underwater habitats from across the globe, as well as a few closer to home. The highlight is the underwater tunnel, which simulates a trip beneath Windermere's surface, complete with carp, char and diving ducks. Alongside the fishy inhabitants, the aquarium is also home to a boa constrictor, a

DON'T MISS

LAKESIDE & HAVERTHWAITE RAILWAY

At the southernmost tip of Windermere is the small landing-station of Lakeside, the southerly terminus for the Windermere cruise boats from Bowness. It also marks the end of the line for the chuffing steam trains of the **Lakeside and Haverthwaite Railway** (www.lakesiderailway.co.uk; Haverthwaite Station, nr Ulverston; standard return adult/5-15yr £6.20/3.10; ⊙mid-Mar–Oct), which was originally built to ferry materials from the Lakeland mines and timber plantations to Ulverston and Barrow, but now serves as one of northern England's most popular vintage railways. Classic carriages decked out in period livery rattle down the line via Newby Bridge to Haverthwaite, near Ulverston; there are five to seven trains daily in season, timed to correspond with the Windermere cruise boats.

Joint tickets are also available for the Lakes Aquarium, Bowness cruises and Motor Museum – see the box, p43.

family of marmosets and a pair of Asian short-clawed otters.

Tickets are up to a third cheaper when bought online.

Lakeland Motor Museum CAR MUSEUM
(www.lakelandmotormuseum.co.uk; Backbarrow; adult/5-15yr £7.50/5, see p43 for combination tickets; ⊙0.30am-5.30pm Apr-Sep, to 4.30pm Oct-Mar) This fabulous collection of vintage automobilia was originally housed at Holker Hall, but it's now installed in a spanking new building at Backbarrow, a couple of miles south of Newby Bridge. There are over 30,000 motor themed exhibits, but it's the classic-car collection that's the real highlight: motors on show range from Morris Minors, Trabants and pedal cars through to iconic Aston Martins, Jaguars and MGs.

A special section of the museum is devoted to the story of Malcolm and Donald Campbell (see p86), with full-size replicas of several of their groundbreaking Bluebird boats. There are also several period shopfront reconstructions, including a re-creation of a local garage forecourt from the 1920s.

Stott Park Bobbin Mill MUSEUM
(EH; adult/child £6/3.60; ⊙11am-5pm Mon-Fri Easter-Oct) Located 1½ miles north of Newby Bridge, this industrial mill was built in 1835 to manufacture the wooden bobbins (thread-spools) used by the industrial looms of Lancashire and northern England's other textile centres. When the textile trade faltered at the end of the 19th century, the mill branched out into making other wooden items such as pick-axe handles, hammer shafts and even yo-yos.

Although the factory closed down in 1971, much of the original machinery is still in place, and admission includes a guided tour and a demonstration of the bobbin-making process (you might even take one home as a souvenir).

🛏 Sleeping & Eating

Knoll GUESTHOUSE ££
(☎015395-31347; www.theknoll-lakeside.co.uk; s £70-100, d £90-150; P🖙) If you're looking to escape the crowded quays of Bowness and Lakeside, this sweet little guesthouse could be just what you're after. It's tucked away in a secluded spot on Windermere's quieter southwestern side. There are just eight rooms, so the feel is intimate and exclusive; posh cotton linen, country-style furnishings and a choice of four-poster or sleigh beds ratchet up the charm, and owner Jen Meads goes out of her way to make your stay a treat. You don't even have to go out for supper; the very decent two-/three-course set menu costs £22/26. Breakfast has some intriguing options too, including beancakes, kedgeree and Manx Kippers.

Swan Hotel HOTEL £££
(☎015395-31681; www.swanhotel.com; Newby Bridge; r Sun-Fri £119-140, Sat £140-210; P🖙🖙) Plonked beside Newby Bridge, the old Swan has been a stop-off for travellers for centuries. The whitewashed facade looks olde worlde, but the interior is actually quite modern: tasteful rooms are divided into standard, deluxe and suite classes, with extra cash buying luxuries such as in-room espresso machines, iPod docks and lake views. The inn serves beers and light bites; for sit-down dinners there's the more upmarket River Room. Saturday stays incur a premium.

❶ Getting There & Away

In addition to the lake cruises and the railway, several buses stop at Newby Bridge:

X35 (hourly Monday to Saturday, three on Sunday) Stops at Newby Bridge en route from Kendal (40 minutes), then runs south to Backbarrow and Haverthwaite (two to three minutes for the motor museum and railway), Ulverston (15 minutes) and Barrow (40 minutes).

618 (five daily Monday to Saturday) Follows a similar route from Barrow, then runs north along the lake to Bowness, Windermere, Troutbeck Bridge and Ambleside.

Lyth & Winster Valleys

To the east of Fell Foot Park, a twisting road (signed towards Kendal) leads northeast past Gummer's How into the little-explored Lyth and Winster Valleys. Spotted with remote farms and timber plantations, these quiet valleys still feel wonderfully remote, even though they're only a short drive from Windermere – a quality which no doubt appealed to Arthur Ransome, who lived nearby at Low Ludderburn while penning *Swallows and Amazons*.

The Lyth and Winster Valleys are principally known for their bumper crops of Westmorland damson, a soft, delicate fruit related to the plum that's used to flavour everything from jam and juices to chocolate and gin. In late summer you'll often see little stalls by the side of the road selling damson-flavoured goodies; the **Westmorland Damson Association** (www.lythdamsons.org.uk) has details of local growers and a downloadable map.

The area is also home to a rare limestone ridge known as the **Whitbarrow Scar**, which supports many unusual species of birds and butterflies. July and August are the best months for butterfly spotting: follow signs to Witherslack, and turn right at Witherslack Hall to find the reserve's small car-park. An OS map will come in handy in case you get lost.

🛏 Sleeping & Eating

TOP CHOICE Punch Bowl Inn PUB ££
(☏015395-68237; www.the-punchbowl.co.uk; Crosthwaite; mains £10.25-14.99, r £160-310; ℗) A cracking dining pub, run by the owners of the equally excellent Drunken Duck near Hawkshead. Inside it feels more country bistro than Lakeland inn: most of the clutter's been cleared out in favour of clean lines, tasteful furnishings and the odd agricultural knick-knack. The upstairs rooms are small but elegantly appointed: they're named after Crosthwaite vicars, and feature fancy spoils such as Roberts radios and roll-top baths. The real attraction's the grub and grog, though: homebrewed ales come from the inhouse Barngates Brewery, and the menu showcases sophisticated country food with a strong Gallic flavour. The pub's in Crosthwaite, about 5 miles southwest of Bowness off the A5074. Definitely worth the drive.

Mason's Arms PUB ££
(☏015395-68486; www.masonsarmsstrawberry bank.co.uk; r £75-135, cottages £110-165; ℗) Perched on the forbiddingly steep fellside of Strawberry Bank, this fine inn is well worth the trip from Windermere. Wonky rafters, slate floors and an antique cast-iron range give the interior plenty of rustic character, and the menu revolves around hearty country fare: pork and damson bangers, or slow-cooked Cartmel lamb served with hotpot potatoes. The pleasant rooms and lovely self-contained cottages have to-die-for views across the valley, as does the lovely outside patio. The inn is just west of Bowland Bridge, about 3 miles east of Windermere; follow the road past Gummer's How, and watch out for the hairpin turns on the way down.

Brown Horse PUB ££
(☏015394-43443; www.thebrownhorseinn.co.uk; mains £10.95-19.95) Another posh pub in Winster, whitewashed outside, polished up inside, as popular with local country folk as with foodie visitors. The interior is an odd melange of styles: retro-chic chandeliers meet squeaky leather and stag's antlers in the dining room, while the bar blends carved oak pews, scuffed slate floors and spotlights. Meat, game and veg is mostly produced on the Brown Horse Estate, and there are two bespoke ales (Old School and Best Bitter) from the new microbrewery – although standards are more posh pub than proper restaurant. It's on the A5074, a few miles past Blackwell House.

Staveley

Four miles east of Windermere off the A591 is Staveley, hunkered down on the banks of the River Kent. The town originally grew up around a busy medieval market and

17th-century timber and bobbin mill, and the tradition of Staveley woodworking remains strong to this day. These days the village is better known for its foodie credentials, with an enticing helping of bakeries and breweries around the redeveloped Mill Yard.

◉ Sights & Activities

Hawkshead Brewery   BREWERY

(www.hawksheadbrewery.co.uk) Set up by former BBC foreign correspondent Alex Brodie, this celebrated alehouse has been based in Staveley since 2006, and now delivers its award-winning beers to pubs all across the Lake District and northern England. Its core ales include the original Hawkshead bitter, plus fruity Red, Lakeland Gold and the dark Brodie's Prime stout, but there are always a few seasonal ales on tap.

You can sample some of the in-house brews in the glossy **beer hall** (⊘noon-6pm Mon & Tue, to 6pm or later Wed-Sun), overlooked by a blackboard beer menu and two gigantic stainless steel vats. If you'd like to take a peek behind the scenes, tours of the brewery are also available at 1pm, 2pm or 3pm on Saturdays (or by arrangement).

LucyCooks   COOKERY COURSES

(www.lucycooks.co.uk) Lucy Nicholson's culinary empire might have fallen on hard times recently (see p63), but her cookery school is still going strong. It offers a huge range of culinary courses, from seafood masterclasses to baking your own bread: prices start at around £125. Check the website to see what's on offer.

Wheelbase   BIKE SHOP

(✆0870 600 3435; www.wheelbase.co.uk; ⊘9am-5.30pm Mon-Sat, 10am-4pm Sun) This vast bike shop – the largest in England, apparently – is housed in an enormous barn in the middle of Staveley. It sells a massive range of bikes, gear and accessories, and the shop produces custom trail maps to some of the area's most popular rides. Bike hire is available for £14/18 per half-/full day. Prices are the same for adults and kids.

✖ Eating

More?   BAKERY £

(www.moreartisan.co.uk) An award-winning bakery known for its speciality breads and cakes, as well as local flours and yeasts. You can watch the bakers at work on the top floor, or hire the services of owner Patrick Moore for baking masterclasses. His infamous More Muddees are guaranteed to satisfy even the most hardcore chocoholic.

KENTMERE VALLEY

If you're fed up with the hectic trails of the central fells, the Kentmere Valley might be the sanctuary you're looking for. Stretching north of Staveley beyond the gushing weir at Barley Bridge, this remote valley was once a centre for the milling industry, but is now better known for the classic **Kentmere Round** (12 miles, seven hours), a superb high-level hike that takes in the summits dotted around the head of the valley, including Yoke, Ill Bell, Froswick, Thornthwaite Crag, Mardale Ill Bell, Harter Fell, Kentmere Pike and Shipman Knotts.

For something less strenuous, you could join one of the NPA's free **guided walks** (www.lakedistrict.gov.uk/index/visiting/events.htm) in Kentmere, which start at Wilf's Café in Staveley. Walks usually start at 10.45am, but there's no need to book; check the website for the next date, or call the events line on ✆0845 272 0004.

Halfway along the valley you'll pass **Kentmere Pottery** (✆01539-821621; gordon .fox4@btinternet.com), where local ceramicist Gordon Fox makes all his wares completely by hand. If he's in, he'll happily show you around his small shop and studio.

The only place to stay is **Maggs Howe** (✆01539-821689; www.maggshowe.co.uk; Lowfield Lane; dm £10, r £30 per person), which offers simple B&B rooms in the farmhouse and basic bunks in the nearby camping barn. Large groups can hire out the whole bunkhouse for £100 per night.

Parking in the valley is limited to a few spaces by the church and village hall – get there very early in summer to be sure of a space. Sadly, the 519 Kentmere Rambler bus has recently been axed, so your only other option is to hoof it the 4 miles from Staveley.

Wilf's Café
CAFE £

(www.wilfs-cafe.co.uk; mains £4-10; ☺10am-5pm) This cheery cafe specialises in filling fare, ideal for a pre- or post-hike feed: jacket spuds, veggie chillis and tasty rarebits. The cafe is sometimes open for speciality food nights on Fridays (£20.50 for three courses) and 'Slide & Supper' evenings (from £7.15). The cafe is also the starting point for ranger-guided hikes into the Kentmere Valley (see p55).

ⓘ Getting There & Around

Staveley is on the branch railway between Windermere (£2.50, five minutes) and Kendal (£2.70, nine minutes). The best bus option is the 555 Lakeslink, which stops in Staveley on the way from Kendal (20 minutes) to Windermere (10 minutes), Grasmere (40 minutes) and Keswick (one hour).

Troutbeck

Travelling from Kentmere as the crow flies, the next valley east is Troutbeck, nestled among glossy green fields and bisected by the clattering course of its namesake river. Hill farming has been the main industry here for centuries, although it's the tourist traffic that largely keeps the valley's two pubs ticking over these days.

There are two roads through the valley, one on either side of the beck. On the right bank, the A592 leads north to the precipitous climb over Kirkstone Pass; en route, it passes the groomed gardens of **Holehird** (www.holehirdgardens.org.uk; admission free, but donations welcome; ☺10am-5pm Apr-Oct), home of the Lakeland Horticultural Society and its renowned collections of hydrangeas, astilbes and ferns.

The more scenic road is on the river's left bank, and climbs past the beautifully preserved farmhouse of **Townend** (NT; Troutbeck; adult/child £4.50/2.25; ☺guided tours 11am & noon, unguided visits 1-5pm Wed-Sun Mar-Oct), built for a wealthy yeoman farmer in the 17th century. Topped by pepperpot chimneys and grey slate tiles, the house contains antique artefacts, books and farming tools, plus original wood panelling and furniture carved by the Browne family, who owned the house until 1943.

The road then winds past a higgledy-piggledy collection of slate-topped houses and rural cottages before rejoining the A592 just south of Raven Crag. The stride up to Wansfell Pike starts on Nanny Lane, near the post office.

🛏 Sleeping & Eating

Windermere YHA
HOSTEL £

(☎0845 371 9352; windermere@yha.org.uk; Bridge Lane, Troutbeck; dm £11.95-16.95; ☺mid-Feb–Nov, reception 7.30-11.30am & 1-11pm; Ⓟ@) This super YHA is halfway up the steep back lane towards Townend. The stately manor house has been converted into spacious dorms (mostly four-berth or smaller), plus a well-stocked shop, a canteen, a kitchen, a gear-drying room and a bar. The nearest buses stop at Troutbeck Bridge, from where it's a steep uphill hike of a mile to the hostel.

Queen's Head
PUB ££

(☎015394-32174; www.queensheadhotel.com; Troutbeck; mains £11.95-16.95; Ⓟ) The first of Troutbeck's two pubs began life as a coaching inn in the 17th century, and while its whitewashed exterior, oak bar and crackling fires feel antique, the menu is altogether more contemporary: you'll find fancy stuff like chantenay carrots and celeriac mash served alongside the ham hock and lamb shank. Happily, it still feels like a proper country pub rather than a dressed-up restaurant, so it's just as good for an honest pint of XB as for a sit-down meal.

Mortal Man
PUB ££

(☎015394-33193; www.themortalman.co.uk; Troutbeck; mains £8.95-14.95, r weekdays £95-145, weekends £120-170; Ⓟ) Another venerable choice overlooking the Troutbeck Valley, especially popular for a Sunday roast or an afternoon pint on the fell-view terrace. The gabled, whitewashed building dates back to 1689, and its rooms have a flavour of a bygone era; nearly all have top-drawer views, and one has a stonking great four-poster. The food mainly centres on 'pub classics' such as bangers and mash and shepherd's pie. In case you're wondering about the curious name, have a look at the pub sign on your way in – it's taken from an old Lakeland rhyme.

ⓘ Getting There & Away

The 517 Kirkstone Rambler (three daily mid-July to August, weekends only mid-March to July and September to October) climbs up the A592 from Windermere to the top end of Troutbeck before travelling over the Kirkstone Pass to Ullswater.

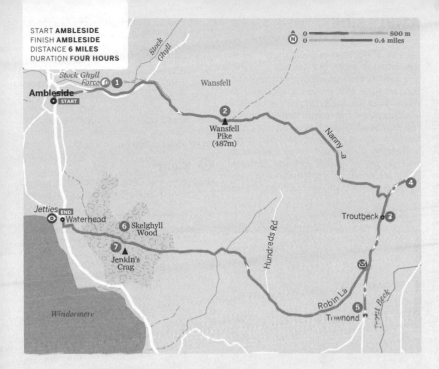

Hiking Tour
Wansfell Pike

This moderate hike from Ambleside takes in the summit of Wansfell Pike (1588ft), which offers a grand outlook despite its low profile.

The trail starts on Stock Ghyll Lane behind the Market Hall. Follow the path up through the woods to the waterfall of ❶ **Stock Ghyll Force**, which tumbles and clatters down the hill right into the centre of Ambleside.

After viewing the falls, take the path leading to the right through a cast-iron Victorian turnstile. Turn left and follow the paved lane, then take the right-hand path leading sharply up the fell-side (signed to Wansfell Pike). It's punishingly steep in places, although a stone staircase has been constructed at the worst bits.

You should reach the summit of ❷ **Wansfell Pike** after around half an hour of climbing. The 'Pike' is actually one of two separate summits on Wansfell; Baystones (1601ft) to the northeast is higher; but Wansfell Pike is considered the superior summit thanks to its impressive outlook over Windermere and the distant Langdale range.

From the fell-top, follow the path east across the fells. After 20 minutes or so, the path joins up with a rough stone track known as Nanny Lane, which meanders steeply downhill into the pretty hamlet of ❸ **Troutbeck**. The nearby ❹ **Mortal Man** makes an excellent place for a pint-stop, or you could head down through the village for a visit to the medieval farmhouse at ❺ **Townend**.

Just past the post office, take the rough track signposted as Robin Lane. Keep with the main track and follow the signs; after a while you'll pass High Skelghyll Farm and drop downhill into the NT-owned ❻ **Skelghyll Wood**. About halfway through the wood, a side-track leads to the famous outlook of ❼ **Jenkin's Crag** – try to time your arrival for late afternoon, when the sinking sun lights up Windermere and the Langdale Pikes.

Return to the main path and follow the main track through the woods to Ambleside, emerging near the Waterhead jetties.

AMBLESIDE

POP 3382

Nestled at the head of Windermere beside the clattering waters of Stock Ghyll, Ambleside couldn't feel more different to the brash, bustling quays of Bowness a few miles to the south. With its lively bistros, well-stocked outdoors shops and independent cinemas, it still feels like a proper Lakeland town rather than simply a place to serve the tourist traffic.

Handily positioned between Grasmere, Windermere, Ullswater and the Langdale Valley, within easy reach of many of the classic Lakeland fells, Ambleside makes an ideal launch-pad for exploring the central sights of the national park. And while it's always busy, it's one of the few Lakeland towns where you'll actually find plenty of things to keep you entertained once the sun goes down.

Ambleside is split into two main areas: the town centre, which is about a mile inland from the lakefront, and Waterhead, from where cruiseboats putter across the water towards Bowness and the southern half of Windermere.

◉ Sights

Ambleside was once an important centre for several Lakeland industries, including

Ambleside

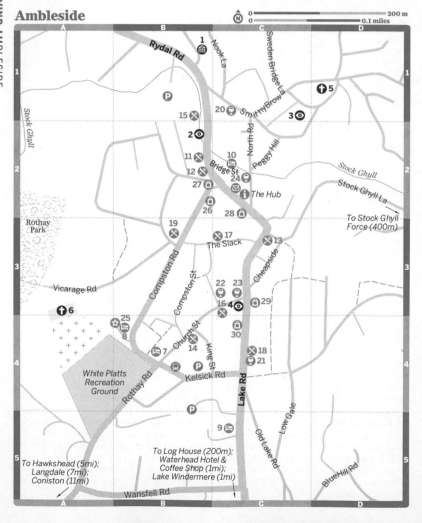

tanning, brewing, milling, smithing and bobbin-making. In their 19th-century heyday, the town's pounding mills and clacking waterwheels must have made an almighty racket (which probably explains Bridge St's former nickname of Rattle Ghyll). Little of the town's industrial architecture now remains, although you can still see one of the old town waterwheels on the side of the Old Mill Tea Room.

The oldest area of town is situated around the warren of streets above Stock High Bridge; the sprawling stone farmhouse of **How Head** is the oldest inhabited building in Ambleside, dating back to the 16th century. Directly opposite is **St Anne's Chapel**, built in 1812 on the site of a much earlier village church. The area 'Above Stock' officially lay in the parish of Grasmere, so until the 19th century deceased parishioners had to be lugged down Nook Lane onto the old Corpse Rd, which leads to St Oswald's Church in Grasmere.

Bridge House
BUILDING
Ambleside's best-known (and certainly most photographed) landmark is the tiny Bridge House, which straddles the waters of Stock Ghyll a little way downhill from Market Cross. The building is now occupied by a National Trust shop, but was originally used as an apple store for the nearby orchard belonging to the (demolished) Ambleside Hall; one local legend claims that constructing it above the river was a clever wheeze to avoid incurring land tax.

Old Stamp House
LANDMARK
As you stroll down Church St, look out for the blue plaque which marks the town's former Stamp House, where William Wordsworth worked following his appointment as Distributor of Stamps for Westmorland in 1813 (a positioned which earned him a handsome annual salary of £400 and the thinly veiled disgust of many of his poetic contemporaries).

Armitt Museum
MUSEUM
(www.thearmittcollection.com; Rydal Rd; adult £2.50; ☉10am-5pm) This tiny town museum is worth a visit for local history: look out for a few mushroom watercolours by Beatrix Potter, a collection of prints by pharmacist-turned-photographer Herbert Bell, and some moving paintings by German painter Kurt Schwitters, who was exiled here during WWII.

St Mary's Church
CHURCH
Overlooking the town bowling green soars the skyscraper steeple of Ambleside's main church, constructed by architect George Gilbert Scott (who also designed London's St Pancras Station and the Foreign and

WINDERMERE & AROUND AMBLESIDE

Ambleside

⊙ Sights

⊜ Sleeping

⊗ Eating

⊜ Drinking

⊕ Entertainment

⊜ Shopping

RUSHBEARING

Ambleside's oldest festival is the annual **rushbearing ceremony**, which sees local parishioners parading around the town's streets carrying big bundles of rushes, reeds and grasses, carried in sheafs or arranged into ornamental shapes. The tradition dates back to the days when local churches had mud rather than slate floors, and rushes were laid underfoot to keep the church interior dry (and also to mask any smells from the graveyard next door).

The ceremonies largely died out following the introduction of stone floors during the 19th century, but it still lives on in Ambleside, and is usually held on the first Saturday in July. Nearby Grasmere holds its rushbearing ceremony on the third Saturday in July.

Commonwealth Office in Whitehall). Inside is a mural depicting Ambleside's rushbearing ceremony, painted by artist Gordon Ransom in 1944; St Mary's marks the official end for the rushbearing procession, which takes place on the first Saturday of July every year.

Galava Roman Fort   RUIN

The site of present-day Ambleside was first earmarked by the Romans, who constructed a fort known as Galava in around AD 79. The site is just west of the modern-day jetties at Waterhead; you can still (just about) make out the foundations of the fort, including the gates, officer's lodgings and granary stores. The land is now owned by the National Trust and is free to visit.

🏃 Activities

Stock Ghyll Force   WALKING

Ambleside's most popular walk is the easy stroll up to Stock Ghyll Force, a picturesque waterfall about half a mile from the town centre. The path starts behind the old Ambleside Market Hall; if you fancy extending it into a longer walk, you could continue on the walk to Wansfell Pike.

Under Loughrigg & Rydal Park   WALKING

This is a really easy amble across the flat fields around Ambleside, circling round via Wordsworth's former home at Rydal Mount. The path starts on Vicarage Rd, then leads through Rothay Park to Pelter Bridge; en route you'll pass the former home of the educationalist Matthew Arnold at Fox How and a set of famous stepping stones across the River Rothay, mentioned by Dorothy Wordsworth in her Lakeland Journals. The path then circles back to Ambleside through the grounds of Rydal Park. All told it's a round trip of around 2.5 miles; count on two to three hours, longer if you stop to visit Rydal Mount or the tea-room at Rydal Hall.

Low Sweden Bridge
& High Sweden Bridge   HIKING

For a longer walk, you could follow the trail up to the packhorse bridges at Low and High Sweden Bridge. The route starts on either Sweden Bridge Lane or Nook Lane, depending on which order you want to visit the bridges; either way, it's a round trip of about 4 miles or three hours. The path can be muddy in wet weather.

Low Wood Watersports   SAILING

(☎015394-39441;   www.elh.co.uk/watersports /index.aspx) Attached to the Waterhead Hotel, this well-run water-sports centre hires row boats (£15 per hour), sit-on-top kayaks (two/four/eight hours £16/21/32), canoes (two/four/eight hours £20/30/45) and motor boats (from £20 per hour). Instruction lessons are available for beginners.

🛏 Sleeping

Ambleside has lots of B&Bs, but as elsewhere last-minute rooms can be hard to come by in July and August and during school holidays. The Hub information centre keeps lists of available rooms.

TOP CHOICE **Randy Pike**   GUESTHOUSE £££

(☎015394-36088; www.randypike.co.uk; r weekdays £180, weekends £200; P🐾) This delightful detached house (once a hunting lodge) is run with enormous charm by owners Andy and Chrissy Hill (who also own the Jumble Room in Grasmere). It feels more like a stay with friends in the country than a night in a B&B. Both rooms are named after family relatives, and wouldn't look out of place in an interior-design magazine: distressed wood floors, quirky furniture, vast bespoke bathrooms with a choice of slate-tiled shower or freestanding bath. It's a devil to find though: ask for directions or get Andy to pick you up from the station.

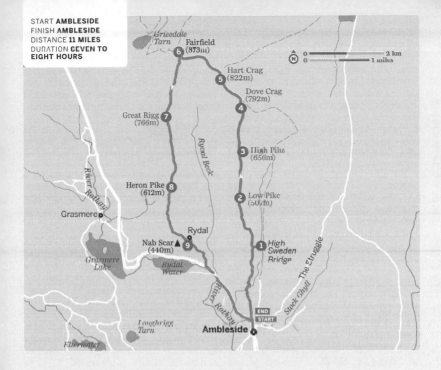

Map labels:

Grisedale Tarn
Fairfield (873m) 6
Hart Crag (822m) 5
Dove Crag (792m) 4
Great Rigg (766m) 7
Rydal Beck
High Pike (656m) 3
Heron Pike (612m) 8
Low Pike (507m) 2
Grasmere
River Rothay
Nab Scar (440m)
Rydal 9
Grasmere Lake
Rydal Water
High Sweden Bridge 1
The Struggle
Scandale Gill
River Rothay
Loughrigg Tarn
END START
Ambleside
Elterwater

0 — 2 km
0 — 1 miles

Hiking Tour
Fairfield Horseshoe

❯ For proper hikers, the 11-mile Fairfield Horseshoe is one of the main targets around Ambleside. It's a strenuous full-day walk, but it allows you to tick off a bumper crop of Wainwrights in a single day. It's best saved for clear weather: cloud will obscure the views and make navigation difficult. There's a lot of elevation involved, too, so be prepared for stiff climbs and lofty drops.

The route starts in Ambleside, where you can stock up with supplies. Head up Smithy Brow and turn left onto Sweden Bridge Lane, climbing northwards past cottages and farmhouses into the valley of Scandale Beck. Before long you'll reach the side trail to **1 High Sweden Bridge**, a good place for a rest stop before the next stage of ascent.

Follow the path west from the bridge, then north, climbing steadily up to the ridge of **2 Low Pike** (507m/1666ft). The path then leads directly north, climbing up and over **3 High Pike** (656m/2155ft) onto the summit of **4 Dove Crag** (792m/2603ft). This is another good place for a break, or you

can head northwest to nearby **5 Hart Crag** (822m/2698ft), overlooking the impressive valleys of Dovedale and Deepdale.

From Hart Crag, the path drops along the rocky incline of Link Hause, following cairns to the lofty crest of **6 Fairfield**, at 873m/2863ft the highest point of the route. It's one of the most dramatic lookouts in the eastern lakes: to the north you'll see Helvellyn, Striding Edge and the other Ullswater peaks, and to the west the brooding Scafells and Langdales. It's also exposed and often windy, so pack an extra layer to avoid the chill.

From Fairfield, the path traces an airy ridge across the final Fairfield summits of **7 Great Rigg** (766m/2513ft) and **8 Heron Pike** (612m/2003ft). It continues down the valley, passing a turn-of-the-century aqueduct near Nab Scar before dropping down into the sweeping grounds of **9 Rydal Hall** and the trail back to Ambleside.

Lakes Lodge
B&B ££

(☎015394-33240; www.lakeslodge.co.uk; Lake Rd; r from £79; P🛜) This modish 16-room mini-hotel makes a refreshing change from frilly bedspreads and net curtains. Slate-floored bathrooms and big photographic wall murals make this feel closer to a city hotel than a Lakeland B&B: ask for one of the upper-floor rooms rather than the basement annexe. Breakfast is served buffet style, and can be a bit of a free-for-all when the hotel's full. The large car park is a major plus point, too.

Gables
B&B ££

(☎015394-33272; www.thegables-ambleside.co.uk; Church Walk; s £50-60, d £80-110; P🛜) This large double-fronted house occupies a prime spot overlooking the town bowling green. Rooms are sweet and simple, livened up by bright scatter cushions and quirky cartoon watercolours on the walls. Guests receive a discount at Sheila's Cottage restaurant, run by the B&B's owners. The wi-fi rules are rather odd – you have to sign a form at reception before they'll give you the access key.

Waterwheel
B&B ££

(☎015394-33286; www.waterwheelambleside.co.uk; 3 Bridge St; r £85-100) Fall asleep to the sound of the rushing river at the dinky Waterwheel, a lovingly converted cottage with three small but perfectly formed rooms. Top choice is Stockghyll, finished with brass bed knobs, china-blue wallpaper and clawfoot bath; Rattleghyll is cosily Victorian; while Loughrigg is squeezed up on the 2nd floor with views over Ambleside's rooftops. The riverside location is lovely, but parking is a real bear: you'll have to unload first, then head for the town car park 250m away.

Riverside
B&B ££

(☎015394-32395; www.riverside-at-ambleside.co.uk; Under Loughrigg; d £98-116; P) Ambleside can feel hectic in high season, which makes this detached Victorian villa down by the River Rothay a welcome retreat. The rooms are light and airy, but it's the spoils that really sell the place: Pure Lakes bath products in the bathrooms, Hawkshead relishes and local bacon on the breakfast table, and a little wooden sun deck out back. Ask for a spa-bath room for maximum luxury.

Waterhead Hotel
HOTEL £££

(☎08458 504503; www.elh.co.uk/hotels/waterhead; r £150-215; P🛜) If only a proper hotel will do, then there's no better choice in Ambleside than the Waterhead. It's awash with four-star features: ice-white rooms with plenty of wood, slate and chrome; wonderful lake views through bay windows; and spa and leisure facilities at its sister hotel at nearby Low Wood. Guests have a choice of two restaurants plus a lakeside cafe across the road. Booking online gets a decent discount.

Easedale Lodge
B&B ££

(☎015394-32112; www.easedaleambleside.co.uk; Compston Rd; s £55-75, d £86-120; 🛜) Another enormously attractive B&B in the centre of Ambleside on the corner of Compston Rd. The rooms are small, but decked out in cutesy style with jolly curtains and stripy bedspreads. It's worth bumping up to 'Deluxe' for extra space.

Compston House
B&B ££

(☎015394-32305; www.compstonhouse.co.uk; Compston Rd; d £56-136; 🛜) Run by ex-New Yorkers, each of the rooms at this B&B has an American theme. Maine has a stripy four-poster and Cape Cod bedspread, New York has Manhattan maps and Big Apple posters, and Arizona has a sunbaked colour scheme. Breakfast has an American flavour, too, including blueberry muffins and pancakes with maple syrup.

Low Wray
CAMPGROUND £

(☎015394-32810; www.ntlakescampsites.org.uk; sites for adult, tent & car £8-12, extra adult £5, child 5-15yr £2.50, dogs £1.50; ⊙check-in 3-7pm Sat-Thu, to 9pm Fri, campsite open Easter-Oct; 🛜) One of three National Trust campsites in the Lake District, but the only one lodged right by the lakeshore. There's waterside access for canoes or lake-going vessels, and the usual facilities including laundry, shop and wheelchair-accessible loo. Pitches with a lake view cost £7.50 extra per night, or £10 if you want to be on the lakeshore; timber 'eco-pods' cost £25 to £42.50, or £5 more for a family-size. Online booking is now available – see p213. The campsite is 3 miles along the B5286; turn left at Clappersgate and follow the signs. Bus 505 stops about a mile from the site.

Yurts and tipis are also available. **4Winds Lakeland Tipis** (☎01539-821227; www.4winds lakelandtipis.co.uk; tipis £370-520 per week) has pre-rigged tipis in 12ft, 16ft and 18ft sizes; book well ahead in summer. **Long Valley** (☎01539-731089; www.long-valley-yurts.co.uk; yurts £395-465 per week) has Moroccan-style yurts complete with wood-burning stoves, while **Wild in Style** (☎07909 446381;

www.wildinstyle.co.uk; yurts £350-450) has more luxurious yurts, with wooden floors, gas hob kitchens and electric lighting.

Ambleside YHA
HOSTEL £

(☎0845 371 9620; ambleside@yha.org.uk; Windermere Rd; din £13.95-17.95; ☺reception 7.15am-11.45pm; P@☎) This enormous lakeside mansion has more space than your average country hotel, with facilities to match. Loads of rooms, ranging from 10-bed dorms to private doubles (some with waterfront views), plus a great cafe-bar, wi-fi, bike hire and organised activity trips

✗ Eating

For several years, Ambleside's dining scene was dominated by the ever-growing empire of local celeb chef Lucy Nicholson, but her culinary empire has fallen on hard times: it went into liquidation in early 2011, and several of her restaurants were forcibly closed. Her best-known restaurant, Lucy's on a Plate, is still trading on Church St, but it's a shadow of its old self.

Fellini's
VEGETARIAN ££

(☎015394-32487; www.fellinisambleside.com; Church St; mains £11.95; ☺dinner) Ambleside's only vegetarian restaurant is the latest project of the team behind Zeffirelli's and Yewfield, and it's fast gaining a reputation as one of the best places to eat in town. The food is a long way from veggie chillis and nut roasts – here you could find yourself dining on lemony cheese quenelles with saffron sauce, or squash and butternut stew laced with fragrant pesto.

Glass House
BRITISH ££

(☎015394-32137; www.theglasshouserestaurant.co.uk; Rydal Rd; lunch £9-12, dinner £12.95-18.50; ☺lunch & dinner) A smart modern British restaurant with one of Ambleside's most interesting dining rooms, featuring an original waterwheel and vintage machinery left over from the building's former incarnation as a fulling mill. The food is British with a Euro twist: Lakeland pork, chicken and lamb are dressed with dauphinoise potatoes, pancetta crisps and truffle oil.

Log House
BRITISH ££

(☎015394-31077; www.loghouse.co.uk; Lake Rd; mains £14.30-22.95, 2-/3-course menu £15/17.50; ☺dinner Tue-Sun) This extraordinary clapboard building was originally shipped over from Norway and used as a studio by well-known Lakeland artist Alfred Heaton

Cooper. The food is reliable and rather pricey, and sticks mainly to the classics: beef fillet, pork belly with champ potatoes, sea bass with chips. The real highlight is the building itself: if you fancy staying, there are three rooms squeezed in under the rafters (£82 to £92.25).

Zeffirelli's
ITALIAN ££

(☎015394-33845; www.zeffirellis.com; Compston Rd; pizza £5.50-7.45; ☺cafe from 10am, restaurant 5.30-11pm) This funky brasserie/cinema/jazz bar (known just as Zeff's to Amblesiders) is a buzzy place for schmoozing and boozing over pizza and antipasti. The large basement dining room always has a lively vibe, with spotlights and a cosmopolitan bistro feel. Upstairs is a jiving jazz bar, and next door is Ambleside's excellent indie cinema: the 'Double Feature' deal includes two-course dinner and a movie ticket.

Dodd's
EUROPEAN ££

(☎015394-32134; Rydal Rd; mains £11.25-14.25; ☺lunch & dinner) A Mediterranean menu of pizzas, pastas and Italian-influenced dishes underpins this small, popular bistro with a small, cosy dining room decked out in rough brick and rustic wood.

Doi Intanon
THAI ££

(☎015394-32119; Market Pl; mains £8.50-15.50; ☺dinner) A reliable Thai restaurant lodged inside Ambleside's old Market Hall. The usual range of red, green and yellow curries are on offer, as well as regional specialities such as *pla datdiow* (steamed sea bass with mango) and *laab* (Thai herb salad).

Apple Pie
CAFE £

(www.applepieambleside.co.uk; Rydal Rd; lunches £4-12) This sunny cafe on the main street is permanently crammed with lunchtime punters popping in for fresh butties, calorific cakes or one of the trademark apple pies. Pine tables inside, a riverside patio outside, or you can order at the counter to go. They'll be adding rooms soon, too – watch the site for details.

Sheila's Cottage
BRITISH ££

(☎015394-33079; The Slack; £9.50-19.95; ☺noon-5pm & 6-9pm) This cute cottage is all about hearty country food – pork belly, Cumberland sausage, lamb's liver – dished up beneath beams, brass knick-knacks and rough stone ceilings.

Tarantella
ITALIAN ££

(☎015394-31338; 10 Lake Rd; mains £9.95-15.95; ☺noon-2pm & 5.30-11pm, also 8.30am-noon Sat

& Sun) Another authentic Italian, with the usual range of risottos, pastas and wood-fired pizzas.

Waterhead Coffee Shop
CAFE £

(Waterhead; lunches £3-10) The Waterhead's small cafe is perfect for coffee and cake by the lake. Call before noon and they'll pack you a takeaway picnic for the following day.

Drinking

Unicorn
PUB

(North Rd) The locals' choice, a rough-and-ready little pub with bags of charm, but which can get rowdy at weekends. Inside you'll find old-fashioned pub decor and a range of Robinsons and Hartleys real ales, plus local musicians at least one night a week.

Golden Rule
PUB

(Smithy Brow) Country prints and the odd brass horseshoe dot the walls at this ale-drinkers' haven, with a line-up of brews including Old Stockport Bitter, Robinson's Hatters Mild and Hartleys XB, plus pork pies and scotch eggs for the peckish.

Royal Oak
PUB

(Market Pl) The town's most central pub is always busy, especially on summer evenings when the front patio overflows with drinkers. The carpets are old and the tables are shabby, but it's an honest place for a pint of Black Sheep or India Pale Ale.

Lake Road Wine Bar
WINE BAR

(10-14 Lake Rd) Wine and cocktails take the place of real ales at this modern bar, with the requisite deep sofas and pop-art prints. DJs man the decks at weekends.

Lucy4
WINE BAR

(2 St Mary's Lane; tapas £4-8) Another laid-back refuge from the town's pub scene, this continental-style tapas bar is ideal for tasty snacks washed down with European lagers.

☆ Entertainment

Zeffirelli's Jazz Bar
JAZZ

(Compston Rd) Live jazz finds its way onto the bill several nights a week at Zeffirelli's upstairs bar, where you can sip a gimlet at the bar or pick your spot at one of the stage-view booths. You don't need a reservation at the restaurant, and entry is usually free unless there's a big name playing.

Zeffirelli's Cinema
CINEMA

(☑bookings 015394-33845; Compston Rd; tickets after 6.45pm £5-7, £1 discount for earlier shows) The town's independent cinema is split across three buildings. Latest releases are shown at the Main Building (on Compston Rd) and **Zeff's by the Park** (in a converted church beside the bowling green). Arthouse and indie, plus live concert link-ups, are shown in the new upstairs screen above Fellini's restaurant.

🔒 Shopping

If those tired old trail boots have seen better days, don't worry – Ambleside has more outdoors suppliers than any other town in the lakes. Prices can be high, although you can often pick up a bargain at end-of-season sales.

Gaynor Sports
OUTDOOR EQUIPMENT

(www.gaynors.co.uk; Market Cross) Ambleside's largest outdoors shop (and one of the biggest in the UK) is the best place for general supplies, and stocks most of the major brands (North Face, Mountain Equipment, Berghaus and Rab). There are five floors to browse, with good sections for clothing, footwear and camping supplies.

Mountain Factor
OUTDOOR EQUIPMENT

(www.themountainfactor.com; 5 Lake Rd) This much-recommended shop offers a smaller but higher-quality range of gear, focusing on top-end brands such as Fjallraven, Haglöfs and Paramó.

Climber's Shop
OUTDOOR EQUIPMENT

(www.climbers-shop.com; Compston Rd) Mainly sells specialist gear for rock climbers and alpinists.

Black's
OUTDOOR EQUIPMENT

(42 Compston Rd) Large branch of the national outdoor chain.

Wearings
BOOKS

(Lake Rd) Superb little independent bookseller, with lots of maps, guides and local-interest titles, plus some gorgeous coffee-table books if you fancy taking home a photographic souvenir.

ℹ Information

Ambleside Library (Kelsick Rd; internet access per hr £3; ◎10am-5pm Mon & Wed, to 7pm Tue & Fri, to 1pm Sat)

Ambleside Police Station (0845 33 00 247; Rydal Rd)

Barclays (Market Pl; ⊘9am-4.30pm Mon-Fri)

HSBC (Market Pl; ⊘9am-4.30pm Mon-Fri)

The Hub (☑015394-32582; tic@thehubof ambleside.com; Market Cross; ⊘9am 5pm) This central building houses the tourist office and post office, and sells everything from guidebooks to bus passes.

Langdale and Ambleside Mountain Rescue Team (☑01539-432580; www.lamrt.org.uk; Lowfold, Lake Rd)

Post office (Market Cross; ⊘9am-5.30pm Mon-Fri, to 12.30pm Sat) In the tourist office building.

www.amblesideonline.co.uk Online access to all things Ambleside.

❶ Getting There & Around

Bus

Lots of buses run through Ambleside. The main bus stop is on Kelsick Rd opposite the library.

555 To Grasmere and Windermere (hourly, 10 on Sunday)

505 To Hawkshead and Coniston (10 Monday to Saturday, six on Sunday, mid-March to October)

516 To Elterwater and the Langdale Valley (six daily, five on Sunday).

Bike Hire

Bike Treks (☑015394-31505; www.biketreks .net; Rydal Rd; per half-/full day £14/18) Excellent bike shop that sells cycling gear and clothing and rents out bikes.

Ghyllside Cycles (☑015394-33592; www .ghyllside.co.uk; The Slack; per day £16) Opening hours can be erratic: phone ahead.

Car

Ambleside's main car park is on the north side of town, just off Rydal Rd. The town's one-way system can be confusing: if approaching from Windermere on Lake Rd, you need to turn left on either Wanstell Rd or Church St, then follow the one-way system through town.

You will need a free timed parking disc to park on Ambleside's streets. You can pick them up from the Hub and many shops around town, or just ask at your B&B or hotel.

Grasmere & the Central Lake District

Best Places to Eat

» Jumble Room (p73)

» Eltermere Inn (p78)

» Sara's Bistro (p73)

» Chesters Cafe by the River (p77)

» Three Shires Inn (p77)

Best Places to Stay

» Eltermere Inn (p78)

» Moss Grove Organic (p73)

» Old Dungeon Ghyll (p79)

» How Foot Lodge (p71)

» Great Langdale Campsite (p81)

Why Go?

The broad bowl of Grasmere acts as a geographical junction between the east and west of the Lake District, sandwiched between the rumpled peaks of the Langdale Pikes and the gentle hummocks and open dales of the eastern fells. It's a wonderfully scenic corner of the national park, ringed by craggy peaks and spotted with woodland, tarns and seemingly endless green fields.

The area is perhaps best known for its literary connections, largely thanks to William Wordsworth, who lived for most of his adult life near Grasmere. Wordsworth and his contemporaries spent countless hours wandering the surrounding hilltops, and the area is dotted with literary landmarks, as well as an excellent museum devoted to the Romantic movement. Grasmere is also the gateway to one of Lakeland's great hiking heartlands, Great Langdale, where walkers set out on classic routes across the high tops of the Crinkle Crags and the Langdale Pikes.

When to Go

Grasmere is one of the Lake District's most popular spots, and the village gets very crowded in summer, especially during school holidays and around the village's traditional sports day on the August bank holiday. For the best hiking weather in Langdale, late spring and early autumn are usually the most reliable times, although, as always, conditions can be changeable on the fells. Dove Cottage and Rydal Mount often have special events to mark Wordsworth's birthday on 7 April.

Grasmere & the Central Lake District Highlights

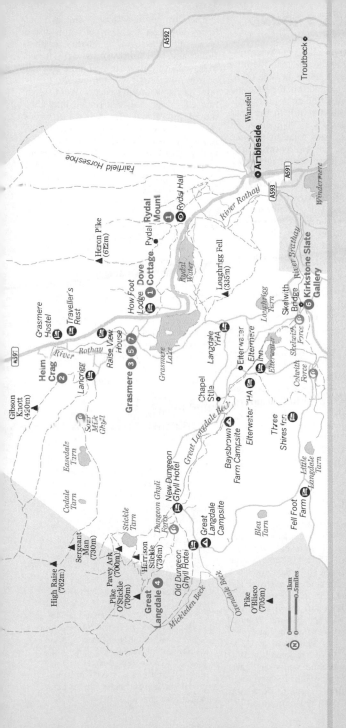

1 Peek into the private life of William Wordsworth at **Dove Cottage** (p68) and **Rydal Mount** (p74)

2 Follow in the footsteps of generations of walkers on Grasmere's classic fell, **Helm Crag** (p72)

3 Sample a slab of the trademark gingerbread from **Sarah Nelson's Gingerbread Shop** (p69)

4 Marvel at the panoramic majesty of the views in **Great Langdale** (p79)

5 Time your visit to coincide with Grasmere's eccentric **traditional sports day** (p74)

6 Pick up some slate souvenirs from the **Kirkstore Slate Gallery** (p77)

7 Stop off for a tale or two courtesy of the exuberantly outfitted Taffy Thomas at the **Storyteller's Garden** (p69)

GRASMERE & AROUND

POP 1458

If it's Romantic connections you're searching for, then look no further than the little village of Grasmere – home for nigh-on 50 years to the grand old daddy of the Lakeland Romantics himself, William Wordsworth. After his long-awaited return to the Lake District in the late 1790s, William never felt too much desire to stray from his adopted home in Grasmere, and two centuries after his death, his spirit still looms large over the village.

The poet's former houses at Dove Cottage and Rydal Mount are both open to the public (another, at Allan Bank, is privately owned), and you can also visit the village school where he taught (now a celebrated gingerbread shop) as well as his family tombs sheltered under the spreading yew trees of St Oswald's Churchyard.

Grasmere's literary cachet has its drawbacks, though: the village's streets are crammed to bursting throughout the summer months, and the modern-day rash of gift shops, tearooms and coach-tour hotels has done little to preserve the quiet country charm that drew Wordsworth here in the first place. Still, the setting is stunning, and if it all gets too frantic you can seek refuge around the shores of Grasmere Lake or out on the airy summits of nearby Helm Crag and Loughrigg Fell.

There's no library, laundrette, bank or tourist office in Grasmere. The **Grasmere Post Office** (Red Lion Sq; ⊘9am-5pm Mon-Wed & Fri, 9am-12.30pm Thu & Sat) has the village's only ATM.

◉ Sights

Dove Cottage   HISTORIC BUILDING
(☏015394-35544; www.wordsworth.org.uk; adult/child £7.50/4.50; ⊘9.30am-5.30pm) Covered with climbing roses, honeysuckle and tiny latticed windows, Dove Cottage seems hardly to have changed since the days when William Wordsworth and his beloved sister Dorothy moved here in December 1799. Originally a coaching inn called the Dove and Olive, Dove Cottage became William and Dorothy's first permanent Lake District home since their childhood in Cockermouth. In 1802 they were joined by William's new wife (and childhood sweetheart) Mary Hutchinson, followed by the first three Wordsworth children – John, Dora and Thomas – born in 1803, 1804 and 1806.

The tiny house became a cramped but happy home for the growing family and a never-ending stream of literary visitors. Eventually the Wordsworths were forced to leave Dove Cottage to find more space at nearby Allan Bank in 1808, but the family (and perhaps more strongly Wordsworth himself) never truly felt settled until they moved into Rydal Mount in 1813, where they remained until William's death in 1850. After the Wordsworths' departure, Dove Cottage was leased by Wordsworth's opium-eating young friend Thomas de Quincey, who remained at the house on and off for the next 20-odd years.

Now owned and restored by the Wordsworth Trust, the tiny cottage provides a fascinating insight into the daily lives of the Wordsworth family. Entry is via timed ticket, and includes an absorbing guided tour with one of the cottage curators.

There are fascinating artefacts dotted throughout the house. Look out for Wordsworth's paper passport in one of the bedrooms, a portrait of one of his favourite dogs, Pepper (given to him by Sir Walter Scott), and a cabinet containing a pair of Wordsworth's spectacles, his shaving case and razor, Dorothy's needlework box, and a set of scales reputedly used by de Quincey to weigh out his opium. Perhaps most

WORDSWORTH MUSEUM & ART GALLERY

Admission to Dove Cottage also includes entry to the **Wordsworth Museum** (same details as Dove Cottage) next door, which houses the largest archive relating to the Romantic movement. The museum moves through the lives and works of most of the great figures of British Romanticism in roughly chronological order; among the intriguing items on display are Thomas de Quincey's beloved blackthorn walking stick and a glass cabinet containing Wordsworth's court suit, cloak, umbrella and favourite hat. Eeriest of all are the haunting life masks of Wordsworth and John Keats, which bring you, literally, face to face with two of England's most illustrious poets. The collection changes throughout the year, and the museum also hosts regular poetry readings and literary seminars.

interesting of all is the little room used as a bedroom for the Wordsworth children, which Dorothy insulated with pages from the daily newspapers.

At the back of the house is the magical little cottage garden, described by Wordsworth as his 'domestic slip of mountain', where the family spent many happy hours declaiming William's latest poetry in the summer house or planting blooms, shrubs and vegetables.

St Oswald's Church   CHURCH

Sheltering under the spreading boughs of several great yew trees at the centre of Grasmere is St Oswald's, parts of which date back to the 13th century. The inside of the church is worth a look for its fine interweaving oak rafters and a marble memorial to Wordsworth, outside are the family graves of William, Mary and Dorothy, as well as their children Dora, Catherine and Thomas, and Coleridge's carousing son Hartley.

Sarah Nelson's Gingerbread Shop   SHOP

(www.grasmeregingerbread.co.uk; Church Stile; ⊘9.15am-5.30pm Mon-Sat, 12.30-5pm Sun) Beside the church in the village's former schoolhouse is this famous gingerbread shop, where ladies in frilly pinnies and starched bonnets have been cooking traditional gingerbread from the same secret recipe for the last 150 years (so secret that the original recipe is locked in a bank vault in Ambleside). Part sticky cake, part crumbly biscuit, the gingerbread comes in greaseproof packets of six (£2.50) or 12 slabs (£3.50). You can also pick up jars of Sarah Nelson's homemade rum butter, along with other Lakeland specialities, including Penrith fudge and toffee, Cartmel sticky toffee sauce and Kendal mintcake. Be prepared to queue – or order online if you prefer not to wait.

FREE Heaton Cooper Studio   ART GALLERY

(www.heatoncooper.co.uk; ⊘9am-5.30pm Mon-Sat,11am-5.30pm Sun) Alfred Heaton Cooper (1864–1929), a Manchester-born artist who was heavily influenced by Turner and Constable, became one of the most celebrated painters of Lakeland landscapes during the late 19th century, and established this studio in Grasmere to display his work. The artistic tradition was continued by his son William (1903–95), another fine landscapist and rock climber, and his wife, the

THE STORYTELLER'S GARDEN

The Lake District has always attracted its share of inspirational eccentrics, but they don't get much more inspirational than the marvellous Taffy Thomas, Britain's first Storyteller Laureate, who created a magical **Storyteller's Garden** (☑015394-35641; www.taffy thomas.co.uk) in his cosy cottage near the shores of Grasmere Lake. A former drama teacher, folk singer and actor, Taffy has devoted his latter years to the fine art of storytelling, and he often opens his garden during school and bank holidays for family story sessions, sometimes with musicians, puppetry and jugglers thrown in for good measure. Check his website for details of forthcoming events.

sculptor Ophelia Gordon Bell (1915–75). Members of the Heaton Cooper family are still exhibiting at the gallery, including William's son Julian (born 1947).

The gallery sells prints, postcards and canvases from all of the Heaton Cooper artists, as well as books and art materials.

Grasmere Lake & Rydal Water   LAKE

From the centre of the village, Redbank Rd leads southwest towards the lakeshore and the **Facryland Tea Garden** (⊘10am-6pm Mar-Oct), where you can hire a rowboat and scull out to the wooded island at the centre of the lake (one of Wordsworth's favourite evening pastimes).

Just to the west is the neighbouring lake of **Rydal Water**. A lovely lakeshore trail connects the two, with an optional side-trip up to **Rydal Cave**, a deep, damp cavern left over from the days when Loughrigg Fell was used as a slate quarry.

🏃 Activities

By far the best-known walk in Grasmere is to the top of **Helm Crag** (p72), which Wainwright described as 'the best known hill in the country'. You can download an MP3 version of his route from www.golakes .co.uk/downloads/podcasts/wainwright .aspx, read by Nik Wood-Jones, who provided the voice of AW in the popular BBC series *Wainwright Walks*.

Grasmere

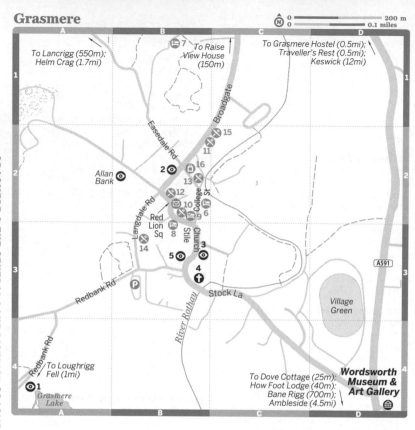

To Lancrigg (550m);
Helm Crag (1.7mi)

To Raise
View House
(150m)

To Grasmere Hostel (0.5mi);
Traveller's Rest (0.5mi);
Keswick (12mi)

Easedale Rd

Broadgate

15
11

Allan
Bank

2

16
13

College St

Langdale Rd

12
10
9
6

Red
Lion
Sq

8

Church Stile

14

5
3
4

Stock La

A591

Redbank Rd

River Rothay

Village
Green

Redbank Rd

To Loughrigg
Fell (1mi)

1
Grasmere
Lake

To Dove Cottage (25m);
How Foot Lodge (40m);
Bane Rigg (700m);
Ambleside (4.5mi)

**Wordsworth
Museum &
Art Gallery**

Old Coffin Trail   WALKING

For hundreds of years St Oswald's in Grasmere was the district's only parish church, and deceased parishioners from outlying areas (including Ambleside, Elterwater and the Langdale Valley) had to be carried along a network of 'coffin trails' or 'corpse roads' to be buried at Grasmere.

You can follow one of them from just behind Dove Cottage, leading across White Moss Common to the grounds of Rydal Mount. The trail is signposted as a public bridleway at both ends; look out for the stone slabs along the route that once allowed coffin carriers to rest their burdens without having to lay them on the ground.

On its own, it's a walk of just over a mile lasting about 45 minutes. For a longer stroll, cross the bridge over the River Rothay opposite the entrance to Rydal Mount, and follow the path west along Rydal Water back to Grasmere. It'll add an extra couple of miles to the walk; count on two to three hours for the loop including the Coffin Trail.

Sour Milk Ghyll & Easedale Tarn   HIKING

If you don't feel like a full-on fell walk, the easy path to the clattering waterfall of **Sour Milk Ghyll** is a great option. The path starts at the end of Easedale Rd and leads for about 1.5 miles along Easedale Beck, the first part is paved and wheelchair accessible, but it gets rougher the closer you get to the falls.

The ghyll apparently got its name from the milky colour of the water as it foams and rushes down the fellside. You can clamber up the side of the cascade to nearby **Easedale Tarn**, which Thomas de Quincey considered 'gloomily sublime'. From here, a trail connects to the Easedale Round.

On the way down, you could stop for afternoon tea at Lancrigg; look out for the driveway to the hotel just before you get back to Easedale Rd.

Grasmere

◎ Top Sights
Wordsworth Museum & Art
  Gallery..D4

◎ Sights
1 Faeryland Tea Garden..........................A4
2 Heaton Cooper Studio B2
3 Sarah Nelson's Gingerbread
  Shop...B3
4 St Oswald's Church..............................B3
5 Taffy Thomas' Storyteller's
  Garden..B3
  Wordsworth Graves ....(see 4)

⊜ Sleeping
6 Beck Allans..B2
7 Butharlyp Howe YHA B1
8 Heidi's Grasmere Lodge B3
9 Moss Grove Organic............................B2

◈ Eating
10 Baldry's Tea Room..............................B2
11 Co-op..B2
12 Croft House Bakery..............................B2
13 Greens..B2
   Heidi's of Grasmere ....(see 8)
14 Jumble Room..B3
15 Sara's Bistro..C2

◉ Shopping
16 Sam Read Booksellers.........................B2

Loughrigg Fell · HIKING
Halfway along the footpath along the southern side of Grasmere Lake, a short, steep path leads straight up to the summit of Loughrigg Fell (335m/1099ft). It may be small, but packs a mighty punch, with wraparound views encompassing Windermere and the Langdale Pikes. It's a round-trip of around two hours from Grasmere.

Silver How · HIKING
Another popular fell within easy reach of Grasmere is Silver How (394m/1292ft). The traditional route from Grasmere travels past Allan Bank, before cutting south over Wray Gill to the summit and circling back down to the village near the Faeryland Tea Garden. This route takes about two hours and is 3 miles.

Easedale Round · HIKING
Helm Crag (see p72) can also be combined with a long circular route known as the Easedale Round (8.5 miles), a long six- to seven-hour circuit which takes in all the summits of the Easedale Valley – Gibson Knott (420m/1379ft), Calf Crag (537m/1762ft) and Sergeant Man (730m/2394ft) – before dropping down past Easedale Tarn and Sour Milk Ghyll back to Grasmere.

🛏 Sleeping

Heidi's Grasmere Lodge · GUESTHOUSE ££
(☎015394-35248; www.harwoodhotel.co.uk; Red Lion Sq; d £99-115; P🐾) Perched above Heidi's Cafe, this button-cute little guesthouse sits in a prime spot right in the centre of the village. The rooms are sweet but might be a bit feminine for some: heart-shaped scatter cushions, floral wallpapers, and a palette of pinks, peaches and creams. They all have underfloor heating and 'splash TVs' in the bathrooms – and check out the futuristic shower in room 3. Parking can be a problem as the nearest car park is on the edge of the village.

Raise View House · B&B ££
(☎015394-35215; www.raiseviewhouse.co.uk; White Bridge; d £106-116; P🐾) Not everywhere in Grasmere can offer a room with a view, but Raise View has plenty: fells unfurl from the windows of Helm Crag and the double-aspect Stone Arthur, while others overlook green fields. It's quite traditional inside, but offers indulgent touches, such as Gilchrist & Soames bath products and fresh Farrer's coffee at breakfast.

How Foot Lodge · B&B ££
(☎015394-35366; www.howfoot.co.uk; Town End; d £70-78; P) Six rooms finished in elegant shades of fawn and beiges, just a cherry-stone's throw from Dove Cottage. Ask for the one with its own private sun lounge, or better still go for the newly redone suite, which has a separate sitting room and a choice of either shower or bath. It's a bit of a steal at this price.

Lancrigg · HOTEL £££
(☎015394-35317; www.lancrigg.co.uk; Easedale; r £140-210; P) Vegetarian food meets country house frilliness at this stately hotel overlooking Easedale. The house was once owned by the Arctic adventurer John Richardson, and the rooms have an antique feel: Whittington is reached via a private staircase, Franklin has Middle Eastern rugs and a four-poster, while the Richardson room has a claw-foot bath hidden behind lace curtains. It's half a mile along Easedale Rd down a private

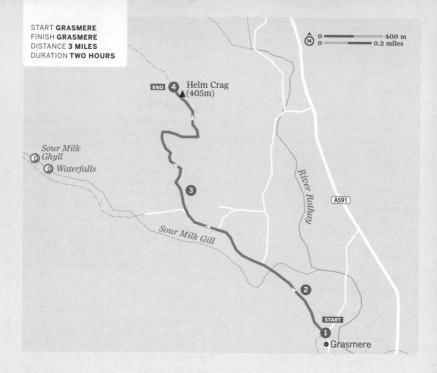

Sour Milk
Ghyll

Waterfalls

Helm Crag
(405m)

END **4**

3

Sour Milk Gill

River Rothay

A591

2

START

1

Grasmere

Hiking Tour
Helm Crag

❭ If you only do one fell walk in Grasmere, make sure it's Helm Crag. Sometimes referred to as the 'Lion and the Lamb', after the twin crags that sit atop its summit, it's a rewarding two-hour climb, but it's dauntingly steep in places, with around 1100ft of elevation gain – so wear proper boots and don't expect to canter up it.

The trail starts on **1** **Easedale Rd**. Follow the road past the turning to **2** **Butharlyp How YHA**. After about 10 minutes you'll pass a public bridleway on the left, signed to Easedale Tarn. Ignore the path and continue along the lane, passing a couple of old farmhouses and the smart country house hotel of **3** **Lancrigg**. Take the track up past the front of the house and follow the signed path as it climbs through pleasant woodland onto the main Helm Crag track.

The first bit of the path is clear but steep; the worst sections have been stepped, but it's still a slog. You'll pass an old stone quarry on your left, cut out from the slopes underneath Jackdaw Crag. The quarry makes

a good place to take a break before pushing on to the summit.

You should reach the top of **4** **Helm Crag** after about an hour of climbing. From the distinctive rock outcrops known as the Lion and the Lamb, you'll be treated to wonderful views south over Grasmere and north towards Dunmail Raise – it's a simple scramble to the top, but as always take care.

Another rocky outcrop, known as the Howitzer after its distinctive cannon-shaped profile, can be reached via a short walk northwest along the ridge. Wainwright always lamented not having climbed it, but in truth it's best left for experienced climbers.

From here, you could set out on the Easedale Round (p71). Alternatively, retrace your steps back to Grasmere, perhaps rewarding yourself with tea at Lancrigg.

track. Afternoon tea is served to passing hikers in summer.

Moss Grove Organic D&B £££
(☎015394-35251; www.mossgrove.com; r depending on season £129-325; P 🛜) Grasmere's B&Bs are pricey by any standards, and Moss Grove is no exception – but at least it's a lot sexier than most. The 11 rooms are impeccably appointed – gloss-wood floors, handmade beds, vast bathrooms – and boast ecofriendly touches, such as organic paints and sheep's wool insulation. Breakfast is served buffet style in the communal kitchen.

Beck Allans B&B ££
(☎015394-35563; www.beckallans.com; College St; d £80-86, apt £365-595 per week; P) There's a choice of self-catering apartments and simple B&B rooms at this modern slate house near the centre of the village. The B&B rooms offer no great surprises, tastefully toned in cream and yellow; the apartments are more spacious and have views across the gardens to the River Rothay.

Butharlyp Howe YHA HOSTEL £
(☎0845 371 9319; grasmere@yha.org.uk; dm £12.40-20.40; ⏰daily Feb-Nov, weekends Dec-Jan, reception 7am-11pm; P @) Since the historic Thorney Howe hostel became independent in 2011, Butharlyp Howe is now the YHA's only outpost in Grasmere. It's housed in a former Victorian mansion off Easedale Rd, overlooking woodland and trimmed lawns. Bright, modernish dorms (including private doubles and quads) and a decent cafe (serving everything from puddings to Perry cider) make this a great option for budget backpackers – though the large rooms are chilly when the weather's cold.

Grasmere Hostel HOSTEL £
(☎015394-35055; www.grasmerehostel.co.uk; Broadrayne Farm; dm £19.50; P) This indie hostel offers a few more spoils than your average hostel: fell views from the dorms, two stainless-steel kitchens, a comfy lounge and even a Nordic sauna. They'll even look after your luggage while you're on the trail. It's a mile from Grasmere near the Traveller's Rest pub; bus 555 stops nearby.

Eating

Grasmere is awash with expensive hotel restaurants and country cafes, but quality can be variable – stick with the suggestions here and you won't go wrong.

COTE HOW ORGANIC GUEST HOUSE

If it's an ecoconscious sleep you're after, **Cote How** (☎015394-32765; www.bedbreakfastlakedistrict.com; Rydal, near Ambleside; s £98-£108, d £120-160; P 🛜) is the place – it's one of only three UK B&Bs licensed by the Soil Association. Food is 100% local and organic, power's sourced from a green supplier, and they'll even lend you wind-up torches and candles (5% discount if you arrive by bus, too). The three rooms are elegantly Edwardian, with cast-iron beds, roll-top baths and fireplaces. The house is in Rydal, just outside Grasmere.

Self-caterers in Grasmere can pick up supplies at the **Co-op** (Broadgate; ⏰8.30am-8pm Mon-Sat, 10am-6pm Sun) and the **Croft House Bakery** (Red Lion Sq).

TOP CHOICE **Jumble Room** INTERNATIONAL ££
(☎015394-35188; Langdale Rd; mains £13-23; ⏰lunch & dinner Wed-Sun) This boho little bistro has carved out a loyal local following thanks to its quirky style and even quirkier owners, Andy and Chrissy Hill (who also run Randy Pike in Ambleside). The dining rooms are a riot of kitsch cushions, primary colours and quirky artwork, and the magpie menu dabbles in everything from Italian gnocchi and Asian soups to jellied ham and Urswick steaks. Owner Andy's a real music nut, too: show some interest in what's on the stereo and you'll likely have a friend for life.

Sara's Bistro BRITISH ££
(☎015394-35266; Broadgate; mains £9.95-15.95; ⏰cafe 10am-4pm, bistro 6-9pm Tue-Sun) Fresh local produce and unpretentious cooking in a sweet little cafe-cum-bistro a few strides from the village centre. The feel's homespun rather than haute cuisine – roast chicken, cheese soufflé and braised lamb, dished up with a minimum of faff and fuss. Book for the Early Bird tables between 6pm and 6.30pm and you'll be treated to a free bottle of wine.

Heidi's of Grasmere CAFE £
(Red Lion Sq; lunch mains £3-8; ⏰9am-5.30pm) Grasmere has no shortage of cafes to choose from, but Heidi's cosy little corner is by far the cutest. Thick-cut sandwiches and fresh salads are accompanied by a

GRASMERE SPORTS

Grasmere is fiercely proud of its annual **sports day**, when local lads and lasses get the chance to test their mettle at a selection of traditional sports on the village green. The event usually takes place on the Sunday of the August Bank Holiday, and has been held practically every year since 1852. In its heyday more than 50,000 spectators flocked to the village to enjoy the show; these days audience figures are a more modest 10,000, but the event remains one of the highlights of the Grasmere calendar.

Among the more unusual events on display are **hound trailing**, in which dogs race each other along a pre-marked scented trail; **guides racing**, the Grasmere equivalent of fell running, in which runners slog up and down a selection of fells in pursuit of the fastest time; and **Cumberland and Westmorland wrestling**, which has much in common with forms of wrestling practised in Celtic areas such as Cornwall and Brittany. Dressed in the traditional wrestler's garb of white long johns, patterned trunks and a white vest, contestants aim to unbalance their opponent during a series of three bouts.

Grasmere also has its own annual **rushbearing ceremony**, similar to the one held every year in Ambleside (p60). The procession takes place on the Saturday nearest to St Oswald's Day (5 August).

daily home-made soup and 'cheese smokeys', served with tomato salsa.

Baldry's Tea Room   CAFE £
(Red Lion Sq; lunch mains £4-8; ◷10am-5pm)
Dainty cakes, treacle tart and cream teas are very much the modus operandi at Baldry's, by far the village's best bet for afternoon tea. With its little round tables and bone china crockery, it's a little slice of old England, with service to match.

 Greens   CAFE £
(College St; mains £5-12; ◷breakfast & lunch, closed Thu) It doesn't look like much from the outside, but give Greens a go and you're likely to be pleasantly surprised. The menu mainly sticks to cafe standards, such as hot paninis, baked spuds, salads and pies, many of which are vegan or gluten-free, and made using sustainable and fair trade ingredients. The footpath tables go like lightning on sunny days, so grab 'em quick at lunchtime.

☖ Drinking

Traveller's Rest   PUB
(on the A591, Grasmere) A fine old coaching inn hunkering under slate roofs and low ceilings on the road to Dunmail Raise. There are several rambling bars to choose from, but the food can be hit-and-miss, so best stick to the Jennings beers.

🔒 Shopping

Sam Read Booksellers   BOOKS
(Broadgate; ◷9am-5.30pm Mon-Sat) General bookshop, good for hiking maps and guides.

Cotswold Rock Bottom   OUTDOORS
(Red Lion Sq; ◷9.30am-6pm) Discounted and end-of-line clothing, equipment and outdoor gear, run by the Cotswold Outdoors chain.

❶ Getting There & Away

The main A591 between Ambleside and Keswick runs along the east side of the village. The expensive main car park is just off Stock Lane; if you can find a space you can park for free at the large lay-by on the A591 near the Traveller's Rest. Bus options:

555 (hourly, 10 on Sundays) The Lakeslink stops at all points along the A591 from Windermere, including Grasmere, Rydal Mount and Keswick.
599 (two to three per hour mid-Mar–Aug) Open-top bus from Grasmere to Ambleside, Troutbeck Bridge, Windermere and Bowness. From September to February, the bus only runs from Ambleside to Bowness.

Rydal Mount

Though tiny Dove Cottage receives most of the visitors, Wordsworth actually spent three times as long living at **Rydal Mount** (www.rydalmount.co.uk; adult/5-15yr £6.50/3, gardens only £4; ◷9.30am-5pm Mar-Oct, 10am-4pm Wed-Sun Nov, Dec & Feb). The poet moved here in 1813, following the sudden deaths of two of his children, Catherine and Thomas, the year before, and remained here until his death in 1850.

That Wordsworth was able to afford a move to Rydal Mount was a mark of his newfound financial security, which derived largely from his appointment as Distributor of Stamps for Westmorland in 1813 rather than the relatively modest proceeds from his poetry and lecturing. It proved to be a happy home for the Wordsworths, and the house (still owned by the poet's descendants) offers a much more revealing portrait of Wordsworth's life in the Lake District than the poky charm of Dove Cottage.

The house is packed with original furniture, manuscripts and possessions relating to the poet's life and work. The heart of the house is the grand book-lined library and smart dining room, where Wordsworth liked to entertain his many literary and political visitors. Much of the room's furniture dates from Wordsworth's residency, and the glass display cases contain some fascinating artefacts, including the poet's own pen, inkstand, picnic box and ice skates. The large portrait of Wordsworth above the fire is by the American painter Henry Inman, who stayed at Rydal Mount in 1844; the picture is reputed to have been one of Mary's favourite paintings of her husband.

Upstairs you can browse around the family bedrooms (including the room belonging to Wordsworth's sister Dorothy, who never married and remained with the family until her death in 1855). On the top floor is Wordsworth's study, containing his encyclopaedia and a sword belonging to his younger brother John, a naval officer who was killed in the shipwreck of the *Earl of Abergavenny* in 1805. There's also a letter from Queen Victoria informing Wordsworth of his appointment as Poet Laureate in 1843, although ironically he never actually managed to write an official line of verse.

Outside the house, you can stroll through a hectare of formal gardens and landscaped lawns, most of which were laid out according to Wordsworth's own designs. You can even rest your legs in the little summerhouse where the poet liked to try out his latest verses on anyone who happened to be in earshot.

Below the house is **St Mary's Church** (built in 1824) and the wooded walk through **Dora's Field**, now owned by the National Trust. Wordsworth originally bought the site with the intention of building a home for his daughter Dora and her husband Edward Quillinan; the house never materialised, and following Dora's death from tuberculosis in 1847, William and Mary planted the field with daffodil bulbs in memory of their eldest daughter.

Rydal Hall

Across the lane from Rydal Mount is Rydal Hall, the family seat of the le Fleming family since 1576, and the home of Wordsworth's erstwhile landlords. It's now a Christian conference centre, but you're free to stroll through the grand gardens of **Rydal Park** before having tea at the rather lovely **Old School Room Tea Shop** (tea & sandwiches £3-6; ⊙10am-5pm, shorter hours in winter).

The grounds also provide a grand setting for a collection of luxurious Mongolian yurts owned by **Full Circle** (www.lake-district-yurts.co.uk; yurts per weekend £320, per week £495), supplied with wooden floors, wood-burning stoves, gas hobs for cooking and – best of all – real beds with springy mattresses.

ⓘ Getting There & Away

All buses to Grasmere also stop at Rydal Church, opposite the entrance to Rydal Mount.

THE LANGDALE VALLEYS

Few places sum up the essence of the Lake District better than the twin valleys of Great Langdale and Little Langdale, which snake westwards from Skelwith Bridge all the way to the brooding bulk of the Scafell range. Carved out by vast glaciers during the last ice age, Langdale derives from the Old Norse for 'long valley', although the area was settled long before the Vikings arrived – during Neolithic times the area served as a centre for stone quarrying and tool making, and Langdale axes have been found as far afield as Ireland and the Mediterranean.

These days the Langdales are a hiking heartland, with access to a range of iconic fells including the Langdale Pikes and the Crinkle Crags, as well as less-trodden routes to Scafell Pike and its sister peaks. The valleys are also home to a selection of fine country inns, which make perfect pint-stops after a long day on the fells.

ⓘ Getting There & Away

To reach the Langdales, follow the A593 from Ambleside to Skelwith Bridge, where the road splits in two: the A593 heads southwest into Little Langdale en route to Wrynose Pass, while the other fork travels northwest (as the B5343) to Elterwater and Great Langdale. A steep, narrow road connects the valleys, passing Side Pike and Blea Tarn en route.

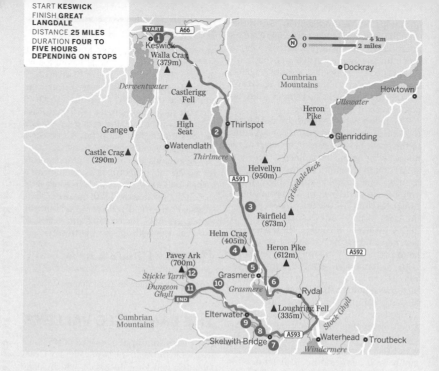

START **KESWICK**
FINISH **GREAT LANGDALE**
DISTANCE **25 MILES**
DURATION **FOUR TO FIVE HOURS DEPENDING ON STOPS**

Driving Tour
Grasmere & Around

❭ Begin this drive in ❶ **Keswick**, 12 miles to the north of Grasmere, and head south along the A591. The road tracks the east bank of ❷ **Thirlmere**, which has served as a reservoir since the late 19th century. As you drive south, you'll have a fine view of the western flanks of the Dodds and Helvellyn on your left, almost matched in grandeur by the Wythburn Fells on your right.

About 10 miles south from Keswick, you'll travel across the dramatic pass of ❸ **Dunmail Raise**, gorged out by a glacier. Look out for the distinctive profile of ❹ **Helm Crag** on the left as you travel south into ❺ **Grasmere**. You can stop here for a guided tour of Wordsworth's house at ❻ **Dove Cottage**, followed by a quick wander around the Wordsworth Museum and a stroll around the village's busy streets.

Drive on through Ambleside and take the A593 west towards ❼ **Skelwith Bridge**. Stop to browse the slate craft at the Kirkstone Gallery, historically one of the Lake District's most important industries. Have lunch in the chic setting of Chester's Cafe next door to the gallery. Leave some time for a stroll to see the well-known waterfall at ❽ **Skelwith Force**, perhaps followed by a quick pint at the Britannia Inn in nearby ❾ **Elterwater**.

Follow the narrow B5343 as it twists and veers into the beautiful valley of ❿ **Great Langdale**. The mountain scenery on either side of the road becomes ever grander as you head further west. Park near ⓫ **Dungeon Ghyll** and take a short stroll to see the waterfall, or tackle the longer hike up to ⓬ **Stickle Tarn**. Once you're back down in the valley, round things off with some hearty grub and ale in one of the local pubs – the classic choice is the Old Dungeon Ghyll Hotel, a favourite haunt for generations of hikers and climbers.

Bus 516 (the Langdale Rambler, six Monday to Saturday, five on Sunday, slightly reduced service in winter) is the only scheduled bus service, with stops at Ambleside, Skelwith Bridge, Elterwater, and the Old Dungeon Ghyll Hotel in Great Langdale.

Skelwith Bridge

Three miles south of Grasmere, Skelwith Bridge itself is little more than a knot of cottages lined up along the banks of the River Brathay. Since the 19th century this small village has been a hub for slate quarrying, and you can still view examples of local slate craft at the **Kirkstone Slate Gallery** (www.kirkstone.com; ☺9am-5pm Mon-Sat, 10am 4pm Sun). There are three types of local slate (Kirkstone Light Sea Green, Kirkstone Silver Green and Brathay Blue Black), each with its own subtly different colour and texture; nameplates, ornaments and other items can be made to order from the gallery shop.

There's another good reason for a stop in Skelwith, and that's the stroll to **Skelwith Force**, a modest 15ft tumble of water about a 10-minute walk from the village. You can extend the walk to nearby **Colwith Force**, which plunges down a series of 46ft rock steps about a mile west of the village. A popular circular route loops around the lake at **Elterwater**, making a round-trip of around 4.5 miles, or 2½ hours. The path to the falls starts near Chester's Cafe.

🛏 Sleeping & Eating

Skelwith Bridge Hotel HOTEL **££**
(☎015394-32115; www.skelwithbridgehotel.co.uk; s £50-55, d £100-120; Ⓟ🖥) Plonked beside Skelwith Bridge, this venerable hotel mainly attracts travellers of a certain age, but it's well worth a look – there are often excellent off-season deals including three-course dinner, bed and breakfast. Admittedly, it's old-fashioned, more country inn than contemporary hotel, and cheaper rooms are in a separate lodge building beside the car park. The homey Talbots Bar is often busy with Langdale locals, and serves a good line-up of Lakeland ales.

Chesters Cafe by the River CAFE **££**
(☎015394-32553; www.chestersbytheriver.co.uk; lunch mains £8-14; ☺10am-5pm) The third establishment in the Drunken Duck portfolio is run along the same gastro-gourmet lines (onion-and-gruyère tart rather than steak-and-ale pie). The trendy style feels a bit at odds with the rural surroundings, but the riverside terrace is a beauty – get there very early for a table. There's a shop next door selling gifts and home furnishings.

Little Langdale

Separated from Great Langdale by the hefty bulk of Lingmoor Fell (469m/1540ft), the valley of Little Langdale traditionally marks the juncture between the old counties of Cumberland, Westmorland and Lancashire – a point officially marked by the **Three Shire Stone**, positioned near the steep summit of Wrynose Pass. The stone was broken into bits when it was hit by a wayward motorist in 1997; it was restored the following year by a local stonemason thanks to the generous donations of Langdale residents and the National Trust.

The valley is a popular hiking base, with several possible destinations including Blea Tarn, Little Langdale Tarn and Lingmoor Fell. For a shorter stroll, it's well worth taking the short path from the Three Shires Inn to **Slater's Bridge**, a pretty little 17th-century humpback bridge once used by workers carrying slate from the nearby slate quarry of Cathedral Cavern.

Beyond the pub, the road crawls up to the high passes of Wrynose and Hardknott (see p103) before dropping down into Eskdale en route to the Cumbrian Coast.

🛏 Sleeping & Eating

Three Shires Inn PUB **££**
(☎015394-37215; www.threeshiresinn.co.uk; Little Langdale; mains £11.95-18.95, d from £90; Ⓟ🖥) Halfway up the road to Wrynose Pass, this inviting 19th-century inn makes an ideal place to break the climb. Ales from Coniston, Hawkshead and Jennings are on tap in the Slaters Bar, accompanied by generous slabs of game, lamb and venison in the dining room. The terrace is the place to sit if the weather's warm, with a grand outlook towards the profiles of Wetherlam and the Tilberthwaite Fells. Insist on a fell-view room if you're staying overnight.

Fell Foot Farm FARMSTA **£**
(☎015394-37149; www.fellfootfarm.co.uk; s £40-50, d £50-60; Ⓟ) If you want to get away from it all, this wonderfully remote farmhouse is the place. It's owned by the National Trust and is still a working sheep farm, so you'll be

able to glimpse Herdwicks from your window. The two rooms are freshly decorated, although the layouts are a bit quirky due to the age of the house – there's a separate cottage if you need more space (from £250 for a minimum of three nights). Breakfast is cooked on the Aga, and fell views unfold in every direction. The farm's about a mile west of the Three Shires Inn.

Elterwater

Named by Norse settlers after the colonies of whooper swans that still swoop across its surface every winter, Elterwater (literally, 'swan lake') presents the picture-postcard image of a traditional Lakeland village, with its tree-fringed lake and clump of slate-roofed cottages gathered around a maple-shaded village green. Somewhat bizarrely for such a peaceful spot, Elterwater originally grew up around the industries of slate quarrying, farming and gunpowder manufacture, but these days the main trade is in tourism – only around a quarter of the village houses are occupied year-round, with the rest used as holiday homes.

If you have time, it's worth making the half-mile trek up to **Chapel Stile**, northwest of the village, where you'll find a collection of quarrymen's cottages constructed from the area's distinctive green slate, and a sturdy mid-19th-century church, notable for its delicate Victorian stained glass.

Sleeping & Eating

TOP CHOICE **Eltermere Inn**　　　　HOTEL £££
(☏015394-37207; www.eltermere.co.uk; Elterwater; d from £110-200; P) New owners Mark and Ruth Jones have given the old Eltermere Hotel a much needed spruce-up, and the interior now more than lives up to the lakeside setting. The 12 rooms each have quirks: Stone Arthur hunkers under beams, Robin Ghyll has an antique four-poster and slate bathroom, and Lingmoor has bags of space and fine fell views. The bar's a treat: crackling grate, stone hearth and well-worn furniture inside, lovely grounds rolling down to the shores of Elterwater outside. The hotel even has its own private jetty (ask to borrow the row boat). Even if you're not staying, it's worth stopping in for tea on the front lawn terrace, or better still for the excellent three-course Sunday lunch (£24.50), overseen by the owners' son and head chef, Ed.

Britannia Inn　　　　PUB ££
(☏015394-37210; www.britinn.net; Elterwater; mains £11.50-18, d £90-120; P) This hugger-mugger inn overlooks Elterwater's village green, and has been in business for five centuries. Hearty plates of lamb henry, Flookburgh shrimps and Cartmel duck are served in the beamed restaurant, and the front terrace makes a tempting place for a pint or three of Coniston Bluebird – although it gets uncomfortably crowded on warm days. People travel for miles to see the pub's annual fireworks display and beer festival, both held in November.

Elterwater YHA　　　　HOSTEL £
(☏0845 371 9017; elterwater@yha.org.uk; Elterwater; dm £16.40-18.40; ☺Easter-Oct; ☺reception 7.30-10am & 5-10.30pm; @) Elterwater's oldest farmhouse now serves as Elterwater's youth hostel, much favoured by walkers setting out on the Langdale trails. It's looking a bit tired in spots – especially in the rather dated lounge – but the rural location is a treat. Accommodation is in two-, four- or six-bed dorms, and amenities include bike hire, basic kitchen and an evening meal. Parking is very limited, but if you get stuck on the fells, you'll be in luck – the hostel manager Nick Cook also happens to be the leader of the Langdale Mountain Rescue Team.

Langdale YHA　　　　HOSTEL £
(☏0845 371 9748; langdale@yha.org.uk; High Close, Loughrigg; dm £16.40-18.40; ☺Mar-Oct; P @) Halfway between Grasmere and Elterwater, this huge Victorian hostel (officially owned by the National Trust) is a favourite for activity groups, so you'll need to book well ahead. Extensive grounds and period features are the selling points, but some of the dorms are enormous (one has 16 bunks) and the central heating doesn't always live up to the task.

Langdale Co-op　　　　SHOP, CAFE £
(Chapel Stile; lunches £4-8; ☺9am-5pm) There's been a shop in Chapel Stile since 1884, and it's still going (despite the fact that it now has to be staffed by volunteers). Tinned goods and fresh food, including fruit and veg are sold downstairs, while upstairs the Brambles Café is famous for its tiffin cake and hiker's picnic pack (sandwich, salad and cake for £5.50). They'll even refill your Thermos with hot tea or coffee.

Wainwrights' Inn　　　　PUB £
(Chapel Stile; mains £8.95-12.95) Chapel Stile's only pub is a regular in the good beer guides,

PARKING IN LANGDALE

Hiking is very much the main attraction in Great Langdale, but it's notoriously popular – during the summer you might find that all the official car parks are full by 10am. There are National Trust car parks at Stickle Ghyll and the Old Dungeon Ghyll Hotel (free for NT members), plus one run by the NPA (£2.50/4.50/6.50 for two/four/12 hours) opposite the New Dungeon Ghyll.

Roadside parking isn't allowed in the valley, so to cope with demand, there are a couple of unofficial car parks in privately owned fields which open in summer. The one at New Dungeon Ghyll Hotel costs £4 all day, and includes a 10% discount on food; find a space then pay at the hotel bar.

Many people find it easier to follow in Wainwright's footsteps and clamber aboard the Langdale Rambler bus instead, which trundles up and down the valley six times a day during the high season.

and is usually busy with an even split of hikers and locals.

Great Langdale

West of Elterwater, the sky opens out and the mountain tops stack up along the horizon as you move ever deeper into the broodily breathtaking valley of Great Langdale, one of the Lake District's most naturally dramatic (and photogenic) spots.

Isolated farmsteads, snaking drystone walls and the occasional pocket-sized cottage dot the broad valley floor, while in the far distance rise some of the true giants of the Lakeland fell roster - **Bowfell** (902m/2960ft), the five summits of the **Crinkle Crags** and the chain of summits known as the **Langdale Pikes**: Pike O' Stickle (709m/2323ft), Loft Crag (682m/2238ft), Harrison Stickle (736m/2415ft) and Pavey Ark (700m/2296ft).

Activities

Langdale Pikes HIKING
The high circuit around the Langdale Pikes is probably the valley's most popular hike, allowing you to tick off between three and five Wainwrights depending on your chosen route. Though the fells are relatively small in height, the walk up is very steep – especially the first section along Dungeon Ghyll towards Stickle Tarn. See p80 for a detailed route description.

Crinkle Crags & Bowfell HIKING
Perhaps the most rewarding Langdale fell walk – among the very best in the park, according to AW – is the trek along the rumpled series of five peaks known as the **Crinkle Crags**, followed by the ascent of nearby **Bowfell**. The classic route climbs up via Oxendale and Red Tarn, before winding out over a ridge trail across the jagged 'crinkles', providing a fantastic outlook over the valley. The only real challenge (apart from the steep ascent) is a section of scrambling over the rocky obstacle of the 'Bad Step' – not quite full-blown rock climbing, but still a challenge for many hikers.

Further north beyond the Crinkles looms the distinctive dome-shaped summit of **Bowfell** (902m/2959ft), from where the trail runs back down to Angle Tarn and Langdale. All told, count on a walk of around 9 miles and six hours, depending on your route. It's very exposed in places, and navigating can be difficult and potentially dangerous in thick cloud, so leave this one for a clear day.

Scafell Pike HIKING
We've detailed the classic route up to Scafell Pike from Wasdale on p109, but there's an alternative route up the mountain's western approach from Langdale, ascending via Angle Tarn, Esk Hause and Great End (910m/2984ft). It's a longer proposition than the ascent from Wasdale (count on around 11 miles and seven hours on the mountain), but this route allows you to explore the remote western section of Langdale, and offers stunning views of the surrounding valleys.

Sleeping & Eating

Old Dungeon Ghyll Hotel HOTEL ££
(015394-37272; www.odg.co.uk; d with bathroom £105-115, 2-night minimum at weekends; P) Huddled under rocky fells, with jaw-dropping views unfurling from every window, this is the classic hikers' hotel in Langdale. It's a long way from luxury, and rooms look a

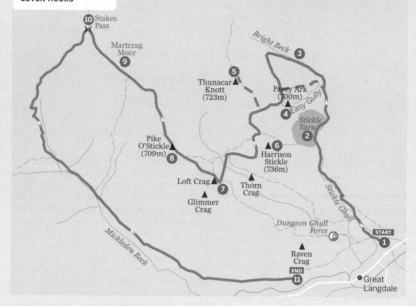

START **NEW DUNGEON GHYLL HOTEL**
FINISH **OLD DUNGEON GHYLL HOTEL**
DISTANCE **7 MILES**
DURATION **SIX TO SEVEN HOURS**

Hiking Tour
The Langdale Pikes

❭ This strenuous walk is the most popular hike in Langdale and crosses over a series of lofty summits, with stirring views over the Langdale and Mickleden Valleys.

The trail starts behind the ❶ **New Dungeon Ghyll Hotel**, leading steeply up the ravine of Stickle Ghyll. The easiest path starts on the beck's left bank, then crosses over stepping-stones halfway up, climbing to ❷ **Stickle Tarn**.

Take a breather at the tarn and admire the craggy views of your next target, Pavey Ark. There are several routes to the summit, including the treacherous scramble up the face of Pavey Ark known as 'Jack's Rake'. A marginally easier scramble leads up Easy Gully, but the most achievable ascent is the route dubbed by Wainwright as ❸ **North Rake**. The trail leads up Bright Beck, and climbs a steep scree gully on its way to ❹ **Pavey Ark's summit**; the views are some of the loftiest in Langdale, but take care near the edge.

Pavey Ark is actually an outlying peak of ❺ **Thunacar Knott**, so peak-bagging purists will want to head northwest for 500m to the summit. There's no path; just head across the grass for the highest point.

From here, pick up the well-worn trail along the cliff from Pavey Ark, and follow it to the top of ❻ **Harrison Stickle**, at 736m/2415ft the highest of the Langdale Pikes. From here, the path drops down the fell's west side, climbs over the rubbly ridge of ❼ **Loft Crag**, and leads northwest to the distinctive hump of ❽ **Pike O' Stickle**. There's a bit of scrambling involved in getting to the top – the drops are daunting but the views are worth it, so take your time and be sure of your footholds.

Once you've conquered the Pikes, follow the faint path across the grassy slopes of ❾ **Martcrag Moor** to the junction at ❿ **Stakes Pass**. Turn south and follow the zigzagging trail for around 3 miles into the Mickleden Valley, ending with a well-deserved pint at the ⓫ **Old Dungeon Ghyll Hotel**.

touch shabby in places, but it's impossible to fault the location. There's a choice of shared or en-suite rooms (some with rickety brass bedsteads, others four-posters). Downstairs, hikers congregate in the bar to swap tall tales and Lakeland ales.

New Dungeon Ghyll Hotel   HOTEL **££**
(☏015394-37213; www.dungeon-ghyll.co.uk; d £98-128; P) If the ODG is full, this well-worn slate hotel makes a useful back-up. Cream walls and country patterns define the rooms: some have four-poster beds, nearly all have views, but the decor throughout is looking rather tired. There's good pub food in the Walkers' Bar (mains £9 to £14) or more sophisticated meals in the sit-down restaurant (set menu £29.50).

TOP CHOICE **Great Langdale Campsite**   CAMPGROUND **£**
(☏015394-37668; www.ntlakescampsites.org.uk; sites for tent, adult & car £8-12, extra adult £5, child £2.50, dogs £1.50, camping pods £25-42.50; ⊙check-in 3-7pm Sat-Thu, 3-9pm Fri, campsite open year-round; P) This gloriously remote National Trust campsite is located about a mile up the valley from the Old Dungeon Ghyll Hotel. With panoramas of the Langdale Fells stretching in every direction, it unsurprisingly fills up quickly, but online booking is now available – see p213. Aim for one of the edge pitches if you prefer things quiet; glampers might want to upgrade to a camping pod, with its own lockable front door and sheep-wool insulation, or one of two yurts provided by Long Valley. The reception area and shop has recently been upgraded, complete with a brand-spanking new oven that delivers fresh bread in season. All in all, one of the best campsites in Lakeland.

Stickle Barn   PUB **£**
(☏015394-37356; Great Langdale; mains £5-12; dm £10-12) This ever busy hikers' retreat is a popular alternative to the valley's hotels, with a cockle-warming menu of casseroles, stews and curries (mains £5 to £10). If the campsites are full, the bunkhouse is also a useful fall back – as always, you'll need your own sleeping bag and camping supplies.

Raysbrown Farm   CAMPGROUND **£**
(☏015394-37300; www.baysbrownfarm.com; sites from £8) A large field campsite on a 320-hectare Herdwick sheep farm, accessed by a humpbacked bridge and hemmed in on all sides by the Pikes, Bow Fell and Crinkle Crags. Facilities onsite include his-and-hers shower block and a washing-up room, but groups of more than four adults aren't allowed. You can pitch where you like, but the farm only accepts cash.

Coniston, Hawkshead & Around

Includes »

Best Places to Eat & Drink

» Drunken Duck (p93)

» Church House Inn (p88)

» Black Bull Inn (p88)

» Jumping Jenny (p84)

» Tower Bank Arms (p96)

Best Places to Stay

» Yewfield (p93)

» Summer Hill Country House (p87)

» Bank Ground Farm (p87)

» Yew Tree Farm (p87)

» Graythwaite Hall (p96)

Why Go?

Windermere might be bigger, Wastwater may be wilder, but Coniston Water maintains a rare air of serenity even on the busiest days. Stretching for 5 miles beneath the Old Man of Coniston, the lake is still famous for the speed attempts made here by Malcolm and Donald Campbell, but today it's altogether more tranquil – the only boats you'll see skimming across its surface are a couple of solar-powered launches and an antique steam yacht.

Cloaked with woodland and criss-crossed by winding lanes, this is a famously picturesque corner of the Lake District. It's also well known for its literary connections: John Ruskin lived here, William Wordsworth went to school here and Arthur Ransome was inspired to write *Swallows and Amazons* while staying here. But as always, it's Beatrix Potter who looms largest: she adored the countryside around Coniston and Hawkshead and wrote some of her most famous tales at the idyllic little cottage of Hill Top in Near Sawrey.

When to Go

This is a popular part of the Lake District, so it can get crowded in summer and the Easter holidays. If you're visiting beauty spots such as Hill Top, Hawkshead and Tarn Hows, you'll enjoy them more by visiting outside these times. September and October are great times of year, as the forests around Tarn Hows and Claife Heights are set ablaze with autumnal colours. Key festivals to look out for include Coniston's Water Festival in July and the Coniston Walking Festival in September.

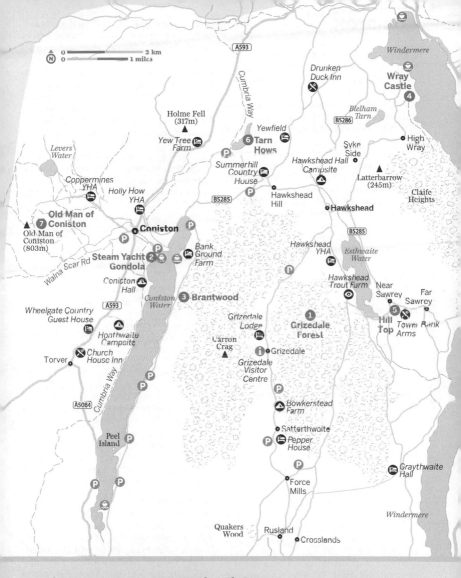

Coniston & Hawkshead Highlights

❶ Explore the bike trails and outdoor artwork of **Grizedale Forest** (p94)

❷ Take a trip across Coniston Water on the restored steam yacht **Gondola** (p86)

❸ Visit John Ruskin's lakeside sanctuary at **Brantwood** (p84)

❹ Follow the beautiful lakeshore trail through Claife Heights to **Wray Castle** (p97)

❺ Brave the throngs at Beatrix Potter's cottage at **Hill Top** (p95)

❻ Pack a picnic and head for the shores of **Tarn Hows** (p95)

❼ Admire the sights from the summit of the **Old Man** (p89)

CONISTON

POP 1948

Hunched beneath the slate summit of the Old Man of Coniston (803m/2276ft), the little village of Coniston grew up as a centre for the local copper-mining industry, but nowadays the only obvious reminders of the town's industrial heyday are the abandoned quarries and mineshafts littering the surrounding hilltops.

Modern-day Coniston is mostly geared towards tourism: cruise boats putter across the lake to John Ruskin's former home at Brantwood, and the town makes an ideal base for exploring the peaceful trails of nearby Tarn Hows and Grizedale Forest. But the town is still inextricably linked with Malcolm Campbell and his son Donald, who embarked on a string of world-record speed attempts here between the 1930s and 1960s.

◎ Sights

Brantwood   HISTORIC BUILDING

(www.brantwood.org.uk; adult/5-15yr £6.30/1.35, gardens only £4.50/1.35; ⊘11am-5.30pm mid-Mar–mid-Nov, 11am-4.30pm Wed-Sun mid-Nov–mid-Mar) This stately house on Coniston Water's east bank was the lifelong home of John Ruskin (1819–1900), the Victorian polymath, philosopher and critic. During an illustrious writing career that spanned over 60 years, Ruskin expounded views on everything from Venetian architecture to the finer points of shell collecting, and in many ways was incredibly ahead of his time. Though best known for his art criticism, he was also a pioneering social reformer, proposing early concepts for community housing, the minimum wage and the welfare state. He was also an unstinting champion for the value of traditional arts and crafts over factory-made materials, a concept that he put into practice during his own renovation of Brantwood.

Ruskin acquired the house as a derelict shell in 1871. Over the next 20 years, he slowly expanded the house and grounds in the pursuit of his concept of 'organic architecture', inspired by natural forms and handcrafted materials. The result is a living monument to his aesthetic principles: every inch of the house, from the furniture to the gardens, was designed according to his painstaking instructions (he even dreamt up some of the wallpaper designs).

Highlights include the grand but surprisingly cosy drawing room, the tome-filled study, and the tiny upstairs bedroom decorated with some of his favourite watercolours (mostly by JMW Turner, and mostly copies of the originals). In the corner of the room is the little circular turret where Ruskin whiled away hours looking out across the lake and pondering the great issues of the day. Later in life he was afflicted by bouts of deep depression, and suffered some kind of mental collapse in the room. He never slept in there again.

As well as being a great thinker, Ruskin was also an inveterate collector: look out for his enormous shell collection and a cornucopia of *objets d'art* collected on his travels. Though better known as a critic, Ruskin was also a talented painter in his own right, and the walls of the house are covered with his watercolours of Lakeland flora and fauna.

Outside the house, 100 hectares of gardens and terraces stretch up the fell-side (Brant derives from a Norse word meaning steep). Of particular note are the Hortus Inclusus, a herb garden modelled along medieval designs, and the Zig-Zaggy, inspired by the purgatorial mount in Dante's *Inferno*. The best views are from the High Walk, designed by Ruskin's cousin Joan Severn.

Brantwood is about 3 miles from Coniston. By car, you can follow the B5285 east of town and follow the signs, but a much better way to arrive is aboard a cruise boat from Coniston.

While you're waiting for the next connection, hot soups, cream teas and homemade pies are served at the lovely **Jumping Jenny** (lunches £4-8; ⊘same as house) cafe, lodged inside Brantwood's former coach house.

Coniston Water   LAKE

Coniston's main attraction is undoubtedly its lake, which at 5 miles long and half a mile across is the third largest in the Lake District (after Windermere and Ullswater). It has two small islands, both of which are owned by the National Trust: **Fir Island** lies close to the eastern shore, while **Peel Island** sits at the lake's southern end, and was supposedly one of the main inspirations for Wild Cat Island in *Swallows and Amazons*.

Coniston Water is a half-mile walk from the village along Lake Rd. Boats can be hired from the Coniston Boating Centre opposite the Bluebird Café.

The lakeshore offers lovely walking, especially the 4-mile stretch that leads along

Coniston

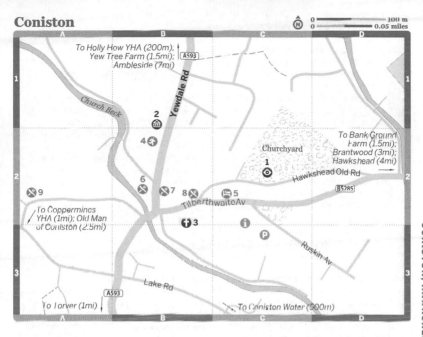

Coniston

◉ Sights
1 Donald Campbell's Grave.................. C2
2 Ruskin Museum B1
3 St Andrew's Church............................ B2

✪ Activities, Courses & Tours
4 Summitreks... B2

🛏 Sleeping
5 Lakeland House C2

🍴 Eating
6 Black Bull Inn...................................... B2
7 Harry's.. B2
8 Meadowdore Cafe B2
9 Sun Hotel A2

the lake's west side, from Sunny Bank across Torver Common to the village. There are several jetties around the lake, but only the ones at Coniston and Brantwood are served by both the Coniston Launches and the *Gondola.*

Ruskin Museum   MUSEUM
(www.ruskinmuseum.com; Yewdale Rd; adult/child £5.25/2.50; ◷10am-5.30pm Easter–mid-Nov, 10.30am-3.30pm Wed-Sun mid-Nov–Easter)

Coniston's quirky little village museum is a treasure trove of Lakeland history. Founded at the turn of the century by Ruskin's long-time compatriot and amanuensis WG Collingwood, the museum houses displays of prehistoric and Bronze Age artefacts, and provides plenty of background on copper mining, drystone walling, sheep farming and local crafts such as linen and lace making. There's also an extensive section on John Ruskin, with displays of his writings, watercolours and sketchbooks. A recent addition is Arthur Ransome's row boat, *Mavis,* which he used to explore Coniston's wooded islands while writing *Swallows and Amazons.*

A new extension to the museum was completed in 2011, which in future years will house Donald Campbell's historic *Bluebird K7* boat following its restoration. In the meantime you can view the boat's Orpheus engine, as well as a comprehensive archive exploring the Campbell story. The museum also runs occasional guided walks around the village, covering points of interest related to the Campbells; they cost adult/child £7/3.50, including admission to the museum.

Discount tickets combing entry to Brantwood and the Coniston cruise boats are available: ask at the ticket office.

THE CAMPBELL STORY

Coniston Water seems like a rather unlikely location for setting world speed records, but between the 1930s and the 1960s, this quiet corner of the Lakes was the setting for a series of audacious attempts by Sir Malcolm Campbell and his son, Donald, to break the world water-speed record.

Coniston's speed connections stretch back to the late 1930s, when Malcolm (already a national motorcycle champion, Grand Prix racer and holder of nine land-speed records) chose the lake as the location for his latest attempt to break the water-speed record, which he had already broken three times (on Lake Geneva, Lake Maggiore in Italy and Lake Halwell in Switzerland). On 19 August 1939, piloting the revolutionary jet-fuelled powerboat *Bluebird K4,* Campbell achieved a speed of 141.74mph – a record that was still intact a decade later when he died at home in Surrey in 1948.

Malcolm wasn't the only Campbell to be bitten by the speed bug, however. Having watched his father's speed attempts as a boy, ex-RAF pilot Donald Campbell set about redesigning the K4 powerboat to mount his own challenge on the water-speed record, spurred on by several other racers who were attempting to steal his father's title.

In June 1950 the record was finally broken by American pilot Stan Sayers, who achieved a new speed of 160.32mph in his boat *Slo-mo-shun IV.* It was five years before Campbell finally regained the record in the revolutionary jetboat *Bluebird K7,* first with a speed of 202.32mph on Ullswater, followed the same year by 216.1mph at Lake Mead in the United States. Campbell smashed the water-speed record several more times over the next decade, culminating at Lake Dumbleyung in Western Australia, where he reached 276.3mph in 1964, having already achieved the land-speed record (403.1mph) just a year before.

Tragically, the Campbell story ended in disaster back at Coniston Water on 4 January 1967. Having already clocked 297mph, Donald decided to make another attempt on the record without allowing sufficient time for the wake from his previous run to subside. Near the end of her return run, at an estimated 328mph, the *Bluebird*'s bow rose out of the water, flipped and struck the lake nose-first, killing Donald instantly. Thirty seconds later the boat had sunk without trace.

Controversially, the remains of the boat and its pilot were recovered from the lakebed in March 2001. Campbell's remains were buried in the village churchyard of St Andrews, and the boat itself is currently being restored (hopefully to full working order) by local engineer and wreck diver Bill Smith, with the blessing of Campbell's daughter Gina. Eventually the boat will be housed at the new extension at the Ruskin Museum, but it's been a long and arduous process: find out the latest news on the restoration at www .bluebirdproject.com.

🏃 Activities

Gondola
CRUISE

(www.nationaltrust.org.uk/gondola; ☺Apr-Oct) For a dash of Victorian elegance, you can't top the puffing steam yacht *Gondola*, originally launched in 1859 and restored to its former glory in the 1980s by the National Trust. Looking like a cross between a Venetian vaporetto and an English houseboat, complete with cushioned saloons and polished wooden seats, it's a stately way of seeing the lake, especially if you're visiting Brantwood. And you don't need to fret about carbon emissions from the *Gondola*'s steam-plume; she's switched from mucky coal to eco-friendly waste-wood logs, cutting her carbon footprint by 90%.

There are several cruises on offer, all of which run weather permitting. All boats stop at the jetties at Coniston, Monk Coniston and Brantwood; only the Explorer and Wild Cat Cruises stop at the southern jetty at Parkamoor.

The **Standard Cruise** (adult/5-15yr £9.90/4.90) runs for 45 minutes, while the 90-minute **Explorer Cruise** (adult/child £21/10.50; ☺2-3.45pm Mon, Thu & Sun) takes in the southern half of the lake, and includes guided commentary. The **Wild Cat Island Walkers Cruise** (adult/child £21/10.50; ☺11am Sun) is a weekly trip to Wild Cat Island, stopping at Brantwood, Monk Coniston and the new Parkamoor jetty stop.

Coniston Launches
CRUISE

(www.conistonlaunch.co.uk) The two original timber-hulled Coniston Launches (*Ruskin* and *Ransome*) date from the 1920s, but they've been powered almost entirely by solar panels since 2005. They were recently joined by a third vessel, *Campbell*, launched in 2011.

There are two circular routes, which run 10 times daily in summer, five times daily in winter. You can either buy a round-the-lake ticket, allowing you to jump on and off, or just buy a single fare to a particular jetty. Special weekly cruises covering the Campbells and Arthur Ransome run only in summer.

The launches stop at several jetties around the lake: at Brantwood and Water Park on the east side, and Lake Bank, Sunny Bank, Torver, Coniston and the Waterhead Hotel on the west side.

The **Northern Service** (adult/5-16yr £9.50/4.95) stops at the northern jetties, including Coniston, Waterhead, Brantwood and Torver; the **Southern Service** (adult/5-16yr £13.50/6.75) includes the southern lake, with stops at the Water Park, Lake Bank and Sunny Bank jetties. The **Campbells on Coniston** (adult/5-16yr £12/6; ⊗12.30pm Tue Apr-Sep) is a cruise with commentary on the Campbell story, while the **Swallows & Amazons** (adult/5-16yr £12.50/6.25; ⊗12.30pm Wed Apr-Sep) is a 110-minute cruise including a visit to Wild Cat Island.

Coniston Boating Centre
BOATING

(☑015394-41366;www.lakedistrict.gov.uk/coniston boatingcentre) For self-propelled lake exploration, the boating centre hires out row boats (from £10 per hour for two people), kayaks (£15 per person for two hours), Canadian canoes (£25 per hour) and electric motor boats (from £20 per hour), plus dinghies (from £40 for two hours) for more experienced sailors.

There's a car park next to the boating centre, but it's usually full in summer.

Summitreks
OUTDOORS

(☑015394-41822; 14 Yewdale Rd) Outdoor equipment, camping and hiking supplies and organised activities.

★☆ Festivals & Events

Coniston Water Festival
LAKE FESTIVAL

There's been a lake festival on Coniston since the mid-19th century. These days it's held in July and hosts everything from sailing displays to plastic duck races.

Coniston Walking Festival
WALKING

Hikers congregate in Coniston in September for a festival of guided walks, talks and hiking-themed events.

🛏 Sleeping

If you're really stuck for a room, most of the town pubs offer basic B&B.

TOP CHOICE Summer Hill Country House
GUESTHOUSE ££

(☑01539-436180; www.summerhillcountryhouse .com; Hawkshead Hill; d £96 116; P🐾) It's a few miles' drive from Coniston, but there's no doubt that this chic country house (built in the early 1700s) is the place to stay if you're after a rural retreat. Owners Patsy and Mike have created five rooms filled with spoils: Gilchrist & Soames bath goodies, fresh fruit, DAB radios and even a Mac Mini for getting online. Our favourite is Room Four, with its monochrome colour scheme and bay window overlooking the gardens. The garden summer house is a gorgeous place to soak up the evening rays.

Bank Ground Farm
B&B ££

(☑015394-41264; www.bankground.com; East of the Lake; d £90, cottages £475-695 per week; P) This lakeside farmhouse offers both history and heritage in a gorgeous Grade II listed building, parts of which date from the 15th century. It oozes low-ceilinged, oak-beamed charm, and the seven rooms are primly done in plump pillows and country-style fabrics. It even boasts literary cachet – Arthur Ransome used it as the blueprint for 'Holly Howe Farm' in *Swallows and Amazons*, and it featured heavily in the 1974 film adaptation. For longer stays, there are self-catering cottages and a huge three-floored converted barn.

Yew Tree Farm
FARMSTAY ££

(☑015394-41433; www.yewtree-farm.com; r £100-124; P) Seen *Miss Potter*? Then you might find this whitewashed farmhouse familiar – it doubled in the film as Beatrix's house at Hill Top. It's still very much a working farm, so you'll fall asleep to a soundtrack of assorted moos and bleats: the three rooms are surprisingly luxurious, especially 'Tarn Hows' with its cruck rafters and king-size four-poster. Sadly, the tea room is no longer open to non-guests. The farm's about 1.5 miles north along Yewdale Rd.

Lakeland House B&B ££

(☑015394-41303; www.lakelandhouse.co.uk; Tilberthwaite Ave; s £40-50, d £74-100; 🐾) This basic B&B is short on frills, but it's the best option if you want to stay in the heart of the village. Perched above Holland's cafe, the en suite rooms are clean but spartan (a bed, a tea tray and a shower is about all you'll get): ask for the attic Lookout Suite for the most space. Remember to choose your breakfast the night before by chalking it up on the blackboard.

Holly How YHA HOSTEL £

(☑0845 371 9511; conistonhh@yha.org.uk; Far End; dm £16.40-19.99; ⊙reception 7.30-10am & 5-10pm) Another fine gabled house turned smart YHA, along the road to Ambleside. The communal areas include a lounge (with original plasterwork ceiling) and a bright, sunny cafe serving evening meals; the dorms, however, are rather bland. It's a school-trip and activity-group favourite, so book ahead.

Coppermines YHA HOSTEL £

(☑0870 770 5772; dm £16.40-19.99; ⊙reception 7-11am & 5-10pm Easter-Oct) This former mine manager's cottage is hidden away in the hills surrounded by piles of slate and old mine workings. It's pretty basic, with a simple kitchen and bunks in three four-bed dorms and two larger dorms, but makes an ideal head-start for trips to the Old Man and Wetherlam. It's 1¼ miles from Coniston along an unsealed track that starts off Yewdale Rd.

Coniston Hall CAMPGROUND £

(☑015394-41223; sites for 2 adults & car £13; ⊙Easter-Oct) The village's main campsite is about a mile south of town off the A593. The site is spread out over 12-odd hectares along the lakeside, with showers, an on-site laundry and a small shop.

Hoathwaite Campsite CAMPGROUND £

(☑015394-63862; nationaltrust.org.uk; adult/child £6/3, £1 discount outside summer) This new National Trust campsite occupies a prime lake-view spot between Coniston and Torver, but at the moment it's primitive: facilities are only offered between May and October, and even then they're limited to two electric showers and four toilets in an old barn. At other times of year, you'll have to bring your own portaloo(!). The lower field is reserved for groups; the top field has space for tents, campervans

and caravans. Cash and cheque only. It's just off the A593, about a mile from Coniston; look out for the sign on the left-hand side just before you reach Torver.

Wheelgate Country Guest House B&B £

(☑015394-41418; www.wheelgate.co.uk; Little Arrow; d £80-90) Chintzy but cosy B&B in a clematis-clad farmhouse, 1½ miles south in Little Arrow.

✕ Eating & Drinking

For lunch or afternoon tea, there's nowhere better in Coniston than the Jumping Jenny cafe at Brantwood.

Church House Inn PUB ££

(☑01539-441282; www.chuchhouseinntorver.com; Torver; mains £11.25-14.25) While the crowds stick to Coniston's pubs, more discerning diners head for this traditional little inn in Torver, which has a well-deserved reputation for its food thanks to its talented chefs Michael and Jimmy, who both polished their skills at the Drunken Duck. The food's rich and hearty (game pie, old spot pork, tattie hotpot), but done with real panache; even the chutneys and breads are homemade. The Sunday roast is a beaut, too – but you'll have to get in early to beat the locals.

Sun Hotel PUB ££

(☑015394-41248; www.thesunconiston.com; mains £11-15) Campbell connections abound at this venerable coaching inn, as Donald had his HQ here during his final fateful campaign. The grand, gabled building is perched up a little incline behind the village, with a choice of tables either in the conservatory, the beamed, slate-floored bar, or the grassy front garden. Pub grub specials are chalked up on blackboards, while guest ales are poured from barrels right behind the bar.

Black Bull Inn PUB ££

(www.conistonbrewery.com; Yewdale Rd; mains £6-14) This whitewashed village inn is one of the best small-scale breweries in the Lakes; the Bluebird Bitter and Old Man Ale have scooped awards from some of Britain's top real ale associations. Inside black-and-white photos of Coniston in its heyday line the walls of the rambling bar, while the front patio is always packed with post-hike drinkers on sunny days.

Bluebird Café CAFE £

(Lake Rd; lunches £4-8; ⊙breakfast & lunch) This busy lakeside cafe was originally built by the

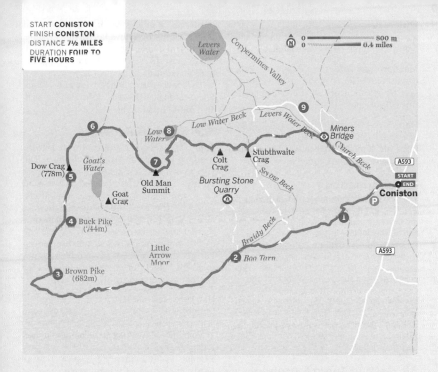

Hiking Tour
The Old Man of Coniston

❯ Hunkering above Coniston like a benevolent giant, the Old Man (803m/2276ft) presents an irresistible challenge. The most popular route is up the east side along the Coppermines Valley, but it's an unrelentingly steep slog. Instead, this route circles behind the Old Man via the spectacular ridge between Brown Pike and Dow Crag.

Start in Coniston and follow the road past the Sun Inn for half a mile to the start of the ❶ **Walna Scar Rd** (you can park here if you've got a car). Go through the gate and head west along the track, admiring the view across the barren expanse of Torver High Common.

The path leads west, passing the tiny pond of ❷ **Boo Tarn** after about a mile. Ignore the side-trail north towards Goat's Water and continue west, following the trail up as it climbs the south flank of ❸ **Brown Pike** (682m/2238ft) and traces the ridgeline across ❹ **Buck Pike** (744m/2441ft) and ❺ **Dow Crag** (778m/2552ft). The views east across Goat's Water to the Old Man are

superb, but the drop is severe; take care near the edge, especially when it's windy.

From Dow Crag, the trail circles round the northern side of Goat's Water, dropping into the saddle of ❻ **Goat's Hause** before following a leg-sapping incline up the west side of the Old Man. At the ❼ **summit**, you'll be rewarded with a glorious 360-degree panorama, east over Coniston Water, north towards Wetherlam and west towards the trio of fells you've just climbed. On a clear day, you'll see south all the way to Morecambe Bay.

From the cairn at the top, a zigzag trail tracks sharply down the mountain's northern side. Follow the slippery path down to ❽ **Low Water**, and then east through the abandoned slate quarries beneath Colt Crag. A stone staircase has been cut out at points, but it's still very steep. The path winds down the valley along the southern back of Levers Beck, passing the ❾ **Coppermines YHA** en route back to the village.

Furness Railway Company, but it now makes a perfect place for a sandwich, spud or salad before you jump on the lake launch.

Meadowdore Cafe   CAFE £

(Hawkshead Old Rd; £4-7) Fill up on standards such as fish and chips and filled baguettes at this village cafe.

Harry's   CAFE £

(4 Yewdale Rd; mains £6.95-11.90) Wine bar offering a snack menu of pasta standards, pizzas and Aberdeen Angus burgers.

ℹ Information

The only bank in Coniston is a small branch of Barclays, but it weirdly has no ATM; there are fee-charging Link machines at the post office and petrol station.

Coniston Tourist Office (☎015394-41533; www.conistontic.org; Ruskin Ave; ⊙9.30am-5.30pm Easter-Oct, to 4pm Nov-Mar; ☎) This community-run super-efficient information centre sells walking leaflets (£1) and the Coniston Loyalty Card (£2), which offers local discounts. Wi-fi is available for a small donation.

Holland's Cafe (Tilberthwaite Ave; internet per 15min £1; ⊙9am-5pm Mon-Fri, 8am-5pm Sat & Sun) Internet access.

ℹ Getting There & Around

For information on the Cross-Lakes Experience, see p224.

The Ruskin Explorer ticket (adult/child £16/7.30) includes the bus fare from Windermere, plus a Coniston launch ticket and admission to Brantwood. Pick it up from the tourist office or the bus driver.

Useful bus routes:

505 (six to eight daily March to October) Hawkshead (15 minutes), Ambleside (36 minutes), Brockhole (45 minutes) and Windermere (50 minutes). Two buses a day continue to Kendal (1 hour 20 minutes).

X12 (five daily Monday to Saturday) To Ulverston (30 minutes).

HAWKSHEAD

POP 1640

As Lakeland villages go, they just don't get much more picture-perfect than tiny Hawkshead. With its cob cottages, narrow alleys and criss-crossing lanes, it feels like a medieval relic from a bygone age – or at least it would, if it weren't for the streams of trippers who mill around its cobbled streets by the score throughout the summer months. The

crush can be oppressive in peak season, but the proximity of Esthwaite Water, Grizedale Forest and Claife Heights thankfully mean there's always somewhere to escape the madding crowds.

The **Hawkshead Post Office and Village Shop** (Main St; ⊙7.30am-5.30pm Mon-Sat, 8am-4pm Sun) is on Main St.

◉ Sights & Activities

Traffic is banned in the centre of Hawkshead, so it's a great place for strolling. The village owes its existence to monks from Furness Abbey, who founded Hawkshead as a centre for the medieval wool trade. Following the dissolution of the abbey under Henry VIII, Hawkshead was granted its own market charter by James I, and became one of the main trading villages in the central Lakes. Several of the lanes still bear names that hint at their former usage – look out for Leather, Rag and Putty Sts, for example.

Hawkshead Grammar
School   HISTORIC BUILDING

(www.hawksheadgrammar.org.uk; admission £2; ⊙10am-1pm & 2-5pm Mon-Sat, 1-5pm Sun Apr-Sep, 10-1pm & 2-3.30pm Mon-Sat, 1-3.30pm Sun Oct) Despite its diminutive appearance, Hawkshead's village school was once renowned as Lakeland's foremost seat of learning. Well-to-do young gentlemen were sent here from across the region to receive a grounding in Latin, Greek, mathematics, rhetoric and classical literature. Among the school's famous alumni were William Wordsworth and his older brother John, who arrived in Hawkshead following their mother's death in 1778. William remained in Hawkshead for the next nine years, boarding in the house now known as Ann Tyson's Cottage before leaving in 1787 to continue his education at Cambridge.

The schoolroom has been left largely unchanged since the school closed in 1909. In Wordsworth's day pupils would have sat here for up to 10 hours a day, covering such weighty subjects as Euclidean geometry, Pythagorean arithmetic, Platonic debate and Greek and Latin rhetoric – so it's little wonder that naughty young Will felt the urge to scratch his name into one of the school desks (no doubt earning a birching for his trouble).

Upstairs you can also view the headmaster's former study – one of the schoolmasters during Wordsworth's scholastic days was Edward Christian, the older brother of Fletcher Christian (of mutiny

Hawkshead

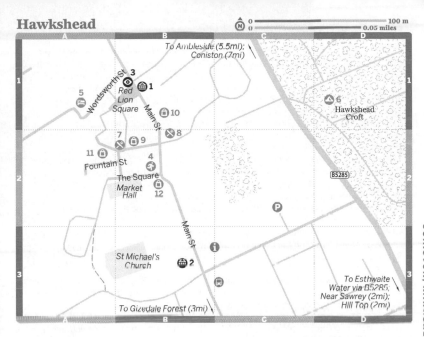

Hawkshead

on the *Bounty* fame). Both the Christian brothers were born in nearby Cockermouth.

Beatrix Potter Gallery ART GALLERY
(NT; ☎015394-36355; www.nationaltrust.org.uk /main/w-beatrixpottergallery; Main St; adult/child £4.60/2.30; ☺10.30am-5pm Sat-Thu Jun-Aug, 11am-5pm Sat-Thu Apr-May & Sep-Oct, 11am-3.30pm Feb-Mar) In the centre of the village are the former offices of Beatrix Potter's husband, solicitor William Heelis, whose firm had been based in Hawkshead since the mid-19th century. The offices have now been converted into this intriguing little art gallery, displaying a collection of watercolours, sketchbooks and studies from the National Trust's Beatrix Potter archive.

While she is best known for her children's books, Beatrix was also a perceptive student of nature and wildlife, and her botanical sketches of flowers, animals and particularly fungi provide an intriguing counterpoint to her more famous work.

The gallery also has some informative displays on Beatrix' work as a conservationist, especially her long campaign to protect the natural landscape of the Lakes from over-development by buying up local land and farms.

Entry is by timed ticket. Discounts are available if you've already visited Hill Top.

St Michael's Church CHURCH
Lodged on a slight rise just behind the village, St Michael's largely dates from the 16th century, although parts of the building (including the eight-belled tower) are thought to be older. The church is notable

BEATRIX POTTER

Of all the Lake District's literary figures, none commands a more fanatical following than Helen Beatrix Potter (1866–1943). More than a century after the publication of her first book, *The Tale of Peter Rabbit*, her anthropomorphic children's fables continue to sell by the bucketload, and her former house at Hill Top remains one of the most visited tourist attractions in Northern England, receiving in excess of 65,000 visitors every year.

Born to a privileged family in South Kensington in 1866 (her father was a barrister, her mother the wealthy daughter of a cotton magnate), Beatrix Potter's connections with the Lake District date back to a family holiday to the region in 1882. A shy and lonely child (thanks to her strict governess education and isolation from other children), the young Beatrix was fascinated by animals, botany and nature, and she instantly felt an extraordinary kinship with the Lake District landscape. Over the course of several summer holidays in the Lakes, she whiled away hours sketching flowers, trees and fungi, not to mention her ever-growing menagerie of pets: frogs, newts, toads and ferrets, as well as a pair of bunny rabbits named Peter and Benjamin Bouncer (who she liked to parade around on a lead).

Though her parents initially frowned on her creative leanings, Beatrix was encouraged to pursue her artistic ambitions by the local vicar and family friend Canon Hardwicke Rawnsley, who recognised her talent and encouraged her to complete her first book, *The Tale of Peter Rabbit*.

Though initially rejected by several publishers, the book was eventually printed by the small firm Frederick Warne & Co in 1901, and was an almost instant smash hit, selling in excess of 25,000 copies in its first year. Its financial success enabled Potter to buy her farm at Hill Top – the first of many property purchases in the Lakes – and spawned a series of 22 more books over the next 20 years, culminating with *The Tale of Little Pig Robinson* in 1930.

While her literary life was an unquestionable success, she had her share of hardships. Her first engagement to her publisher, Norman Warne, ended tragically in 1905 when he died suddenly of anaemia. She later married local solicitor William Heelis in 1913, who she met during the purchase of her second property in Lakeland, Castle Farm.

After she married, Beatrix became increasingly interested in hill farming and animal husbandry: during the 1920s and '30s she established her own prize-winning flock of Herdwick sheep, became a respected agricultural judge and president of the Herdwick Sheep Breeders' Association, and worked tirelessly to protect the Lakeland landscape she so adored.

She died in 1943 at the age of 77, bequeathing her 1600-hectare estate to the National Trust. Some of her early work is displayed at the Armitt Museum in Ambleside and the Beatrix Potter Gallery in Hawkshead.

---

for its elegant central nave, lined with circular pillars and decorative arches, as well as a striking war memorial designed by Ruskin's secretary, WG Collingwood (apparently inspired by his interest in Cumbria's pre-Norman crosses).

Summitreks   OUTDOOR ACTIVITIES
(☑015394-36655; The Square) Small outlet for this experienced activity provider.

Esthwaite Water   LAKE
To the south of Hawkshead, surrounded by overhanging trees and dappled woodland, Esthwaite Water is an oasis of peace and quiet compared to some of the better-known lakes. It's one of only a handful without any shoreline trail: the only place with public access to the lakeshore is the small car park at Ridding Wood, near the southern end.

Esthwaite is also home to the largest **trout fishery** (www.hawksheadtrout.com) in northwest England, as well as a healthy population of pike, perch, rudd and roach. Courses are available if you'd like to learn the finer points of line casting and fly tying; tuition costs £110 for a full day including tackle hire and boat, plus £50 for every extra person.

A shore permit costs £28 per day and includes a 'catch and release' limit of up to four fish. A boat permit costs £41.50/67.50 for one/two people and includes boat hire and four fish.

Cheaper evening permits starting at 4pm are also available, and there are also 'novice fishing packages' designed specially for adults and children.

🛏 Sleeping & Eating

TOP CHOICE Drunken Duck   PUB £££

(☏015394-36347; www.drunkenduckinn.co.uk; Barngates; mains £12.95-21.95; ℗) The renowned Drunken Duck is much more than a gastropub – it's a brewery, boozer, bistro and boutique inn all rolled into one. Inside, the 400-year-old building blends rustic architecture with country chic: slate bar, oak beams and vintage signs in the bar, offset by leather chairs and wood floors in the dining room. Home-brewed ales come from the Barngates Brewery behind the pub, but it's the food people travel for – venison loin, duck confit, lamb rump, served (of course) with champ and cavallo nero rather than plain mash and broccoli. Rooms offer chic spoils such as Roberts radios, enamel baths and rolling views. Unfortunately, the Duck's fame precedes it – it's one of the Lake District's most desirable dining destinations, and you'll need military precision to bag a table in summer. Lunch is a better bet, as it doesn't take bookings. It's halfway between Skelwith Bridge and Hawkshead; look out for the brown signs on the B5285 and B5286.

Yewfield   GUESTHOUSE ££

(☏015394-36765; www.yewfield.co.uk; Hawkshead Hill; d £98-124; ℗🖥) Zen aesthetics mingle with Victorian Gothic at this swish guesthouse on Hawkshead Hill, run by the owners of Zeffirelli's in Ambleside. Oak panels meet Oriental bedspreads in the rooms, but there's a more austere feel to the grand tower suite. Downstairs there's a stylish lounge complete with a grand piano, and the veggie breakfast features home-baked bread, muesli and fresh fruit. It's a bit tricky to find, on a minor road off the B5285 between Coniston and Hawkshead.

Ann Tyson's Cottage   B&B ££

(☏015394-36405; www.anntysons.co.uk; Wordsworth St; s £35-75, d £66-74) Both the Wordsworth boys once lodged at this tiny cottage down one of Hawkshead's narrow backstreets, where they were looked after by the genial 'old dame' Ann Tyson. These days the house is snug and chintzy, crammed with padded bedheads, low ceilings and tiny windows, as well as an antique bed that once belonged to John Ruskin.

Hawkshead YHA   HOSTEL £

(☏0845 371 9321; hawks head@yha.org.uk; dm £10.40-18.40; ⊙reception 7.30am 10pm, hostel open year-round; @) Hawkshead's hostel is lodged inside a regal Regency house near Esthwaite Water, decked out with original cornicing, panelled doors and even a veranda. As usual the dorms are nothing fancy, but there's bike rental, a cafe (meals £3 to £6) and buses stop outside the door. Unfortunately it's another of the Lake District YHAs which has recently been put up for sale, and may or may not be open by the time you read this – check the YHA website for the latest news.

Hawkshead Hall Campsite   CAMPGROUND £

(☏015394-36221; www.hawksheadhall-campsite.co .uk; 2 people, tent & car £15; ⊙mid-Mar–mid-Oct) Basic tap-and-tent site a quarter of a mile north of the village. It's mainly geared towards families and couples (ie no stag nights or hens parties). Facilities are limited to a portacabin shower block.

Hawkshead Croft   CAMPGROUND £

(☏015394-36374; www.hawkshead-croft.com; 2 people, tent & car £15.75 18.75; ⊙mid-Mar mid Sep) Caravans rule the roost here, although there's a rather cramped field that's reserved for tents. Facilities include a coin-op laundry, games room and modern shower block.

Queen's Head   PUB ££

(www.queensheadhotel.co.uk; Main St; mains £12-17.50, d £40-90; ℗) Oak-panelled character abounds in this ancient village pub, and the menu is surprisingly upmarket, with such fare as woodland venison, Gressingham duck and Winster Valley pork. It's crammed with nooks and crannies to hide away in, and the atmosphere is pleasantly antique.

King's Arms   PUB ££

(www.kingsarmshawkshead.co.uk; The Square; mains £8-14) Another 500-year-old inn, serving steak pie, Cumberland bangers and bean chilli among beams and brass horseshoes.

🛍 Shopping

Hawkshead Relish Company   FOOD

(www.hawksheadrelish.com; The Square) This famous relish company sells a tempting range of chutneys, relishes and mustards, from classic piccalilli to fruity Westmorland Chutney.

Honeypot   FOOD

(The Square) The village deli has a great selection for packing your own picnic, including Cumbrian cheeses, honeys and bottled ales.

Poppi Red   GIFTS

(www.poppi-red.co.uk; The Square) Frilly and ultra-feminine gift shop with a cutesy stock of home furnishings, pottery and craftwork, and a small tea-room that's drowning in polka dots.

 Getting There & Around

For information on the Cross-Lakes Experience, see p224.

Useful bus routes:

505 (10 Monday to Saturday, six Sunday mid-March to October)

X31 (four daily April to September) Circular bus from Coniston to Hawkshead via Tarn Hows. A couple of buses continue to Ulverston.

AROUND HAWKSHEAD

Grizedale Forest

Stretching for over 6000 acres across the hilltops between Coniston Water and Esthwaite Water is **Grizedale Forest** (www.forestry.gov.uk/grizedalehome), a dense conifer forest whose name derives from the Old Norse *griss-dale,* meaning 'valley of the pigs'. Though it looks lush and unspoilt today, the forest has been largely replanted over the last 100 years; by the late 19th century, the original woodland had practically disappeared thanks to the demands of the local logging, mining and charcoal industries.

Criss-crossed by hiking trails and mountain-bike routes, as well as a high-wire adventure park strung between the trees, the forest makes a fantastic all-day outing. But it's not just worth visiting for its natural attractions; since 1977 artists have created over 60 outdoor sculptures around the forest, including a wooden xylophone, a wave of carved ferns and a huge Tolkienesque 'man of the forest'. Many of the artworks nestle almost invisibly among the trees, so keep your eyes peeled on your walk around.

Grizedale Information Centre (01229-860010; grizedale@forestry.gsi.gov.uk; 10am-4pm) has a small shop and cafe, and also sells maps detailing the forest trails and outdoor sculptures.

 Activities

Forest Trails   WALKING, BIKING

Alongside the artworks, there are eight marked walking trails through the forest,

from the relatively short routes around **Ridding Wood** (1 mile/one hour; marked in blue) and **Machell's Coppice** (1.5 miles/one hour; marked in purple) through to the tough hike to the forest's highest point at **Carron Crag** (3 miles/two hours; marked in red) and the long-distance **Silurian Way** (9 miles/five hours; marked in green).

There are also five different way-marked bike routes – some are easy family rides, while others, including the new 16km **North Face Trail**, are designed for experienced mountain bikers.

Maps of all the trails are sold at the visitor centre, while hire bikes, route guides and trail maps are available from **Grizedale Mountain Bike Hire** (01229-860369; www.grizedalemountainbikes.co.uk; per day adult £26-50, child £16; 9am-5.30pm Mar-Oct, last hire 2pm in winter, 3pm rest of year).

Go Ape   OUTDOORS

(0870 458 9189; http://goape.co.uk/sites/grizedale; adult/child £30/20; 9-5pm Easter-Oct, closed Tue during term time) This treetop assault course is one of two in the Lake District (the other is in Whinlatter Forest, near Keswick). It features a dizzying network of rope ladders, bridges, platforms and ziplines that takes about two hours. There's a minimum age limit of 10 years, and you'll need to be more than 4ft 7in (1.4m) in height. Needless to say, you'll also need to have a head for heights – regardless of whether you're a gorilla (adult) or baboon (child).

Sleeping

Grizedale Lodge   GUESTHOUSE **££**

(015394-36532; www.grizedale-lodge.com; d £95-100; P) Despite the rather grand tag of 'Hotel in the Forest', this is in fact just a seriously nice B&B, in a lovely private spot in the middle of the forest. Rooms are done out with tester beds, puffy pillows and frilly fabrics, and for breakfast there's whisky-laced porridge and a full-on fry-up. You might even spot a deer grazing on the lawn.

Bowkerstead Farm   CAMPGROUND **£**

(01229-860208; www.grizedale-camping.co.uk; Satterthwaite; adult/child £6/2.50, pods £25, yurt £50) Just outside Satterthwaite, about a mile south of the Grizedale Visitor Centre, this is a campsite from the old school, with several spacious camping fields on a wooded farm, but unashamedly frugal facilities (the his-and-hers shower block is very basic). The site can get boggy in heavy rain, but there's

TARN HOWS

Two miles off the B5285 from Hawkshead, a twisting country lane wends its way to the famous lake of Tarn Hows. Nestled in a natural bowl surrounded by sun-dappled woodland, it's one of the Lake District's best-known (and most popular) beauty spots – but in fact the lake isn't natural at all. It was created in 1862 by wealthy landowner and MP James Marshall, who owned the surrounding land as part of his family estate at Monk Coniston Hall.

In an effort to attract visitors to the area, he combined the original three small tarns into one, designing a new shoreline with plantations of pine, larch and spruce alongside the native oak and birch trees. The strategy worked: within 50 years the tarn was a regular stop on the route for tourist charabancs from Ambleside and Windermere, and it's still one of the national park's most popular picnic spots.

The tarn and over 4000 acres of surrounding land was bought by Beatrix Potter in 1930, and subsequently bequeathed to the National Trust. Since 1965 it has been a SSSI (Site of Special Scientific Interest), and supports lots of rare flora and fauna, including water lobelia, water lilies and bog-bean, as well as juniper bushes and unusual lichens. Red squirrels can sometimes be spotted racing through the treetops, too, so bring some good binoculars. Less palatably, the tarn is also home to a small population of medicinal leeches, which were once fairly common in British lakes, but are now surprisingly scarce.

There's an easy circular stroll around the lake, with plenty of scenic viewpoints en route where you can stop and admire the view. It takes about an hour, but can be very busy in summer: if the crowds are a problem, there are several side paths around Tarn Heights to explore, or you could tackle the exciting hike to the top of nearby Holme Fell (317m/1040 ft).

Parking is free for National Trust members, but finding a space can be difficult on busy summer weekends. The newly built visitor centre near the National Trust car park explores the history of the lake and some of the people involved in its development.

The seasonal X31 bus stops on Hawkshead Hill, about a mile from the lake. If you prefer, you could walk up to the tarn from Coniston along the woodland paths through the Monk Coniston estate at the northern end of Coniston Water. It's a 5- to 6-mile round trip, taking around three hours.

a yurt and a few camping pods for extra shelter.

Pepper House B&B **££**
(☏01229-860206; www.pepper-house.co.uk; Satterthwaite; s £42, d £74; P) Three no-nonsense B&B rooms in a cruck-framed farmhouse near Satterthwaite. It's a good spot for animal lovers: assorted cats and dogs roam the house, and outside there's a small flock of Herdwicks and Swaledales, and a horse named Oliver.

❶ Getting There & Away

The main Grizedale car park, where you'll find the visitor centre and bike-hire centre, is about 3 miles south of Hawkshead. Several other small car parks are dotted around the edge of the forest.

The only bus that serves the forest is the X30 (four daily Easter to November), which makes a loop via Hawkshead, Grizedale, Lakeside, Newby Bridge and Haverthwaite as part of the Cross-Lakes Experience route.

Hill Top & Near Sawrey

If there's anywhere in the Lakes where you can still discern the spirit of the real Beatrix Potter beneath all the kitschy clutter, it's **Hill Top** (NT; www.nationaltrust.co.uk/hilltop; Near Sawrey; adult/child £7/3.50; ⊙house 10am-4.30pm or 5pm Apr-Oct, 10.30am-3.30pm Feb & Mar, closed Fri year-round; shop & garden open daily except Jan) Beatrix purchased this picture-perfect farmhouse in the shady hamlet of Near Sawrey in 1905 (largely on the proceeds of her first book, *The Tale of Peter Rabbit*), and went on to write a string of bestsellers at the house, although after 1913 she mostly lived at nearby Castle Farm and used Hill Top mainly as a base from which to administer her rapidly expanding property portfolio.

The house has hardly changed since Potter's death in 1943, and still contains much of her original pottery, china and furniture (as stipulated in her will). Dedicated

THE ART OF BUSHCRAFT

If your camp skills only stretch as far as heating a can of beans over a propane stove, then it might be a good idea to book yourself in for a bushcraft course with **Woodsmoke** (☑01900-821733; www.woodsmoke.uk.com). Courses are run on a private estate near Esthwaite Water, and cover everything from the basics of fire-lighting, foraging and shelter construction through to advanced skills such as tracking and bow-making.

Courses are held throughout the year; the three-day introductory Trailbreaker Course costs £225 per person.

Potterites will spot countless decorative details that Beatrix wove into her tales – particularly in the kitchen, garden and vegetable patch.

As one of Lakeland's key visitor attractions, Hill Top can be a serious scrum in summer, especially since the success of the 2006 biopic *Miss Potter*. Entry is by timed ticket to avoid overcrowding, but the queues can still be horrendously long (tickets are often sold out by 2pm, and don't even think about trying to visit on a Bank Holiday). It's particularly popular with Japanese visitors, so many of the information signs are bilingual.

From Near Sawrey, the B5285 runs southwest for about a mile along the west side of Esthwaite Water, passing through Far Sawrey before dropping downhill to Ferry House and the Windermere ferry.

🛏 Sleeping & Eating

Tower Bank Arms　　　　　PUB **££**
(☑015394-36334; www.towerbankarms.co.uk; Near Sawrey; mains £8-14, s/d £50/80) Eagle-eyed Potter fans might recognise this village pub, as it famously featured in *The Tale of Jemima Puddleduck*. Covered in climbing roses and with a neat little clock above the porch, it makes a fine spot for lunch after a visit to Hill Top. There's a sweet little beer garden out back overlooking farmland and fields, plus a handful of teeny bedrooms upstairs, all christened after Cumbrian numbers. Food is rich and filling (beef and ale stew, mushroom stroganoff) and there's a choice of Hawkshead and Barngates ales at the bar.

Graythwaite Hall　　　HOLIDAY COTTAGES **££**
(☑015395-31351; www.graythwaiteholidays.co.uk; cottages from £490 per week) Holiday digs on the sprawling 6000-acre estate of Graythwaite Hall, ranging from cute estate worker's cottages for two to a beautiful lakeside house sleeping 10. All the houses are different, but have mod-cons including kitchens, dishwashers and Sky TV. The estate has its own swimming pool and fitness hall, and ample grounds to explore.

Sawrey House　　　　　　HOTEL **££**
(☑015394-36387; www.sawreyhouse.com; Near Sawrey; s £52-62, d £120-164; ℗) This splendid Victorian mansion is literally steps from Hill Top. The building's a real beauty, all tall chimneys and elegant gables, and is leased by the owners from the National Trust. The feel throughout is old-fashioned – ruffles, ruches and floral fabrics in the bedrooms, country magazines and sofas in the lounge – but the countryside views from the rear rooms are amazing. Dinner and B&B packages are good value.

Buckle Yeat　　　　　　COTTAGE **££**
(☑015394-3644; www.buckle-yeat.co.uk; Near Sawrey; d £80-90; ℗) You can actually sleep inside a Beatrix Potter tale at this gorgeous 17th-century cottage, which featured in *The Tale of Tom Kitten*. The six rooms are snug in a country farmhouse way, if a little overpriced.

Sawrey Hotel　　　　　　　PUB **££**
(☑01539-443425; www.sawrey-hotel.co.uk; Far Sawrey; d £70, mains £12-16; ℗) Just about the only place for a pint and a pie between Ferry House and Near Sawrey is the Sawrey Hotel, whose black-and-white bulk sits just behind the B5285 road. The rooms are drab, so it's best visited for a bit of pub nosh and a pint in the Claife Crier bar (apparently built using wood from local shipwrecks).

Garth Country House　　　SELF-CATERING **££**
(☑015394-36346; www.thegarthcountryhouse.co.uk; Near Sawrey; cottages £300-625 per week) Three self-catering properties surrounded by ornamental shrubs and ordered lawns. The best is the original Aspland Place villa, which boasts original Victorian tiles, fireplaces and bay windows; the smaller houses at Garth Court and Gardener's Cottage are both charming.

ℹ Getting There & Away

Near Sawrey is 2 miles south of Hawkshead. The Cross-Lakes Experience minibus (p224) travels

CLAIFE HEIGHTS

South of Wray Castle stretch the dense woodlands of Claife Heights, which during the 19th century was one of the most popular areas for Victorian visitors, largely thanks to guidebook author Thomas West, who eulogised the area in his 1778 *Guide to the Lakes*.

Several 'viewing stations' were established around Claife Heights to enable well-heeled visitors to admire the views without muddying up their bustles and britches. The only surviving example is at **Claife Station**, which is accessible along a (sometimes steep and slippery) public footpath between Ferry House and Far Sawrey, starting near the small National Trust car park at Ash Landing.

In its heyday in the 1830s and '40s, this viewing station would have been luxuriously appointed with fine furniture, fashionable fabrics and attendants serving afternoon tea; the windows of the drawing room would have been tinted in different colours to simulate the effect of changing light on the landscape (light blue for winter, green for spring, yellow for summer and dark blue for moonlight).

Sadly, the building has fallen into disrepair and is currently fenced off to the public, but you can still explore the lovely lakeshore walk from Ferry House through the Claife Heights woodland to the second car park at Red Nab.

For a whole-day circuit, you could circle round via the summit of **Latterbarrow** (245m/803ft), which has wonderful views across Windermere, Grizedale Forest and the Coniston Fells. If you include Latterbarrow, it's a round-trip of around 7 to 8 miles, shorter if you just do the short circuit along the lakeshore.

through the village on its way from Ferry House to Hawkshead.

Graythwaite Hall Gardens

These lavishly landscaped **gardens** (⏰10am-6pm Apr-Aug; adult/under 14yr £3/free) were one of the first commissions of Thomas Mawson, Lakeland's answer to Lancelot 'Capability' Brown. Created in 1896, the gardens spread across a wooded valley of around 12 acres, and incorporate many exotic species brought back by plant hunters from the Far East, especially rhododendrons and azaleas. There are also some fine areas of lawn, formal terraces and ornamental planting, as well as a fragrant rose garden, a 'Dutch' garden and an endearing little dogs' cemetery.

The gardens are clearly signed off the minor road along the west side of Windermere, about 2½ miles south of Ferry House.

Wray Castle

Overlooking the northwest side of Windermere are the splendid turrets, gateways and battlements of Wray Castle, an imposing mansion built in typically ostentatious Victorian style during the heyday of the Gothic Revival in 1840. It was built for a retired Liverpudlian surgeon, Dr Dawson, partly by plundering funds from his wife's gin fortune, but sadly it proved an unhappy project – his wife apparently loathed the house so much she utterly refused to live there and the house almost immediately fell into disuse. Later the house served as a lavish holiday home for the young Beatrix Potter and her family, who rented the property during their first sojourn to the Lakes in 1882. Eventually Wray Castle and its 25-hectare estate were gifted to the National Trust in 1929, largely thanks to the persuasive powers of Canon Hardwicke Rawnsley, one of the trust's founder members.

The estate is still owned by the National Trust. There have been plans to re-open the house for many years, and the Trust is currently in negotiations to turn it into an upmarket hotel. Regardless of the house's future, the sweeping grounds remain open to the public year round. The estate is particularly notable for its trees, including fine examples of sequoia, lime, redwood and beech, as well as a spreading mulberry that was allegedly planted by Wordsworth.

Western Lake District

Best Places to Eat

» Wasdale Head Inn (p109)
» Pennington Hotel (p101)
» Shepherd's Arms Hotel (p111)
» Low Wood Hall (p109)
» Strands Inn (p109)

Best Places to Stay

» Wasdale Head Inn (p109)
» Stanley House (p103)
» Wasdale Head Campsite (p109)
» Wastwater YHA (p107)
» Coachman's Quarters (p101)

Why Go?

In many ways this is the quintessential Lakeland landscape. Studded with silvery lakes, mist-shrouded fells, country pubs and hill farms, this side of the national park feels much rawer and wilder than its more pastoral neighbour to the east. It's a place saturated with superlatives: home to England's smallest church (St Olaf's in Wasdale), highest mountain (Scafell Pike), deepest lake (Wastwater) and steepest roads (Hardknott and Wrynose), not to mention some of its wildest scenery.

As always, the best way to appreciate the landscape is to get out and explore. A string of high fells stand like sentinels across the western reaches of Ennerdale and Wasdale, including Great Gable, Scafell and Scafell Pike, providing irresistible targets for peak-baggers. If you prefer to hike alone, however, you might prefer to head for the little-visited Duddon Valley, where you can walk for hours with only the odd Herdwick sheep for company.

When to Go

Wet weather and low cloud can make it hard to appreciate the views in this part of the Lake District, so most people visit in summer – but it's worth avoiding half-terms and school holidays if you'd prefer to climb Scafell Pike in peace. Early autumn can be a good time to visit, with relatively few crowds and fairly settled weather.

The Santon Bridge Inn holds its famous World's Greatest Liar Competition in November, and Muncaster Castle offers special twilight walks and Victorian-themed Christmas tours in late November and early December.

RAVENGLASS & AROUND

Flung out on the western border of the national park, the little harbour of Ravenglass is quiet these days, but a couple of millennia ago it was home to the thriving naval base of Glannaventa, one of the most important Roman ports in northwest England.

Few traces of the Roman occupation now remain, save for the ruins of a Roman bathhouse just behind the harbour. Most of present-day Ravenglass dates back to the 19th century, when the harbour was redeveloped as a link between northern England's thriving industrial ports and the iron-rich Eskdale mines to the east, accessed via the miniature trains of the Ravenglass and Eskdale Railway.

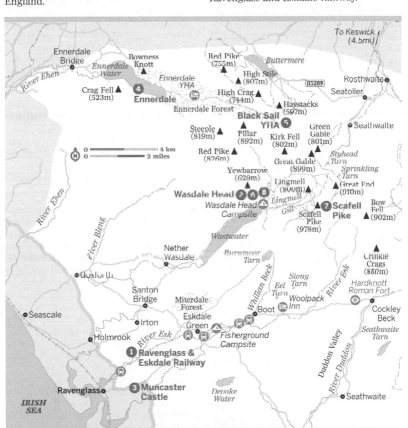

Western Lake District Highlights

❶ Ride the miniature choo-choos of the **Ravenglass and Eskdale Railway** (p100)

❷ Drink in the wraparound views from **Wasdale Head** (p107)

❸ Go ghost-spotting at one of England's most haunted castles, **Muncaster** (p100)

❹ Leave the crowds behind in the unspoilt valley of **Ennerdale** (p110)

❺ Sleep out in the wilds at the **Black Sail YHA** (p111)

❻ Discover hiking history and home-brewed beers at the **Wasdale Head Inn** (p109)

❼ Stand on top of the roof of England, **Scafell Pike** (p108)

❽ Duck under the ancient roof-beams of England's most minuscule church, **St Olaf's** (p107)

There's not much to keep you in Ravenglass long, although the flat, sandy beach and stout seafront cottages lend the village a certain stark charm. Take a stroll at sunset to see it at its best.

◉ Sights

Ravenglass & Eskdale Railway   RAILWAY
(☎01229-717171; www.ravenglass-railway.co.uk) Steam enthusiasts will be in seventh heaven aboard the miniature carriages of the Ravenglass and Eskdale Railway, affectionately known as La'al Ratty (a Cumbrian term roughly translating as 'little passage'). The teeny steam trains chug for 7 miles along a gloriously scenic track into the vale of Eskdale and the foothills of the central fells, terminating at Dalegarth Station, near Boot.

The narrow-gauge railway was originally built in 1876 to ferry iron ore from the nearby Eskdale mines to the coast, but huge extraction costs, difficult working conditions and fluctuating metal prices meant that the railway never managed to turn a profit. After teetering close to collapse several times throughout its history, it's now owned and operated by the Ravenglass and Eskdale Railway Preservation Society, and under its careful stewardship it has become one of Cumbria's top tourist attractions: over 120,000 passengers take a trip on the railway every year.

The railway begins at Ravenglass and makes several request stops in Eskdale at Muncaster Mill, Irton Rd (for Eskdale Green), Fisherground and Beckfoot en route to Dalegarth.

There are between seven and 14 trains every day during the main season (April/October); trips run at other times of year to coincide with school holidays (see the website for a full timetable).

Single fares are £7/3.50 per adult/child aged five to 15 years. Day tickets allow unlimited travel on the railway for £12/6. Dogs cost £1.50; bikes can be carried on the trains for £3.50, but you'll need to pre-book by phone.

While you wait for your train, there's a small museum exploring the railway's history across the car park from the La'al Ratty platform, next to the Ratty Arms pub.

FREE Roman Bathhouse   RUIN
No self-respecting Roman settlement would be complete without its bathtub, and Glannaventa was no exception. Ravenglass' Roman Bathhouse is one of the tallest Roman structures still standing in England, and although only a few of the original walls remain, it's still possible to make out the essential footprint. Sadly, the underfloor heating system (known as the 'hypocaust') hasn't survived, but you can still see the wall niches which would have housed votive statues or, possibly, fragrant oil dispensers.

Across the road from the bathhouse, you can still see the flattened plateau and protective ditchworks of the Glannaventa fort in a nearby field, although all the stone has long since been carted away for other uses, and today the foundations are completely covered by grass.

The easiest way to the bathhouse is to follow the road past the Ravenglass Camping and Caravanning Campsite, which is clearly signposted on the main road into town. The bathhouse is 500m past the campsite on the left-hand side. Alternatively, a small tunnel leads under the railway tracks and emerges at the southern end of the beach.

Muncaster Castle   CASTLE
(www.muncaster.co.uk; adult/5-15yr incl owl centre, gardens & castle £12/8; ☉gardens 10.30am-6pm or dusk, castle noon-4.30pm Sun-Fri Feb-Nov) A mile east of Ravenglass is Muncaster Castle, the ancestral seat of the Pennington family, built around a 14th-century pele tower designed to resist raids from across the Scottish border. The house is a sumptuous affair, with a wealth of stately rooms including a great hall, a dining room, an extraordinary octagonal library and a collection of historic oils by artists including Joshua Reynolds and Thomas Gainsborough.

The house is also famous for its spooks, including a ubiquitous White Lady, the Muncaster Boggle (said to be the spirit of a girl murdered outside the castle gate in the 1800s) and the malevolent jester Tom Skelton (aka Tom Fool, hence the word 'tomfoolery'), who was purportedly chums with William Shakespeare and is often cited as the last official jester in England. Budding ghost-hunters can arrange their own overnight **ghost sit** (per group Mon-Thu £460, Fri & Sun £499, Sat £560) in the castle's Tapestry Room, supposedly the most haunted in the castle.

In its heyday the estate encompassed a whopping 23,000 acres, although these days the grounds have dwindled to a more

RICHARD WOODALL'S BUTCHERS SHOP

One of Cumbria's top butchers is in the little village of Waberthwaite. **Woodall's of Waberthwaite** (☑01229-717237; www.richardwoodall.com; Waberthwaite) supplies bangers and bacons to none other than HM The Queen, so you can't quibble with the provenance – and it's been in business for eight generations, so they should know how to stuff a sausage by now. The dry-cured bacons and smoked hams are especially renowned.

modest 1800 acres. Alongside the formal gardens, the estate also provides a home for the **Muncaster Owl Centre**, which has one of the world's largest captive owl populations. Pygmy owls, barn owls, eagle owls, and a range of other winged beasties, including herons, waders and birds of prey, all spread their wings at the centre; there's a daily talk and aerial display at 2.30pm, and you can watch the heron feeding at 3.30pm.

In winter the castle itself is closed except for special events, such as the regular 'Victorian Christmas' guided tours. The owl centre and gardens remain open year-round

🛏 Sleeping & Eating

Pennington Hotel   HOTEL **££**
(☑01229-717222; www.muncaster.co.uk/pennington-hotel; Ravenglass; r £90-120; P🛜) In Ravenglass near the seafront, this former coaching house partly dates from the 16th century, but you'd never guess from the inside: the Pennington family (owners of Muncaster Castle) have given it a thoughtful overhaul, with light, neutral rooms complete with flat-screen TVs and wi-fi. The restaurant's equally good, with a choice of budgets in the contemporary bar or the more formal restaurant.

Coachman's Quarters   B&B **££**
(☑01229-717614; www.muncaster.co.uk/muncaster039s-coachman039s-quarters; d £80; P) If you'd prefer to stay on the estate itself, this former coachhouse has been converted into pleasant B&B digs, tastefully done in lemons and creams, with patches of exposed brick and wooden rafters for period character. Entry to the gardens and owl centre is included,

and breakfast's served at the Creeping Kate Kitchen.

Ratty Arms   PUB **£**
(☑01229-717676; Ravenglass) This no-nonsense pub is plonked beside the station platform in Ravenglass, and has plenty of railway atmosphere: one room bears more than a passing resemblance to a train carriage, and lots of photos and memorabilia relating to La'al Ratty are dotted round the place. The food's generous but not great, so it's probably best for a quick pint while you wait for your train.

❶ Getting There & Away

Bus G/X6 from Whitehaven stops at Ravenglass and terminates at Muncaster (70 minutes, four or five daily).

Ravenglass is also on the Cumbrian Coast train line, and as such is included in the Cumbrian Coast Day Ranger ticket (see p226). Sample single fares:

DESTINATION	FARE (£)	DURATION (HOURS)
Carlisle	11.40	1¾
Whitehaven	4.50	½
Ulverston	7.80	1¼
Grange-over-Sands	11.30	1½
Arnside	12.20	1¾

ESKDALE

Inland from Ravenglass, the chugging engines of La'al Ratty chunter along the base of the Eskdale Valley before reaching journey's end at Dalegarth Station, a stone's throw from the scattered houses and whitewashed inns of Boot.

Further east along the valley, the road snakes up into the hilltops before reaching the high mountain passes of Hardknott and Wrynose into Little Langdale.

Eskdale Green

Whether you're arriving by road or rail, the first village you'll reach from the west is Eskdale Green, a tiny hamlet that marks the junction of the minor roads from Wasdale, Santon Bridge and the coast.

There's been some kind of settlement here since at least Roman times, and quite possibly long before, and the village became an important gateway into the Eskdale Valley following the arrival of the La'al Ratty railway, which stops on the edge of the village at the station at Irton Rd. There's another request stop near the Fisherground campsite.

The village is at its liveliest in late summer for the **Eskdale Fete**, a family-friendly fete held in the grounds of the Outward Bound centre on the Sunday of the August Bank Holiday. Even more important to the local community is the annual **Eskdale Show**, held on the last Saturday in September in a field near the King George IV pub. This traditional country gathering is the largest Herdwick sheep show in the whole of Cumbria, and attracts breeders from all over northern England; there are also displays of hound trailing, fell running and local craftwork.

You can find general supplies at the **Eskdale Green Village Store** (☑019467-23229).

Sights & Activities

FREE Giggle Alley   WOOD, GARDENS
In the 1890s the village formed part of the Gatehouse estate, founded as a country retreat by the Liverpudlian coal merchant James Rea. The house itself has been an Outward Bound centre since the 1950s, but the bamboo plantations, maple trees, azaleas and ornamental pools of its lovely Japanese garden, designed by renowned Victorian landscaper Thomas Mawson, are slowly being restored to their former glory by the Forestry Commission and local volunteers after decades of neglect.

The gardens can be reached via a public footpath through Giggle Alley Wood, near the car park beside the little chapel of St Bega, which has small displays on the Eskdale Valley.

Outward Bound   ACTIVITY CENTRE
(☑0870 513 4227; www.outwardbound-uk.org) A long-standing British favourite, especially among school and youth groups. Rafting, canoeing, abseiling – you name it, they do it. On-site accommodation is available at both of the activity centres in Eskdale and Ullswater.

🛏 Sleeping & Eating

Fisherground Farm   CAMPGROUND £
(☑019467-23349; www.fishergroundcampsite.co.uk; Eskdale Green; adult/3-15yr/car/dogs £6/3/2.50/1.50; ☺Mar-Oct) This convivial family-

orientated campsite is popular with hikers and overnighters on La'al Ratty, with lots of space spread out over a couple of farm fields, and separate his-and-hers bathroom blocks with coin-op showers and a nearby laundry. There's even a little adventure playground for the kids.

King George IV   PUB £
(www.kinggeorge-eskdale.co.uk; Eskdale Green; r £60-72; ℗) The best of the local pubs, clad in beams, flagstones and climbing ivy, and surrounded by rolling countryside. Expect solid pub standards and a decent ale selection.

Dalegarth & Boot

Two miles east of Eskdale Green brings you to the last stop on the La'al Ratty line at **Dalegarth** (☑019467-23226; ☺when trains are running). The trains turn round here on an iron turntable before making the return journey to Ravenglass; while you wait, you can have a cup of tea in the station cafe, or perhaps hire a bike from the visitor centre (half-/full day £8/14).

Half a mile further east brings you to the shoebox-sized village of Boot, the last sign of human habitation before the tortuous slog up to Hardknott. The village largely dates from the Eskdale iron-mining boom in the 19th century, and the surrounding hilltops are pockmarked with abandoned quarries, shafts and mine works.

Boot hosts its own annual **beer festival** (www.bootbeer.co.uk) in mid-June.

◉ Sights

Stanley Ghyll Force   WATERFALL
Opposite Dalegarth station, a short trail leads to the 60ft waterfall of Stanley Ghyll Force, one of the Lake District's most photogenic waterfalls, cut into a narrow ravine flanked by lush ferns and overhanging trees. Nearby is the little chapel of **St Catherine's**, parts of which date from the 12th century.

Eskdale Mill   HISTORIC SITE
(☑019467-23335; admission £1.50; ☺11am-5.30pm Apr-Sep, sometimes closed on Mon or Sat) Just behind Boot village, across the 17th-century humpback bridge over Whillans Beck, is one of England's oldest working mills, built in 1578. The twin waterwheels were once employed to grind flour and grain, and were still in use into the 1920s; they were later used to generate electricity

until the valley was hooked up to the national grid in the mid-1950s. Admission includes a guided tour around the mill and its wooden machinery in the company of Dave King, the genial miller who's been in charge of the site for the last 17 years. Phone ahead to make sure the mill's open.

Fold End Gallery ART GALLERY

(019467-23335) Small gallery between Dalegarth and Boot, displaying local sculptures, ceramics, paintings and hand-blown glass

🛏 Sleeping & Eating

Stanley House GUESTHOUSE ££

(019467-23327; www.stanleyghyll-eskdale.co.uk; Eskdale; s £64, d £100-120, f £140-160; P 🛜)
Recently taken over by new owners Harry and Paddington Berger, this detached house halfway down the valley near Beckfoot Station is by far the nicest place to kip in Eskdale. The 12 thoroughly refurbed rooms err towards the classic rather than the contemporary, but they're very comfy and have surprising spoils such as HD TVs and a complementary DVD library. Heating and hot water comes almost entirely from sustainably sourced log fuels, produced on site.

Woolpack Inn PUB £

(019467-23230; www.thewoolpackinn.co.uk; Boot; r £85-145, mains £12.50-19.50; P) This venerable Boot pub is under new management, and behind its whitewashed exterior has received a total refit, including a biomass boiler, wood-fired pizza oven and stripped-out interior that's more urban gastropub than rural inn. It might have gone too far for some tastes, as precious little of the rustic interior remains – although the rooms are lighter, brighter and much more contemporary than of old. Food can be very erratic – until it sorts out its standards, you're better off just having a pint of Peroni in the garden.

Boot Inn PUB ££

(0845 130 6224; www.bootinn.co.uk; Boot; s/d £45/90, mains £7.95-9.95; P) Traditionalists will much prefer this old country boozer, which sticks to a tried-and-tested formula: solid grub, weekly quiz nights, pool and darts (plus a Nintendo Wii) and plenty of ale choices at the bar. The beer garden is particularly nice, with an outside play area and plenty of sun-trap tables to soak up the rays. Rooms are standard B&B, heavy on the frills.

Brook House Inn PUB £

(019467-23288; www.brookhouseinn.co.uk; Boot; s/d £55/79, mains £9.95-14.95; P) This old Eskdale inn is the choice for beer drinkers: there are six or seven ales on tap, including the ever-present Hawkshead bitter and a range of guest brews from local producers. Food and rooms are ordinary, but the position's lovely, surrounded by green fields and drystone walls.

Eskdale YHA HOSTEL £

(0870 770 5824; eskdale@yha.org.uk; Boot; dm from £16.40; ⏰Easter-Oct) This purpose-built hostel is in a wonderfully out-of-the-way position, a bit further up the Eskdale road from the Woolpack Inn. Clad in stone and commanding views across the valley, it's a favourite with walkers and travellers on La'al Ratty, so tends to get busy. The dorms and communal lounge are small, but the cafe dishes up a great-value daily meal for £9.95/11.95 for 2/3 courses. The hostel sits in ample grounds; it's currently trying to raise £4000 to develop 15 acres into a wildlife habitat.

Hollins Farm CAMPGROUND £

(019467-23253; www.hollinsfarmcampsite.co.uk; Boot; adult £7.66-9.19, child £2.66-2.86, camping pod £40.85; P) Another quiet farm site aimed squarely at family campers, with a strict no-music, no-fires and no-rowdiness policy. The camping field is spacious and sheltered by tall pines, with a little village of 10 eco-pods, as well as a really nice camping barn for groups (£112.34 per night).

Hardknott & Wrynose Passes

There are two ways to get to the Cumbrian Coast from the central fells. You could, like most people, choose the easy way and follow the circuitous route along the A593 and A595. Alternatively, you could take the heart-in-the-mouth, seat-of-the-pants option and brave the twin passes of Wrynose and Hardknott, two of England's highest road passes, which top out at 393m above sea-level and tackle gradients that occasionally reach a forbidding 1 in 3.

Originally a packhorse route developed by the Romans, and later used by generations of traders, shepherds and drovers, it's without doubt one of the Lake District's most infamous stretches of highway. Every year there's yet another tale of an

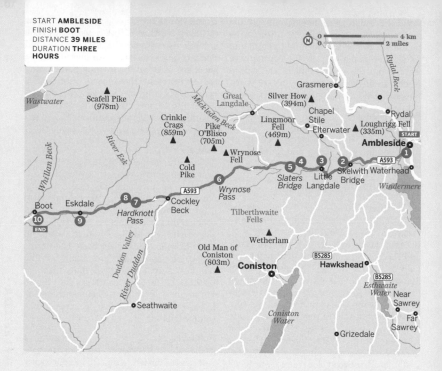

Driving Tour
Wrynose & Hardknott Passes

❯ Is this the nation's most spectacular drive? Many seasoned drivers seem to think so, and you certainly won't be the only one doing it on a summer weekend. Traversing both of the steepest passes in England and reaching 30% gradients in some places, it's a real roller-coaster. You can do the drive in either direction, but east–west gives you the best views. Be prepared for other drivers coming the opposite way.

Start out in ❶ **Ambleside** and follow the A593 to ❷ **Skelwith Bridge**, stopping for breakfast at Chesters Café by the River and a stroll to Skelwith Force. Just after Skelwith Bridge, take the sharp right-hand turn onto the steep road into ❸ **Little Langdale**.

It's here that things get steep. The road crawls up towards Little Langdale Tarn, offering craggy views of Wetherlam and the Tilberthwaite Fells as it passes the ❹ **Three Shires Inn**. You can pause here and take a walk to the quaint packhorse crossing at ❺ **Slaters Bridge**, then continue the climb up to ❻ **Wrynose Pass**. At the top of the

pass, the views across the fells become increasingly wild and empty, and you'll really start to feel like you've left civilisation a long way behind. Near the summit is the Three Shire Stone, which marks the spot at which the counties of Cumberland, Westmorland and Lancashire historically met.

From Wrynose, the road plunges into the valley of Cockley Beck. You'll pass a left-hand fork leading towards Duddon Valley; ignore this and follow the right-hand fork, tracing a series of long hairpins up to ❼ **Hardknott Pass** at 393m (1289ft). The vistas here are magnificent: you'll be able to see all the way to the coast on a clear day.

From the pass, the road drops into another set of very sharp, steep hairpins, passing the Roman ruins of ❽ **Hardknott Fort**, before dropping down into the green sweep of ❾ **Eskdale**. Have a pint at one of the pubs around ❿ **Boot** – you've earned it.

unsuspecting minibus or coach getting stranded on one of its hairpin bends, but it's perfectly driveable as long as you take things slowly and carefully.

There are two important things to note if you're taking it on. Firstly, be prepared for the fact that it's single carriageway all the way from Little Langdale to Eskdale, and there are no road markings anywhere on the route. If you meet another car coming in the opposite direction, one of you will have no choice but to reverse to the last passing place – not always an easy prospect if it happens to be one of the steep sections with a hair-raising drop to one side.

Secondly, make sure your tyres and brakes are in good working order before you set out, and top up the water in your radiator – you'll do most of it in first or second gear, so your engine will get hot. Try to use gear braking as much as possible to avoid unnecessary wear to your brake pads.

Apart from the wonderfully wild views, the other main reason to tackle the road is the chance to visit the remote **Hardknott Roman Fort**, perched in a commanding spot just beneath the high point of Hardknott Pass.

Known to the Romans as Mediobogdum, the fort was built between AD 120 and AD 138 to guard the important supply route between the harbour at Ravenglass and the inland forts at Galava (present-day Ambleside) and along Hadrian's Wall.

Though the building itself has been almost entirely plundered for building materials, you can still make out its essential foundations, including the parade ground, watchtowers, baths and commandant's house. You can't help feeling a little sympathy for the legionaries stationed here, most of whom were conscripts from the Dalmatian Coast in Croatia; with its freezing snows and bone chilling winds, it must have been a formidably tough posting for soldiers raised on Mediterranean climes.

WORTH A TRIP

DUDDON VALLEY

Halfway along the road between Wrynose and Hardknott, a branch road leads into the delightful Duddon Valley. With no lakes and no big-name hills to explore, it's overlooked by most visitors and remains one of the least-visited of the Lake District's valleys. As such, it's an excellent place to escape the crowds, and if you're really lucky you might even spot a peregrine falcon soaring above the hilltops.

Stretching from the tip of Cockley Beck down to the little village of Ulpha, near the edge of the Duddon Sands, this remote valley was a favourite of Wordsworth's – he even wrote 34 sonnets devoted to it. It hardly seems to have changed since he was here: sheep still outnumber people by a sizeable margin, and the rolling fells and tawny slopes are home to just a few farmhouses and tumbledown barns.

The hills here may be relatively small in Lakeland terms, but they're almost guaranteed to be free of the crowds that plague the better-known summits. Two of the best options are **Wallowbarrow Crag** and the conical hump of **Harter Fell** (653m/2142ft), which Wainwright thought was one of the few fells that could really be described as beautiful.

Accommodation is thin on the ground, but there's a gloriously remote campsite at **Turner Hall Farm** (☎01229-716420; turnerhall@ktdinternet.com; sites from £12) near Seathwaite, and basic bunk digs at the **High Wallabarrow Farm Camping Barn** (☎01229-715011; www.wallabarrow.co.uk; dm £10) near Ulpha, which also has a converted farm cottage for rent (£425 to £500 per week). For seasonal B&B, see the listings on the valley's website.

Pubs are even scarcer: the only option in the valley proper is the homely **Newfield Inn** (☎01229-716208; www.newfieldinn.co.uk; Seathwaite; no credit cards), with an impressive slate-floored bar and a no-nonsense line-up of ales, pork chops and shepherd's pies. If you like to drink your pint in peace, take our word for it – there's probably nowhere better in Lakeland.

For B&B listings, holiday cottages and other information, visit www.duddonvalley .co.uk.

WASDALE

If it's a wilderness hit you're after, few places in the Lakes can match up to the unruly emptiness of the Wasdale Valley. Closer to the wide-open vistas of the Scottish highlands than the gentle dales of the eastern Lakes, Wasdale (pronounced 'woz', rather than 'waz') still feels thrillingly remote: the only signs of human habitation are a historic hiker's inn, a web of drystone walls and a handful of slate-roofed farm cottages, all dwarfed by the backdrop of brooding peaks and the inky black expanse of Wastwater, England's deepest lake.

The views become increasingly dazzling as you venture into the valley from the western gateway at Nether Wasdale; the road tracks the west shore of the lake all the way to Wasdale Head, overlooked by a moody cluster of some of the national park's highest mountains, including the sister mountains of Scafell and Scafell Pike.

Shops are few and far between in the valley – the only place for supplies once you get beyond Nether Wasdale is the **Barn Door Shop** (☎019467-26384; Wasdale Head), which sells food, outdoor gear and hiking supplies, and also runs the useful community website www.wasdaleweb.com.

❶ Getting There & Away

There's no public transport except for the **Wasdale Taxibus** (☎019467-25308), which runs between Gosforth and Wasdale Head twice daily on Thursday, Saturday and Sunday. It's run by Gosforth Taxis; you need to ring to book a seat.

There's a public car park at the northeastern end of the valley next door to the Wasdale Head Inn.

Gosforth & Santon Bridge

Other than a smattering of pubs, shops and B&Bs, there's not too much to keep you in either of the villages at the western end of Wasdale – but it's worth finding the time to visit the 14ft **Gosforth cross** in the churchyard of St Mary's, one of the few 10th-century stone crosses to survive in mainland England. Its four carved faces are notable for their mix of pagan and Christian influences, intermingling elements of the Norse sagas with Biblical imagery – the lower parts of the cross are decorated with interlocking foliage, thought to represent *Yggdrasil,* the Norse tree of life, while the upper surfaces depict various warriors and figures (including one said to be either a depiction of Christ on the cross or the resurrection of the Viking god Baldur).

A rather less impressive cross, also dating from the 10th century, can be seen in the churchyard at **Irton** nearby.

🛏 Sleeping & Eating

Rainors Farm B&B **££**
(☎019467-25934; www.rainorsfarm.co.uk; Gosforth; s £45, d £65-70, yurts per week £525-595) Dinky little B&B in a whitewashed farmhouse cottage, offering two rooms prettied up with crimson spreads and country views. There's a choice of traditional or veggie breakfasts, and campers can bunk down in a back-garden yurt (one in a paddock, the other by the stream).

Gosforth Hall Hotel HOTEL **££**
(☎019467-25322; www.gosforthhallhotel.co.uk; Gosforth; mains £9.95-15.95; ℗) Off-kilter floors, spiralling staircases and even an original 'priest's hole' hint at the age of

---

FIBBING & FACE PULLING

Cumbrians are well known for their propensity for telling tall tales, but Will Ritson, a 19th-century landlord at the Wasdale Head Inn, took the tradition to a different level. Will was known throughout the region for his outlandish stories; one of his most famous tales concerned a Wasdale turnip that was so large that local residents burrowed into it for their Sunday lunch, and later used it as a shelter for their sheep. He also claimed to own a cross between a foxhound and a golden eagle that could leap over drystone walls.

In honour of Will's mendacious tradition, the Santon Bridge Inn holds the **World's Biggest Liar** competition (www.santonbridgeinn.com/liar) every November. Cumbrian dialect is allowed, but lawyers and politicians are barred from entering. Recent winner Paul Burrows took the title in 2010 with his outrageous claim that the mountains of Essex had been stolen centuries ago and moved to Cumbria, explaining why Essex is now flat as a proverbial pancake.

this Grade-II listed building, formerly a 17th-century manor. The old kitchen has been turned into a pub, serving generic food including rump steaks and a huge 'hunger annihilation' pie. Rooms (doubles £70 to £120) are tired but will do in a pinch.

Bridge Inn PUB ££
(www.santonbridgeinn.com; Santon Bridge; mains £8-15; 🛜) Near the junction of the road between Santon Bridge and Nether Wasdale, this black-and-white coach stop packs in the punters thanks to its annual fibbing competition (see boxed text), but it's also a reliable bet for lamb in Jennings bitter or battered haddock, served amid wood stanchions and country trinkets.

Wasdale Head

The road into Wasdale Head is one of the most memorable in the Lakes. You can almost feel the wildness closing in: great green-brown fells recede into the far distance, marking the course of the long-gone glacier which carved out the valley. It all feels fantastically wild and rather un-English: catch it on a stormy day, when the lake's cloaked in spidery mist and great black clouds are rolling across the fell-tops, and it feels like driving into a forgotten world.

◉ Sights

Wastwater LAKE
In his *Guide to the Lakes,* Wordsworth described Wastwater as 'long, narrow, stern and desolate', and it's a description that still seems apt. The lake itself is owned by the National Trust, and is the deepest body of water in the national park (around 258ft at its deepest point).

It's also one of the coldest and clearest; very little life can survive in its inhospitable waters, apart from the hardy Arctic char. On the lake's southern side, the huge scree slopes reach a height of up to 2000ft, created by thousands of years of natural erosion on the surrounding mountains.

St Olaf's CHURCH
This tiny chapel near Wasdale Head is reputed to be the smallest in England. The foundations of the church date back to at least the 16th century, but it's probably much older – the central roof beam is rumoured to have been fashioned from the

hull of a Viking longboat. Despite its age, the churchyard was officially unconsecrated until 1901, meaning that the dead had to be carried along the old coffin route over Eskdale Moor and Burnmoor Tarn to be buried at the church in Boot.

🏃 Activities

Walkers have an almost endless choice in Wasdale – classic routes to several of the Lake District's loftiest peaks start at Wasdale Head, including **Great Gable** (899m/2949ft), **Scoat Fell** (841m/2759ft) and **Lingmell** (800m/2624ft).

But it's undoubtedly **Scafell Pike** (978m/3209ft) that the vast majority of hikers want to tick off their list first. Though the hike to the top and the views from the summit actually aren't as grand as some of Wasdale's other mountains, there's an inevitable sense of achievement that comes from standing on top of England's highest point. The mountain is connected to its neighbour, **Scafell** (964m/3162ft), by the famous Mickledore Pass, but the old scramble up Lord's Rake is now considered unsafe due to unstable rockfall.

For proper peak-baggers, the **Mosedale Horseshoe** (10.2 miles) is one of the most popular long-distance routes from Wasdale, taking in Pillar, Scoat Fell, Steeple, Red Pike and Yewbarrow.

Carolclimb (📞019467-26424; www.carolclimb .co.uk; Wasdale) is a husband-and-wife team, Carol Emmons and Richard Sagar, that provides everything from tailored hikes to alpine skills training.

🛏 Sleeping & Eating

Wastwater YHA HOSTEL £
(📞0845 371 9350; wastwater@yha.org.uk; Wasdale Hall, Nether Wasdale; dm from £15.95; ⏰reception 8am-10am & 5-10.30pm, open year round by advance booking) This gloriously located hostel has a position that would be the envy of any country hotel: nestled on the shores of Wastwater, with top-drawer views across the lake towards Wasdale Head. Originally the manor of Wasdale Hall, built in 1829, the house still bears many of its original features, with wood panelling, gabled roof and cornicing, and although it's leased by the YHA, it's actually owned by the National Trust. Two of the dorms are large, with 10 beds – try to get one of the quads if you can – and the homely cafe is worth a look even if you're only passing through.

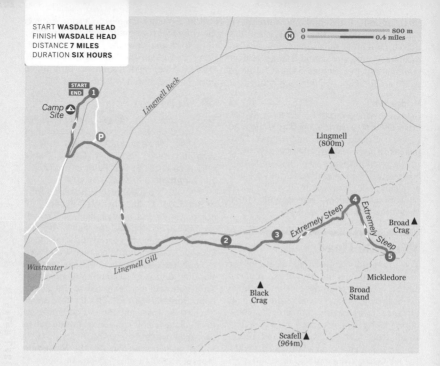

0 ——————— 800 m
0 ——————— 0.4 miles

START END ①

Camp Site

P

Lingmell Beck

Lingmell
(800m) ▲

④ Broad
Crag ▲

Extremely Steep

② ③ Extremely Steep ⑤

Wastwater

Lingmell Gill

Mickledore

Black
Crag ▲

Broad
Stand

Scafell ▲
(964m)

Hiking Tour
Scafell Pike

❯ Every year thousands of hikers set out to conquer **Scafell Pike**. Despite its height, it's achievable as long as you're fit, equipped and prepared for a slog. The exposed summit and altitude makes this walk dangerous and difficult to navigate during bad weather. Proper supplies, a compass and a map are essential whatever the weather. Stick to the path wherever possible, as trail erosion is becoming a big problem on Scafell Pike.

There are several routes to the top, but this classic ascent starts from the ① **Wasdale Head car park**. Head south over Lingmell Beck and follow the path up towards Lingmell Gill. Cross the stones over the beck and continue climbing steeply up the track along ② **Brown Tongue**, overlooked to the south by the stern cliffs of Black and Scafell Crags.

You'll soon reach a junction: the right fork leads to an alternative ascent of the peak via the scree-covered pass of Mickledore. Take the left fork instead, traversing the boulder-strewn expanse of ③ **Hollow Stones** onto a

long zigzagging trail up to ④ **Lingmell Col**, where the route ascends southeast over a shattered plain of rocks, scree and boulders all the way up to the highest point in England.

A large cairn marks the actual ⑤ **summit** (978m/3209ft). You almost certainly won't be alone: even on the worst days, someone seems to set out to conquer the mountain, and on sunny days it can be uncomfortably crowded. The views across the valley overlook the interlocking panorama of peaks to the north, including Great Gable, Kirk Fell, Green Gable and Pillar. Scafell looms to the southwest, across the narrow ridge of Mickledore; look out for rock climbers tackling the classic challenge of Broad Stand nearby.

Once you've basked in the views, retrace your steps from the summit plateau all the way back down to Wasdale Head. Pat yourself on the back – you've just conquered the nation's loftiest hiking challenge.

Wasdale Head Campsite
CAMPGROUND £

(☑019467-26220; www.ntlakescampsites.org.uk; sites for tent, adult & car £8-12, extra adult £5, child £2.50, dogs £1.50, camping pods £25-42.50; ⊙check-in 5-7pm weekdays, 8-10.30am & 5-6pm weekends, campsite open year round; ℗) This National Trust campsite is in a wonderfully wild spot, nestled beneath the Scafell range a mile from Wastwater. Facilities are similar to the other NT sites, but this is the only one that has electric hookups for caravans and campervans. The views are, needless to say, rather fine – but note the rather short check-in times.

Low Wood Hall
HOTEL ££

(☑019467-26111; www.lowwoodhall.co.uk; Nether Wasdale; s £60-85, tw £80-90, d £75-120; ℗) The valley's only real hotel offers two categories of room – the cheaper ones in the annexe are dowdy, but the superior rooms in the main building have a prim doll's-house appeal, with prissy fabrics and puffy sofas. The restaurant (mains £15 to £20) is about the closest thing to fine dining in Wasdale – expect traditional cordon bleu food served in rather starchy style. Ask for a table in the conservatory if you like to dine with a view.

Burnthwaite Farm
B&B ££

(☑019467-26242, www.burnthwaitefarm.co.uk; Wasdale Head; d with/without bathroom £68/58; ℗) Down-to-earth farmhouse style lodgings with the usual low ceilings, floral-print duvets, and cholesterol-heavy brekkie. Two rooms are en suite, others share facilities.

Strands Inn
B&B, PUB ££

(☑019467-26237; www.strandshotel.com; Nether Wasdale; s £56-65, d £82-90, ste £115-145, ℗) Popular pub in Nether Wasdale which brews its own beer (ask the barman for the story behind the curiously named 'Errmmm...' ale). The building dates from around 1800, and still feels vintage, especially in the beamed bar, and 14 pleasant B&B rooms are available upstairs (most with showers, a couple with baths).

Barn Door Campsite
CAMPGROUND £

(☑019467-26384; Wasdale Head; per person £2.50) Wasdale's other campsite is next door to the Barn Door Shop. It's back-to-basics – luxuries are limited to a cold tap and a toilet – but it's cheap and there's nearly always room. No reservations – just pay at the shop when you arrive.

Murt Camping Barn
HOSTEL £

(☑01946-758198; www.campingbarns.co.uk; Nether Wasdale; dm £8.50) About 250m from Nether Wasdale, this simple stone barn sleeps around eight people in chilly but dry surroundings. There's a single loo and shower, and hot water on tap, but you'll need bedding and camping supplies. The farm also makes its own cheese.

Lingmell House
B&B ££

(☑019467-26261; www.lingmellhouse.co.uk; Wasdale Head, d £60; ℗) Bare-bones B&B in a former vicarage, run by a member of the Wasdale Mountain Rescue Team. It's basic – no phones, no TVs – but the setting is grand.

WESTERN LAKE DISTRICT WASDALE HEAD

DON'T MISS

WASDALE HEAD INN

Few places in England feel as thrillingly out-of-the-way as the **Wasdale Head Inn** (☑019467-26229; www.wasdale.com; Wasdale Head; d £108-118; ℗), a favourite meeting place for generations of hill walkers, climbers and peak-baggers. It's stuffed with hiking history – one of its former owners, Will Ritson, helped pioneer the sport in the late 19th century, and vintage climbing memorabilia and dog-eared photos of Victorian gents in tweed britches and hobnailed boots decorate the wood-panelled walls. You can even browse tattered visitor books dating back to the mid-19th century. The snug rooms are small but charming, and more spacious superior rooms and self-catering flats are available in the converted barn. The restaurant serves surprisingly sophisticated food, but it's the hugger-mugger bar that's the real heart of the inn: beers are home-brewed by the Great Gable Brewing Company, and have locally themed names such as Yewbarrow, Wry'nose and Wasd'ale. Management of the inn has recently been taken over by born-and-bred Wasdale man Adam Naylor, nephew of the legendary fell-runner Joss Naylor.

ENNERDALE

Over the windswept fell-tops to the north of Wasdale is the neighbouring valley of **Ennerdale**, often cited by seasoned Lakelanders as the most scenic corner of the national park.

In many ways it feels even more remote than Wasdale – most of the valley is taken up by the blue-green 2.5-mile arc of Ennerdale Water, with the rest taken up by dense conifer plantations put in place by the Forestry Commission in the 1930s. The lake is one of the only ones in the national park not ringed by an access road, so it's entirely free of the traffic jams, cruise boats and crowds that plague some of the more accessible beauty spots. If the landscape looks uncannily familiar, don't be surprised – the valley featured in the closing sequence of Danny Boyle's British zombie flick *28 Days Later*.

More recently, the Forestry Commission (in partnership with the National Trust and United Utilities) has made a concerted effort to return Ennerdale to its former wild state as part of the **Wild Ennerdale Project** (www .wildennerdale.co.uk). Timber felling is being scaled back and wild cattle have been reintroduced to the area.

🏃 Activities

Unsurprisingly, Ennerdale is fantastic walking country. The easiest option is the 7-mile trail that loops round the lake from the car park at Bowness Knott. Fierce storms in 2008 damaged some sections of the trail, but it's still perfectly doable; the only slightly tricky section is at the rocky outcrop of Angler's Crag. More walking routes can be downloaded from the Wild Ennerdale website.

For something more challenging, you might think about tackling the **Ennerdale Round**, tracing a 22.4-mile course around all the major peaks overlooking Ennerdale, including Red Pike, Haystacks, Green Gable, Kirk Fell, Pillar and Steeple. Most hikers opt to break the hike into two days, overnighting at the fantastically remote Black Sail YHA.

The valley is also on the long-distance **Coast-to-Coast Walk** from Whitehaven, which cuts through Ennerdale Bridge before climbing over Black Sail Pass into Borrowdale and Seatoller.

Bradley's Riding Centre (☎01946-861354; www.walk-rest-ride.co.uk) offers horse-riding trips into Ennerdale, lasting from half an hour to a full day.

🛏 Sleeping & Eating

With no B&Bs or hotels in the valley, accommodation is limited to either hostels or camping. Alternatively, you could look for B&B digs in nearby Ennerdale Bridge.

Ennerdale YHA HOSTEL **£**
(☎0845 371 9116; ennerdale@yha.org.uk; Cat Crag, Ennerdale; dm from £15.95; ⏰reception 8am-10am

---

THREE PEAKS CHALLENGE

Most people struggle to get to the top of Scafell Pike in a single day, but for a select bunch of souls scaling England's highest summit just isn't enough – so how about tackling Britain's two other highest summits for good measure? The gruelling Three Peaks Challenge is one of the toughest tests any British hill walker can tackle, and involves reaching the three highest points of the British mainland – Ben Nevis (1344m/4409ft) in Scotland, Snowdon (1085m/3560ft) in Wales and, the baby of the bunch, Scafell Pike (978m/3209ft) in England – all in under 24 hours.

Thousands of hopefuls attempt the route every year, but only a hardy few ever make it across the finishing line. A few hardcore purists have even tried to complete the challenge without the use of motorised vehicles, using relay teams of cyclists and runners.

The standard route starts in the late afternoon with the ascent of Ben Nevis, followed by a six-hour overnight dash to scale Scafell Pike before breakfast, topped off by another three-hour drive and then the climb to the top of Snowdon. To successfully complete the challenge, participants have to make it back to the bottom of Snowdon before the clock ticks round to the 24-hour mark.

The generally accepted record is held by the heroic fell runner Joss Naylor, who completed the challenge in just under 12 hours in the early 1970s. Increased traffic on the motorways means his record is unlikely to be broken in the foreseeable future.

BLACK SAIL YHA

Lost among the fells to the east of Ennerdale Water, **Black Sail YHA** (📞07711-108450; dm £13.95; ☺Apr–mid-Oct, by arrangement at other times) is an absolute legend among Lakeland walkers. It sits in an amazing spot at the top of the Black Sail Pass, 6 miles east of Bowness Knott, and is only accessible on foot. Converted from an old shepherds' bothy, the facilities are simple bordering on spartan. The two dorms (one four-bed, one eight-bed) are cramped, there's no phone reception, no TV and no electric power, and the lounge doubles as a drying room for wet boots and smelly socks. But you don't come to Black Sail for luxury – you come for the privilege of staying in one of the Lake District's wildest and most unspoilt valleys, and to get a head start on the numerous hiking trails that pass right outside the hostel's front door. Bookings are essential – especially if you want to be treated to one of the hostel manager's three-course meals, which even come with a choice of wine or beer. Oh – and did we mention the views?

& 5-8pm; P) Purpose-built hostel converted from forestry cottages, tucked away in green woodland at the eastern end of the lake. Power is supplied by the hostel's own hydroelectric generator, so it's as green as hostels come. The decor is modern throughout and the dorms are limited to two six-bed and three four-bed configurations. It's a popular hikers' hostel, so book well ahead. The YHA also runs a camping barn nearby (from £9 per night).

Shepherd's Arms Hotel PUB ££
(📞01946 861249; www.shepherdsarmshotel.co.uk; s/d/f £49.50/79/99; P🛜) Terrific village pub

that doubles as Ennerdale's handiest stopover on the C2C route, offering smartly refurbished rooms decked out with hefty wooden sideboards, thick throws and big digital TVs. There's a stripy-walled lounge for guest use, complete with magazines and original fireplace, a line-up of beers certified by the Campaign for Real Ale (CAMRA), and the usual pub standards on the blackboard (mains £8 to £16).

ⓘ Getting There & Away

Ennerdale is no longer served by bus. There are two car-parks: Bleach Green at the lake's eastern end, and Bowness Knott on the northern shore.

Keswick & Derwentwater

Best Places to Eat

» Pheasant Inn (p124)
» Kirkstile Inn (p126)
» Cottage in the Wood (p126)
» Quince & Medlar (p129)
» Morrel's (p120)

Best Places to Stay

» Howe Keld (p118)
» Swinside Lodge (p120)
» Old Homestead (p128)
» Winder Hall (p126)
» Seatoller Farm (p132)

Why Go?

Pocked with islands, fringed by pebbled shores and over-looked by the hulking dome of Skiddaw, there are few lakes with such an immediate wow factor as Derwentwater. Neither as touristy as Windermere nor as wild as Wastwater, it's a place that seems to encapsulate all the essential qualities of the Lake District landscape. If you like nothing more than cruising on the water or wandering the hilltops, there are few places where you'll be better served.

The lively market town of Keswick makes a convenient base. South of town are the twin valleys of Borrowdale and Buttermere, while Bassenthwaite Lake and its wild ospreys is a few miles north. To the west you'll find the conifer forests of Whinlatter, the peaceful fields of Lorton, and the market town of Cockermouth, thoroughly polished up since 2009's floods and now (nearly) as good as new.

When to Go

In terms of festivals and events, May and June are definitely the best months to visit Keswick: the town hosts lively celebrations devoted to beer, jazz and mountain sports. July and August can be oppressively busy, although it's well worth catching the gruelling Borrowdale Fell Race in August if you can. Mid-September brings one of the region's largest country meets, the Borrowdale Show, when local farmers bring out their prize Herdwicks, and there are traditional wrestling contests, fells races, sheep-shearing competitions and even a classic tug-of-war to watch.

KESWICK

POP 5257

Nestled at the head of Derwentwater among a thicket of towering fells, Keswick is one of the handsomest of all the Lake District's market towns. Centred on a lively cobbled marketplace crammed with enough outdoors stores to launch an assault on Everest, the town is the northern Lakes' main commercial centre – so don't be surprised if you encounter some crowds in the summer.

Countless classic fell walks criss-cross the encircling hilltops, while barges and row boats scull out from the northern shores of the lake near Crow Park. And if the weather turns, you can always head indoors to browse the curious exhibits of the Keswick Museum, or settle in for some grub at one of the town's tempting pubs and cafes.

History

Keswick's name derives from the Old Norse *cese-wic* (cheese farm), and agriculture was an important industry throughout the Middle Ages, following the endowment of the town's market charter in 1276. The town later became an important industrial centre, especially for slate and graphite (then known as plumbago, or black lead), which was discovered at Seathwaite in 1555.

In 1864 a railway between Cockermouth, Keswick and Penrith opened up the area to tourists and industrialists, leading to a building boom around Keswick, Hope Park and Fitz Park. The line was closed during the Beecham cuts of the 1960s and '70s, and now forms a lovely section of the Sea to Sea Cycle Route (C2C).

◎ Sights & Activities

Derwentwater   LAKE
Studded with islands and ringed by scowling fells, Derwentwater is, for many people, the prettiest of all the Lakeland lakes. It stretches for 3 miles from the green expanse of Crow Park, a short walk from Keswick town centre, to the 90ft tumble of Lodore Falls at the lake's southern end.

The lake is famous for its islands: the largest is **St Herbert's**, named after the 'hermit of Derwentwater', who supposedly lived there in the 7th century, while the smallest is **Rampsholme Island**. In the northeastern corner is **Lord's Island**, formerly the property of local earls, while nearby **Derwent Island** was owned by eccentric aristocrat Joseph Pocklington, who built the island's wonderful Italianate house (Wordsworth thought it was an eyesore and tried to get it pulled down). The island now belongs to the National Trust and is rented to tenants, who are required to open the house to the public five days a year. Phone ☎017687-73780 for details of the next opening days.

Paths wind almost the whole way around the shores of Derwentwater, but it's a long walk from end to end, so it's probably more sensible just to follow the first section to the famous viewpoint of **Friar's Crag**, 15 minutes' walk from the Keswick jetties.

As always, the best way to explore the lake is by boat, either motorised or paddlepowered. The **Keswick Launch Company** (www.keswick-launch.co.uk) calls at seven landing stages around the lake: Ashness Gate, Lodore Falls, High Brandlehow, Low Brandlehow, Hawse End, Nichol End and Keswick.

There are eight daily boats from mid-March to mid-November, dropping to three a day from mid-November to mid-March. A circular trip costs £9/5 per adult/child. You're free to hop off and walk to the next jetty if you wish; single fares to each landing stage are also available. In summer there's also a twilight cruise at 7.30pm, plus special Father Christmas cruises in December.

FREE **Keswick Museum & Art Gallery**   MUSEUM
(Station Rd; ◎10am-4pm Tue-Sat Feb-Oct) Tucked along Station Rd overlooking the orderly lawns of Fitz Park, this endearingly oddball museum has hardly changed since its opening in 1898. Glass display cabinets house a hotchpotch of exhibits including a Napoleonic teacup, a penny farthing bicycle, a rare fish pickled in a jar, a mounted golden eagle, a spoon made from a sheep's leg bone and a cluster of letters from Southey, Wordsworth, de Quincey and Ruskin.

But the museum's most famous exhibits are its mummified cat (allegedly 664 years old) and the Musical Stones of Skiddaw, fashioned from hornsfel rock in 1827 by stonemason Joseph Richardson. The stones' plink-plonk melody was a famous 19th-century tourist attraction, and even featured in a gala performance for Queen Victoria.

Cumberland Pencil Museum   MUSEUM
(www.pencilmuseum.co.uk; Southey Works; adult/child £3.75/2.50; ◎9.30am-5pm) Plumbago, or graphite, has been an important export for Keswick since the 16th century. Local

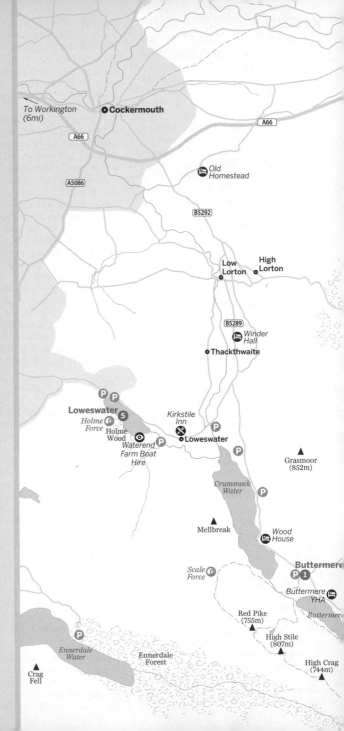

Keswick & Derwentwater Highlights

1 Camp among the green pastures and glowering fells in **Buttermere and Borrowdale** (p129)

2 Row a boat out to one of Derwentwater's idyllic woodland **islands** (p113)

3 Survey the scenery from the top of **Castle Crag** (p131)

4 Venture deep underground into the slate mines of **Honister** (133)

5 Leave the crowds well behind on the quiet shores of **Loweswater** (p126)

6 Pay your respects to Alfred Wainwright on top of **Haystacks** (p134)

7 Admire the ambition of the ancient architects of **Castlerigg Stone Circle** (p122)

8 Take an evening hike up to the hidden tarn of **Watendlath** (p132)

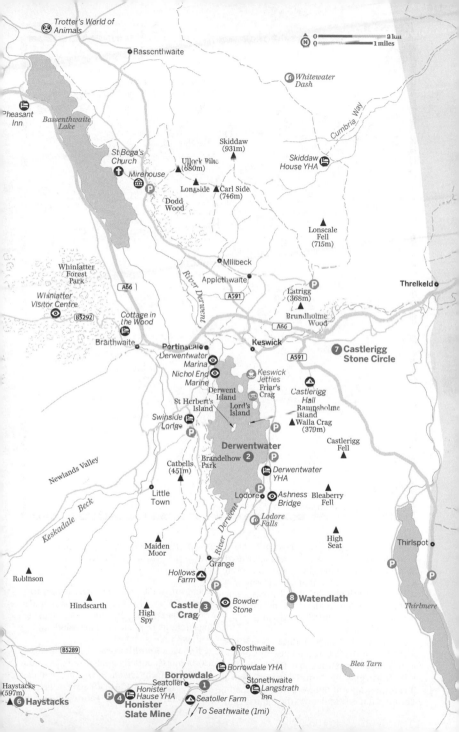

Keswick

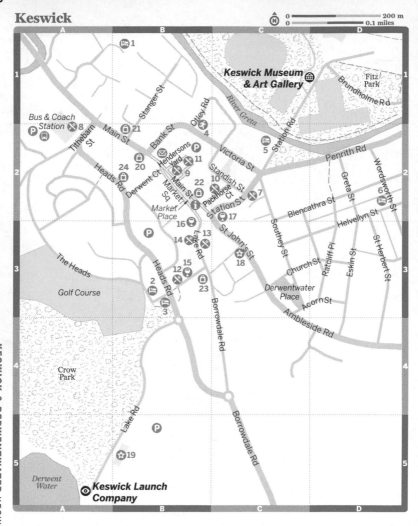

shepherds used graphite for years to mark their sheep, and the mineral was later used as a rust proofer, a metal lubricant and even a cure for stomach ailments, but it was only when some bright spark in Florence stuck it into a wooden holder and invented the pencil that the graphite industry in Keswick really took off.

The first industrially produced pencil was made here in 1832, and the museum's exhibits include a reconstruction of the Seathwaite slate mine and the world's longest pencil (measuring an impressive 26ft tip to end). The museum is next door to the Cumberland Pencil Factory, which still manufactures luxury Derwent colouring pencils.

Hiking

There are some awesome fells within easy reach of Keswick. One of the most popular options is Catbells, but the more challenging summits of Blencathra and Skiddaw are both within easy reach.

Keswick Rambles (www.keswickrambles.org .uk) organises a daily guided walk from the Moot Hall from Easter to October. Full-day hikes (adult/child £15/7.50) start at 9am or 10am returning around 4pm or 5pm, and

Keswick

cover distances of 8 to 10 miles. Half-day walks cost £7.50/4 – see the website for the latest schedule.

Mike Wood (07931 639910; www.mikewood mountain.co.uk) is another recommended local guide, who offers courses in navigation and wild camping, and charges a flat rate of £90 per day for guiding services.

Several route guides can be downloaded from www.keswick.org/walks app.

Catbells
HIKING

The miniature mountain of Catbells (451m/1481ft) packs an impressive punch considering its modest height. In Book 6 of his *Pictorial Guides*, Wainwright called it 'one of the great favourites, a family fell where grandmothers and infants can climb the heights together'. That's certainly true, but the family will still need to be fit. The climb to the top is quite steep in places, but the views provide ample reward: Skiddaw, the Newlands Valley, Borrowdale and the pointy peak of Castle Crag are all visible from the top.

The traditional path starts near the Hawse End jetty on the lake's west side, then climbs up over the summit and loops back along the lakeshore via Brandlehow Park. It's a round-trip of around 3 miles to the jetty, or an extra mile if you walk back to Keswick.

Walla Crag
HIKING

The easterly lookout at Walla Crag (379m/1243ft) is easily reached from the town centre. Start on Ambleside Rd and follow the path through Springs Wood to Castlerigg Hall and Camping Park. A trail leads south from the end of the road to the crag, which has a great view west over Derwentwater.

You can turn it into a loop route by descending south over Falcon Crag and following the lakeshore trail back to town, a total distance of around 6 miles.

Latrigg
HIKING

A low hump just behind Keswick, utterly dominated by nearby Skiddaw, Latrigg (368m/1203ft) is another easy summit with top-drawer views. Follow the first section of the Skiddaw route (p119), and look out for

WORTH A TRIP

THRELKELD QUARRY

A century ago Threlkeld was a hive of industrial activity thanks to its rich deposits of granite, lead and copper. The **Threlkeld Quarry & Mining Museum** (www.threlkeldminingmuseum .co.uk; Threlkeld; mine tour adult/child £5/2.50, museum £3/1.50; 10am-5pm Mar-Oct) revisits the village's mining heyday; you can take a fascinating underground mine tour, browse vintage mining machinery in the museum, and even take a ride on 'Sir Tom', a restored narrow-gauge locomotive built in 1926.

the right-hand turn just before you reach the Underscar car park. Once you've reached the top, you can either retrace your steps or continue east via Brundholme Wood, returning to town along the Threlkeld railway path.

Blencathra
HIKING

Sometimes known by its alternative name of Saddleback (the name coined from the shape of the mountain when seen from the east), Blencathra (868m/2848ft) looms along the skyline northeast of Keswick, and (alongside Skiddaw) represents the toughest hiking challenge in the area.

There are several routes to the top. The usual one starts in the village of **Threlkeld**, and loops around the fell's unforgiving east side, a steep but straightforward climb to the summit. There's a more challenging route to the top via the rocky ridge of **Halls Fell**, but the third route via **Sharp Edge** is best left for experienced scramblers and rock-climbers – it involves sheer thousand-foot drops and makes Helvellyn's ridges look like child's play.

Threlkeld Railway Path
WALKING

This disused railway path runs for around 3 miles from Keswick to Threlkeld via a series of tunnels, embankments and bridges; it makes a great walk and also forms part of the Sea to Sea Cycle Route (C2C). You can pick up the trail on Station Ave near the Keswick Leisure Pool and Fitness Centre.

Boat Hire

Traditional row boats can be hired beside the Keswick Launch, or you can rent canoes, kayaks and dinghies from one of the lake marinas: **Nichol End Marine** (☏017687-73082; www.nicholendmarine.co.uk) or **Derwentwater Marina** (☏017687-72912; www.derwentwatermarina.co.uk).

Other Activities

Newlands Adventure Centre OUTDOORS
(☏017687-78463; www.activity-centre.com) This well-run multi-activity centre is a great place to try your hand at several different outdoor sports in a day. You can choose from ghyll scrambling, climbing, abseiling, orienteering, archery and several other activities: each one costs £25 per person, or you can stay overnight in the dorm and build your own multiday course.

The centre is in the lovely Newlands Valley, about 2 miles from Keswick.

Keswick Climbing Wall ROCK CLIMBING
(☏017687-72000; www.keswickclimbingwall.co.uk; ☺10am-9pm Tue & Fri, 10am-5pm Sat-Mon) Practise your skills at one of the northwest's largest indoor rock-climbing centres. Group sessions for novice climbers cost £10/15 for one/two hours, or £30 for private lessons. The centre is in a new purpose-built location on Goosewell Farm; follow Penrith Rd east from town and look out for the signs.

⚜ Festivals & Events

Keswick has one of the busiest calendars in the Lake District. Highlights include the following.

Keswick Mountain Festival OUTDOORS
(www.keswickmountainfestival.co.uk) Guest speakers from the worlds of climbing, biking, hiking and adventure sports come to Keswick for this mid-May festival. Big discounts are usually available on gear.

Keswick Jazz Festival MUSIC
(www.keswickjazzfestival.co.uk) Jazz acts old and new play at various venues around town in mid-May.

Keswick Beer Festival BEER
(www.keswickbeerfestival.co.uk) Beer brewers from across the lakes and much further afield descend on Keswick for a four-day ale-fest in June.

🛏 Sleeping

Practically every house along Blencathra, Helvellyn and Eskin Sts has been turned into a B&B – they're generally on the simple side, but handy for last-minute rooms.

There's another cluster of B&Bs on the Heads, overlooking the golf course – the houses are grander on the outside, but bog-standard B&B on the inside.

Howe Keld TOP CHOICE B&B ££
(☏017687-72417; www.howekeld.co.uk; 5-7 The Heads; s £45, d £80-90; 🛜) The nearest thing to a proper boutique B&B in Keswick, and a distinct cut above the other guesthouses round town. All 14 rooms have been totally overhauled and now feature luxury touches such as goose-down duvets, slate-floored bathrooms and furniture made by a local carpenter. It's sleek and very contemporary, and the breakfast is an utter spoil, with a choice of home-made smoothies, vegetarian rissoles, French pancakes and make-your-own muesli.

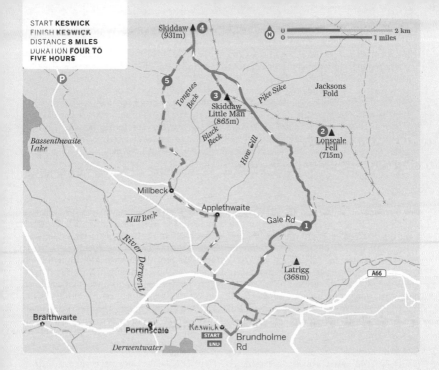

Hiking Tour
Skiddaw

> Cumbria has four mountains that top 3000ft – Scafell Pike, Scafell, Helvellyn and Skiddaw (931m/3054ft), which completely dominates Keswick's northern skyline. It's a long puff to the top, but on a clear day the mountain's all-round panorama more than matches the other top three – although as with all high peaks, 'Keswick's Matterhorn' is not just steep, it's also exposed, windy and very hard to navigate in fog and cloud. Plan accordingly.

The route starts on Brundholme Rd in Keswick and follows Spooney Green Lane. You'll reach the ① **Underscar car park** at the end of Gale Rd after about an hour. If you're feeling lively you could add an ascent of Latrigg, otherwise stick to the trail and take the next left-hand fork, which begins the long plod to the fell-top.

Look out for a ruined building known as the Halfway House on your right as you ascend past ② **Lonscale Fell** (715m/ 2344ft). Victorian tourists would once have paused here for refreshments, but these days you'll have to bring your own.

After another long climb you'll reach a left-hand detour to ③ **Skiddaw Little Man** (865m/2838ft). Stick to the main trail and carry on up the steep path for around half a mile over a series of 'tops'; you'll know you've reached Skiddaw's true ④ **summit** when you're standing next to the Ordnance Survey trig-point and the memorial commemorating the Queen's Silver Jubilee.

Famously, William Wordsworth and Robert Southey climbed Skiddaw in 1815 to celebrate Napoleon's defeat at Waterloo; at the top, they tucked into a lunch of roast beef, plum pudding and punch. If the weather's clear, you should be able to glimpse all the main Lakeland ranges, including Helvellyn and the Scafells, and, on a really good day, the Scottish peaks.

There are several possible descents, including a classic ridge trail over ⑤ **Carl Side**, but retracing your steps allows you to take in the summit of Skiddaw Little Man on the way down.

GRETA HALL

It's not often you get the chance to stay in a house occupied by two of England's greatest poets, but that's exactly what's on offer at **Greta Hall** (☏017687-75980; www.gretahall.net; Main St; £350-1490 per week). Robert Southey and Samuel Taylor Coleridge both lived here, and the house witnessed a stream of literary visitors including de Quincey, Byron, Shelley, Keats and, of course, William Wordsworth (comedy fans might also recognise it from an episode of the BBC series *The Trip*, starring Rob Brydon and Steve Coogan).

Owners Jeronime and Scott Palmer have lovingly renovated the house and now offer three gorgeous self-catering apartments, including the two-floored Coleridge Wing, where you warm yourself by the very same fireplace where the poet like to sit and compose his verse. There's also a large coach-house that sleeps up to 11 people, or a cosy cottage for two in the old wash house.

Powe House   B&B ££
(☏017687-73611; www.powehouse.com; Portinscale; s £40-60, d £80-84; P🐾) If you don't mind being a bit further out of town, this chic little guesthouse in Portinscale makes a very decent alternative. All six rooms are great value: the roomiest are 3 and 5, both with double sash windows overlooking trimmed gardens. Room 6 is cosy but you can glimpse the summit of Skiddaw through the window.

Swinside Lodge   HOTEL £££
(☏017687-72948; www.swinsidelodge-hotel.co.uk; Newlands; d incl dinner £176-276; P) This swish hotel has scooped awards for its gourmet food and Georgian finery. It's classy without being chi-chi; rooms are furnished in countrified style, and the house is a reassuring mix of creaky floorboards, cosy lounges and book-stocked shelves. A four-course supper at the bistro is included. It's in Newlands, a couple of miles' drive from Keswick.

Highfield Hotel   HOTEL £££
(☏017687-72508; www.highfieldkeswick.co.uk; The Heads; d £170-210; P) This turret-covered Victorian mansion is the poshest of the Heads guesthouses. The feel's formal: the best rooms boast Crow Park views, but many are surprisingly squashed considering the price tag. Go for room 5 for double-aspect views, rooms 9 and 15 for elbow-room, and the Woodford for a regal Rococo bed.

Oakthwaite House   B&B ££
(☏017687-72398; www.oakthwaite-keswick.com; 35 Helvellyn St; d £64-78) One of the best choices in the B&B-heavy zone around Blencathra St. The rooms are elegantly finished in blues, creams and greys – ask for one of the king-size rooms if you're after space, as the dormer room is shoebox-small.

Keswick YHA   HOSTEL £
(☏0870 770 5894; keswick@yha.org.uk; Station Rd; dm £14.40-22.40; 🐾) This riverside YHA is in a great location overlooking Fitz Park, and was recently refurbished from scratch thanks to the generosity of a retired doctor. The rooms, dorms and kitchens have been stripped out and polished up, and the hostel now has its own in-house cafe on the ground floor. Some rooms even have riverfront balconies.

Castlerigg Hall   CAMPGROUND £
(☏017687-74499; www.castlerigg.co.uk; Rakefoot Lane; adult £8.30, child 5-16yr £4.30, car £3) Keswick's largest campsite is on a hilltop off the A591, about 1.5 miles from the town centre (take Penrith Rd and follow signs to Castlerigg and Rakefoot). There are separate fields for caravans and campers. Facilities are good: there's a shop, a restaurant, a laundry and a campers' kitchen, for which you'll need 50p to work the microwave and hobs. No advance reservations.

**Keswick Camping
& Caravanning Club**   CAMPSITE £
(☏017687-72392; www.campingandcaravanning club.co.uk/keswick; Crow Park Rd; adult £9.15, child £2.85; ☉Feb–mid-Nov) Great choice for lakeside camping, with 250 pitches spread out across a 5-hectare field at the northern end of Derwentwater. Some of the lakeside pitches get muddy in wet weather, and it gets very busy in season – extra space is available at a sister site nearby. You'll need to be a member to book online.

🍴 Eating

Morrel's   EUROPEAN ££
(☏017687-72666; Lake Rd; mains £13.95-17.50, 3-course menu £16.95; ☉dinner Tue-Sun)

Keswick's top table is this glossy restaurant, smoothly done in shades of cappuccino, cream and chocolate, enlivened by gloss wood floors and pop art movie prints. Expect classic bistro food spiced by the occasional Spanish, Italian and Oriental touch. Several self-catering apartments (£450-650 per week) are available above the restaurant.

A Different Taste   BISTRO ££
(017687-80007; 20 Station St; mains £11-15; ☺dinner Tue-Sun) A refreshingly unpretentious and reassuringly homely little restaurant, serving bistro staples such as pork escalopes, beef stroganoff and lamb chump, all cooked with care and attention by owner-chef Debra Brown. The space is snug, and it's popular with Keswickians at weekends, so you'd be wise to book.

Abraham's Tea Rooms   CAFF £
(2 Borrowdale Rd; mains £4-10; ☺breakfast & dinner) This fine cafe is lodged among the roof-beams of the George Fisher outdoor store, in the former studio belonging to the Abraham brothers, who pioneered the art of mountain photography in the Lake District. It's a refined affair, good for hearty rarebits, mackerel pâté on toast and crunchy salads, or afternoon cream tea with homemade jam.

Bryson's   BAKERY £
(42 Main St; cakes £2-5) For breads, buns and biscuits just like Grandma used to make, Bryson's is the place. The shelves are stocked with currant-heavy fruit cakes, Battenburgs, coconut fancies and chocolatey florentines, or for local flavour try some Borrowdale Teabread – perfect fare for munching on while you stalk the fells.

Lakeland Pedlar   CAFE £
(www.lakelandpedlar.co.uk; Hendersons Yard; mains £3-10) This veggie cafe–cum–bike shop is an old fave among cyclists and hungry walkers, with a daily pot of home-made soup, plus burritos, stews, casseroles and chunky doorstep sandwiches.

Pumpkin   CAFE £
(19 Lake Rd; lunches £4-10; ☺Mon-Sat) This modish cafe was formerly owned by celebrity chef Peter Sidwell, and the menu still owes much to his culinary ethos. The coffee's top-notch, the chalkboards are crammed with Continental salads and made-to-order flatbreads, and the glass cabinets proffer a tempting assortment of pastries, muffins, cakes and fresh-baked patisserie. Even sans-Sidwell, tables are as scarce as ever at lunchtime, so arrive early.

Sweeney's   BISTRO, BAR ££
(www.sweeneysbar.co.uk; 18-20 Lake Rd; 2/3 courses £11.95/13.95) Laid-back wine bar that does a decent line in burgers, pizzas and steaks, with plenty of deep leather sofas to sink into after supper.

Cheese Delicatessen   CHEESE SHOP
(www.keswickcheesedeli.co.uk; 9 Packhorse Ct) Pick up local cheeses at this small shop in Packhorse Ct.

Booth's   SUPERMARKET
(Tithebarn St; ☺8am-6pm Mon-Sat, 11am-4pm Sun) Large supermarket on the edge of town.

🍷 Drinking

George Hotel   PUB
(St John's St) Originally known as the George & Dragon, this is supposedly the oldest inn in Keswick. It's where the locals go for a pint and a pie, with a comprehensive line-up of Jennings beers on tap and a popular quiz night on Tuesday.

Dog and Gun   PUB
(2 Lake Rd) Sporting prints, scruffy bench seats and russet-faced punters are all on show at this venerable old inn just off the main street. 10p from every pint of 'Thirst Rescue' goes into the coffers of the Keswick Mountain Rescue Team.

Cafe-Bar 26   WINE BAR
(26 Lake Rd) Swish bar that's ideal for a glass of merlot or a continental beer, perhaps accompanied by some tapas or bruschetta. Leather, wood and chrome give things a metro-chic feel.

☆ Entertainment

Theatre by the Lake   THEATRE
(017687-74411; www.theatrebythelake.com; Lakeside) This smart venue hosts new and classic drama, as well as touring bands and musical acts.

Alhambra   CINEMA
(017687-72195; www.keswick-alhambra.co.uk; St Johns St) Keswick's town cinema hub shows mainstream releases, plus occasional indie and art-house films courtesy of the Keswick Film Club.

KESWICK & DERWENTWATER KESWICK

DON'T MISS

CASTLERIGG STONE CIRCLE

Of all the Lake District's stone circles, none has the drama of Castlerigg, perched on a lonely hilltop a mile above Keswick. Constructed between 3000 and 4000 years ago, the circle contains between 38 and 42 stones (depending on which ones you count), with a further rectangle of stones set inside the main ring; the tallest is around 8ft high, and the largest weighs over 16 tons.

Quite how the ancient Britons dragged these massive lumps of rock to this isolated spot remains a mystery, and archaeologists are still divided over its purpose – some think it's a prehistoric market place or monument, while others believe it's a celestial calendar that marked the passing seasons.

The circle is signposted off the A66 and A591, near the Castlerigg Hall campsite.

🛍 Shopping

Keswick has one of the best selection of gear shops in the Lakes, including branches of **Cotswold Outdoor**, **Black's** and **Planet Fear**, but the oldest and best is **George Fisher** (www.georgefisher.co.uk; 2 Borrowdale Rd), in business for almost a century and still the one to beat. It's spread over three levels, with well-stocked departments devoted to camping, climbing and clothing, and its boot-fitting service is second to none.

Bookends (☑017687-75277; 66 Main St) is an excellent local bookshop selling walking guides and maps.

ℹ Information

Branches of Natwest, Lloyds, Barclays and HSBC are in Market Pl.

Keswick Library (Heads Rd; internet per ½hr £1; ☉10am-7pm Mon & Wed, 10am-5pm Tue & Fri, 10am-12.30pm Thu & Sat) Internet access.
Tourist office (☑017687-72645; keswicktic@lake-district.gov.uk; Moot Hall, Market Pl; ☉9.30am-5.30pm Apr-Oct, to 4.30pm Nov-Mar) In the old Moot Hall at the top of Market Pl. Sells discount launch tickets.
U-Compute (48 Main St; per ½hr/hr £2/3; ☉9am-5.30pm) Internet cafe above the post office.
www.keswick.org Useful town website.

ℹ Getting There & Around
Bike Hire
Keswick Mountain Bikes (☑017687-75202; www.keswickbikes.co.uk; ☉9am-5.30pm Mon-Sat, 10am-5.30pm Sun) The town's largest bike shop has three outlets: a workshop and hire centre near the Climbing Wall, a retail shop on Otley Rd, and another shop above the Lakeland Pedlar. Bike hire costs £15 to £40 per day depending on the model.

Whinlatter Bikes (☑017687-74412; www.whinlatterbikes.com; Tithebarn St; ☉9am-5.30pm Mon-Sat) Similar prices.

Bus
Useful buses:
555 Hourly to Ambleside (40 minutes), Windermere (50 minutes) and Kendal (1½ hours).
X5/X50 (hourly Monday to Saturday, six on Sunday) East–west route that stops in Workington, Cockermouth and Keswick, then becomes the X50 to Threlkeld and Penrith.
77/77A (four daily in summer) Main bus to Borrowdale and Buttermere. The 77 goes in an anticlockwise direction via Whinlatter, Lorton, Buttermere, Honister Pass and the Borrowdale hamlets, then runs along the west side of Derwentwater through Portinscale and back to Keswick. The 77A does the same route in a clockwise direction.
78 (twice-hourly Monday to Saturday, eight on Sunday) Runs down east-side Derwentwater via Lodore Falls (10 minutes), Grange (15 minutes), Rosthwaite (20 minutes) and Seatoller (25 minutes).

AROUND KESWICK

Keswick is handily positioned for exploring the northern Lakes, including the reservoir of Thirlmere, the wooded shoreline of Bassenthwaite Lake, the rural haven of Back O' Skiddaw and the secluded valley of Lorton.

Thirlmere

A couple of miles southeast of Keswick is Thirlmere, one of the Lake District's largest reservoirs, created from two separate lakes at the end of the 19th century to supply drinking water to Manchester. The project was passionately opposed by environmental campaigners including John Ruskin, who felt the new reservoir would irrevocably alter the local landscape.

Looking at Thirlmere's tree-fringed shores these days, you'd be hard put to see what the fuss was all about, but the project wasn't without its costs: the hamlets of Armboth and Wythburn were both drowned during the construction of the dam at the valley's northern end.

The main reason for visiting is to wander the woodland around the lake (keep your eyes peeled for red squirrels) or to tackle an alternative route up the west side of Helvellyn, via Birk Side and Nethermost Pike (891m/2920ft).

The A591 runs along the reservoir's east side to Grasmere, and there's a second minor road along the west side. There are car parks at Swirls and Wythburn. The 555/556 bus stops at both en route to Grasmere and Windermere.

Bassenthwaite Lake

Pub pedants like nothing better than to remind you that the Lake District actually only has one lake: Bassenthwaite Lake (the others are actually all meres, waters or tarns).

Three miles north of Keswick, nestling in the shadow of the Skiddaw range, Bassenthwaite is one of the few lakes undisturbed by cruise boats and pleasure vessels. Surrounded by pine and beech forest, it's become a haven for wildlife, including red squirrels, wintering water birds and, famously,

THE NEWLANDS VALLEY

Comparatively few people make the trek to the Newlands Valley, the hidden valley that runs southwest for 7 miles from the village of Braithwaite, just west of Keswick, all the way to Buttermere, climbing over the high point of **Newlands Hause** (1093ft) en route.

It's a wild and almost completely empty landscape, only interrupted by a handful of remote farms and cottages, so it's ideal hiking country. The classic circuit is the 9- to 10-mile **Newlands Horseshoe**, which runs from the tiny village of Little Town and over the tops of Robinson, Hindscarth, Dalehead, High Spy and Maiden Moor.

the Lake District only pair of ospreys. The wild show continues under the water, too: Bassenthwaite is one of only two English lakes (along with Derwentwater) that harbours wild vendace, a highly endangered whitefish that became stranded here at the end of the last ice age.

Much of the shoreline of Bassenthwaite is privately owned, so the best way to get down to the lake is to visit the grounds of Mirehouse. The lake's namesake village is actually half a mile inland from Bassenthwaite's northern tip: there's not much to see, save for a homely village pub and the imposing edifice and grounds of Armathwaite Hall, now an extremely pricey country hotel.

☉ Sights

Dodd Wood & the
Bassenthwaite Ospreys   WILDLIFE RESERVE
In 2001 the first ospreys to breed in England for 150 years set up home at Bassenthwaite. These magnificent birds of prey were once widespread, but were driven to extinction by hunting, habitat loss and egg collectors. The last wild pair was destroyed in Scotland in 1916, but following years of conservation, the ospreys have slowly recolonised several areas of the British Isles, including Bassenthwaite.

In recent years the birds have been returning every April, spending the summer at Bassenthwaite before heading for Africa in late August or early September. No-one knows how long they'll continue to do so, so you'd be wise to enjoy the spectacle while you can.

Two bird hides have been constructed in Dodd Wood, roughly 3 miles north of Keswick on the A591. The **lower hide** (☉10am-5pm) is 15 minutes' walk from the car park at Mirehouse, and the **upper hide** (☉10am-5.30pm) is another half-hour further through the forest. Telescopes are provided, but your own pair of binoculars will come in handy.

If you don't spot the birds, there's a live video feed at the Whinlatter Visitor Centre. Find out the latest news on the birds at www.ospreywatch.co.uk.

Mirehouse   HISTORIC HOUSE
(www.mirehouse.com; house & gardens adult/child £7/3, gardens only £3.50/1.50; ☉gardens 10am-5.30pm Apr-Oct, house 2-5pm Sun & Wed Apr-Oct, plus 2-5pm Fri Aug) Built in 1666, the lakeside manor of Mirehouse has been occupied

since 1802 by the Spedding family, and in many ways still feels more like a family residence than a stuffy museum piece.

The house's hallways are stuffed to the rafters with furniture, literary memorabilia and quirky antiques. Among the items on display are vintage rocking chairs, a collection of clay pipes and an array of letters from eminent writers including Robert Southey, Thomas Carlyle, John Constable and Wordsworth, as well as Alfred Tennyson, who stayed at the house while writing his epic poem *Morte d'Arthur* in the company of his friend James Spedding (the first biographer of Francis Bacon).

Outside, azaleas, roses, a rhododendron tunnel, a collection of Cumbrian fruit trees and adventure playgrounds are dotted around the grounds, and you can detour through a wildflower meadow planted to attract honey bees. A lakeshore path leads through Catstocks Wood to the tiny church of **St Bega**.

The nearest car park is at Dodd Wood, 10 minutes' walk from the house. Tickets are sold at the Old Sawmill Tearoom next to the car park; an admission discount of £3 is refundable against the car parking fee.

Trotters World of Animals   ZOO
(www.trottersworld.com; adult/3-14yr £7.75/5.75; ⊙10am-5.30pm) You'll meet everything from a Canadian lynx to Asian fishing cats and the world's titchiest otters at this animal park, at the northern end of Bassenthwaite Lake. Unlike most zoos, here handling the animals is positively encouraged – if you're feeling brave you could get hands-on with a boa constrictor or a red-kneed tarantula, although more cautious types will probably prefer to stick to stroking the billy goats and Shetland ponies. Regular flying demonstrations with the park's collection of owls, vultures, hawks and falcons are held throughout the day.

🛏 Sleeping & Eating

Highside Farm   B&B **££**
(☑017687-76952; www.highside.co.uk; d £70-80; 🅿) Don't be taken in by the rustic facade: behind the slate roof and whitewashed cob, this rural farmhouse conceals some flashy interiors. Rooms in the main house are named after Lakeland fells, but for luxury you'll want the Lake View suite, with a deluxe bathroom and a home cinema housed in a converted barn. The lounge, with its inglenook hearth and cosy sofas,

SKIDDAW HOUSE YHA

It doesn't quite feel as 'ends-of-the-earth' as Black Sail, but **Skiddaw House** (☑07747-174293; skiddaw@yha .org.uk; ⊙8-10am & 5-10.30pm) still feels a long way from civilisation. It's the highest hostel in England, variously used as a ghyllie's lodge and shepherd's bothy, and now offering extremely basic bunk accommodation for up to 15 people. Limited meals are available from the hostel manager if you reserve ahead; remember to bring a torch, as there's only battery-powered lighting. Ring ahead before setting out to make sure there's space, as it's a good 3 miles' hike from the nearest road at Whitewater Dash. Camping is also available for £6 per night.

feels more traditional. It's on a minor road to Orthwaite, a mile south of Bassenthwaite Village.

Pheasant Inn   PUB **££**
(☑017687-76234; www.the-pheasant.co.uk; near Dubwath; lunch mains £8-14, dinner mains £14-25; 🅿) This much-vaunted Bassenthwaite inn is dressed up in time-honoured country garb: wood panelling, sporting prints and hunting trophies, with proper beer pumps and vintage whiskies behind the bar. The menu is full of cockle-warming dishes such as Old Spot pork and pan-fried pigeon, served with rich gravy and red wine jus, and the inn also does a rather fine afternoon tea, complete with hot buttered scones, finger sandwiches and fruit cake.

ⓘ Getting There & Away

The main A66 road to Cockermouth runs along the lake's western shore, while the minor A591 runs along the east side via Dodd Wood.

A few buses serve Bassenthwaite in summer; the handiest is the 555, which runs along the lake's eastern side three or four times daily in summer, stopping at Mirehouse (10 minutes).

Back O' Skiddaw

Secreted away beyond the northern edge of Skiddaw, along the uppermost border of the national park, is the area locally known as Back O' Skiddaw, a little-explored region that's well off the beaten track and remains largely untroubled by the tourist hordes. Patchwork fields and quiet villages are dotted around the countryside, including the solid farming hamlets of Uldale and Ireby, and the quaint village of Hesket Newmarket, arranged around a grassy green.

Most attractive of all is **Caldbeck**, whose name derives from the Norse for 'cold stream'. Notable landmarks include **St Kentigern's Church**, dedicated to the 6th-century saint who purportedly first preached the Christian gospel in this corner of England, and the **Priest's Mill**, which began life as a corn mill and has now reinvented itself as an arts and community centre.

Most people visit this corner of the lakes to hike, either on their way along the long-distance Cumbria Way, or to explore the little-known Caldbeck Fells. One of the best-known targets is the high point of **Carrock Fell** (661m/2169ft), from where the views stretch east all the way to the Eden Valley.

🛏 Sleeping & Eating

Boltongate Old Rectory B&B £
(☎016973-71647; www.boltongateoldrectory.com; d £115-125, P) If you're after somewhere to stay, the best place by far is this sparkling little number in nearby Boltongate. It has scooped a bevy of awards, and justly so; bedrooms and bathrooms glimmer with brass beds and soothing shades, while sophisticated food is on offer in the restaurant.

Old Crown PUB ££
(www.theoldcrownpub.co.uk; mains £7-16; P) Hesket Newmarket's super village inn is one of the first co-op owned pubs in Britain, with around 100 local stakeholders who got involved when the pub was teetering on the brink of closure. It brews a formidable line-up of beers including Blencathra Bitter, Old Carrock Ale and Great Cockup Porter, and you'll find solid pub mains (casseroles, pies, curries) to accompany the brews. The well-known mountaineer Chris Bonington (who lives in Caldbeck) has even been known to stop in on occasion.

Watermill Cafe CAFE £
(www.watermillcafe.co.uk; Caldbeck; ☉9am-5pm mid-Feb–Oct, 9am-4.30pm Nov-Jan; 🐾) This endearing cafe is squeezed among the stone walls and A-frame rafters of the old Priest's Mill in Caldbeck. Find your spot at one of the wooden tables and tuck into a hearty ploughman's lunch or a slice of sticky lemon cake. The cafe does an excellent Sunday lunch, and sometimes opens for special dinner evenings.

❶ Getting There & Away

The Caldbeck Rambler runs once a day from Carlisle to Caldbeck (as the 74), then trundles on to Hesket Newmarket, Threlkeld and Keswick as the 73. It operates a slightly different route on Saturdays; there are no buses on Sunday.

Whinlatter, Lorton & Loweswater

West of the lake, the B5292 veers sharply off the main A66 near Braithwaite, and begins a long, snaking climb into the conifer forests around Whinlatter Pass before dropping down into the lovely Vale of Lorton.

The views as you climb over the pass at 1043ft above sea level and descend the other side towards Loweswater are outstanding, but take care during winter, as the pass is often icy or even snowbound.

WHINLATTER FOREST PARK

Encompassing 1200 hectares of pine, larch and spruce, Whinlatter is England's only true mountain forest. The forest was planted around a century ago in order to counter a chronic timber shortage following WWI, but it's now better known for its wildlife – the forest is one of the best places in Cumbria to see red squirrels.

You can watch live video feeds from squirrel-cams dotted around the forest at the **Whinlatter Visitor Centre** (☎017687-78469; www.forestry.gov.uk/whinlatterforestpark; Whinlatter Forest Park; ☉10am-5pm), which also houses information panels and video displays for the Bassenthwaite ospreys, and a small cafe.

Mountain-bikers can tackle two challenging trails in the forest: the twin loops of the 17km Altura Trail and the new 8km Quercus Trail. They're both fairly challenging routes, incorporating berms, downhills, boards and jumps – so are probably best left for experienced bikers. **Cyclewise** (☎017687-78711; www.cyclewise.co.uk), next to the visitor centre, hires bikes and also runs skills sessions and training courses.

The forest also has a tree-top assault course run by **Go Ape** (☎017687-78469; http://goape.co.uk/sites/whinlatter; adult/10-17yr

£30/20; ⊘9am-5pm mid-Mar–Oct, closed Mon & Fri in term-time).

🛏 Sleeping & Eating

TOP CHOICE Cottage in the Wood BISTRO ££
(☎017687-78409; www.thecottageinthewood.co.uk; Whinlatter Forest; dinner 3-/4-/5-courses £30/36/42, d £110-180; P) This elegant restaurant-with-rooms has a growing reputation as one of the most attractive weekend hideaways in the northern lakes. It's nestled among lofty conifers on the road towards Whinlatter Pass, and you'll be treated to wraparound woodland views from the accomplished bistro, which recently took top honours in the prestigious Taste of Cumbria competition. Standard rooms are decorated in cottage style: for a spoil, ask for the attic suite, with its glass skylights and claw-foot tub, or the garden room, with its super-luxurious slate-tiled wet-room.

LORTON & LOWESWATER

From the high point of the Whinlatter Pass, the B5292 traces a long, lolloping course down the fell-side into the jade-green Vale of Lorton, scattered with farmhouses, beech copses and rickety barns.

After 3 miles the road passes through the twin hamlets of Low Lorton and High Lorton en route to the tiny National Trust–owned lake of Loweswater, one of the smallest, shallowest and most secluded of all the Lakeland lakes. Barely a mile across and averaging just 60ft deep, it's a supremely peaceful spot, unsullied by the traffic, crowds and touristy razzmatazz of many other lakes.

The NT has a handful of traditional row boats moored alongside the lake shore, which can be booked from the warden's house at **Watergate Farm** (☎01946-816944) or at the opposite end of the lake from **Waterend Farm** (☎01946-861945).

Otherwise, Loweswater is for walking. The distinctive rocket-shaped summit looming on the lake's southern side is **Mellbreak** (512m/1676ft); alternatively, follow the peaceful trail around the shoreline, and keep your eyes peeled for woodpeckers and red squirrels around **Holme Wood** and the tinkling tumble of **Holme Force**.

🛏 Sleeping & Eating

TOP CHOICE Kirkstile Inn PUB ££
(☎01900-85219; www.kirkstile.com; Loweswater; mains £12-16, s £61.50-90, d £93-107; P) A quainter country pub you simply could not find. Hidden away on a lane near Loweswater, the Kirkstile's a joy from start to finish: old photos on the walls, hearty portions of pork fillet and ham-and-leek pudding, and home-brewed ales (including Melbreak Bitter and Kirkstile Gold) that have won awards from the beer-quaffers at CAMRA. Upstairs rooms are tastefully Tudor, and some have views onto Lorton Vale. There's also a newly converted self-catering cottage next door.

Winder Hall HOTEL ££
(☎01900-85107; www.winderhall.co.uk; Low Lorton; d £135-185; P) Supposedly the oldest building in Lorton, this charming family hotel has architectural elements dating back to Tudor and Jacobean times, and the house is full of creaky charm. It's surrounded by delightful grounds, and even has a Nordic sauna in the summer house. Rooms are old-fashioned but pretty, and the restaurant's a winner for Sunday lunch.

Wheatsheaf Inn PUB £
(☎01900-85199; www.wheatsheafinnlorton.co.uk; Low Lorton; mains £9.95-13.95) Lorton's much-loved local makes a friendly place for a pint, with Jennings ales on tap and of course an open fire to warm your toes by. Camping is available in summer.

❶ Getting There & Away

The 77/77A bus trundles four times daily from Keswick via Whinlatter, Lorton and Buttermere, before travelling over Honister Pass and tracking Derwentwater's west shore, with stops including Seatoller, Catbells and Portinscale, before terminating again at Keswick.

COCKERMOUTH

POP 8225

Plonked in flat fields beyond the northerly fells, the Georgian town of Cockermouth was hitherto best known as the birthplace of William Wordsworth and the home base of one of Cumbria's largest breweries, Jennings, but in November 2009 the town hit the national headlines after flash floods inundated the town centre, causing millions of pounds of damage and forcing the evacuation of many residents by RAF helicopter.

Ironically, Cockermouth's recent trials may actually have had a positive outcome. The town centre has been comprehensively

Cockermouth

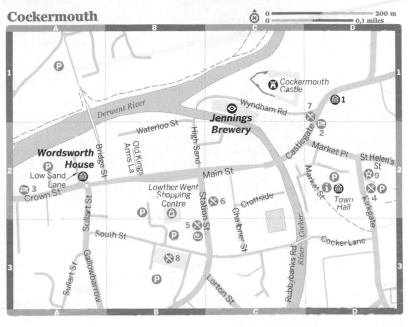

Cockermouth

renovated post-flood, and the only obvious signs of damage you'll see are the occasional empty shop or high-water mark halfway up a building. It's a friendly and attractive town, and makes a much quieter base for exploring the northern Lakes than nearby Keswick.

⊙ Sights

Wordsworth House HISTORIC HOUSE
(NT; www.wordsworthhouse.org.uk; Main St; adult/child £5.90/2.95; ⊙11am-4.30pm Mon-Sat mid-Mar–Oct) At the eastern end of Main St, this elegant Georgian mansion is the celebrated birthplace of all five Wordsworth children (William was the second to arrive, born on 7 April 1770, followed a year later by Dorothy). Built around 1745, the house has been painstakingly restored using authentic materials based on family accounts from the Wordsworth archive.

Happily, the house narrowly escaped devastation during the 2009 floods: the floodwaters stopped inches short of the ground floor, although the front wall and the back garden (mentioned in Wordsworth's epic biographical poem *The Prelude*) were seriously damaged. The front gates were literally torn from their posts: one was subsequently recovered, but the other's thought to be somewhere out in the Irish Sea.

Since the floods, the house has been dried out, dehumidified and given a fresh lick of paint, and it's now (almost) business as usual. Don't miss the flagstoned kitchen, the grand 1st-floor drawing room and the bedroom thought to have belonged to wee Willie himself. Costumed guides sometimes

THE COCKERMOUTH FLOODS

On the night of 19 to 20 November 2009, some of the heaviest rain ever seen in Britain fell across northwest England. An estimated 314mm (12.4in) fell in just over 24 hours, topping the previously held record of 279.4mm (11in) recorded in Martinstown, Dorset, in July 1955. Bridges, roads, walls and buildings across much of Cumbria were swept away as the region's rivers swelled and burst their banks, Cockermouth was by far the worst affected.

The town's position at the confluence of two major rivers, the Cocker and Derwent, meant that the floods rose higher and faster here than anywhere else: at their peak, the waters reached a height of 2.5m (8ft). Key bridges were destroyed, the town centre and Main St were flooded, and thousands of businesses and homes were left without electricity, water and other essential supplies – in some cases for several weeks.

Cockermouth has since rallied in impressive fashion, although it's thought that it could take several years before the town has fully recovered. Flood trail leaflets can be picked up at the tourist office; all proceeds go towards the ongoing reconstruction effort.

wander around the house for that extra bit of period authenticity. A small exhibition also details the story of the flood and the subsequent restoration work.

Jennings Brewery BREWERY
(www.jenningsbrewery.co.uk; adult/over 12yr £6/3) The town's historic brewer, in business since 1874, fared less well in the floods: they left the brewery's main site under around 5ft of water, and production was halted until mid-January 2010.

The brewery is now very much back in business, however, and you can take a guided tour around the site, including a tasting session in the Cooperage Bar: look out for core ales including Cocker Hoop and Sneck Lifter, as well as seasonal brews such as Laughing Gravy, Tizzie Wizzie and Soggy Bottom. Admirably, since the floods Jennings has donated 10p from every pint to the Cumbria Flood Recovery Fund.

Tours run twice daily at 11am and 2pm from March to October, although Sunday tours only run in July and August. See the website for other times.

Castlegate House Gallery ART GALLERY
(www.castlegatehouse.co.uk; Castlegate; ⊙10.30am-5pm Mon, Fri & Sat) This small Georgian gallery just uphill from the centre hosts regular exhibitions by artists from across northern England and Scotland. The rear garden is delightful and well worth a look.

🛏 Sleeping

TOP CHOICE Old Homestead B&B ££
(☎01900-822223; www.byresteads.co.uk; Byresteads Farm; s £60, d £80-100; P) This spankingly good farm conversion is 2 miles west of Cocker-

mouth. The farmhouse clutter has been cleared to leave light, airy rooms with just a few rustic touches for character (a wood rafter here, a stone tile or hardwood mirror there). Top choices are the Cruck rooms (with burnished leather sofas) and the Master's Room (with handcrafted four-poster bed), all with vistas across the working sheep farm. It's on the back roads between Cockermouth and Lorton; phone for directions.

Six Castlegate B&B ££
(☎01900-826749; www.sixcastlegate.co.uk; 6 Castlegate; s £42, d £65-75; ☏) Saved from the floods by its fortunate position on a slight rise at the far end of Main St, this Grade II–listed town house offers Georgian heritage with a modern twist. Feathery pillows, lofty ceilings and shiny showers make this Cockermouth's top B&B sleep.

Trout Hotel HOTEL £££
(☎01900-823591; www.trouthotel.co.uk; Crown St; d £154-224; P☏) A complete renovation has transformed this time-worn inn into a surprisingly swish sleep, with rooms decked out in contemporary fabrics and funky mosaic-tiled bathrooms with White Company bathstuffs. It's expensive for what it is, though, so you might prefer to stop in for some food – there's a choice of relaxed grub in the bar, al fresco eating in the Terrace, or gourmet in the Derwent.

Cockermouth YHA HOSTEL £
(☎0845 371 9313; cockermouth@yha.org.uk; Double Mills; dm £14.40-16.40; ⊙reception 7.30-10am & 5-10.30pm Apr-Oct) A simple hostel in a converted 17th-century watermill, 10 minutes' walk from town. Camping space and cycle storage are available.

✗ Eating & Drinking

Cockermouth has a big **Sainsbury's** (43 Station St; ⊙8am-8pm Mon-Sat, 10am-4pm Sun) and a **Co-op** (12 Station St; ⊙7am-10pm), both near the town centre.

Quince & Medlar
VEGETARIAN ££

(☎01900-823579; 13 Castlegate; www.quinceand medlar.co.uk; mains £12-16; ⊙dinner Tue-Sat; ☑)
This renowned veggie establishment was another fortunate flood escapee, and it's a good thing too: it serves some of the fanciest meat-free food you could ever hope to taste. Burnished panels, candles and squeaky leather chairs give it the atmosphere of a private gentlemen's club, and the imaginative food is a whole world away from nut roasts and veggie bangers.

Merienda
CAFE £

(7a Station St; mains £4-8; ⊙breakfast & lunch, to 10pm Fri) Savour light lunches and open-faced sandwiches at this sunny cafe-diner, with an admirable penchant for fair-trade goods, local produce and specialist coffees.

Bitter End
PUB ££

(☎01900-828993; www.bitterend.co.uk; Kirkgate; mains £9.25-11.50) This is one of Cumbria's finest pub-cum-microbreweries, with boutique beers including Cockermouth Pride, Lakeland Honey Beer and the fantastically named Cuddy Lugs. It's also got a great reputation for food, mainly generous grub along the lines of Cumberland sausage with champ and gravy, or Boston beef with rosemary potatoes. The bar is dressed in wood-panelled walls, low lighting and period etchings.

☆ Entertainment

Kirkgate Arts Centre
ARTS CENTRE

(www.thekirkgate.com; Kirkgate) Housed in a converted school, the town's art centre hosts occasional concerts and readings, as well as regular film screenings.

ℹ Information

Library (☎01900-325990; Main St; internet per ½hr £1; ⊙10am-7pm Mon & Wed, to 5pm Tue & Fri, to 12.30pm Thu, to 1pm Sat)
Tourist office (☎01900-822634; cockermouthtic@co-net.com; ⊙9.30am-5pm Mon-Sat, 10am-2pm Sun Jul & Aug, 9.30am-4.30pm Mon-Sat Apr-Jun, Sep & Oct, 9.30am-4pm Mon-Fri, 10-2pm Sat Nov-Mar) Inside the town hall.
www.cockermouth.org.uk Useful town guide.

ℹ Getting There & Away

The X4/X5 (13 Monday to Saturday, six on Sunday) travels from Workington via Cockermouth on to Keswick (35 minutes) and Penrith (1¼ hours).

BORROWDALE & BUTTERMERE

Ask many people for their quintessential image of a Lakeland dale, and chances are they'll come up with something close to Borrowdale and Buttermere. Backed by craggy fells, cloaked in bottle-green pastures and stitched together by mile upon mile of drystone walls, these twin valleys are like a vision of the Lake District in miniature.

In previous centuries this area was dominated by two local industries – farming and slate mining – and much of the original forest cover was cleared to make way for grazing cattle and agricultural land. These days the valleys are much favoured by walkers striking out for the fells around the lakes of Buttermere and Crummock Water, considered by Wainwright to be among the 'very best vintage' – and even if you're not here to walk, you'll find it hard not to fall for the views.

ℹ Getting There & Away

A single narrow road (the B5289) runs south from Keswick into Borrowdale, climbing across Honister Pass into Buttermere en route to Lorton and Cockermouth.

For details on the 77 and 78 buses, see p122.

Lodore, Grange & Rosthwaite

Beyond the southern end of Derwentwater, the B5289 traces the course of the River Derwent right into the heart of the Borrowdale Valley, meandering through a picturesque landscape of chimney-topped cottages, oak copses, green fields and fells.

◉ Sights & Activities

Lodore Falls
WATERFALL

At the southern end of Derwentwater, this famous waterfall was the subject of a splendidly verbose 1820 poem by Robert Southey, 'The Cataract of Lodore', but it dries up to a dribble in dry weather and is only worth a visit after a good spell of rain. (something

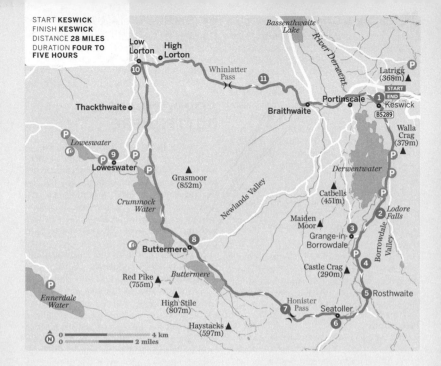

START **KESWICK**
FINISH **KESWICK**
DISTANCE **28 MILES**
DURATION **FOUR TO FIVE HOURS**

Driving Tour
Borrowdale & Buttermere

❯ This is one of the Lakes' most beautiful road trips, taking in the unspoilt scenery of the Borrowdale, Buttermere and Lorton Valleys. The roads are good, although they're narrow and winding, and there's a steep ascent up Honister Pass.

Pick up some trip supplies in ❶ **Keswick**, then head along the B5289 into the Borrowdale Valley. First stop is ❷ **Lodore Falls**, followed by a detour to the little hamlet of ❸ **Grange-in-Borrowdale**. If your legs are feeling lively the village is a great place from which to tackle Castle Crag, one of Borrowdale's best-known hills.

Otherwise carry on to the huge boulder known as the ❹ **Bowder Stone**, shifted into position by the mighty glacier which carved out the Borrowdale Valley. Pootle on to ❺ **Rosthwaite** for tea and cake at the Flock-In Tea-Room, or continue to ❻ **Seatoller** for lunch at the Yew Tree Inn.

In the afternoon, tackle the steep crawl up to ❼ **Honister Pass**, where you can pick up some slate souvenirs or take an underground mine tour. From here, the road swings and veers down into the beautiful valley of ❽ **Buttermere**. Spot the zigzag peaks of High Stile, Haystacks and Red Pike looming on your left-hand side over the lake, stop off for a drink at the Fish Hotel, and remember to pay your respects to Wainwright inside St James' Church.

Continue along the shore of Crummock Water past ❾ **Loweswater**, where you could make an optional but very worthwhile detour via the excellent Kirkstile Inn. From nearby ❿ **Low Lorton**, a right-hand turn carries you over Whinlatter Pass to ⓫ **Whinlatter Forest Park**. The forest park makes a good spot for a late-afternoon stop; there's a pleasant cafe at the visitor centre, as well as displays on the local red squirrel and osprey populations.

From Whinlatter, it's a downhill drive to the A66 junction at Braithwaite back to Keswick.

Borrowdale gets plenty of, thankfully). The falls are actually in the grounds of the Lodore Hotel; there's an honesty box for donations.

Bowder Stone LANDMARK

South of Lodore, the road winds past the small hamlet of Grange-in-Borrowdale into the **Jaws of Borrowdale**, a dramatic valley hollowed out by a gigantic glacier during the last ice age. A mile further south from Grange is the Bowder Stone, a house-sized lump of rock weighing 1870 tons, thought to have been dumped here by the glacier when it melted at the end. A set of steep wooden stairs lets you climb up to the top and look out across the valley.

There's a small National Trust car park near the stone.

Platty+ BOATING

(②017687-76572; www.plattyplus.co.uk) Near the Lodore landing jetty, you can get out onto the lake by hiring kayaks, canoes and dinghies. If you've got a few friends, you can even rent a Chinese dragon boat or a Viking longboat for a day.

Castle Crag WALKING

Borrowdale has several fells to conquer, but one of the most spectacular also happens to be one of the smallest. Little Castle Crag (290m/985ft), half a mile south of Grange, was once used as a stone quarry, and its pockmarked top now provides amazingly good views across the valley.

The easiest starting point is the double-arched footbridge in Grange. Take the path south past Hollows Farm campsite and follow signs to the base of the crag. It's a short but very steep walk up, with one section near the summit that zigzags up a mass of shattered slate: take care here, as the stone is very slippery underfoot. The old quarry is full of upstanding stones arranged by previous hikers, but the best views are from the grassy plateau just above.

On the way back, you can take an alternative path east across fields to the little village of **Rosthwaite**, which marks the starting point for the **Borrowdale Fell Race**, usually held on the first Saturday in August.

🛏 Sleeping & Eating

Hotels in Borrowdale tend to be pricey, so you're better off with B&Bs if you're on a budget.

Hazel Bank HOTEL £££

(②017687-77248; www.hazelbankhotel.co.uk; Rosthwaite; r £160-192; P) A neo-Gothic manor languishing in private grounds, reached via its own humpbacked bridge. Rooms ooze country refinement: Bowfell glitters in green and gold, while Great Gable boasts a king-sized four-poster that Henry VIII would have envied. Afternoon tea is served on the lawn in view of the Borrowdale fells.

Yew Tree Farm & Flock-In Tea-Room R&B, CAFE ££

(②017687-77675; www.borrowdaleherdwick.co.uk; Rosthwaite; d £75; P) Not to be confused with the *other* Yew Tree Farm near Coniston, this cute-as-a-button farmhouse is a sanctuary of chintz. Floral motifs snuggle under low ceilings; bathrooms are titchy, and there are no TVs, so you'll have to make do with the views. Even if you're not staying, don't miss afternoon tea at the Flock-In Tea-Room across the lane, where you can scoff some of Borrowdale's best jam sponges and homemade scones.

Hollows Farm CAMPGROUND £

(②017687-77298; www.hollowsfarm.co.uk; Grange; adult/child £6/3; P) A ravishing little campsite near Grange, with a choice of fields offering views of open fells or sheltered woodland. It's short on luxuries (cold water sinks, basic loo block) but the setting is superb. B&B is offered in the farmhouse (doubles £56 to £64)

Borrowdale Gates HOTEL £££

(②017687-77204; www.borrowdale-gates.com; Grange; d £190 250; P🌐) Traditional hotel set in 2-acre grounds near Grange, with a swish silver-service restaurant and rooms that are looking much more up-to-date after a recent revamp.

Borrowdale YHA HOSTEL £

(②0870 770 5706; borrowdale@yha.org.uk; Longthwaite; dm £14.40-18.40; ☺reception 7.30am-10pm) Modern cedar-clad hostel, set back from the Rosthwaite road and heavily geared towards outdoorsy types. It's popular with activity groups, so book ahead.

Grange Bridge Cottage CAFE £

(Grange; teas & lunches £3-8; ☺10am-5pm) Another sweet cafe snuggled by the river in Grange, serving up a tempting assortment of fresh soups, chunky cakes and hot pies to its loyal clientele of hikers and motor-tourers. Take your pick from tables inside the cottage or the cute riverside garden.

ASHNESS BRIDGE & WATENDLATH

About 2½ miles south of Keswick, a minor road leads sharply away from the east side of Derwentwater towards the National Trust–owned tarn of Watendlath, a famously picturesque stretch of water cradled in a photogenic bowl of green fells. En route, the single-lane road leads across Ashness Bridge, without doubt one of the most photographed packhorse bridges in the Lake District, and the stirring lookout at Surprise View, which offers a panoramic vista across the fields, farms and cottages of Borrowdale.

There's a small car park and tearoom at Watendlath, but the road to the tarn is very narrow, and driving is more trouble than it's worth in summer. Save it for a spring or autumn evening, or better still hike up the steep path from Rosthwaite in Borrowdale, which begins near the Hazel Bank Hotel.

Scafell Hotel   PUB £
(☎017687-77208; www.scafell.co.uk; Rosthwaite; ℗) This old coaching inn is popular with walkers looking for a pint of Theakston's and some unfussy grub. It's also the traditional start point for the Borrowdale Fell Race: you can see a list of previous winners behind the bar.

Stonethwaite, Seatoller & Seathwaite

Beyond Rosthwaite, the road trundles on past a cluster of little hamlets, utterly dwarfed by the surrounding fells that dominate the skyline on every side.

First port of call is Stonethwaite, little more than a gaggle of cottages huddled along a country track, which marks the beginning of the remote fell-walking country around the Langstrath Valley. A mile further on is tiny Seatoller, huddled beneath the arduous climb up to Honister Pass, which originally grew up as a village to house workers employed in the nearby slate mines.

From Seatoller, a single-track lane leads west to Seathwaite, which holds the dubious honour of being the wettest inhabited place in Britain – an average of 140in of rain falls in the village every year, and during the 2009 floods the village notched up over 12in in 24 hours – the highest amount since records began.

There is a positive note to this precipitation, however; **Taylor Ghyll Force** is one of the Lakes' most impressive waterfalls, tumbling down 82ft through a series of cascades about a mile's walk from Seathwaite village.

For hardcore walkers, Seathwaite is also the start point for alternative routes up to Great Gable, Pillar and Scafell Pike. The lane is often lined with bumper-to-bumper cars on sunny days, so you might find it easiest to park at the small NT car park in Seatoller.

🛏 Sleeping & Eating

Langstrath Inn   PUB, B&B ££
(☎017687-77239; www.thelangstrath.com; Stonethwaite; d £94-110; ◷closed Sun & Mon; ℗🗟) Stonethwaite's solitary inn is a find: behind its sturdy whitewashed exterior you'll discover smart, stripped-back rooms in sleek whites and neutral tones, offset by original beams, slate-tiled bathrooms and ethnic knick-knacks. Downstairs in the snug bar, the excellent food (mains £10.95 to £15.95) comes from local suppliers (Yew Tree lamb, Newlands beef) and there's heaps of stout stone character.

Seatoller House   B&B ££
(☎017687-77218; www.seatollerhouse.co.uk; Seatoller; s £60, d £90-120; ℗) All the rooms at this Potteresque hidey-hole have their own eccentricities – ground-floor Badger has a hearth and garden views, Rabbit has pine wardrobes and a window overlooking Glaramara, and Osprey boasts rafters and skylight. The cottage sits in a tiny terrace in Seatoller.

Seatoller Farm   CAMPGROUND £
(☎017687-77232; www.seatollerfarm.co.uk; Seatoller; camping adult/child £6/3, s £46-60, d £54-70; ℗) Rolling campsite with a choice of fields (riverside or woodside) on a 500-year-old farm in Seatoller. It feels very secluded, and the pitches are nicely spread out, with views of fells in all directions. The site can get damp in wet weather – bring some bug spray to deter the midges. B&B rooms are available in the farmhouse if the weather turns intolerable, or you could hire a yurt.

Yew Tree Inn
CAFE £

(Seatoller; mains £8-18; ⊙10am-6pm) Now run by the owners of Honister Slate Mine, this attractive cafe is lodged inside an ancient cottage next to Seatoller House (the sign above the door dates from 1628). Inside, farm tools and an old wheelbarrow dangle from the ceiling, and a tempting line-up of paninis, jacket spuds, coffees and cakes are served up at the counter. If the weather's sunny, take your goods out to the dinky back garden.

Honister Pass

From Seatoller, the road crawls up the switch-backing road to the bleak, wind-lashed Honister Pass. This was once one of the most productive quarrying areas in the Lake District, and still produces much of the region's grey-green slate, but economic uncertainties meant the site was teetering on the verge of financial collapse when local entrepreneur Mark Weir took it over in 1997.

Over the next 14 years, Weir transformed the mine into one of the Lake District's great success stories, opening the underground chambers up for guided tours, reinvigorating the slate-mining business

and even adding the UK's first 'Via Ferrata' (although his controversial plan to place a zip line on the summit of nearby Fleetwith Pike was scuppered by local opposition). Tragically, Weir was killed in a helicopter crash during a routine flight near Honister in March 2011.

⊙ Sights & Activities

The large car park at Honister costs £5 per day; the cost is refunded if you take a mine tour or spend over £10 in the slate shop.

Honister Slate Mine   UNDERGROUND TOUR
(☑017687-77230;   www.honister-slate-mine.co
.uk, adult/child £9.95/4.95; ⊙tours 10.30am, 12.30pm & 3.30pm Mar-Oct) You can take a tour around three of the original mines, including the Kimberley and Honister; a tour into the 'Cathedral' mine runs on Friday by request (£19.75), but you'll need eight people. Whichever tour you choose, it's cold and wet underground, so come suitably dressed.

Via Ferrata   ROCK CLIMBING
(adult/under   16yr/16-18yr   £19.50/9.50/lb).
Modelled on the century-old routes across the Italian Dolomites, this vertiginous clamber follows the cliff trail once used by

---

FELL RUNNING

Forget marathons, triathlons and pentathlons – the ultimate British endurance sport has to be fell running, a muscle-shredding cross-country race that makes the Iron Man Challenge look like child's play.

The rules are simple – competitors battle it out over a series of fells in a bid for the fastest time – but give little idea of the truly gruelling nature of the sport. Races take place in all weathers and traverse some of Lakeland's most challenging fells. Courses usually aren't marked, so competitors are expected to navigate the best route for themselves. Needless to say, broken limbs and sprained ankles are par for the course, and only the toughest competitors make it to the finish line.

Wasdale, Ennerdale and Borrowdale all hold their own annual fell races, but the most famous event is the Bob Graham Round (BGR), a gruelling challenge that entails climbing 42 peaks in under 24 hours, covering over 40 miles and 28,500ft of ascent en route. The event is named after Bob Graham, a local gardener and guesthouse owner, who first completed the 'round' in 1932. The current record for the BGR is held by legendary fell runner Billy Bland, who completed the circuit in a mindblowing 13 hours and 53 minutes in 1982.

As if the standard BGR wasn't enough, the challenge has been extended by some runners to see how many summits they can notch up in the allotted time. The current record is held by Mark Hartell, who conquered 77 summits in 1997, an achievement so far unmatched by any other runner. The women's record is held by Anne Stentiford, who managed 62 peaks in 1994.

For more information on the sport, see the website for the official Fell Runners Association at www.fellrunner.org.uk, or pick up a copy of Richard Askwith's excellent account of his time as a fell runner, *Feet in the Clouds: A Tale of Fell-Running and Obsession*.

the Honister slate miners using a system of fixed ropes and iron ladders. It's exhilarating and great fun, but unsurprisingly you'll definitely need a head for heights.

🛏 Sleeping

Honister Hause YHA HOSTEL £
(☎0870 770 5870; Seatoller; dm £16.40-20.40; ☺daily Easter-Oct, Sat & Sun Nov) Next to Honister, these former quarry-workers' lodgings have been turned into another bare-bones walkers' hostel, with functional cooking facilities and a lounge that doubles as a drying room.

Buttermere & Crummock Water

Up and over the pass, the road drops sharply into the deep bowl of Buttermere, gouged out by a steamroller glacier and backed by a string of emerald-green hills. The valley's twin lakes, Buttermere and Crummock Water, were once joined, but became separated by glacial silt and rockfall; the little village of Buttermere sits halfway between the two, and provides a wonderfully cosy base for exploring the rest of the valley.

Buttermere's jagged skyline occupies a special place in the hearts of many hill walkers, since it was one of Wainwright's favourite walking destinations – and also marks his last resting place. After his death in 1991, as requested in his will, his ashes were carried to the top of **Haystacks** (597m/1958ft) by his second wife Betty, and scattered near the lonely shores of Innominate Tarn. A window plaque inside **St James' Church**, in Buttermere village, commemorates the great man and looks directly out over the summit of his favourite fell.

🏃 Activities

We've detailed the walk up Haystacks, but if you'd like to extend the walk, you can include the mountain in a fantastic circuit around the valley's main fells.

The route starts in Buttermere, crosses the land bridge between Buttermere and Crummock Water and climbs up to **Scale Force**, at 170ft one of Lake District's highest waterfalls. It then dips and climbs over the summits of **Red Pike** (755m/2479ft), **High Stile** (807m/2644ft) and **High Crag** (744m/2443ft) en route to Haystacks, descending via the steep trail into Warnscale Bottom. All told it's a circuit of around 8.5 miles, lasting around seven hours.

🛏 Sleeping & Eating

Wood House B&B ££
(☎017687-70208; www.wdhse.co.uk; Buttermere; d £100; P) B&Bs are rare in Buttermere, which makes this prim and proper retreat even more of a find. Rooms are effortlessly elegant, decked out in restrained tones of fawn and cream; most have Buttermere views, and there's fresh-baked bread and Woodall's bacon on the breakfast table. The house even has artistic cachet – it featured in a 1798 landscape by JMW Turner – but it might be a bit too olde-worlde for some.

Buttermere YHA HOSTEL £
(☎0870 770 5736; buttermere@yha.org.uk; dm £16.40-22.40; ☺reception 8.30-10am & 5.30-10.30pm; P) Even in the YHA's stellar line-up of hostels, Buttermere still manages to impress. It's perched in a perfect position on the Honister–Buttermere road: the best rooms look out across the lake, and the decor is smart, colourful and surprisingly modern. There's a great cafe-kitchen, and

---

THE MAID OF BUTTERMERE

The Fish Inn is famous as the home of the legendary beauty Mary Robinson, the so-called Maid of Buttermere. After Joseph Palmer described her beauty in *A Fortnight's Ramble in the Lake District* in 1792, visitors were soon trekking from across the Lakes to see if Mary's beauty lived up to its reputation. Wordsworth was impressed, although the rakish Coleridge was apparently less dazzled.

Mary's fame unfortunately drew an unwelcome admirer in the shape of John Hatfield, an unscrupulous con man who passed himself off as an army colonel and MP in order to win her hand in marriage; within a year Hatfield had been exposed as a bankrupt and a bigamist, and was sentenced to death by hanging.

Despite her terribly public embarrassment, Mary soldiered on and married a more reliable farmer-type from Caldbeck. Together they ran the inn until Mary's death in 1837. The tale is retold in Melvyn Bragg's novel *The Maid of Buttermere*.

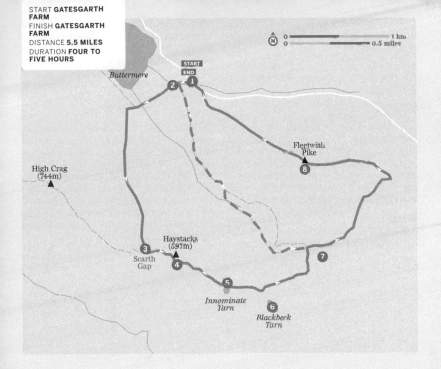

Buttermere

START END ❶

❷

Fleetwith Pike ❽

High Crag (744m)

Haystacks (597m)

❸ Scarth Gap

❹

❺

❼

Innominate Tarn

❻

Blackbeck Tarn

Hiking Tour
Haystacks

❭ 'For a man trying to get a persistent worry out of his mind, the top of Haystacks is a wonderful cure.' So said AW in Book 7 of his *Pictorial Guides*, and if anywhere sums up what Wainwright loved about the Lakeland fells, it's Haystacks. This route follows Wainwright's favourite ascent from Gatesgarth, and descends via the dramatic arête of Fleetwith Pike. As always, an OS map will come in handy as the paths can be confusing.

Park at ❶ **Gatesgarth Farm** (or catch the 77A bus from Buttermere). Head southwest across ❷ **Peggy's Bridge**, and follow the path as it winds up to the saddle of ❸ **Scarth Gap**, a good place for a breather before you tackle the rocky buttress of Haystacks itself.

The climb to the summit is steep but not too testing, although there are a few bits where you'll need hands as well as feet. After 20 minutes you'll reach the ❹ **summit**, with its twin cairns and cluster of little pools. The panorama from the top is grand, stretching northwest across Buttermere,

west into Ennerdale and south towards Great Gable.

From here, the path meanders eastwards past two high tarns: ❺ **Innominate Tarn**, where Wainwright's ashes were scattered in 1991, and the reedy pool of ❻ **Blackbeck Tarn**. As you descend, you'll pass a left-hand path into Warnscale Bottom, an easy descent if you don't feel like tackling Fleetwith Pike.

Otherwise, descend towards the slate piles of ❼ **Dubs Quarry**, and follow the quarry roads before cutting west under Honister Crag. From here. the path leads straight to the summit cairn of ❽ **Fleetwith Pike**, with a mind-blowing prospect due west across Buttermere and Crummock Water.

From the top, a clear path leads steeply down the spine of the pike; it's not too difficult, but it is steep and rubbly in places, so take care. Eventually the path levels out onto grassy slopes and descends back to Gatesgarth.

plenty of quads and six-bed dorms. The only drawback is the shortage of private rooms, but it's a quibble.

Syke Farm CAMPGROUND **£**
(☑017687-70222; Buttermere; adult/child £7/3, cheaper rates Nov-Feb) Set on a lumpy riverside site not far from the Buttermere pubs, Syke Farm is undeniably simple, but you'll wake up to views of Red Pike, High Stile and Haystacks. The site is quite small and feels cramped when it's busy; come in the shoulder months and things are a lot more comfortable. Check-in at the farm shop in the village first, and don't forget to sample some of the homemade ice cream.

Bridge Hotel HOTEL **£££**
(☑017687-70252; www.bridge-hotel.com; Buttermere; r £130-150; ℗) The better of Buttermere's brace of inns is (as its name suggests) right beside the village bridge. Rooms are classy but frilly, and there are no tellies due to the dodgy signal. Downstairs, there's a beamed bar and a table d'hôte restaurant serving braised venison, slow-roasted lamb and the valley's best Sunday lunch.

Fish Inn PUB **£**
(☑017687-70253; www.fishinnbuttermere.co.uk; mains £6.50-12.50; ℗) The village's second pub is short on decorative dazzle, but the convivial bar is a friendly place to tuck into filling plates of Crummock trout and Cumbrian tatie pot, washed down with that essential pint of ale. There's a choice of four different brewers, including beers from Bitter End and the Hesket Newmarket Brewery.

Ullswater

Best Places to Eat

» George and Dragon (p147)
» Rampsbeck Country Hotel (p141)
» Howtown Hotel (p146)
» Le Mardale (p148)
» Sharrow Bay (p141)

Best Places to Stay

» Lowthwaite Farm (p143)
» Boathouse at Knotts End (p145)
» Howtown Hotel (p146)
» Beckfoot Country House (p148)
» Haweswater Hotel (p148)

Why Go?

Second only in stature to Windermere, Ullswater cuts a regal 8-mile sweep through the eastern fells. Gouged out by a long-extinct glacier, it's arguably one of the most dramatic of the valleys, with each shore flanked by serrated summits, including the unmistakeable razor ridges of Helvellyn, England's third-highest mountain.

It's a great lake for cruising, with a fine fleet of old 'steamers' plying the waters between the small villages of Pooley Bridge, Glenridding and Patterdale. Overlooking the lake are the woodland parks of Gowbarrow and Glencoyne, whose springtime daffodil displays were canonised by Wordsworth in one of his best-loved poems. And while the west side of the lake can feel jammed in summer, you can usually find solitude in the little-visited valleys on the eastern side, or by detouring away from the lake to the rolling parkland of the Lowther estate and the wild valley of Haweswater out to the southeast.

When to Go

As elsewhere in the Lake District, Ullswater isn't at its best in the height of the summer crush. Much better to visit early or late in the season, especially if you can time your visit with the local walking festival, held between the end of September and the start of October, which is also one of the best seasons to climb the summit of Helvellyn. Look out for a series of festivals throughout the year at Dalemain, including a deliciously eccentric Marmalade Festival in February.

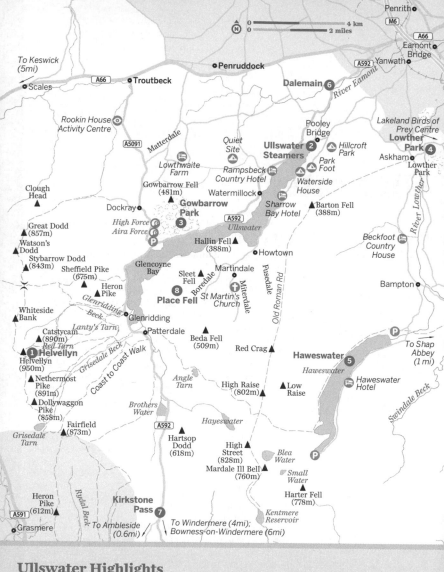

To Keswick (5mi)

Scales

Troutbeck

A66

Penrith

M6

A66

Eamont Bridge

Yanwath

A592

Penruddock

Dalemain ⑥

River Eamont

Rookin House Activity Centre

A5091

Matterdale

Pooley Bridge

Lakeland Birds of Prey Centre

Lowther Park ④

Quiet Site

Ullswater Steamers ②

Hillcroft Park

Askham

Lowther Park

Lowthwaite Farm

Rampsbeck Country Hotel

Park Foot

Gowbarrow Fell (481m)

Waterside House

Clough Head

Great Dodd (857m)

Dockray

Gowbarrow Park ③

Watermillock

Sharrow Bay Hotel

Barton Fell (388m)

Beckfoot Country House

River Lowther

Watson's Dodd

Stybarrow Dodd (843m)

High Force
Aira Force

A592

Ullswater

Hallin Fell (388m)

Howtown

Bampton

Sheffield Pike (675m)

Heron Pike

Glencoyne Bay

Sleet Fell

Martindale

Whiteside Bank

Glenridding Beck

Place Fell ⑧

St Martin's Church

Mirkdale

Old Roman Rd

Catstycam (890m)

Red Tarn

Glenridding

Lanty's Tarn

Patterdale

Beda Fell (509m)

Red Crag

Haweswater

P

To Shap Abbey (1 mi)

Helvellyn ①

Helvellyn (950m)

Nethermost Pike (891m)

Coast to Coast Walk

Grisedale Beck

Haweswater ⑤

Haweswater Hotel

Swindale Beck

Dollywaggon Pike (858m)

Angle Tarn

High Raise (802m)

Low Raise

Fairfield (873m)

Brothers Water

Hayeswater

Grisedale Tarn

A592

Hartsop Dodd (618m)

High Street (828m)

Blea Water

Heron Pike (612m)

A591

Rydal Beck

Kirkstone Pass ⑦

To Ambleside (0.6mi)

Mardale Ill Bell (760m)

Small Water

Harter Fell (778m)

Kentmere Reservoir

To Windermere (4mi);
Bowness-on-Windermere (6mi)

Grasmere

N

0   4 km
0   2 miles

Ullswater Highlights

① Tame your nerves on the tightrope walk along Striding Edge to **Helvellyn** (p144)

② Hop aboard one of Ullswater's historic **'steamers'** (p139)

③ Wander among the daffodils of **Gowbarrow Park** (p141)

④ See a restoration work-in-progress at **Lowther Park** (p147)

⑤ Scan the skies above **Haweswater** (p147) for one of England's last golden eagles

⑥ Soak up the country-house splendour of **Dalemain** (p139)

⑦ Drive over Lakeland's highest stretch of road at **Kirkstone Pass** (p146)

⑧ Leave the crowds well behind on the summit of **Place Fell** (p143)

ULLSWATER & AROUND

There's a real sense of grandeur as you drive along the western side of Ullswater, glimpsing flashes of the fell-tops and the lakeshore through a cover of hedgerows and overhanging trees. The lake has both scale and scenery in its favour: dramatically framed by lofty hills including Place Fell, Hallin Fell, Helvellyn and the Dodds, it has one of the most naturally impressive settings in the national park.

The two-lane A592 tracks the lake's northern shore, passing through the hamlets of Pooley Bridge, Glenridding and Patterdale. A second minor road runs along the southern shore from Pooley Bridge to tiny Howtown, where it dead-ends.

Dalemain

Driving southwest along the A592 road from Penrith, you can't miss the striking salmon-pink facade of Dalemain (www.dalemain .com; adult/under 16yr £7.50/free, gardens only £3; ◎11.15am-4pm mid-Mar–Sep, closes 1hr earlier in Oct, gardens open Feb-Dec), a mile from Ullswater's northern tip.

With a name deriving from the Old Norse for 'manor in the valley', this elegant country estate traces its roots back to the reign of Henry II. The Georgian facade was constructed during the mid-18th century, but behind its orderly frontage are the remnants of a 12th-century pele tower and an Elizabethan manor.

Inside it's the picture of an English country house – half *Gosford Park* set, half three-dimensional *Cluedo* board, with a bewildering maze of passages, spiralling staircases and interconnecting rooms. Since 1679 the house has been owned by the Hasell dynasty; family photos and heirlooms are dotted around among the antiques, Chippendale furniture and priceless oil portraits. Highlights include the Chinese Room, with its handmade oriental wallpaper, the Tudor Fretwork Room, with its oak panelling and ornate plaster ceiling, and the fascinating servants' quarters. Tea is served in the medieval Great Hall.

Outside, the grounds feature a Tudor knot garden and a wonderful rose walk. The 16th-century Great Barn houses two small agricultural museums, while in the base of the Norman pele tower is a museum dedicated to the Westmorland and Cumberland Yeomanry regiment, founded in 1819 and disbanded shortly after WWI.

The house hosts lots of festivals and events throughout the year, including country shows, tractor meets, classic car displays and a very British Marmalade Festival.

Guided tours run throughout the day starting at 11.15am, or you can wander around on your own after 11.45am until the house closes at 4pm (3pm in October). The lovely tea room opens slightly earlier and later.

Pooley Bridge

Nestled at the head of the lake alongside the babbling River Eamont, the tiny hamlet of Pooley Bridge is little more than a gaggle of pubs, cottages and teashops. The main reason to stop here is to climb aboard one of the **Ullswater 'Steamers'** (www.ullswater -steamers.co.uk), which putter out for the southern reaches of the lake, stopping at Howtown and Glenridding.

The company's oldest vessels have been in service on Ullswater for over a century: *Lady of the Lake* was launched in 1877, followed by *Raven* in 1889. They were recently joined by two new boats, the *Lady Dorothy* (transported from Guernsey in 2001) and the *Totnes Castle* (launched in 2007 as the *Lady Wakefield*). The boats would originally have been steam-powered and still boast their original chimneys, though they're now run on diesel.

Up to 11 daily ferries run in summer, dropping to three or four in winter. Return fares are available from Pooley Bridge to Howtown (adult/child £9.30/4.60) or Glenridding (adult/child £8/4), or you could by a Round the Lakes Pass (£12.70/6.35), allowing a day's unlimited travel.

Bikes and dogs can be carried depending on space, and wheelchair access is usually possible (although the height of the lake sometimes causes problems, so it's worth ringing ahead).

Located in Watermillock, **Distant Horizons** (✆017684-86465; www.distant-horizons .co.uk; Ullswater) provides guided climbing, classic scrambles, canyoning and winter navigation.

🛏 Sleeping & Eating

The choice around the northern end of the lake is mainly limited to pricey hotels or bargain-basement campsites. For a quick

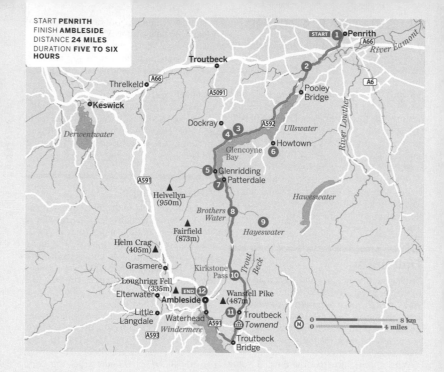

Driving Tour
Around Ullswater

❯ This scenic spin takes in the best bits of the Ullswater Valley, with a trip across the lake thrown in for good measure.

Kick the day off in ❶ **Penrith**, with an early-morning detour to the stately home of ❷ **Dalemain**. Then it's west along the A592, regularly cited as one of Britain's top 10 drives; the road swings and swerves all the way along the lake shore of Ullswater, offering sweeping views over the lake and the cloud-covered fells to the east.

Stop off at ❸ **Gowbarrow Park** and stretch your legs with a woodland stroll up to ❹ **Aira Force**, followed by a ploughman's lunch and a pint at the homely Royal inn in Dockray.

After lunch, drive on into ❺ **Glenridding** and indulge in a leisurely afternoon cruise across the lake on one of the Ullswater 'Steamers'. It's well worth stopping off for tea or a pint at the ❻ **Howtown Hotel** on the opposite side of the lake, followed perhaps by a walk to the top of Hallin Fell for end-to-end lake views.

The most spectacular stretch of driving is saved for last. From Glenridding, the road rolls past ❼ **Patterdale** and to the small lakes of ❽ **Brothers Water** and ❾ **Hayeswater**, then climbs spectacularly to the top of ❿ **Kirkstone Pass**, the highest road pass in the Lake District. There's a handy car park near the summit of the pass from where you'll have a sweeping view over the surrounding fells.

Once you've taken your snaps and admired the views, hop back in the motor for the downhill section to ⓫ **Troubeck**. It's worth stopping at the historic yeoman's farmhouse of Townend, now owned by the National Trust, and the village's oldest inn, the Mortal Man.

The road trip ends in the busy town of ⓬ **Ambleside**, where you can treat yourself to a gourmet supper at either the Glass House or veggie-friendly Fellini's.

evening meal, the pubs in Pooley Bridge are handy if unexciting.

Rampsbeck Country Hotel HOTEL £££
(017684-86442; www.rampsbeck.co.uk; Watermillock; s £145-300; P) This family-run hotel is surrounded by striped lawns and lush gardens, and boasts one of the best lakeside spots on Ullswater. It offers traditional service from start to finish: rich fabrics and half-tester beds in the rooms, afternoon tea served on the lawn, and four-course dinner service (£55) in the grand dining room, from where Ullswater views unfold through floor-to-ceiling windows.

Sharrow Bay HOTEL £££
(017684-86301; www.sharrowbay.co.uk; d £270-420; P🖥) This legendary Lakeland getaway is one of England's most famous country hotels, and there are still few places to top it. It's now owned by the Relais & Chateaux Group, but the feel is as exclusive as ever: gilded mirrors, antique armchairs and ornate chandeliers in the public rooms, matched by a swash of swags, ruches and canopied beds in the over-the-top boudoirs. Of course, there's a Michelin-rated restaurant, plus a private jetty and boathouse too.

Ullswater View B&B ££
(017684-86286; www.theullswaterview.co.uk; Watermillock; d £72-100; P🖥) The name's a giveaway – all the rooms at this modernised stone house in Watermillock have a lake outlook, and a thoughtful refurbishment has spruced up the decor with beige-tiled bathrooms, fancy sinks and flat-screen TVs.

Waterside House CAMPGROUND £
(017684-86332; www.watersidefarm-campsite .co.uk; sites for 2 adults, tent & car £14-24; ⊙Mar-Oct) Lovely lakeside camping, with separate fields for general and family campers, and electric hook-ups for campervans and caravans. Canoes, row boats and 'sea cycles' are available for hire if you feel like getting out on the water.

Hillcroft Park CAMPGROUND £
(017684-86363; Roe Head Lane; sites £12-20; ⊙Mar-Oct) The handiest campsite for Pooley Bridge, on a hilly plot five minutes' walk from the village. There's a teeny on-site shop, plus a few camping pods for hire and some electric hook-ups. The site gets very busy due to its proximity to Pooley Bridge.

Park Foot CAMPGROUND £
(017684-86309; www.parkfootullswater.co.uk; Howtown Rd; sites for 2 adults, tent & car £14-28; ⊙Mar-early Nov) Further south on the Howtown road, this site is best for families, with tennis courts, bike hire, pony trekking and an adventure playground. Ask for the Aikbeck Field if you want to be near the lake. Electric hook-ups cost £4 extra.

Sun Inn PUB ££
(017684-86205; www.suninnpooleybridge.co .uk; mains £5-12) The pick of Pooley Bridge's pubs is a Jennings establishment, with a carte du jour of chicken-and-ham pies and haddock lasagnes, a pleasant beer garden and a play-fort to keep the youngsters entertained. Rooms (£75 to £80) are frill-heavy and small, but will do at a pinch.

ⓘ Getting There & Away

There are two car parks in Pooley Bridge (one on either side of the bridge), but they fill up early in summer.

Bus 108 (six daily, four on Sunday) travels from Penrith via Pooley Bridge, Glenridding and Patterdale.

Gowbarrow Park & Aira Force

Southwest of Pooley Bridge, the A592 ducks and dives along Ullswater's western shore. After 5 miles you'll reach the small NT car park at Gowbarrow Park, founded by the Howard family (owners of nearby Greystoke Castle) as a hunting park and leisure garden, but now run by the National Trust.

The car park marks the start of the half-hour stroll to one of the most famous waterfalls in the Lake District, Aira Force. The 230ft cascade makes for a furious sight after heavy rain, with its clashing waters tumbling down into a densely wooded ravine lined with spruce, fir, pine and cedar. Red squirrels are frequent visitors to the woods around the falls, so keep your eyes peeled. If the inevitable crowds around the falls are a little too much, you can continue your walk along the wooded trail to **High Force**, or strike out for the summit of Gowbarrow Fell (481m/1578ft).

The pleasant country pub the **Royal** (017684-82356; Dockray; mains £8-14), makes an ideal place for a pint and a bacon butty before tackling the return walk.

THE ULLSWATER DAFFODILS

Just south of Gowbarrow Park is the little inlet of **Glencoyne Bay**, famous as the inspiration for one of Wordsworth's most celebrated poems. During a springtime walk on 15 April 1802, Dorothy and William stumbled across a sprightly stand of daffodils swaying in the breeze, a sight which inspired perhaps the most quoted lines in English poetry:

> I wandered lonely as a cloud
> That floats on high o'er vales and hills
> When all at once I saw a crowd,
> A host, of golden daffodils;
> Beside the lake, beneath the trees,
> Fluttering and dancing in the breeze.

Interestingly, William didn't actually complete his poem until two years later in 1804, and many of its famous phrases seem to have been inspired as much by his sister's journal as by his own recollections. In her diary she recalls how the daffodils 'rested their heads upon these stones as on a pillow for weariness and the rest tossed and reeled and danced and seemed as if they verily laughed with the wind that blew upon them from over the lake, they looked so gay ever glancing ever changing'.

Needless to say, springtime is the best time to visit if you want to see the blooms, but try to resist the urge to pick them unless you fancy a slap on the wrist from an NPA warden.

Glenridding & Patterdale

Clustered around the lake's southern reaches, 3 miles south of Gowbarrow, the side-by-side hamlets of Glenridding and Patterdale are backed by some of the most striking mountain scenery anywhere in Lakeland.

High in the western hills loom the spectres of Great Dodd, Stybarrow Dodd, Raise, Nethermost Pike and Dollywaggon Pike, connected by the high point of Helvellyn and its twin ridge walks via Striding Edge and Swirral Edge. Thousands of plucky hikers descend on the villages every year to tackle the trails and admire the Lakeland scenery, but apart from the views and the lake there's not much to keep non-walkers entertained.

⊙ Sights & Activities

Originally Glenridding was established as a mining settlement to tap the lead reserves at nearby Greenside Mine. Power was provided by several waterwheels along the beck, and much later by a series of dams at High Dam and Keppel Cove, which infamously burst its banks in 1927 causing widespread devastation in the valley below.

The lead mines closed down in the mid-1960s and Glenridding has since turned its attention almost entirely to tourism, with a smattering of tearooms, outdoors shops,

B&Bs and grocery shops. A mile further south from Glenridding, Patterdale is little more than a conglomeration of cottages and a large slate-fronted hotel.

Helvellyn   HIKING
For the vast majority of visitors, the villages are simply convenient staging posts for exploring the fells. The main target is Helvellyn (p144), and thousands of visitors clamber up to the summit every year. It was a favourite walk of Wainwright's, and seems also to have exercised a peculiarly powerful hold over Wordsworth: the mountain crops up frequently in his work, and he continued to climb it well into his 70s. One of the most famous portraits of the poet, completed by painter Benjamin Haydon in 1842, depicts Wordsworth deep in thought with Helvellyn as a suitably Romantic backdrop.

In addition to the route we've detailed, an alternative descent is to turn south from the summit over Dollywaggon Pike (858m/2810ft), past Grisedale Tarn and up onto Fairfield (873m/2864ft), followed by a dramatic descent along the sharp ridge of St Sunday Crag. This walk offers one of the best panoramas of the Ullswater valley – better, some think, than the traditional Helvellyn route.

The Dodds   HIKING
Another popular option for peak-baggers is to strike out for the **Dodds**, a string of

ater Tourist Office (☑017684-82414; watertic@lake-district.gov.uk; ⊙9am-0pm Apr-Oct) By the main car park.

w.ullswater.com Local website with advice accommodation, activities and walks.

ℹ Getting There & Around

The Ullswater Bus and Boat ticket (adult/child £13.60/6.85) combines a day's travel on Bus 108 with a return trip on an Ullswater 'Steamer'.

Useful routes:

108 (6 daily, 4 on Sunday) Bus from Penrith to Patterdale via Pooley Bridge and Glenridding.

517 (Kirkstone Rambler; 3 daily Jul & Aug, otherwise weekends only) Travels over the Kirkstone Pass from Bowness and Troutbeck, stopping at Glenridding and Patterdale.

Howtown & Martindale

The narrow, twisty road winding along the lake's eastern edge to the miniscule hamlet of Howtown is best avoided if you're a bad reverser – it's single track pretty much the whole way from Pooley Bridge, and passing places are few and far between. A better way to arrive is via the Ullswater Steamers, which call in at the village jetty en route from Glenridding and Pooley Bridge.

There's precious little to see in the village itself: the main reason for visiting is an expedition into the nearby peaks, either the ascent of Hallin Fell, or the more challenging charge up Fusedale, High Raise and Angle Tarn, taking in the old Roman road of High Street en route.

Apart from the fells, the 2-mile toil up to the church of **St Martin's** is well worth the effort. Sitting high in the hilltops above the Martindale valley, this is one of the most beautiful of all the Lake District's mountain chapels – sheltered under the boughs of a thousand-year-old yew, with a flagstoned interior housing a 17th-century pulpit and a 500-year-old church bell.

🛏 Sleeping & Eating

TOP
CHOICE **Howtown Hotel**   HOTEL **££**

(☑017684-86514; www.howtown-hotel.com; Howtown; d incl dinner from £160, ⊙Apr-Nov) This bewitchingly backward hotel steadfastly refuses to kowtow to the expectations of modern travellers. There are no phones, no TVs and precious few mod-cons, and its interior design seems to have stalled around the early 1900s (think period prints and antique armchairs rather than designer furnishings). Simple country food and rooms with views of fells and fields make this an ideal refuge from the stresses of 21st-century existence. The four self-catering cottages are similarly idyllic escapes. Even if you're not staying, don't miss a pint in the walkers' bar – it's a gem.

LOWTHER & HAWESWATER

Eastwards from the deep valleys and interlocking hills around Ullswater, the countryside opens out onto the broad green pastures of the Lowther Park estate, the family seat of the aristocratic Lowther family, who still own huge swathes of land across the Lake District. To the south, a narrow road runs through the pocket-sized village of Bampton

DON'T MISS

KIRKSTONE PASS

South of Ullswater the main A592 climbs past the modest splashes of Brothers Water and Hayeswater en route to Kirkstone Pass – at 454m/1489ft the highest mountain pass in Cumbria open to road traffic.

It's one of the most scenic stretches of road in the whole national park, but it's not always easy going: the upper section as you pass the whitewashed **Kirkstone Pass Inn** (www.kirkstonepassinn.com) is rather ominously known as the 'Struggle'. Every winter unsuspecting drivers are caught out by surprise patches of black ice and snow, only to find themselves coming to an abrupt stop against a drystone wall.

Historically the surrounding hillsides were important slate-mining areas, and the industry is still in full swing around the Kirkstone Quarry – you can see examples of local slate craft at the Kirkstone Slate Gallery in Skelwith Bridge.

The 517 Kirkstone Rambler travels up and over the pass from Glenridding, stopping outside the inn before heading to Troutbeck, Windermere and Bowness. There are three daily buses in July and August, otherwise the service runs only on weekends.

lofty fells that loom along the horizon to the north of Glenridding. There are many ways to string them together, but one of the most popular routes starts at Dockray (near Gowbarrow Park), then circles round via the tops of Clough Head (726m/2,382ft), Great Dodd (857m/2807ft), Watson's Dodd (789m/2584ft), Stybarrow Dodd (843m/2770ft) and Sheffield Pike (675m/2214ft). It's a long, demanding day on the fells, covering between 9 and 13 miles depending on how many peaks you tackle: there is some difficult terrain and route-finding involved, so plan accordingly.

Other Hikes   HIKING

Several more fells loom temptingly on the lake's southern side, including **Place Fell** (657m/2156ft) and the little summit of **Hallin Fell** (388m/1273ft), probably the best option for a short up-and-down walk, especially when combined with a trip to nearby Howtown on the Ullswater 'Steamers'.

Glenridding Guides   HIKING

(☑017684-82957; www.glenriddingguides.com) For guided walks in the Ullswater area, this experienced guiding company is the outfit to ask: choose your fell and Steve will provide someone to show you the way. He should know what he's talking about – he's a longstanding member of the Patterdale Mountain Rescue team

Prices are £70 per half-day (plus £10 for each extra person) or £120 per full day (plus £20 per extra person). It also runs courses on navigation, wild camping, rock climbing and winter skills.

Glenridding Sailing Centre   BOATING

(☑017684-82541; www.glenriddingsailingcentre.co.uk; the Spit, Glenridding) The lake's main sailing centre hires out canoes (£15/40/65 for one hour/three hours/full day) and kayaks (£10/25/45 for one hour/three hours/full day), as well as various boats and dinghies (£70 to £110 per day).

St Patrick's Boat Landing   BOATING

(☑017684-82393; www.stpatricksboatlandings.co.uk; Glenridding) Charges similar prices to the sailing centre, and also rents out mountain bikes.

Rookin House   OUTDOORS

(☑017684-83561; www.rookinhouse.co.uk) This multi-activity provider offers a varied range of outdoor pursuits. It's one of the best places in the Lake District to try horse riding and pony trekking, but you can also try your hand at archery, clay-pigeon shooting, tree climbing and paintballing, or learn how to drive an argo-cat and a JCB digger.

For a truly bizarre way to spend a day, you could also try out a session of human bowling, which involves climbing inside a giant ball and allowing your friends to aim you at a set of man-sized pins.

The centre is about 3 miles north of Ullswater; take the turn onto the A5091 near Gowbarrow Park, signed towards Dockray and the A66.

🛏 Sleeping

There are a couple of large corporate hotels in Glenridding and Patterdale, but neither are particularly worthy of recommendation.

TOP
CHOICE **Lowthwaite Farm**   B&B **££**

(☑017684-82343; www.lowthwaiteullswater.com; Matterdale; d £76-86; ℙ) Owners Jim and Tine have turned this cob farmhouse into an oasis of laid-back charm. The four rooms are stylish, cosy and individual: most of the furniture comes from Tanzania, where the adventurous pair previously had a tour company arranging trips up Kilimanjaro. The most characterful room is Blencathra, which offers a downstairs lounge and an upstairs sleeping loft in a converted shed. Breakfast's a mix-and-match treat of granola, homemade breads and fresh-baked muffins. The house is in Matterdale, a couple of miles from the lake, and is a bit of a devil to find – phone ahead for directions.

ENGLAND'S HARDIEST HIKERS

While you're tackling the challenges of Helvellyn, spare a thought for the steel-legged Helvellyn Weatherline Assessors, who are employed by the national park to climb the mountain every day between December and March to assess the risk of possible avalanches and routine weather conditions such as wind chill, snow depth and temperature. The information is recorded on the **Lake District Weatherline** (☑0870 055 0575; www.lake-district.gov.uk/weatherline), a vital weather service relied upon by hundreds of thousands of hill walkers every year.

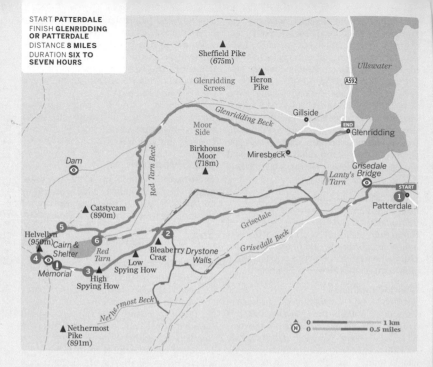

Sheffield Pike (675m)

Glenridding Screes

Heron Pike

Ullswater

A592

Glenridding Beck

Gillside

Moor Side

END *Glenridding*

Birkhouse Moor (718m)

Miresbeck

Dam

Red Tarn Beck

Lanty's Tarn

Grisedale Bridge

START ❶ *Patterdale*

Catstycam (890m)

❺

Grisedale

Helvellyn (950m) *Cairn & Shelter*

❻ ❷

Bleaberry Crag *Drystone Walls*

Grisedale Beck

Red Tarn

❹ ❶ *Low Spying How*

Memorial ❸ *High Spying How*

Nethermost Pike (891m)

Nethermost Beck

0 —— 1 km
0 —— 0.5 miles

Hiking Tour
Helvellyn

❯ After Scafell Pike, the Lake District's second-most popular mountain is Helvellyn, especially the classic ridge route along Striding Edge. It's busy year-round, but it's a challenge even for experienced walkers, with dizzying drops and some all-fours scrambling. It's best avoided if you're wary of heights, and don't even think about it in wintry conditions.

There are several possible routes. This one heads west from ❶ **Patterdale**. After about half a mile, cross Grisedale Beck via a humpback bridge before ascending the flank of Birkhouse Moor. After a long, steep climb you'll reach the ❷ **Hole-in-the-Wall**, a good place to take a breather, with views up to the Helvellyn summit, Red Tarn and the ragged spine of Striding Edge.

Head southwest beneath Bleaberry Crag and over the rocky mound of ❸ **High Spying How**. Then it's onto the ridge itself. Several trails wind their way along the edge, offering various degrees of difficulty; whichever you choose, walk slowly and

carefully. At the end of the ridge there's the option of a scramble over the rock tower known as the Chimney. You can avoid it by following along an easier path on the right.

From here, another sharp, rocky section leads to Helvellyn's ❹ **summit** (950m/3118ft). The views are truly fabulous: southeast to St Sunday Crag, northeast to the pointy peak of Catstycam, west to Thirlmere and east to Ullswater.

Three memorials can be found around the summit. The first is dedicated to Robert Dixon, who slipped off the peak while following a foxhounds' trail, and the second to the climber Charles Gough, who, in 1805, became the first recorded person to fall off the mountain. A third memorial marks the point where two daring pilots, John Leeming and Bert Hinkler, landed their plane on 22 December 1926.

Descend via ❺ **Swirral Edge**, following the path between Catstycam and ❻ **Red Tarn**. You can retrace your steps back to Patterdale or follow the path along Red Tarn Beck to Glenridding.

Boathouse at Knotts End APARTMENT £££
(☎01768-774060, 01539-448081; www.lakescottage holiday.co.uk; Watermillock; apt per night from £195; 🅿) This heart-meltingly pretty boathouse is now one of the loveliest self-catering apartments on Ullswater. It's perched right above the water, with an A-framed ceiling, a cute galley kitchen and a timber balcony overlooking the lake. You couldn't ask for a more romantic location – so unsurprisingly, you'll need to book well ahead.

Old Water View B&B ££
(☎017684-82175; www.oldwaterview.co.uk; Patterdale; d £84; 🅿) Old-fashioned it may be, but this traditional B&B still has bags of charm. The split-level 'Bothy' has a mum-and-dad's double with attic singles for the kids, and 'Place Fell' is jammed under the rafters. Look out for Wainwright's autograph on the wall – according to the owners, this was the room the great man liked to stay in.

Cherry Holme B&B ££
(☎017684-82512; www.cherryholme.co.uk; Glenridding; d £85-125; 🅿🛜) This spacious house on the eastern edge of Glenridding is a cut above, with elaborate pine beds, plush furnishings and a Nordic-style steam room.

Patterdale YHA HOSTEL £
(☎0845 371 9337; patterdale@yha.org.uk; dm from £13.95; ⊙reception 7.30-10am & 5-10.30pm Easter-Oct) Purpose-built modern hostel by the Patterdale shoreline, with a rather institutional atmosphere thanks to its small dorms set around several side wings. The £11.95 menu at the cafe is super value.

Side Farm CAMPGROUND £
(☎017684-82337; andrea@sidefarm.fsnet.co.uk; Patterdale; site for 2 adults & car £10-12; ⊙Easter-Oct) This Patterdale campsite has 70-odd pitches spread out over a spacious farmer's field overlooking Ullswater. By far the best spots are by the lakeshore, but there's no booking, so you'll need both luck and an early start. Facilities include basic shower blocks, a laundry and a small sticky-bun teashop.

Quiet Site CAMPGROUND £
(☎07768727016; www.thequietsite.co.uk; sites £16-30, pods £35-50; ⊙year-round; 🅿🛜) Huddled on the hillside between Pooley Bridge and Gowbarrow, this eco-friendly campsite is one of the best in Ullswater – although prices have sky-rocketed since it was featured in *Cool Camping*. The grassy camping fields have views over Ullswater

(sloping sites are cheaper...
room facilities are hou...
farm buildings. It's eco-fr...
reed-bed sewage treatm...
wastewater and recycling...
is signed from the A592 ju...
Brackenrigg Inn, from where i...
drive of about 1.5 miles.

Gillside Farm CAM...
(☎017684-82346; www.gillsidecaravanand...
site.co.uk; Glenridding; sites for 2 adults, te...
£16; ⊙Mar-Nov) Glenridding's main cam...
is in a part-wooded field, situated on a w...
ing farm run by the Lightfoot family (wh...
gladly supply you with milk and eggs fo...
breakfast). Facilities are fairly rudimentary...
(sinks for dishwashing, a shower block, one...
washing machine) but there's a camping...
barn in case the weather turns. The entrance...
to the farm is on the track to Helvellyn.

🍴 Eating & Drinking

Decent eating options are very thin on the ground in Glenridding.

Fellbites CAFE ££
(Glenridding; lunch £8-12, evening menu 2-/3-courses £17.50/23.50; ⊙lunch daily, dinner Thu-Sat) This converted stone barn beside the main car park is the best all-round option in Glenridding. There's a varied selection of all-day breakfasts, spuds and chunky sandwiches, and more filling mains after dark. Hungry hikers will no doubt want to plump for the daily roast, and veggies will also find they're well catered for.

Traveller's Rest PUB ££
(Glenridding) Decent pub with a fell-view patio; the food isn't up to much, so stick to the beers. The pub's a 500m walk from the A592.

🛍 Shopping

There's a handful of shops in the village for supplies, including the **Glenridding Mini Market** (⊙8am-8pm daily in summer) or **Sharman's of Glenridding** (⊙8am-6pm, later in summer), which has the village's only cash machine and also hires hiking boots in case you've left yours at home.

ℹ Information

Glenridding Cyber Cafe (www.glenridding cybercafe.co.uk; internet access per half hr £1; ⊙10am-11pm) Inside Kilner's Coffee House at the Glenridding Hotel.

146

Ull...
ullsw...
5.3...
w...
on...

ULLSWATER HOW... & PATTERDALE

WORTH A TRIP

SHAP ABBEY

Standing in a lonely spot next to the River Lowther, about half a mile west of its namesake village, **Shap Abbey** was the last great abbey to be founded in England, and the last to be dissolved by Henry VIII's dissolution. It was established in 1199 by a group of Premonasterian canons, and reached the height of its powers during the early 16th century, when the impressive bell tower was added to the abbey's west front. This tumbledown tower is now practically all that remains of this once-splendid abbey; the rest of the stone was carted off to build the walls of Shap Market Hall and nearby Lowther Castle.

to one of the national park's least-developed valleys, Haweswater, while to the southeast you'll find one of the Lake District's most atmospheric ecclesiastical landmarks, the tumbledown ruins of Shap Abbey.

Lowther Park

The Lowthers' domain may have diminished somewhat over the centuries, but their vast family estate of **Lowther Park** (www.lowther .co.uk; ⊙10am-5pm) is still an undeniably impressive affair.

Encompassing great tracts of woodland, forest, hunting park and pasture, the estate's most spectacular feature is the crenellated ruin of **Lowther Castle**. Furnished with turrets, battlements and corner towers, the house was built by Victorian architect Robert Smirke, who also designed the British Museum and the Covent Garden Theatre in London, but its upkeep proved too costly even for the prodigiously prosperous Lowthers.

The house fell into decline during the early 20th century, especially following the infamously profligate antics of Hugh, the 5th Earl of Lonsdale, who bankrupted the family coal mines and spent much of the family fortune. Long-held plans to restore the castle and its once-lavish landscaped gardens are finally coming to fruition thanks to a recent £9 million award from the Regional Development Agency. The renovations to the house and the addition of the new visitor centre are

due to be completed around 2014, but it's thought that it will be a couple of decades before the gardens will be back to their full Victorian glory.

For now, the grounds of the estate are open from 10am to 5pm daily, and sections of the house will be opened to allow visitors to see how the restoration work is progressing. The estate's long-running country show, the Lowther Horse Driving Trials and Country Fair, was relaunched in August 2011 as the Lowther Game and Country Fair. Visit the website for the latest updates.

The grounds also contain the **Lakeland Birds of Prey Centre** (Lowther Castle; adult/child £6/3; ⊙11am-5pm Apr-Oct), which provides daily demonstrations by its population of hawks, falcons, eagles and owls.

🛏 Sleeping & Eating

TOP
CHOICE **George and Dragon** PUB ££
(☎01768-865381; www.georgeanddragonclifton.co
.uk; mains £16.95-25.95; s £70-120, d £90-145) On the edge of the Lowther Estate in the village of Clifton, this pub has been comprehensively refurbished, and sources its produce straight from the estate's organic farm. Reclaimed benches, flagstoned hearths and a fire blazing in the grate make this a delightful stop-off for lunch. Period prints and sepia photos explore the estate's history, while the handwritten blackboards are jam-packed with tasty fare such as saddle of lamb, venison medallions and wild trout. The rooms have been tastefully redone, too, although the rear-facing ones are tiny.

Haweswater

There are few places in Cumbria that feel as wild and empty as the valley of Haweswater, a long grey slash of water ringed by orange-brown fells and lonely hilltops. South of Askham, a minor road runs through the village of Bampton all the way to the car park at Burnbanks at the lake's northern end, before tracking along the eastern shore and coming to a dead stop near the lake's southerly tip (where there's a second car park at Mardale Head).

Seen on a brooding winter's day, topped by clouds and ribbons of mist, the lake makes a powerfully moody sight, but it's actually not a natural body of water. Haweswater was dammed in the early 1930s to create the Lake District's second reservoir, drowning the little farming community of Mardale in the process – an event which inspired Sarah Hall's moving novel, *Haweswater*.

The construction of the dam raised the water level by 95ft, doubling the length of the lake to create the new 4-mile reservoir. Although most of the village was demolished prior to the flooding of the valley, during dry periods the village's bridge and drystone walls sometimes make an eerie reappearance above the waterline.

Haweswater is also home to one of the RSPB's largest **bird reserves** (haweswater @rspb.org.uk), with a population of buzzards, peregrine falcons, ring ouzels and dippers. The star attraction, however, is the chance for a rare sighting of a golden eagle: Haweswater is one of the only places in England frequented by these mighty birds in summer.

There's a special **viewpoint** and **bird hide** in the Riggindale Valley, about 1.5 miles' walk from the Mardale Head car park. RSPB wardens man the hide on weekends from April to October, and can hopefully help you spot the birds.

Apart from birdwatchers, often the only other visitors to the valley are hill walkers setting out on the classic circuit up the Riggindale Valley via High Street (828m/ 2718ft), Mardale Ill Bell (760m/2496ft) and Harter Fell (778m/2552ft).

Sleeping & Eating

Haweswater Hotel   HOTEL **££**
(✆01931-713235; www.haweswaterhotel.com; s £60-80, d £80-120; ℗🖫) Modern it most certainly isn't, but if you're looking for isolation you'll be hard-pushed to beat this marvellously remote hotel, built to replace Mardale's drowned Bull Inn in the late 1930s and still the only place to stay in the valley. Clad in ivy, teeming with antiques and offering views of Haweswater from nearly every room, it's an endearingly old-fashioned refuge from the modern world. A two-/three-course dinner at **Le Mardale** restaurant is available for £24.95/29.95: the feel is fairly formal, with refined dishes such as Gressingham duck, venison medallions and wood pigeon dished up in art Deco inspired surroundings.

Beckfoot Country House   B&B **££**
(✆01931-713241; www.beckfoot.co.uk; near Helton; s £40-50, d £80-110; ☺Mar-Dec; ℗) Halfway between Askham and Bampton, this remote house is surrounded by peaceful paddocks, some of which are grazed by the owner's Shetland ponies. It's a wonderfully backward kind of place, filled with ticking clocks, chaises longues and country knick-knacks, and the rooms are rather huge.

WORTH A TRIP

SHAP ABBEY

Standing in a lonely spot next to the River Lowther, about half a mile west of its namesake village, **Shap Abbey** was the last great abbey to be founded in England, and the last to be dissolved by Henry VIII's dissolution. It was established in 1199 by a group of Premonasterian canons, and reached the height of its powers during the early 16th century, when the impressive bell tower was added to the abbey's west front. This tumbledown tower is now practically all that remains of this once-splendid abbey; the rest of the stone was carted off to build the walls of Shap Market Hall and nearby Lowther Castle.

to one of the national park's least-developed valleys, Haweswater, while to the southeast you'll find one of the Lake District's most atmospheric ecclesiastical landmarks, the tumbledown ruins of Shap Abbey.

Lowther Park

The Lowthers' domain may have diminished somewhat over the centuries, but their vast family estate of **Lowther Park** (www.lowther .co.uk; ⊙10am-5pm) is still an undeniably impressive affair.

Encompassing great tracts of woodland, forest, hunting park and pasture, the estate's most spectacular feature is the crenellated ruin of **Lowther Castle**. Furnished with turrets, battlements and corner towers, the house was built by Victorian architect Robert Smirke, who also designed the British Museum and the Covent Garden Theatre in London, but its upkeep proved too costly even for the prodigiously prosperous Lowthers.

The house fell into decline during the early 20th century, especially following the infamously profligate antics of Hugh, the 5th Earl of Lonsdale, who bankrupted the family coal mines and spent much of the family fortune. Long-held plans to restore the castle and its once-lavish landscaped gardens are finally coming to fruition thanks to a recent £9 million award from the Regional Development Agency. The renovations to the house and the addition of the new visitor centre are

due to be completed around 2014, but it's thought that it will be a couple of decades before the gardens will be back to their full Victorian glory.

For now, the grounds of the estate are open from 10am to 5pm daily, and sections of the house will be opened to allow visitors to see how the restoration work is progressing. The estate's long-running country show, the Lowther Horse Driving Trials and Country Fair, was relaunched in August 2011 as the Lowther Game and Country Fair. Visit the website for the latest updates.

The grounds also contain the **Lakeland Birds of Prey Centre** (Lowther Castle; adult/child £6/3; ⊙11am-5pm Apr-Oct), which provides daily demonstrations by its population of hawks, falcons, eagles and owls.

🛏 Sleeping & Eating

TOP CHOICE **George and Dragon**   PUB ££
(☑01768-865381; www.georgeanddragonclifton.co .uk; mains £16.95-25.95; s £70-120, d £90-145) On the edge of the Lowther Estate in the village of Clifton, this pub has been comprehensively refurbished, and sources its produce straight from the estate's organic farm. Reclaimed benches, flagstoned hearths and a fire blazing in the grate make this a delightful stop-off for lunch. Period prints and sepia photos explore the estate's history, while the handwritten blackboards are jam-packed with tasty fare such as saddle of lamb, venison medallions and wild trout. The rooms have been tastefully redone, too, although the rear-facing ones are tiny.

Haweswater

There are few places in Cumbria that feel as wild and empty as the valley of Haweswater, a long grey slash of water ringed by orange-brown fells and lonely hilltops. South of Askham, a minor road runs through the village of Bampton all the way to the car park at Burnbanks at the lake's northern end, before tracking along the eastern shore and coming to a dead stop near the lake's southerly tip (where there's a second car park at Mardale Head).

Seen on a brooding winter's day, topped by clouds and ribbons of mist, the lake makes a powerfully moody sight, but it's actually not a natural body of water. Haweswater was dammed in the early 1930s to create the Lake District's second reservoir, drowning the little farming community of Mardale in the process – an event which inspired Sarah Hall's moving novel, *Haweswater*.

The construction of the dam raised the water level by 95ft, doubling the length of the lake to create the new 4-mile reservoir. Although most of the village was demolished prior to the flooding of the valley, during dry periods the village's bridge and drystone walls sometimes make an eerie reappearance above the waterline.

Haweswater is also home to one of the RSPB's largest **bird reserves** (haweswater @rspb.org.uk), with a population of buzzards, peregrine falcons, ring ouzels and dippers. The star attraction, however, is the chance for a rare sighting of a golden eagle: Haweswater is one of the only places in England frequented by these mighty birds in summer.

There's a special **viewpoint** and **bird hide** in the Riggindale Valley, about 1.5 miles' walk from the Mardale Head car park. RSPB wardens man the hide on weekends from April to October, and can hopefully help you spot the birds.

Apart from birdwatchers, often the only other visitors to the valley are hill walkers setting out on the classic circuit up the Riggindale Valley via High Street (828m/

2718ft), Mardale Ill Bell (760m/2496ft) and Harter Fell (778m/2552ft).

Sleeping & Eating

Haweswater Hotel HOTEL **££**
(☏01931-713235; www.haweswaterhotel.com; s £60-80, d £80-120; P🕏) Modern it most certainly isn't, but if you're looking for isolation you'll be hard-pushed to beat this marvellously remote hotel, built to replace Mardale's drowned Bull Inn in the late 1930s and still the only place to stay in the valley. Clad in ivy, teeming with antiques and offering views of Haweswater from nearly every room, it's an endearingly old-fashioned refuge from the modern world. A two-/three-course dinner at **Le Mardale** restaurant is available for £24.95/29.95: the feel is fairly formal, with refined dishes such as Gressingham duck, venison medallions and wood pigeon dished up in art Deco inspired surroundings.

Beckfoot Country House B&B **££**
(☏01931-713241; www.beckfoot.co.uk; near Helton; s £40-50, d £80-110; ☺Mar-Dec; P) Halfway between Askham and Bampton, this remote house is surrounded by peaceful paddocks, some of which are grazed by the owner's Shetland ponies. It's a wonderfully backward kind of place, filled with ticking clocks, chaises longues and country knick-knacks, and the rooms are rather huge.

Cumbrian Coast

Best Places to Eat

» L'Enclume (p153)

» Rogan & Company (p153)

» Gillams (p158)

» Hazelmere Café (p151)

» Zest (p163)

Best Places to Stay

» L'Enclume (p153)

» Eden Lodge (p157)

» Lowther House (p161)

» Moresby Hall (p163)

» No 43 (p151)

Why Go?

Most visitors to the Lake District never stray far beyond the boundaries of the national park, but they're missing out on one of the county's forgotten gems – its bleakly beautiful coastline, a gentle panorama of sandy bays and grassy headlands stretching from Morecambe Bay to the shores of the Solway Coast.

Historically, Cumbria's ports developed to serve the local mining, quarrying and shipbuilding industries, and while scattered pockets of industry still remain (principally around Barrow-in-Furness and the nuclear plant at Sellafield), much of the rest of the coast is as ruggedly beautiful as the rest of the Lakeland landscape. Wander the landscaped grounds of Holker Hall, spot seabirds from the RSPB reserve at St Bees Head, admire the views from the top of Black Combe and then wrap things up with some Michelin-starred dining in the medieval village of Cartmel.

When to Go

The Cumbrian Coast receives far fewer visitors than the national park, so it's usually light on crowds even in peak season – although attractions such as the South Lakes Animal Park, The Beacon and the beaches around Millom and Haverigg get busy during the summer holidays. Holker Hall and St Bees Head are best in spring and early summer, while September sees the annual World Gurning Competition in Egremont, a face-pulling contest dating back to the 12th century, when the lord of the manor supposedly handed out sour crab apples to his workers.

Cumbrian Coast Highlights

1 Explore the grand rooms and even grander gardens of **Holker Hall** (p154)

2 Sample the stellar food at Simon Rogan's two restaurants in **Cartmel** (p153)

3 Watch one of the northwest's largest seabird colonies at **St Bees Head** (p165)

4 Delve into the seafaring and rum-running heritage of **Whitehaven** (p160)

5 Pay homage to Ulverston's best-known son at the **Laurel and Hardy Museum** (p157)

6 Step back into the past at the tumbledown **Furness Abbey** (p159)

7 Enjoy a panoramic view across the Cumbrian Coast from the summit of **Black Combe** (p155)

lofty fells that loom along the horizon to the north of Glenridding. There are many ways to string them together, but one of the most popular routes starts at Dockray (near Gowbarrow Park), then circles round via the tops of Clough Head (726m/2,382ft), Great Dodd (857m/2807ft), Watson's Dodd (789m/2584ft), Stybarrow Dodd (843m/2770ft) and Sheffield Pike (675m/2214ft). It's a long, demanding day on the fells, covering between 9 and 13 miles depending on how many peaks you tackle: there is some difficult terrain and route-finding involved, so plan accordingly.

Other Hikes
HIKING

Several more fells loom temptingly on the lake's southern side, including **Place Fell** (657m/2156ft) and the little summit of **Hallin Fell** (388m/1273ft), probably the best option for a short up-and-down walk, especially when combined with a trip to nearby Howtown on the Ullswater 'Steamers'.

Glenridding Guides
HIKING

(☎017684-82957; www.glenriddingguides.com) For guided walks in the Ullswater area, this experienced guiding company is the outfit to ask: choose your fell and Steve will provide someone to show you the way. He should know what he's talking about – he's a longstanding member of the Patterdale Mountain Rescue team.

Prices are £70 per half-day (plus £10 for each extra person) or £120 per full day (plus £20 per extra person). It also runs courses on navigation, wild camping, rock climbing and winter skills.

Glenridding Sailing Centre
BOATING

(☎017684-82541; www.glenriddingsailingcentre.co .uk; the Spit, Glenridding) The lake's main sailing centre hires out canoes (£15/40/65 for one hour/three hours/full day) and kayaks (£10/25/45 for one hour/three hours/full day), as well as various boats and dinghies (£70 to £110 per day).

St Patrick's Boat Landing
BOATING

(☎017684-82393; www.stpatricksboatlandings.co .uk; Glenridding) Charges similar prices to the sailing centre, and also rents out mountain bikes.

Rookin House
OUTDOORS

(☎017684-83561; www.rookinhouse.co.uk) This multi-activity provider offers a varied range of outdoor pursuits. It's one of the best places in the Lake District to try horse riding and pony trekking, but you can also try your hand at archery, clay-pigeon shooting, tree

climbing and paintballing, or learn how to drive an argo-cat and a JCB digger.

For a truly bizarre way to spend a day, you could also try out a session of human bowling, which involves climbing inside a giant ball and allowing your friends to aim you at a set of man-sized pins.

The centre is about 3 miles north of Ullswater; take the turn onto the A5091 near Gowbarrow Park, signed towards Dockray and the A66.

🛏 Sleeping

There are a couple of large corporate hotels in Glenridding and Patterdale, but neither are particularly worthy of recommendation.

TOP CHOICE Lowthwaite Farm
B&B ££

(☎017684-82343; www.lowthwaiteullswater.com; Matterdale; d £76-86; P) Owners Jim and Tine have turned this cob farmhouse into an oasis of laid-back charm. The four rooms are stylish, cosy and individual: most of the furniture comes from Tanzania, where the adventurous pair previously had a tour company arranging trips up Kilimanjaro. The most characterful room is Blencathra, which offers a downstairs lounge and an upstairs sleeping loft in a converted shed. Breakfast's a mix-and-match treat of granola, homemade breads and fresh-baked muffins. The house is in Matterdale, a couple of miles from the lake, and is a bit of a devil to find – phone ahead for directions.

ENGLAND'S HARDIEST HIKERS

While you're tackling the challenges of Helvellyn, spare a thought for the steel-legged Helvellyn Weatherline Assessors, who are employed by the national park to climb the mountain every day between December and March to assess the risk of possible avalanches and routine weather conditions such as wind chill, snow depth and temperature. The information is recorded on the **Lake District Weatherline** (☎0870 055 0575; www.lake-district.gov.uk/weatherline), a vital weather service relied upon by hundreds of thousands of hill walkers every year.

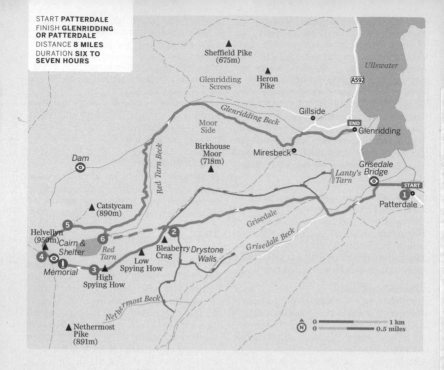

Hiking Tour
Helvellyn

❯ After Scafell Pike, the Lake District's second-most popular mountain is Helvellyn, especially the classic ridge route along Striding Edge. It's busy year-round, but it's a challenge even for experienced walkers, with dizzying drops and some all-fours scrambling. It's best avoided if you're wary of heights, and don't even think about it in wintry conditions.

There are several possible routes. This one heads west from ❶ **Patterdale**. After about half a mile, cross Grisedale Beck via a humpback bridge before ascending the flank of Birkhouse Moor. After a long, steep climb you'll reach the ❷ **Hole-in-the-Wall**, a good place to take a breather, with views up to the Helvellyn summit, Red Tarn and the ragged spine of Striding Edge.

Head southwest beneath Bleaberry Crag and over the rocky mound of ❸ **High Spying How**. Then it's onto the ridge itself. Several trails wind their way along the edge, offering various degrees of difficulty; whichever you choose, walk slowly and

carefully. At the end of the ridge there's the option of a scramble over the rock tower known as the Chimney. You can avoid it by following along an easier path on the right.

From here, another sharp, rocky section leads to Helvellyn's ❹ **summit** (950m/ 3118ft). The views are truly fabulous: southeast to St Sunday Crag, northeast to the pointy peak of Catstycam, west to Thirlmere and east to Ullswater.

Three memorials can be found around the summit. The first is dedicated to Robert Dixon, who slipped off the peak while following a foxhounds' trail, and the second to the climber Charles Gough, who, in 1805, became the first recorded person to fall off the mountain. A third memorial marks the point where two daring pilots, John Leeming and Bert Hinkler, landed their plane on 22 December 1926.

Descend via ❺ **Swirral Edge**, following the path between Catstycam and ❻ **Red Tarn**. You can retrace your steps back to Patterdale or follow the path along Red Tarn Beck to Glenridding.

Boathouse at Knotts End   APARTMENT **£££**
(☑01768-774060,01539-448081;www.lakescottage
holiday.co.uk; Watermillock; apt per night from £195;
P) This heart-meltingly pretty boathouse is
now one of the loveliest self catering apartments on Ullswater. It's perched right above
the water, with an A-framed ceiling, a cute
galley kitchen and a timber balcony overlooking the lake. You couldn't ask for a more
romantic location – so unsurprisingly, you'll
need to book well ahead

Old Water View   B&B
(☑017684-82175; www.oldwaterview.co.uk; Patterdale; d £84; **P**) Old-fashioned it may be, but
this traditional B&B still has bags of charm.
The split-level 'Bothy' has a mum-and-dad's
double with attic singles for the kids, and
'Place Fell' is jammed under the rafters.
Look out for Wainwright's autograph on the
wall – according to the owners, this was the
room the great man liked to stay in.

Cherry Holme   B&B **££**
(☑017684-82512; www.cherryholme.co.uk; Glenridding; d £85-125; **P**🛜) This spacious house
on the eastern edge of Glenridding is a cut
above, with elaborate pine beds, plush furnishings and a Nordic-style steam room.

Patterdale YHA   HOSTEL **£**
(☑0845 371 9337; patterdale@yha.org.uk; dm
from £13.95; ⊘reception 7.30-10am & 5-10.30pm
Easter-Oct) Purpose-built modern hostel by
the Patterdale shoreline, with a rather institutional atmosphere thanks to its small
dorms set around several side wings. The
£11.95 menu at the cafe is super value.

Side Farm   CAMPGROUND **£**
(☑017684-82337; andrea@sidefarm.fsnet.co.uk;
Patterdale; site for 2 adults & car £10-12; ⊘Easter-
Oct) This Patterdale campsite has 70-odd
pitches spread out over a spacious farmer's
field overlooking Ullswater. By far the best
spots are by the lakeshore, but there's no
booking, so you'll need both luck and an early
start. Facilities include basic shower blocks, a
laundry and a small sticky-bun teashop.

✦ Quiet Site   CAMPGROUND **£**
(☑07768727016; www.thequietsite.co.uk; sites £16-
30, pods £35-50; ⊘year-round; **P**🛜) Huddled
on the hillside between Pooley Bridge and
Gowbarrow, this eco-friendly campsite is
one of the best in Ullswater – although
prices have sky-rocketed since it was
featured in *Cool Camping*. The grassy
camping fields have views over Ullswater

(sloping sites are cheaper), and the bathroom facilities are housed in converted
farm buildings. It's eco-friendly, too, with
reed-bed sewage treatment, harvested
wastewater and recycling. The campsite
is signed from the A592 just after the
Brackenrigg Inn, from where it's an uphill
drive of about 1.5 miles.

Gillside Farm   CAMPGROUND **£**
(☑017684-82346; www.gillsidecaravanandcamping
site.co.uk, Glenridding; sites for 2 adults, tent & car
£16; ⊘Mar-Nov) Glenridding's main campsite
is in a part-wooded field, situated on a working farm run by the Lightfoot family (who'll
gladly supply you with milk and eggs for
breakfast). Facilities are fairly rudimentary
(sinks for dishwashing, a shower block, one
washing machine) but there's a camping
barn in case the weather turns. The entrance
to the farm is on the track to Helvellyn.

✖ Eating & Drinking

Decent eating options are very thin on the
ground in Glenridding.

Fellbites   CAFE **££**
(Glenridding; lunch £8-12, evening menu 2-/
3-courses £17.50/23.50; ⊘lunch daily, dinner Thu-
Sat) This converted stone barn beside the
main car park is the best all-round option
in Glenridding. There's a varied selection of
all-day breakfasts, spuds and chunky sandwiches, and more filling mains after dark.
Hungry hikers will no doubt want to plump
for the daily roast, and veggies will also find
they're well catered for.

Traveller's Rest   PUB **££**
(Glenridding) Decent pub with a fell-view
patio; the food isn't up to much, so stick to
the beers. The pub's a 500m walk from the
A592.

🛍 Shopping

There's a handful of shops in the village
for supplies, including the **Glenridding
Mini Market** (⊘8am-8pm daily in summer) or
Sharman's of Glenridding (⊘8am-6pm,
later in summer), which has the village's only
cash machine and also hires hiking boots
in case you've left yours at home.

ⓘ Information

Glenridding Cyber Cafe (www.glenridding
cybercafe.co.uk; internet access per half hr
£1; ⊘10am-11pm) Inside Kilner's Coffee House
at the Glenridding Hotel.

Ullswater Tourist Office (☏017684-82414; ullswatertic@lake-district.gov.uk; ⊙9am-5.30pm Apr-Oct) By the main car park. **www.ullswater.com** Local website with advice on accommodation, activities and walks.

❶ Getting There & Around

The Ullswater Bus and Boat ticket (adult/child £13.60/6.85) combines a day's travel on Bus 108 with a return trip on an Ullswater 'Steamer'.

Useful routes:

108 (6 daily, 4 on Sunday) Bus from Penrith to Patterdale via Pooley Bridge and Glenridding.

517 (Kirkstone Rambler; 3 daily Jul & Aug, otherwise weekends only) Travels over the Kirkstone Pass from Bowness and Troutbeck, stopping at Glenridding and Patterdale.

Howtown & Martindale

The narrow, twisty road winding along the lake's eastern edge to the miniscule hamlet of Howtown is best avoided if you're a bad reverser – it's single track pretty much the whole way from Pooley Bridge, and passing places are few and far between. A better way to arrive is via the Ullswater Steamers, which call in at the village jetty en route from Glenridding and Pooley Bridge.

There's precious little to see in the village itself: the main reason for visiting is an expedition into the nearby peaks, either the ascent of Hallin Fell, or the more challenging charge up Fusedale, High Raise and Angle Tarn, taking in the old Roman road of High Street en route.

Apart from the fells, the 2-mile toil up to the church of **St Martin's** is well worth the effort. Sitting high in the hilltops above the Martindale valley, this is one of the most beautiful of all the Lake District's mountain chapels – sheltered under the boughs of a thousand-year-old yew, with a flagstoned interior housing a 17th-century pulpit and a 500-year-old church bell.

🛏 Sleeping & Eating

TOP
CHOICE **Howtown Hotel** HOTEL ££
(☏017684-86514; www.howtown-hotel.com; Howtown; d incl dinner from £160; ⊙Apr-Nov) This bewitchingly backward hotel steadfastly refuses to kowtow to the expectations of modern travellers. There are no phones, no TVs and precious few mod-cons, and its interior design seems to have stalled around the early 1900s (think period prints and antique armchairs rather than designer furnishings). Simple country food and rooms with views of fells and fields make this an ideal refuge from the stresses of 21st-century existence. The four self-catering cottages are similarly idyllic escapes. Even if you're not staying, don't miss a pint in the walkers' bar – it's a gem.

LOWTHER & HAWESWATER

Eastwards from the deep valleys and interlocking hills around Ullswater, the countryside opens out onto the broad green pastures of the Lowther Park estate, the family seat of the aristocratic Lowther family, who still own huge swathes of land across the Lake District. To the south, a narrow road runs through the pocket-sized village of Bampton

---

DON'T MISS

KIRKSTONE PASS

South of Ullswater the main A592 climbs past the modest splashes of Brothers Water and Hayeswater en route to Kirkstone Pass – at 454m/1489ft the highest mountain pass in Cumbria open to road traffic.

It's one of the most scenic stretches of road in the whole national park, but it's not always easy going: the upper section as you pass the whitewashed **Kirkstone Pass Inn** (www.kirkstonepassinn.com) is rather ominously known as the 'Struggle'. Every winter unsuspecting drivers are caught out by surprise patches of black ice and snow, only to find themselves coming to an abrupt stop against a drystone wall.

Historically the surrounding hillsides were important slate-mining areas, and the industry is still in full swing around the Kirkstone Quarry – you can see examples of local slate craft at the Kirkstone Slate Gallery in Skelwith Bridge.

The 517 Kirkstone Rambler travels up and over the pass from Glenridding, stopping outside the inn before heading to Troutbeck, Windermere and Bowness. There are three daily buses in July and August, otherwise the service runs only on weekends.

SOUTH COAST

Grange-over-Sands

POP 4098

Overlooking the sandy expanse of Morecambe Bay, the quiet seaside town of Grange-over-Sands was founded as a granary store for the monks of Cartmel Priory, but was transformed by the massive boom in Victorian and Edwardian tourism following the arrival of the railway in the mid-19th century.

Hundreds of grand holiday villas and oversized hotels sprang up around the town's hilly streets to cater for the influx of day-trippers and train travellers who arrived en masse to stroll the seafront and breathe in the bracing sea air.

Once you've had a stroll along the seafront promenade, wandered the ornamental gardens and browsed the town's shops, there's not a great deal to keep you entertained, but the town makes a convenient base for exploring the southern coast.

If you're feeling energetic, the half-hour stroll up **Hampsfell** offers great views across the bay and (if the weather plays ball) inland to Coniston, Helvellyn and the Langdale Pikes. The best vantage point is the **Hampsfell Hospice**, a little building constructed in 1846 by the vicar of Cartmel as a travellers' shelter.

The **tourist office** (☑015395-34026; grangetic@southlakeland.gov.uk; Victoria Hall, Main St; ☺10am-4pm Easter-Oct) is on Main St.

🛏 Sleeping

There are some huge Victorian hotels in Grange, but they're generally overpriced and devoid of character.

Lymehurst Hotel   HOTEL ££
(☑015395-33076; www.lymehurst.co.uk; Kents Bank Rd; s £45, d £100-130; P🖤) By far Grange's best guesthouse, in a smart house typical of the town's Edwardian architecture. Light, contemporary rooms keep the clutter to a minimum, opting for pine, cream walls and white linen. The restaurant is worth investigating – chef-owner Kevin Wyper favours bold European flavours (mains £16.50 to £21.50), and also takes charge of breakfast.

Graythwaite Manor   HOTEL £££
(☑015395-32001; www.graythwaitemanor.co.uk; Fernhill Rd; r £138-158; P) Decoratively speaking, this chimney-clad mansion is stuck somewhere around the mid-1930s – a Union-jacked flagpole stands outside, leather armchairs and grandfather clocks fill the corridors, and there's a wood-panelled lounge straight out of a Hercule Poirot novel. Rooms are at the same time spacious and stuffy; latticed windows afford views of trimmed lawns.

TOP CHOICE **No 43**   B&B £££
(☑01524-762761; www.no43.org.uk; The Promenade, Arnside; r £130-185; P🖤) Across the sands of Morecambe in the pleasantly faded resort of Arnside, this brilliant boutique B&B comes as a delightful surprise – with its bespoke wallpapers, Belfast sinks and metro-chic trappings, it'd feel more at home in Soho than the Cumbrian seaside. Some rooms boast Bose hi-fis, others picture-frame fires; ask for No 2 or 7 if you're after an estuary view.

🍴 Eating

TOP CHOICE **Hazelmere Café**   CAFE £
(☑015395-32972; www.hazelmerecafe.co.uk; 1-2 Yewbarrow Tce; sandwiches £4-6, mains £5-12; ☺10am-5pm) This deliciously old-fashioned cafe serves up quite possibly the best afternoon tea in Cumbria – it's even won a national award from the Tea Guild. Take your pick from over 30 different brews, and enjoy the olde-worlde decor of frilly doilies, starched linen and bone china teapots. Classic English dishes define the menu – potted shrimps, rabbit pie and cheese toasties – and there's a veritable bounty of buns, tarts, macaroons and gateaux to choose from under the cake stands. If you don't feel like sitting

CUMBRIAN COAST GRANGE-OVER-SANDS

ℹ FURNESS RAILWAY & CUMBRIAN COAST LINES

The Furness Railway and Cumbrian Coast lines follow a long 120-mile loop from Lancaster to Carlisle, stopping at coastal towns including Grange-over-Sands, Ulverston, Barrow-in-Furness, Millom, Ravenglass, Whitehaven and Workington.

Direct trains run every couple of hours, with extra connecting services north and east from Barrow; services are limited on Sunday.

The **Cumbrian Coast Day Ranger** (adult/5-15yr £17/8.50) covers a day's travel on the Cumbrian Coast line.

South Coast

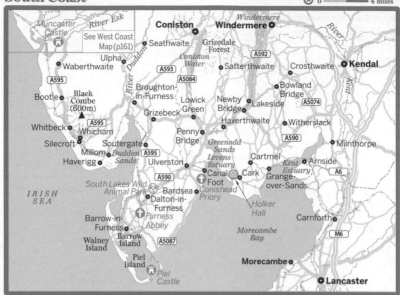

down, you can order something sweet and sticky from the bakery next door.

Higginsons BUTCHER £
(Keswick House, Main St) Head to this renowned butcher for top-quality pies, sausages and steaks.

❶ Getting There & Away

BUS A couple of useful buses stop in Grange:

532 (hourly Monday to Saturday) Travels between Grange, Kents Bank, Flookburgh and Cartmel and back. Five or six buses continue to Kendal.

X35 (hourly Monday to Saturday, four on Sunday) Stops at Grange on its way from Kendal (30 minutes) to Ulverston (30 minutes) and Barrow (1 hour 20 minutes).

TRAIN Grange is on the Furness Railway line, with connections along the Cumbrian Coast (with a change at Barrow-in-Furness), and south to Arnside and Lancaster.

DESTINATION	SINGLE FARE (£)	DURATION
Cark & Cartmel	2.30	8min
Whitehaven	14.40	2¼hr
Barrow-in-Furness	6.60	½hr
Arnside	2	5min
Lancaster	5.60	½hr

Around Grange-over-Sands

CARTMEL
POP 1798

This miniscule medieval village is lost among green fields and flower-filled hedgerows a couple of miles inland from Grange. Arranged around a quaint market square that's barely changed since the Middle Ages, it's an almost impossibly pretty vision of a traditional English village – although the smattering of smart toy shops, vintage booksellers and artisan bakeries hint that the residents are all rather more well-heeled these days.

Cartmel traditionally has three claims to fame – its 12th-century priory, its little racecourse and its sticky toffee pudding – but more recently it's gained recognition as one of Cumbria's most exciting culinary destinations thanks to super-chef Simon Rogan, who now has two restaurants in the village: Michelin-starred L'Enclume, and its sister bistro, Rogan & Company.

◉ Sights

Village Square LANDMARK
Cartmel's market square dates back to medieval times, and although its original

market cross has long gone, the old granite fish slabs where the daily catch would once have been displayed can still be seen. Whitewashed inns and higgledy-piggledy houses line the sides of the square, as well as an original medieval gatehouse leading to Cartmel Priory nearby.

Cartmel Priory
CHURCH

(www.cartmelpriory.org.uk; ⊙9am-5.30pm May-Oct, to 3.30pm Nov-Apr) This village priory is one of the few to have survived the ravages of the Dissolution largely unscathed. The priory's most unusual feature is its square belfry tower, set diagonally across the original lantern tower. Inside, light filters in through the stained-glass **east window**, lighting up the wooden pews and stone tombs set into the floor. Note the skulls and hourglasses carved into many tombstones, designed as *memento mori* to remind parishioners of the transience of life.

Cartmel Village Shop
FOOD & DRINK

(www.stickytoffeepudding.co.uk; The Square; ⊙9am-5pm Mon-Sat, 10am-4.30pm Sun) Cartmel's delightful village shop has earned a nationwide reputation thanks to its recipe for sticky toffee pudding, but it's since branched out into all kinds of indulgent treats. You can buy pre-prepared packs of sticky toffee pudding from the chiller cabinets, alongside the latest pudding recipes for sticky ginger, banana chocolate and summer fruits. Luxury picnic supplies are dotted round the rest of the shop, as well as an ice-cream counter in summer.

Racecourse
HORSE RACING

(www.cartmel-racecourse.co.uk) Racing officially dates back to 1856 in Cartmel, but it's thought that local monks were holding mule races here as far back as the 15th century. These days it's strictly a thoroughbred affair, and on race days the village streets are chock-a-block with wax jackets, shooting sticks and Hunters wellies. Main race fixtures are held between May and August.

🍴 Sleeping & Eating

TOP CHOICE Rogan & Company
BRITISH ££

(☎015395-35917; www.roganandcompany.co.uk; mains £10.50-15.95; ⊙lunch & dinner) Simon Rogan's second Cartmel establishment is more straightforward bistro than gastronomic laboratory, so it'll probably suit most diners better than nearby L'Enclume. It's a chic place to dine, combining the 16th-century shell of the original building with deep leather chairs, sleek white walls and shiny wood tables. Head chef Louie Lawrence's menu sticks to classics with a characteristically inventive spin – shepherd's pie with sweetbreads and *kohlrabi* (German turnip), for example, or wild salmon smoked in tea.

L'Enclume
BRITISH £££

(☎015395-36362; www.lenclume.co.uk; Cavendish St; dinner menu £69-89, rooms £99-159; ⊙lunch weekends, dinner daily) Simon Rogan's much-vaunted and Michelin-starred establishment is rapidly gaining a reputation as one of Britain's best addresses for boundary-pushing cuisine. This is dinner as theatre:

CUMBRIAN COAST AROUND GRANGE-OVER-SANDS

MORECAMBE BAY CROSSING

Before the coming of the railway, the sandy expanse of Morecambe Bay provided the only reliable route into the Lake District from the south of England.

The traditional crossing is made from Arnside on the eastern side of the bay over to Kents Bank, near Grange-over-Sands. It has, however, always been a risky journey. Over 115 sq miles of tidal sand and mud flats (the largest such area in Britain) are revealed at low tide, but the bay is notorious for its treacherous quicksands and fast-rising tide (said to move at the speed of a galloping horse).

Even experienced fishermen have lost carts, ponies and tractors in the capricious sands, and there have been numerous strandings, most recently in 2004, when at least 21 Chinese cockle pickers were tragically caught by the tide and drowned.

It's possible to walk across the flats at low tide, but only in the company of the official **Queen's Guide**, a role established in 1536. Cedric Robinson, a local fisherman, is the 25th official Queen's Guide, and leads walks across the sands throughout the year. You'll need to register a fortnight in advance – ask at the Grange tourist office for details of the next crossing. The 8-mile trudge takes around 3½ hours.

Find out more about this unique waterway at www.morecambebay.org.uk.

Rogan's dishes are designed to create a sensory experience as much as a taste sensation, and you'll experience a madcap assortment of foams, glazes, lollipops and savoury shot glasses on your way through the menu, not to mention a smorgasbord of weird ingredients ranging from goat's milk mousse to onion ashes and tree bark. The restaurant itself provides a suitably sleek setting, with minimal furniture, rendered walls and artful sculptures dotted round the dining room. It also recently acquired its own organic farm at Howbarrow, nearby. Yes, it's pricey and pretentious, but one thing's for sure – you certainly won't leave without forming an opinion. Twelve chi-chi rooms are available in the main house and a separate lodge next to Rogan & Company.

Cavendish Arms PUB **££**
(☑015395-36240; www.thecavendisharms.co.uk; mains £12-18; r £60-90) Behind the medieval gateway, covered with hanging baskets, this is the pick of the town inns – not a full-blown gastropub, but getting there. Sophisticated dishes – guinea fowl supreme, venison steak in Cumberland sauce – are served amid heavy beams, sturdy furniture and a log fire. Rooms are plain but snug.

ⓘ Getting There & Away
The 530/532 travels from Cartmel to Grange (40 minutes, hourly Monday to Saturday), stopping at Cark & Cartmel station, 2 miles southwest of the village.

From here there are trains every couple of hours east to Grange (£2.30, eight minutes) and west to Ulverston (£2.70, eight minutes).

HOLKER HALL
Few of Cumbria's stately homes can top the red-brick splendour of **Holker Hall** (☑015395-58328; www.holker-hall.co.uk; adult/6-15yr house & grounds £11.50/6, grounds only £7.50/4; ⊙house 11am-4pm Sun-Fri mid-Mar–Nov, gardens 10.30am-5pm Sun-Fri mid-Mar–Nov, closes 4pm in shoulder months), owned by just three Cumbrian families (the Prestons, the Lowthers and the Cavendishes) over the last 500 years.

Though parts of Holker Hall date from the 16th century, the west wing was entirely rebuilt following a devastating fire in 1871, complete with mullioned windows, gables and copper-topped turrets. This is the only wing open to the public (the present-day Cavendishes still live in the other one).

Among the highlights are the **Drawing Room**, packed with Chippendale furniture and historic oil paintings, and the **Library**, containing an antique microscope belonging to Henry Cavendish (discoverer of nitric acid) and over 3500 antique books (some of which are fakes, designed to conceal light switches when the house was converted to electric power in 1911). The showstopper is the **Long Gallery**, notable for its plasterwork ceiling and fine English furniture – look out for the 19th-century sphinx-legged table and a wonderful walnut cabinet inlaid with ivory and rosewood.

Holker's stunning landscaped gardens stretch over 10 hectares, and encompass a world-renowned array of formal rose gardens, rhododendron arbours, stately terraces and tinkling fountains. The estate is particularly known for its rare trees: one enormous 72ft lime is thought to be the largest example in England.

The hall's **Courtyard Cafe** (mains £6-12; ⊙10.30am-5.30pm, closes 4pm winter, closed Jan) makes a good spot for lunch after visiting the house, and you can pick up cuts of the estate's venison, steak and saltmarsh lamb from the **Food Hall** (☑015395-59084; www.holkerfoodhall.co.uk; ⊙same hr as cafe).

Ulverston

POP 11670

It might not have the looks of some of the Lake District's better-known towns, but in many ways Ulverston's a more authentic place. It's been a merchant town since the 13th century, and the main square still hosts a lively outdoor bazaar each Thursday and Saturday, with a farmers market on the third Saturday of the month.

During the 18th and 19th centuries, Ulverston became an important centre for leather, copper and iron ore, and the smart Georgian buildings lining the streets hint at the wealth that flowed into the coffers during its industrial heyday. The town's a good deal quieter these days, and while it's a bit short on sights, it's conveniently placed for exploring the southern Lakes, especially for cyclists on the long-distance Cumbria Way. But Ulverston's main claim to fame is undoubtedly as the birthplace of Stan Laurel, the spindlier half of Laurel and Hardy, who's commemorated in a local museum as well as a brand-new statue, unveiled with great fanfare in 2009.

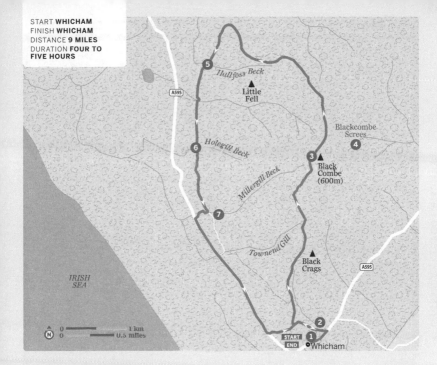

Hiking Tour
Black Combe

❯ This often-overlooked fell is one of Cumbria's best-kept secrets, looming dramatically over the county's western coastline and offering panoramic views all the way from Solway down to the Duddon Sands and Morecambe Bay. Walk Black Combe on the right day and you might even glimpse the distant crests of Snowdonia, a couple of hundred miles to the south.

Start near the little village of ❶ **Whicham**. Follow the public bridleway behind ❷ **St Mary's Church** as it climbs up Moorgill Beck. As you walk, look out over the Irish Sea; you might be able to spot the silhouette of the Isle of Man far out on the western horizon, as well as the dark hump of Walney Island squatting off the Furness Peninsula to the south.

The path passes from bracken into heather and grass as it continues the leg-sapping ascent up to Black Combe's ❸ **summit** at 600m/1969ft, which you should reach after another hour or so of walking. The top is marked by a trig point and

a drystone wind shelter, as well as a small tarn just to the south.

Unlike most of the other Lakeland fells, Black Combe stands almost in isolation, so there's practically nothing to obstruct the 360-degree coastal views to the south and west, and to the distant mountains inland. The only drawback to such an isolated spot is the inevitable breeze – it can be pretty windy up top, so a warm coat and an extra fleece might well come in handy!

The descent route tracks northeast, passing to the left of the ❹ **Blackcombe Screes**, before meandering northwest through disused quarries and sheepfolds. The views as you descend the grassy slope are lovely, so there's no need to rush.

The path then swings south over ❺ **Hallfoss Beck** and ❻ **Holegill Beck**, then meanders beneath the western slopes to the disused ❼ **Whitbeck Mill**, which still has its original waterwheel in place. It then rejoins the path to Whicham.

Ulverston

Ulverston

◉ Sights & Activities

Laurel and Hardy Statue   MONUMENT

A brand-new statue of the bumbling duo was unveiled outside Coronation Hall in 2009. It was created by artist Graham Ibbeson, who also designed the statue of Eric Morecambe on the seafront in Morecambe.

Hoad Monument   LANDMARK

The town's most prominent piece of architecture is the pointy tower on Hoad Hill, built to commemorate the explorer, author and Secretary to the Admiralty Sir John Barrow (1764–1848), who helped map much of the Arctic and participated in the search for the northwest passage. The views are wonderful, stretching north towards Langdale, Coniston and Helvellyn and south to Morecambe Bay. The monument is open (indicated by a flying flag) most Sunday afternoons in summer and on Bank Holidays, but you can visit the hill at any time of year.

Ulverston Canal   HISTORIC SITE

In 1796 England's deepest, widest canal was extended from the coast into Ulverston to enable access to deep-water shipping. Unfortunately the arrival of the Furness Railway in the mid-1840s scuppered the canal's profitability, and it was closed down for good in the early 20th century. It is now owned by the pharmaceutical company GlaxoSmithKline, which has a large factory beside the canal.

The canal towpath starts near **Canal Head**, a 10-minute walk from the town centre, and offers a lovely 2-mile walk to the shores of Morecambe Bay.

Lanternhouse GALLERY
(www.lanternhouse.org; The Ellers; admission varies) This contemporary gallery space hosts everything from digital video to conceptual sculpture. The building is almost as quirky as the artwork – part converted school, part reclaimed barn, part modern concrete tower, topped off by a cast-iron pinnacle.

River Deep Mountain High OUTDOORS
(☎015395-28666; www.riverdeepmountainhigh.co.uk; Ulverston) Multidiscipline company offering many activities, including hiking, scrambling, gorge walking, raft-building and more.

★ Festivals & Events

Ulverston touts itself as a festival town, and there are several intriguing events dotted through the calendar. There's a **town carnival** in early July, a **lantern procession** in September and a lively **Dickensian Festival** in late November, when half the town turns out in Dickensian garb to celebrate the coming of Christmas.

🛏 Sleeping

Eden Lodge HOTEL **££**
(☎01229-587067; www.eden-lodge.com; Bardsea; s £80, d £100-135; P🛜) It's a bit out of town (in the nearby village of Bardsea, in fact), but if you prefer to sleep in comfort this smart detached house is probably the place. It's billed as a hotel, but it's really a posh guesthouse: pleasant neutral rooms have thoughtful touches such as body-jet showers and iPod docks; bump up to the top rooms and you'll get a blu-ray player. Breakfast is served in the new glass conservatory, overlooking the grounds of Conishead Priory.

Bay Horse Hotel HOTEL **££**
(☎01229-583972; www.thebayhorsehotel.co.uk; Canal Foot; d £95-120; P🛜) This old coaching inn is picturesquely positioned on the pebbly sands of the Levens Estuary. The rooms are a bit behind the times (heavy on floral prints and net curtains), but have the option of a balcony overlooking the water. The restaurant is more tempting, blending French flavours with local venison loin and saltmarsh lamb. The 2-/3-course fixed menu at £25/31 is good value, and the conservatory dining room has fine estuary views. Follow signs to Canal Foot from the A590.

Lonsdale House Hotel GUESTHOUSE **££**
(☎01229-581260; www.lonsdalehousehotel.co.uk; 11 Daltongate; s £65-70, d £70-105; P🛜) Georgian building with 20 rooms, some overlooking the walled garden. The venerable building is showing its age – expect creaky floorboards and saggy beds – but it's in a good position for town.

CUMBRIAN COAST ULVERSTON

DON'T MISS

LAUREL AND HARDY MUSEUM

Ulverston's Stan Laurel connections are exhaustively explored at this fabulously quirky **museum** (www.laurel-and-hardy.co.uk; Brogden St; adult/child £4/2; ☉10am-5pm Feb-Dec), founded by the avid Laurel and Hardy collector and former town mayor Bill Cubin back in 1983. The original premises on Upper Brook St was more a shrine than a museum: every last inch of the tiny building was carpeted with movie posters, newspaper clippings, collectibles and film props, and there was even a tiny cinema where you could catch screenings of the duo's flicks.

Cubin died in 1997, and the museum is now run with a similar sense of enthusiasm by his grandson. Long-held plans to move the museum into more spacious premises finally came to fruition in 2008; the collection was moved lock, stock and barrel into Ulverston's old Roxy cinema. All the old floor-to-ceiling memorabilia is still on show, but it's presented in a rather less chaotic fashion than at the former site; there's even a new 15-seat cinema, complete with back-to-back Laurel and Hardy classics.

✕ Eating & Drinking

TOP CHOICE **Gillams**   CAFE £
(www.gillams-tearoom.co.uk; 64 Market St; lunch £3-8; ⊘Mon-Sat) Gillams has been in business since 1892: it started life as the town's grocer, and now serves as Ulverston's best place for lunch. It's run along veggie-organic principles these days (even vegans have a good choice); there are several daily specials on the blackboard, ranging from broccoli tarts to fresh salads, and an ever-tempting array of cakes to choose from on the counter. There's a sweet little slate patio out back, too, just in case the sun decides to make an appearance. You can also pick out posh groceries such as artisan teas and Lakeland biscuits from the next-door shop.

Rustique   BISTRO £££
(☑01229-587373; www.eatatrustique.co.uk; Brogden St; mains £16.50-22.50; ⊘lunch & dinner Tue-Sat) This swish bistro is tucked away in an alley just off Brogden St. The concrete building looks unremarkable from the outside, but it's full of contemporary appeal once you get through the door. Chef Jason Bright's Mediterranean-influenced menu seems more suited to a Riviera bistro than an Ulverston backstreet – seafood and mussel stew with aïoli, or salmon with samphire and truffle oil. He also runs a small **deli** (⊘9.30am-4pm Mon, Tue & Thu-Sat, to 1pm Wed) just along the street, great for handmade ciabattas and takeaway soups.

World Peace Cafe   CAFE £
(www.worldpeacecafe.org; 5 Cavendish St; mains £3-8; ⊘10am-4.30pm Tue-Sat) Realign your chakras over cappuccino and cake at this holistic cafe, an offshoot of the Manjushri Buddhist Centre. Ingredients are organic and fair trade, and there's a meditation centre on the 1st floor for the super-stressed.

Farmers Arms   PUB ££
(www.thefarmers-ulverston.co.uk; 3 Market Pl; mains £6-14) Lively pub on the market square, with a well-deserved foodie reputation. The deli boards include a mix of meats, sausages and cheeses, perfect lunch fare to accompany a pint of XB or Hawkshead Bitter. There are a few tables on the front terrace overlooking the square, otherwise it's inside for a place by the fire or a table in the long dining room.

Hot Mango   CAFE £
(27 King St; lunch £5-8; ⊘9am-4pm Tue-Sat) Cheery cafe on the main street, good for a quick morning cappuccino or a lunchtime panini.

ℹ Information

Library (Kings Rd; internet per ½hr £1; ⊘9am-6pm Mon & Thu, to 5pm Tue & Fri, to 1pm Wed & Sat)

Tourist office (☑01229-587120; ulverston.tourism@southlakeland.gov.uk; County Sq; ⊘9am-5pm Mon-Sat, 10am-4pm winter) Inside the Coronation Hall.

www.ulverston.net Town website.

ℹ Getting There & Away

BUS The hourly X35 travels from Ulverston via Haverthwaite, Newby Bridge, Grange-over-Sands and Kendal. Only four buses on Sunday.

TRAIN Connections from Ulverston:

DESTINATION	SINGLE FARE (£)	DURATION
Cark & Cartmel	2.70	8min
Whitehaven	10.40	1¼hr
Barrow-in-Furness	3.50	25min
Lancaster	8.60	¾hr
Carlisle	10.50 to 14.80	1¾hr

CUMBRIA WAY

Ulverston marks the southerly start of the long-distance hiking route of the **Cumbria Way** (www.ldwa.org.uk/ldp/members/show_path.php?path_name=Cumbria+Way), which winds up through the Lake District via Coniston, Langdale, Keswick, Caldbeck and Carlisle, covering a total distance of around 70 miles (depending on your exact route). The trail was devised by the Ramblers' Association and completed in the mid-1970s, but it wasn't completely waymarked until 2007.

There's also a sister route for cyclists, the **Cumbria Way Cycle Route** (www.cumbriawaycycleroute.co.uk). **Sustrans** (www.sustrans.org.uk) publishes a 30-page booklet on the route, including accommodation and eating tips along the way.

THE DOCK MUSEUM

The busy port city of **Barrow-in-Furness**, sprawling along the coastline to the southwest of Ulverston, isn't the prettiest city in England, but it's worth visiting for the **Dock Museum** (www.dockmuseum.org.uk; admission free; ◷10am-5pm Tue-Fri, 11am-5pm Sat & Sun Easter-Oct), which charts the story of how this modest fishing harbour was transformed into one of the thumping powerhouses of the Industrial Revolution. In its heyday, Barrow was the world's leading iron and steel city, as well as a massive centre for shipbuilding and manufacture (BAE Systems still has a major shipbuilding presence in Barrow). The museum's striking pyramid-shaped building stands above the city's old Victorian dry dock, and houses exhibitions exploring the city's shipbuilding heritage from the days of early steam liners to modern state-of-the-art submarines.

Around Ulverston

CONISHEAD PRIORY

Two miles south of Ulverston along the A5087, **Conishead Priory** (www.nkt-kmc-manjushri.org; admission free; ◷2-5pm weekdays, noon-5pm weekends & Bank Holidays Easter-Oct, 2-4pm Nov-Easter) has variously served as a stately home, a military hospital, a miners' retreat and a spa hotel, but since the mid-1970s the Victorian Gothic mansion has been owned by the Manjushri Buddhist organisation, and it's now home to a Kadampa Buddhist Temple housing Europe's largest bronze Buddha.

Entry to the grounds and the temple is free. Guided tours (including the inside of the main house) are offered at 2pm and 3.30pm on weekends, and cost £3. Meditation retreats are available for those interested in delving a little deeper.

A little further south is the coastal harbour of **Bardsea**, a nice place for a paddle and a picnic when the sun is shining.

FURNESS ABBEY

The Cistercian monks of **Furness Abbey** (EH; adult/child £3.80/2.30; ◷10am-5pm Apr-Sep, 10am-4pm Sat & Sun Oct-Mar) were once among the richest and most powerful in northern England, controlling a huge swathe of land stretching from present-day Lancashire to the Central Lakes. But their dominion was brought to an ignominious end during the Dissolution, and these days the rosy-red ruins offer only the barest hint of the abbey's former grandeur.

An informative audio guide provides an overview of the abbey's history. While the roof and most of the walls have long since been dismantled, you can still discern the abbey's essential footprint: various arches, windows and the north and south transept walls are still standing, along with the shell of the bell tower and the remnants of the underground drainage system. A rather fanciful legend maintains that a subterranean tunnel leads beneath the abbey all the way to Piel Castle, enabling the monks to escape during times of trouble. Before you leave, the small museum is worth a look for two rare knights' effigies and a collection of other stone carvings.

The abbey is 8.5 miles from Ulverston. Several buses, including the hourly X35, stop nearby.

SOUTH LAKES WILD ANIMAL PARK

Budding Doctor Doolittles will love this fantastic **animal park** (www.wildanimalpark.co.uk; Broughton Rd; adult/3-15yr £12.50/8; ◷10am-5pm Easter-Nov, to 4.30pm Nov Easter) just outside Dalton-in-Furness. Beasties and birdies of every shape, size and configuration roam the themed enclosure spaces: spectacled bears, Colombian spider monkeys and capybaras populate South America; wallabies, kangaroos, emus and ibises roam Down Under; lemurs indulge in tree-swinging antics in Madagascar; and Sumatran and Amur tigers stalk the Asian enclosure. As always, though, it's Africa that steals the show, with its menagerie of giraffes, hippos, meerkats, mandrills, baboons and golden-coated lions.

You can join the keepers to feed the giraffes, lemurs and penguins, or go the whole hog and become a keeper for a day (£125).

The park is half a mile east of Dalton-in-Furness, off the A590 from Ulverston. Follow the brown elephant signs.

WORTH A TRIP

MILLOM & HAVERIGG

Tucked away to the west of Duddon Sands, the quiet stretch of coastline between Millom and Haverigg makes an attractive detour, dotted with sandy patches, grassy dunes and quiet coastal paths, ideal for strolling on a blustery day.

This stretch of shoreline was once a bustling centre for iron and steel production: local workers were known as 'red men' because of the coating of iron ore dust that covered them by the end of the day. The area's industrial past is explored at the quaint **Millom Folk Museum** (www.millomfolkmuseum.co.uk; adult/child £4/1; ⊙10.30am-3.30pm Mon-Sat), which also houses a small display on the work of local poet Norman Nicholson, who lived in Millom for over 70 years.

Nearby, the former iron ore works at **Hodbarrow** has been turned into an RSPB bird reserve, with an enclosed lagoon that welcomes seasonal visitors such as coots, swans, geese, terns, teal and great crested grebe. If you're really lucky you might spot a natterjack toad, one of England's most endangered amphibians.

Further along the coast are the small beaches at **Haverigg** and **Silecroft**. The **Murthwaite Green Trekking Centre** (☑01229-770876; www.murthwaitegreen.co.uk; Silecroft; 1/2/3hr ride £23/39/55, half-/full day £71/103) offers pony treks and horse rides across the sands, including a three-hour trot with a picnic on the beach.

WEST COAST

Whitehaven

POP 23,795

It's a little hard to believe today, but the port of Whitehaven was once the third-busiest harbour in England, with a bustling trans-atlantic trade in coal, iron and spices (as well as less salubrious cargoes of illicit liquor and slaves). The town was entirely remodelled in the 17th century by local landowner Sir John Lowther, and its regimented Georgian streets provide a stark contrast to the usual higgledy-piggledy layout of most English harbour towns. These days you're more likely to see swanky yachts rather than spice freighters moored up along its harbour, but there's still a faint trace of seagoing grandeur hanging around its briny old streets.

One of the most notorious incidents in Whitehaven's history occurred during the American War of Independence, when the town was attacked by American naval commander John Paul Jones (actually a Scot, born in Arbigland in 1747). Jones convinced his reluctant crew to mount a daring night raid on Whitehaven, hoping to strike a blow against one of Britain's key ports. Unfortunately for him, strong winds and tides, coupled with a shortage of ammunition, a semi-mutinous crew and the troublesome distractions of Whitehaven's taverns, meant the raid was a total flop; of the 200-odd ships stationed in Whitehaven's harbour, Jones sank just a single lowly coal barge.

⊙ Sights & Activities

The Beacon   MUSEUM

(www.thebeacon-whitehaven.co.uk; West Strand; adult/under 16yr £5/1.50; ⊙10am-4.30pm Tue-Sun) The tall tower at the end of the harbour houses The Beacon, which explores the town's distinguished history of transatlantic trade, shipbuilding and salt making, and its not-so-distinguished history of smuggling and slave trading.

Fresh from a £2.2 million refurbishment, the building is split over four floors, each devoted to a different theme: Work and Play on the 2nd, Tides and Trades on the 3rd and the Viewing Gallery and Weather Zone on the top floor, where you can view the town through a high-powered telescope and try your hand at presenting a TV weather forecast.

Rum Story   MUSEUM

(www.rumstory.co.uk; Lowther St; adult/child £5.45/3.45; ⊙10am-4.30pm) The fun (if tacky) waxworks at the Rum Story delve into Whitehaven's long associations with 'the dark spirit'. Sometimes legally imported, sometimes covertly smuggled, this sweet firewater underpinned the town's success during the 18th century, and probably provided much-needed solace during the darker days that followed. The attraction is lodged inside one of the old warehouses owned by the Jefferson family, who were local kingpins of the rum-running trade. Among the various exhibits you can stop off at an 18th-century sugar workshop, delve into a debauched 'punch tavern' and visit the original rum cellars. Grown-ups will even get a tot of rum at the end of the tour.

FREE **Haig Colliery**
Mining Museum   HISTORICAL SITE
(☎01946-599949; www.haigpit.com; Solway Rd, Kells; ⊙10am-5pm) Along with sea-trading and rum-running, Whitehaven was also once at the centre of one of Cumbria's largest coal-mining industries. Several large pits surrounded the town, including the Haig Colliery, which closed down in 1986, ending almost 500 years of continuous production. It was a dreadfully hard way to make a living, not to mention a dangerous one: it's estimated that 1200 people lost their lives in Cumbria's mines down the centuries, including 100 in a single day at the Wellington Pit Disaster in 1910.

West Coast

⌂ 0 ——— 8km
Ⓝ 0 ——— 4 miles

Silloth

Solway Firth

[B5300]

[A596]

Allonby

Aspatria

Crosby

Maryport

[A596] **Cockermouth**

Lake District National Park

Workington [A66]

[A595] [A5086]

Low Lorton High Lorton

Loweswater

Lamplugh

Crummock Water

Whitehaven

Frizington

Buttermere

Ennerdale

St Bees Head [B5345]

Cleator Bridge Moor

Ennerdale Water

St Bees

Egremont

Wasdale Head

Wastwater

[A595]

Sellafield Nuclear Plant

Nether Wasdale

Gosforth

Santon Bridge

Boot

Seascale

Holmrook

Eskdale Green

IRISH SEA

See South Coast Map (p152)

It's now possible to take a guided tour of the old mine workings, as well as several mine engines that are currently being restored by enthusiasts. The site is open daily in summer.

St Nicholas' Church   CHURCH
This red-brick chapel on Lowther St was savaged by fire in 1971; only the original clock tower remains, with the former nave now taken up by an ornamental garden and a memorial to workers killed in Cumbria's coal pits.

C2C Route   CYCLING
Whitehaven marks the traditional starting point for northern England's most popular long-distance cycling route, the C2C (Sea-to-Sea), which runs for 140 miles east to either Newcastle or Sunderland. It travels through the Lake District National Park, crosses the Pennines and traverses several sections of disused railway through County Durham. You can follow the whole route or just split it up into day-long sections.

For more information on the route, there's the useful online **C2C Guide** (www.c2c-guide.co.uk), or you could buy route guides and trail maps from **Sustrans** (www.sustrans.org.uk). For bike-hire companies and luggage transfers, see the general info on p28.

Michael Moon's   BOOKSHOP
(19 Lowther St; ⊙9.30am-5pm Mon-Sat) Endearingly eccentric antiquarian and secondhand bookshop, perfect for extended browsing.

🛏 Sleeping

Lowther House   B&B ££
(☎01946-63169; www.lowtherhouse-whitehaven.com; s £70, d £90; 🔊) This renovated B&B has been given an overhaul by an interior designer, and it really shows. The house dates from 1860, and there are lots of knick-knacks and decorative touches evoking Whitehaven's seagoing past. All the three light, attractive rooms are named after ships that were once moored at the town's harbour, and boast White Company bedding, wooden shutters and views across the Solway Firth.

Glenfield   B&B ££
(☎01946-691911; www.glenfield-whitehaven.co.uk; s £40, d £65-80; Ⓟ) Traditional brick guesthouse in the heart of Whitehaven's conservation district, offering six rooms decked out in shipshape Victorian fashion: Corkickle is the roomiest, with original fireplace and sofa chairs, while Fleswick and Nannycatch

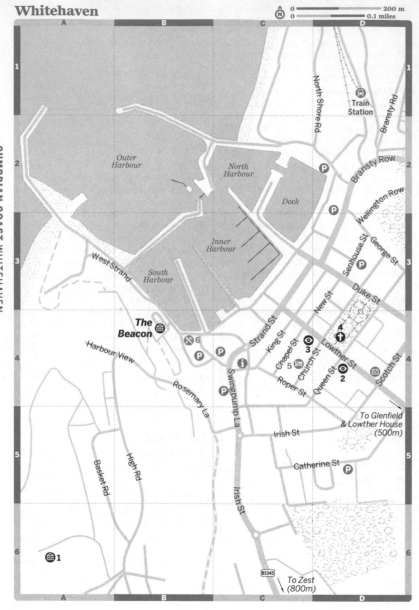

0   200 m
0   0.1 miles

are finished in peachy stripes, and apple-green Ingwell is tailored for single travellers.

Georgian House Hotel HOTEL **££**
(☎01946-696611; www.thegeorgianhousehotel.net; 9-11 Church St; s £89, d £110-125; P🖥) For

hotel digs, try this former sea-captain's residence in the town centre. Period Georgian trappings blend with up-to-date comfort: turned-wood bed frames, flashy wallpapers and thick carpets keep things cosy, although rooms feel rather corporate.

Whitehaven

◎ **Top Sights**
    The Beacon..B4

◎ **Sights**
  1 Haig Colliery Mining Museum A6
  2 Michael Moon's D4
  3 Rum Story C4
  4 St Nicholas' Church............................. D4

🛏 **Sleeping**
  5 Georgian House Hotel........................ C4

✕ **Eating**
  6 Zest Harbourside................................B4

Moresby Hall   HOTEL **£££**

(☏01946 696317; www.moresbyhall.co.uk; Moresby; s £90-105, d £120-150; 🅿) If you feel like playing lord of the manor, then head out of town to this Grade-I listed mansion, replete with antiques, lofty ceilings, ordered lawns, and a frontage dating from 1620. Rooms are conservatively decorated but universally huge: four-posters, hydromassage showers and Gilchrist & Soames bath stuffs set the aristocratic tone.

✕ Eating

Zest Harbourside   CAFE **£**

(☏01946-66981; 8 West Strand; mains £6-12) This buzzy diner is the best place to eat in town, with a chilled bistro menu of blinding butties, crab cakes and spicy meatballs. The inside has a cool maritime feel, with globe lanterns dangling from the ceiling, chrome fixtures and fittings, and a handful of tables right beside the quay.

Zest   BRITISH **££**

(☏01946-692848; www.zestwhitehaven.com; Low Rd; mains £12-18; ⊙dinner Wed-Sat) Zesty by name, zesty by nature, this out-of-town brasserie is the best option for a sit-down dinner. Top-quality local ingredients and fusion flavours have attracted a string of celeb diners, and the feel inside is bright and bang up-to-date. The restaurant is about half a mile along the B5345 towards St Bees.

ℹ Information

Branches of NatWest, Lloyds and HSBC can be found on Lowther St.

Library (Lowther St; internet per ½hr £1; ⊙9.30am-7pm Mon, Tue & Thu, 9.30am-4pm Wed & Sat, noon-4pm Sun)

CUMBRIAN COAST WHITEHAVEN

AN ATOMIC TALE

Few places stir up such a maelstrom of controversy as the billowing chimneys and sprawling reactor halls of **Sellafield Nuclear Plant**, halfway between St Bees and Ravenglass. Originally an ammunitions dump and TNT factory, after WWII the nearby site of Windscale was chosen as the site for Britain's first plutonium-manufacturing reactors (needed to supply the country's nuclear arsenal). In 1956 they were joined by four Magnox reactors at Calder Hall, creating the world's first commercial nuclear power station.

In a country still reeling from postwar rationing, huge unemployment and a shattered national infrastructure, the opening of Windscale seemed to sum up the nation's hopes for a newer, brighter, shinier future. But the dream soon turned sour: in 1957 a fire tore through the Windscale reactor hall forcing its emergency closure, and though the initial fallout was hushed up, it soon emerged that Windscale was the site of the world's first large-scale nuclear disaster. Huge amounts of radioactive material contaminated local land, milk production and animal crops, and eventually drifted as far afield as Wales, Scotland and the Irish west coast.

It was the first of a long line of controversies. The Windscale site, subsequently renamed Sellafield in 1981 and now the UK's largest nuclear-reprocessing facility, has been dogged by nonstop claims of environmental damage and radioactive pollution over the last 50 years – not least by the Irish government, which has long campaigned for an embargo on the release of reactor water into the Irish Sea.

With a new generation of British nuclear power stations on the horizon, Sellafield's own future is still very much in the balance. The site has been scheduled for decommissioning over the next decade, but its closure would represent a huge blow to local employment; many local people have lobbied hard for a new power station to be built on the Sellafield site, while rival environmentalists have lobbied equally strongly for its permanent closure.

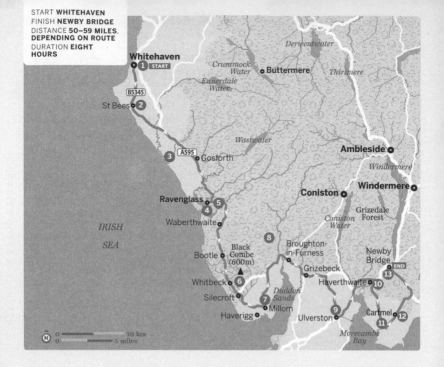

START **WHITEHAVEN**
FINISH **NEWBY BRIDGE**
DISTANCE **50–59 MILES,**
DEPENDING ON ROUTE
DURATION **EIGHT**
HOURS

Driving Tour
Cumbrian Coast

〉 Begin this tour of the Cumbrian Coast in
❶ **Whitehaven**. Take a bracing morning
stroll along the harbourfront, explore the
town's history at The Beacon, and have a
quick coffee and pastry at Zest Harbourside.
Then jump in the car and continue south
on the B5345 to ❷ **St Bees**. You'll spot all
kinds of seabirds nesting at the RSPB reserve
at St Bees Head, so bring binoculars.

Continue southeast from St Bees and rejoin
the A595. Look out for the chimney stacks of
the ❸ **Sellafield** nuclear power station on
your right as you drive towards Gosforth.

About 5 miles from Gosforth you'll reach
❹ **Ravenglass**, another pretty harbour
village that marks the terminus for the La'al
Ratty Steam Railway. Nearby ❺ **Muncaster
Castle** is well worth a visit for its dramatic
architecture and fascinating owl centre.

South of Ravenglass, the coastal views
become increasingly impressive as you travel
past the steep slopes of ❻ **Black Combe**,
the area's highest fell. A turn-off leads south
on the A5093 to the quaint village of

❼ **Millom**, home to a quirky folk museum
and another beautiful RSPB reserve at
Hodbarrow, located in a disused ironworks.

Rejoin the A595 as it loops east towards
Broughton-in-Furness. A minor road leads
north to the eerie stone circle of
❽ **Swinside**, but it's a bit tricky to find
without an OS map, so you might just prefer
to head onwards to the stout market town
of ❾ **Ulverston**. Have lunch at Gillams and
visit the endearingly offbeat Laurel and Hardy
Museum.

Continue on the A590 to ❿ **Haverthwaite**,
and look out for the left-hand turn onto the
B5278 to ⓫ **Holker Hall**, where you can
spend the rest of the afternoon wandering
the stately rooms and landscaped grounds.

Finish up with a gourmet supper in
⓬ **Cartmel** at one of Simon Rogan's
acclaimed restaurants. You can either stay
overnight or head to ⓭ **Newby Bridge** via
the A590.

Tourist office (☏01946-598914; tic@copelandbc.gov.uk; Market Pl; ⊙9.30am-4.30pm) In the Market Hall near the town centre.

❶ Getting There & Away

BUS Useful services:

6 (five daily Monday to Saturday) Travels to Egremont, Gosforth and Seascale. Two buses continue to Ravenglass and Muncaster.

X6 (four Sunday) Follows a slightly different route via St Bees, Gosforth, Ravenglass and Muncaster and on to Bootle, Haverigg and Millom.

20 (six daily Monday to Saturday, four on Sunday) Most useful weekday service to St Bees.

TRAIN Connections every two hours north along the Solway Coast ports to Carlisle (£9, one hour 10 minutes), or south to Ravenglass (£4.50, 30 minutes) and beyond.

Around Whitehaven

To the south of Whitehaven twitchers gather around the rust coloured headland of **St Bees Head** to see the large colonies of guillemots, herring gulls, fulmars and kittiwakes nesting around the RSPB reserve. The headland also marks the start of Alfred Wainwright's classic long-haul **Coast-to-Coast Walk** (see p28).

Further north are the old harbours of **Workington** and **Maryport**, where you'll find the **Lake District Coast Aquarium** (www.coastaquarium.co.uk; South Quay, Maryport; adult/3-16yr £7.50/4.75; ⊙10am-5pm) and its deep-sea denizens, including cuttlefish, conger eels, rays, starfish and sea horses.

North of Maryport a long, flat expanse of windblown dunes stretches past the seafront villages of **Allonby** and neat **Silloth**, marking the start of the **Solway Coast** (www.solwaycoastaonb.org.uk). This protected nature reserve extends along the coast to Rockcliffe Marsh near Carlisle, and is important for its coastal salt marshes and populations of migratory seabirds.

❶ Getting There & Away

Several towns on the Solway Coast are served by the Cumbrian Coast railway from Whitehaven, with stations at St Bees, Workington and Maryport.

The 60 bus runs between Maryport, Allonby and Silloth eight times daily from Monday to Saturday.

Inland Cumbria

Includes »

Best Places to Eat

Best Places to Stay

Why Go?

Bordered by the Scottish frontier, the Lakeland fells and the northern Pennines, inland Cumbria has long served as a historical crossroads. Generations of Picts, Celts, Romans and Reivers have all battled each other for supremacy over this strategic patch of land down the centuries, and 2000 years of conflict have left a permanent smudge on the landscape.

It's one of the best places in Cumbria to get a sense of the county's history. Fortified pele towers, crumbling abbeys and ruined castles litter the hilltops, while the red-brick battlements of Carlisle Castle still stand watch over England's northern border. The most obvious reminder of the region's tempestuous past, however, is the remains of the Vallum Aelium, otherwise known as Hadrian's Wall, which sprawls across Cumbria's northern reaches en route to Wallsend, near the River Tyne. There's no better place to cast your mind back into the past.

When to Go

Inland Cumbria generally stays quieter than the honeypot destinations of the Lake District, so it's a good region to visit year-round – although traffic jams are an inevitable headache during school holidays. There are some interesting festivals to look out for: Appleby's historic horse fair happens in June, while the little village of Langwathby has become famous for its annual scarecrow-making festival, held at the start of July. Kendal hosts a lively street arts festival in September and a major mountain festival in November.

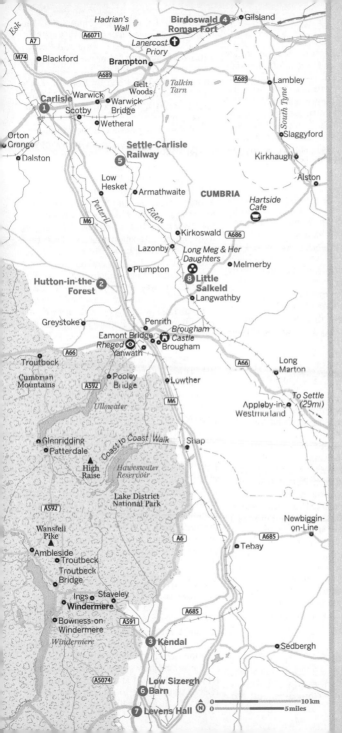

Inland Cumbria Highlights

1 Climb onto the ramparts of **Carlisle Castle** (p168)

2 Play lord of the manor at **Hutton-in-the-Forest** (p179)

3 Investigate the artworks at **Abbot Hall Art Gallery** (p182)

4 Trace the course of Hadrian's Wall to **Birdoswald Roman Fort** (p174)

5 Ride the rails aboard the landmark **Settle–Carlisle Railway** (p172)

6 Browse the shelves of the fantastic farm shop at **Low Sizergh Barn** (p186)

7 Enjoy the surreal topiary of **Levens Hall** (p187)

8 Take a tour of Little Salkeld's working **watermill** (p178)

CARLISLE

POP 69,527

Precariously perched on the stormy border between England and Scotland, the red-brick city of Carlisle has been in the thick of the action for 2000 years. Overlooking the bleak frontier once known ominously as the 'Debatable Lands', it's witnessed more sieges, sackings and pillagings than practically any other city in England, and the remnants of its martial past can still be seen dotted around the city's streets, including the original medieval gatehouses and forbidding rust-red castle.

Much later the city became a thumping powerhouse of the Industrial Revolution, as well as an important terminus for seven Victorian railway companies, but these days most of the heavy industry has moved on, and Carlisle has reinvented itself as a lively centre for shoppers, students and rowdy weekend revellers.

From the M6, the main routes into town are London Rd and Warwick Rd. The train station is south of the city centre, a 10-minute walk from Town Hall Sq (also known as Greenmarket) and the tourist office. The bus station is on Lonsdale St, about 250m east of the square. Most of the town's B&Bs are dotted along Victoria Pl and Warwick Rd.

History

A Celtic camp or *caer* provided an early military station for the Romans, who founded a key stronghold known as Luguvalium, which became the northwest's main administrative centre following the construction of Hadrian's Wall. After centuries of intermittent conflict between Picts, Saxons and Viking raiders, the Normans seized Carlisle from the Scots in 1092. Later, throughout the Middle Ages, the English developed Carlisle as a military stronghold, enlarging the walls, citadels and the great gates, and the city became an important strategic base for Royalist forces during the Civil War. Peace came to Carlisle with the Restoration, and the city developed as an industrial centre for cotton and textiles after the arrival of the railway in the mid-19th century.

◉ Sights

TOP CHOICE **Carlisle Castle** CASTLE
(EH; adult/child £5/3; ⊙9.30am-5pm Apr-Sep, 10am-4pm Oct-Mar) Carlisle was founded as a military city, and its brooding, rust-red

castle provides a timely reminder of the conflicts that have shaped the city's history.

The castle began as a Celtic and Roman stronghold; a Norman motte-and-bailey fort was constructed in 1092 by King William II, and reinforced in stone by Henry I. Later additions were made by Henry II, Edward I and Henry VIII, who tacked on the 'cannon-proof' circular towers.

Thanks to its position in the frontline of England's defences, Carlisle Castle has witnessed a host of sieges. In 1315 the English-held castle was encircled by Robert the Bruce after his victory at Bannockburn, but the castle sat out the siege under its commander, Andrew de Harcla. Another notorious eight-month siege occurred during the Civil War in 1644, when the 700-strong Royalist garrison were starved into submission by the Parliamentarian General Lesley; the defenders survived by eating rats, mice and the castle dogs before finally surrendering in 1645 (a day-by-day account was kept by 18-year-old Isaac Tullie, after whom the city's Tullie House Museum is named). The Jacobite siege of 1745 was less protracted: Bonnie Prince Charlie's army besieged Carlisle for just six days before the defenders caved in.

There are wide-ranging displays covering the castle's history in the central keep. Look out for the Warden's Apartments, furnished in authentic 15th-century style, and the famous 'licking stones', which Jacobite prisoners supposedly lapped for moisture to keep themselves alive. Mary Queen of Scots was imprisoned here in 1568, and you can visit the remains of the tower where she was held. You can also walk along several sections of the castle's crenellated battlements.

Admission includes entry to the **Kings Own Royal Border Regiment Museum**, which explores the history of Cumbria's Infantry Regiment. There are guided tours of the castle from April to September, sometimes in the company of costumed Border Reivers.

Tullie House Museum MUSEUM
(www.tulliehouse.co.uk; Castle St; adult/5-18yr £5.20/50p; ⊙10am-5pm Mon-Sat, 11am-5pm Sun, opens 1hr later on Sun Nov-Mar) Carlisle's excellent museum explores the founding of the city, life under Roman rule and the development of modern Carlisle.

The brand-new **Roman Frontier Gallery**, opened in 2011 at a cost of £1.4 million, really makes a visit to the museum worthwhile. It uses multimedia panels and

INLAND CUMBRIA CARLISLE

interactive displays to tell the story of the Roman occupation of Carlisle, supplemented by a wide range of artefacts dug up around the city: Roman hairpins, gaming dice, tombstones, busts, sculptures and even a few excruciating-looking surgical instruments. Look out for high-profile pieces on loan from other national museums.

The upstairs **Border Galleries** cover the rest of the city's history, from Celtic Carlisle to the Border Reivers and the Jacobite Rebellion. On your way out, look out for the Muckle Toon Bell, which was rung to warn of impending raids, and features a hefty crack in one side sustained during a town hall fire in the 1880s.

On the ground floor is the **Carlisle Life Gallery**, which explores the city's social history through photos, films and recorded stories. Nearby **Old Tullie House** concentrates on fine arts, sculpture and porcelain housed in a wonderful 17th-century Jacobean house, and the basement **Millennium Gallery** is a rather odd mishmash of mineral displays, geology, architecture and a glass-bricked 'whispering wall'.

Once you've done the tour, a subway leads underneath the A595 to Carlisle Castle.

Carlisle Cathedral   CHURCH
(www.carlislecathedral.org.uk; donation £2; ☺7.30am-6.15pm Mon-Sat, 7.30am-5pm Sun) Carlisle's sandstone cathedral – the only one in Cumbria – began life as an Augustinian priory church in 1122, before being elevated to cathedral status 11 years later, when its first abbot, Athelwold, became the first Bishop of Carlisle.

The building's notable features are the 15th-century carved choir stalls, the dramatic barrel-vaulted roof and the delicate column capitals, depicting labours associated with each month, but there's no chance of missing the centrepiece: at over 50ft high, the dramatic 14th-century **East Window** is one of England's largest and most spectacular Gothic windows. During the 1644–45 siege of Carlisle, two-thirds of the nave was torn down by Parliamentarian troops to reinforce their defences, and serious restoration wasn't completed until the mid-19th century.

Other priory buildings dotted around the cathedral include the 16th-century **Fratry** and the **Prior's Tower**.

FREE **Guildhall Museum**   MUSEUM
(Greenmarket; ☺noon-4.30pm Tue-Sun Apr-Oct) This tiny museum is housed in one of Carlisle's oldest buildings, dating from the early 15th century and originally built for Carlisle's trade guilds. At the time of writing it was closed for restoration work; ask at the tourist office for the latest updates.

☞ Tours

FREE **Open Book Visitor Guiding**   GUIDED TOURS
(☎01228-670578; www.greatguidedtours.co.uk) Offers tours of Carlisle from April to September, including visits to Carlisle Castle and Hadrian's Wall.

☐ Sleeping

Carlisle's accommodation is underwhelming – the choice boils down to big, faceless chain hotels in the centre (Travelodge, Ibis and Premier Inn all have a presence) or B&Bs scattered around the outskirts.

Warwick Hall   HOTEL ££
(🖳www.warwickhall.org; Warwick-on-Eden; s £84-90, d/ste £120/150; ◨🐾) If you don't mind staying a little way outside the city, there's no doubt about it – Warwick Hall is far and away the top place to stay near Carlisle. It's a lovely redbrick mansion about 2 miles from the city, in the suburb village of Warwick-on-Eden, and has all the country-house trappings you could wish for: huge rooms, high ceilings, sweeping grounds and even its own river to fish in. Rooms are old-fashioned and furnished with antiques: for maximum space and comfort go for the Garden or River View Suite.

Hallmark Hotel   HOTEL ££
(☎01228-531951; carlisle.reception@hallmarkhotels .co.uk; d from £75-95; ◨🐾) Carlisle has been crying out for a decent city-centre hotel for years, and it's finally got one in the shape of the Hallmark Chain it may be, but it's useful if you want to be in the middle of things. It's a long way from 'boutique' (despite what the brochure says), but it's perfectly comfortable as long as you make sure you get one of the renovated rooms. Train noise might be a problem, as it's right next door to the station.

Premier Inn Carlisle Central   HOTEL ££
(☎0871 527 8210; Warwick Rd; r £65-95; ◨🐾) Yes, yes, we do realise it's a Premier Inn, but don't dismiss it out of hand. It's on Warwick Rd about a mile from the city centre, and the rates offer decent value considering the convenient location. And of course you

Carlisle

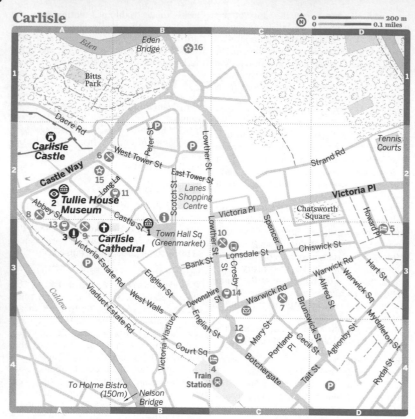

know exactly what you're going to get: identikit furniture and easy-clean fabrics. On the plus side, it's in a modern purpose-built building, there's loads of parking and it has a half-decent restaurant.

Willowbeck Lodge
B&B ££
(☎01228-513607; www.willowbeck-lodge.com; Lambley Bank, Scotby; d £100-130; P 🛜) This impressive detached house makes a great place to escape the Carlisle bustle. It's in a bold modern house about 3 miles' drive from the outskirts. Six deluxe rooms are closer to hotel standard than B&B, offering tasteful shades of beige and taupe, luxurious bathrooms and a 22ft-high gabled lounge overlooking a private pond.

Langleigh Guest House
B&B ££
(☎01228-530440; www.langleighhouse.co.uk; 6 Howard Pl; s £36, d £72; P) This B&B is completely chaotic, but has period charm. It's decorated throughout in well-to-do Edwardian fashion – think brass lamps, antique

clocks and watercolour prints. Look elsewhere if you're not a fan of dogs.

🍴 Eating

Holme Bistro
BRITISH ££
(☎01228-534343; www.holmebistro.co.uk; 56-58 Denton St; mains £11-16; ⊙lunch & dinner Mon-Sat) The top spot to eat in Carlisle right now, bar none. It's a short stroll south from the station and run by a brother-and-sister team, Rob Don and Kirsty Robson. Together they produce modern British bistro food with a minimum of pomp and pretension. The dining room is attractively finished with white walls and wood, and the food is similarly classic: tuck into confit duck, pork escalopes or baked cod, or come on Friday for the steak special. Worth the walk.

Bari
INDIAN £
(☎01228-522970; 21-23 West Tower Street; mains £5.95-11.95; ⊙dinner) Owner Abdul Bari has

Carlisle

INLAND CUMBRIA CARLISLE

really gone to town on the interior at this popular Indian restaurant, with sleek wood floors, mood lighting and smooth leather. It's an attractive setting in which to enjoy some of the city's best Indian cuisine, including unusual dishes such as crab *malabari masala* (white crab with coconut and masala spices) or *adrakhi* (chicken or lamb cooked with olives, ginger and chilli).

David's BISTRO ££
(☎01228-523578; 62 Warwick Rd; lunch £8-12, dinner £14-24; ◷lunch & dinner Tue-Sat) Townhouse dining with a refined air. David's has been a big name on the Carlisle scene for some years, and it's still up there. The interior is all elegant mantelpieces and overhead chandeliers, providing a perfect atmosphere for suave dishes with a classically French influence.

Foxes Café Lounge CAFE £
(18 Abbey St; ◷9.30am-4.30pm Tue-Sat, plus 7.30-11.30pm Fri & Sat) Lively cafe-cum-gallery displaying local art on the walls and providing an outlet for all kinds of creative happenings, from open-mic nights to photo exhibitions. Continental cafe food on the menu, and a good selection of global beers and home-brewed coffees.

Townhouse CAFE £
(34 Lowther St; lunch £3.95-5.95; ◷9am-5pm) This city-centre cafe is a reliable bet for light lunches, crunchy salads and classic tea and cake. There's a slightly bohemian vibe, thanks to the mix-and-match furniture,

fairy lights and chalkboard menus. It's good for a late breakfast – check out the porridge choices and decide whether you're a northerner or a southerner...

Prior's Kitchen Restaurant CAFE £
(Carlisle Cathedral; lunches £4-6; ◷9.45am-4pm Mon-Sat) Formerly a monk's refectory, this stone-vaulted cafe is a popular post-shop cafe, especially with ladies of a certain age. Plump for a cream tea or a hot buttered teacake, or browse the daily selection of quiches, baguettes and sandwich rounds.

🍷 Drinking

Carlisle's nightlife centres on the wall to wall bars around Botchergate, but it gets notoriously troublesome at chucking-out time; if you've ever wondered what the phenomenon of British binge drinking is all about, this is the place to find out. Mind how you go.

Gilded Lily PUB
(6 Lowther St; ◷9am-midnight Mon-Thu, 9am-2am Fri & Sat, noon-midnight Sun) Once a bank, now an upmarket city pub. Indulge in Continental beers and bespoke cocktails beneath the original skylight, and be prepared for plenty of dolled-up punters come the weekend.

Fats PUB
(48 Abbey St; ◷11am-11pm) Slate, steel and an open fireplace attract a classy clientele to Fats. World beers behind the bar, with open-mic nights, scratch sessions and DJs to pull in the punters.

SETTLE–CARLISLE RAILWAY

Britain has its fair share of classic railway journeys, but few can match the history and heritage of the **Settle–Carlisle Railway** (www.settle-carlisle.co.uk), which rattles across the Yorkshire Dales and the Eden Valley from Leeds to Carlisle, with stops at Settle, Kirkby Stephen and Appleby.

It's one of England's most stunning train journeys, traversing a varied landscape of moor, heath, pasture and valley, not to mention 14 tunnels and the 24-arched Ribblehead viaduct, one of the great triumphs of Victorian engineering.

The line required the blood, sweat and graft of 6000 'navvies' to complete at a cost of £3.5 million (twice the original estimate), and work was halted several times due to freezing weather conditions, floods, blizzards and even a smallpox outbreak. The railway was finally opened for business in 1876. Over a century later in 1998, a memorial stone was laid in the churchyard of St Mary's in Mallerstang to commemorate the scores of workers who lost their lives during its construction.

If you're planning on hopping on and off, it's probably worth getting a Settle–Carlisle Day Ranger ticket for £25/12.50 per adult/child, or a longer Rover Ticket allowing four days' travel in eight for £44/22.

Other sample fares from Carlisle:

DESTINATION	SINGLE	DAY RETURN	DURATION (HR)
Appleby	£8.60	£9.10	¾
Leeds	£24.40	£29.40	2½
Settle	£17.80	£21.20	1½
Skipton	£19.70	£25.30	2

Alcoves Café Bar
BAR

(Up Long Lane, 18 Fisher Street; ◷6pm-late Tue-Sat) Easy to miss, but this alleyway hangout near the cathedral is a popular spot for late-night drinks and DJs when you're wanting to evade the Botchergate hullabaloo. Look out for the lane off Fisher St.

Café Solo
BAR

(1 Botchergate) Hispanic-themed cocktails, late-night tapas and Sol beers at a tiny corner bar on the edge of Botchergate.

☆ Entertainment

Sands Centre
EXHIBITION CENTRE

(www.thesandscentre.co.uk) The city's main entertainment and music venue hosts everything from gigs to trade shows. It's about a 10-minute walk from town.

Brickyard
LIVE MUSIC

(www.thebrickyardonline.com; 14 Fisher St) Carlisle's oldest gig venue has had its ups and downs over the years, but it's still the main place to catch new acts and touring bands. It's housed in the former Memorial Hall near the castle.

Information

You'll find branches of all the major banks around Lowther St, Bank St and English St.

Cumberland Infirmary (☎01228-523444; Newtown Rd) Half a mile west of the city centre.

Police Station (☎0845 33 00 247; English St; ◷8am-midnight)

Tourist office (☎01228-625600; www .historic-carlisle.org.uk; Greenmarket; internet per 15min £1; ◷9.30am-5pm Mon-Sat, 10.30am-4pm Sun May-Aug, 10am-4pm Mon-Sat Sep-Apr)

Getting There & Away

Bus

Carlisle is Cumbria's main transport hub. For details on long-distance coaches to London and elsewhere, see p221.

Useful regional bus links:

104 (40 minutes, hourly Monday to Saturday, nine on Sunday) To Penrith.

554 (70 minutes, three daily) To Keswick, where it connects with the 555 Lakeslink to Windermere, Ambleside and Coniston.

600 (one hour, seven Monday to Saturday) To Cockermouth and towns in between.

AD 122 (Hadrian's Wall bus; six daily April to October) Seasonal bus which roughly follows the route of the wall, stopping in Brampton and Hexham.

Train

Carlisle is the county's busiest rail link. For details on train services across northern England and further afield, see p221. It's also the terminus for several regional railways:

Cumbrian Coast Line Loops round the coastline stopping at Maryport, Workington, Whitehaven, Ravenglass and Barrow, linking up with the Furness line to Grange-over-Sands, Arnside and Lancaster.

Settle-Carlisle Line (www.settle-carlisle.co.uk) Historic line which cuts southeast across the Yorkshire Dales.

Tyne Valley Line Follows Hadrian's Wall to Newcastle-upon-Tyne (£13.60, 1½ hours), with stops at Hexham, Alston, Haltwhistle and Brampton.

Getting Around

For taxis in Carlisle, try the following:

Citadel Station Taxis (☑01228-523971)
County Cabs (☑01228-596789)
Radio Taxis (☑01228-527575)

AROUND CARLISLE

While most people make a headlong dash out of Carlisle for the M6, the open countryside around the city is worth taking a couple of days to explore. This is one of the best places to investigate Cumbria's past: to the east, you can make the pilgrimage to the great ecclesiastical seat of Lanercost Priory, before exploring the remains of Hadrian's Wall around Brampton and the crumbling garrison fort at Birdoswald. If you've got time, there's also a famous Anglo-Saxon cross at Bewcastle.

Brampton & Around

The stout sandstone market town of Brampton lies 7 miles northeast of Carlisle and 2 miles west from the remains of Hadrian's Wall. Founded around the 7th century and later an important terminus on the Tyne Valley Railway, the town now makes a good base for exploring the area east of Carlisle, with a smattering of boutiquey B&Bs and a more relaxed feel than the hustle and rush of nearby Carlisle.

◉ Sights

Brampton Town   HISTORIC AREA

Notable for its winding exterior staircase, arched windows and weather-vane turret,

Brampton's octagonal **Moot Hall** was built in 1817 and is now occupied by the **Brampton Tourist Office** (☑016977-3433; tourism@carlisle.gov.uk; ⊙10am-5pm Mon-Sat Easter-Sep, to 4pm Oct-Easter).

The town's other landmark is **St Martin's Church** (www.stmartinsbrampton.org.uk; ⊙9.30am-4.30pm), designed by architect Philip Webb, a key figure in the Pre-Raphaelite movement and a partner in the interior-design company run by artist Edward Burne-Jones, poet-painter Dante Gabriel Rossetti and English designer William Morris (whose workshop made the church's stained-glass windows).

Two miles south of town is the 26-hectare boating lake of **Talkin Tarn**, scooped out by an ancient glacier and now surrounded by walking trails and 48 hectares of quiet woodland. The nearby **Gelt Woods RSPB Reserve** is a popular haven for twitchers and bird spotters.

Lanercost Priory   CHURCH

(www.lanercostpriory.org.uk; suggested donation adult/child £3/1.50; ⊙10am-5pm mid-Mar–Sep, slightly shorter hr at other times) About 3 miles northeast of the town centre is the rosy ruin of Lanercost Priory, situated at the old crossing over the River Irthing.

Second only in stature to the abbey in Furness, Lanercost was founded by Augustinian monks in the mid-12th century, but has a chequered history. Marauding Scottish raiders sacked the building at least four times, and it suffered the same sorry fate as Cumbria's other priories during Henry VIII's Dissolution.

Fortunately Lanercost was saved from total collapse by Victorian architect Anthony Salvin, who restored part of the building and converted it for use as a parish church in the mid-19th century.

In summer, the AD 122 stops directly outside the priory.

Sleeping & Eating

TOP CHOICE Willowford Farm   B&B **££**

(☑016977-47962; www.willowford.co.uk; Gilsland; s £50, d £75-120; P) It'd be hard to find a nicer location than this: Hadrian's Wall steamrollers literally right through the grounds of this eco-conscious farm B&B. It's just outside the village of Gilsland, and offers a choice of rooms in the main house or in a converted milking parlour. It's worth bumping up to a superior room or the family suite, where

BIRDOSWALD ROMAN FORT

Just east of Lanercost Priory, the remains of one of England's great ancient **monuments** (EH; www.birdoswaldromanfort.org; adult/child £5/3; ☺10am-5.30pm mid-Mar–Sep, 10am-4pm Oct–mid-Mar) wind out across the flat fields. The great barrier of **Hadrian's Wall** once stretched for just over 70 miles between Wallsend and Bowness-on-Solway, and was manned by several thousand legionaries operating from garrison forts positioned at key points along the wall's length.

Though most have long since been plundered for building supplies, you can still see the remains of a few, notably at Vindolanda and this one at Birdoswald.

Built to replace an earlier timber-and-turf fort, Birdoswald would have been the operating base for around 1000 Roman soldiers; excavations have revealed three of the four gateways, as well as granary stores, workshops, exterior walls and a military drill hall. A visitor centre explores the fort's history and the background behind the wall's construction.

you'll find a combination of smart design (reclaimed beams, wood, slate) and environmental friendliness (fleece insulation, underfloor heating). The breakfast is really hearty, and there's a set menu every night for £18; ask nicely and they'll even pack you lunch for the next day for £6.

TOP CHOICE Crosby Lodge B&B £££
(☎01228-573618; www.crosbylodge.co.uk; Crosby-on-Eden; lunch/dinner menu £28/38, s £90-100, d £160-185; P) It's on the pricey side, but this 1805 country house, with its obstentatious architecture, makes for a supremely luxurious stay. The decor is positively Austenesque: lofty Georgian windows overlook tended parkland, and the interior is an antique shop of burnished dressers and sleigh beds. The restaurant is one of the most renowned in northern Cumbria – decked out in rich crimsons and oil paintings, with a five-course menu stuffed with amuse-bouches, langoustine, sweetbreads and beef in Béarnaise sauce. Reservations are essential.

Tantallon House B&B ££
(☎016977-47111; www.hadrians-wall-bed-and-breakfast.co.uk; Gilsland; s £55, d £86-90; P🛜) Another lovely gabled B&B in Gilsland, a stone's throw from Birdoswald. The rooms are huge and airy, with Victorian hearths and sash windows overlooking shrub-filled gardens. Don't forget to visit the aviary and say hello to Hoot the owl.

❶ Getting There & Away

BUS Useful buses to Brampton:
685 (hourly Monday to Saturday, four on Sunday) Stops en route from Carlisle and continues to Hexham (one hour 20 minutes) and Newcastle (two hours 20 minutes). Three buses a day run via Gilsland.

95 (20 minutes, two daily Monday to Saturday)
AD 122 (Hadrian's Wall Bus) Seasonal service that runs four times daily from April to October. It runs from Carlisle to Brampton, Lanercost Priory, Birdoswald Fort and Gilsland, then continues to Haltwhistle, the Roman forts at Vindolanda and Chesters, and Hexham. One bus a day continues to Newcastle.

TRAIN There are around six daily trains from Carlisle to Brampton (£4.20, 15 minutes) and Haltwhistle (£6.90, 30 minutes).

PENRITH & THE EDEN VALLEY

POP 14,882

There's a flavour of bygone days hanging around the crimson-bricked streets of Penrith, one of eastern Cumbria's most atmospheric market towns and, until 1070, its capital.

Vintage shopfronts, traditional greengrocers and old pubs line its cobbled alleys and busy shopping arcades, and the focus of daily life still revolves around the medieval market square. While it might not be as pretty as other Lakeland towns, Penrith makes a lively and convenient gateway for exploring the eastern Lakes and the Eden Valley.

History

Penrith's name derives from the Celtic words *penn* and *rid*, meaning either 'hill ford', 'main ford' or 'red hill'. During the 9th and 10th centuries the town was allied with the Scots as part of Strathclyde, and served as the capital of the semi-autonomous kingdom of Rheged until 1070.

It was later annexed by the English in 1295, leading to a century of conflict with the Border Reivers, who sacked the town three times, prompting the construction of a defensive pele tower (later reinforced as Penrith Castle) and a warning beacon at the top of Beacon Hill.

⊙ Sights

Penrith Castle   RUIN
(⊘7.30am-9pm Easter-Oct, 7.30am 4.30pm Oct-Easter) Opposite the station are the ruins of this 14th-century castle, built by William Strickland (later Bishop of Carlisle and Archbishop of Canterbury). The castle was substantially reinforced by Richard, Duke of Gloucester (later Richard III), to resist Scottish raids, which had previously razed the town three times (in 1314, 1345 and 1382). Richard embellished the castle with a new banqueting hall and residential quarters before becoming King of England in 1483 following Edward IV's death; he was killed just two years later at the Battle of Bosworth Field and the castle fell into disrepair.

FREE Penrith Museum   MUSEUM
(⊘9.30am 5pm   Mon-Sat,   1-4.45pm   Sun) Penrith's tourist office houses a quirky museum displaying local historical objects. Look out for antique clocks from the town's heyday as a clock-making centre, ceremonial keys, and a wrestling belt belonging to William Jameson, a former champion Cumbrian wrestler (memorably described as 'a polar bear on its hind legs in a grey flannel shirt').

There's also a display on Percy Topliss, the notorious army fraudster, impostor and con man sometimes known as 'the Monocled Mutineer'. Following a career of forgery, impersonation, black marketeering and general skulduggery, Topliss murdered a taxi driver and wounded two policemen and went on the run; he was eventually killed during a gunfight with local bobbies near Penrith, and was buried in an unmarked grave in Beacon Edge Cemetery. You can see the monocle he often used as part of his disguise in the museum's display cabinet.

St Andrew's Church   CHURCH
Built from the distinctive local red sandstone, St Andrew's Church was constructed

during the 18th century on the site of an earlier chapel, parts of which survive in the 14th-century church tower.

In the churchyard are the weathered remains of two Celtic crosses and four 10th-century tombstones, known as the **Giant's Grave**; local legend maintains they mark the burial site of Owen Caesarius, the rightful king of Cumbria.

Nearby is the **Giant's Thumb**, another badly weathered Norse cross believed to date from the 10th century.

Old Town   HISTORIC BUILDINGS
Penrith was granted its market charter in the 13th century, and grew into an important trading centre, with markets centring on Corn Market, Dockray, Sandgate, Burrowgate, Castle Mart and Market Pl.

Following the arrival of the railway in the mid-19th century, Penrith became a bustling industrial base, especially for tanners, weavers, tailors, coopers and saddle makers; in 1907 the town boasted 57 inns (each associated with a particular trade or guild) for a population of just over 9000 people. Many of the town's streets still bear reminders of the old trades with which they were once associated.

Brougham Castle & Around   RUIN
(EH; ☎01768-862488; adult/child £3/1.50; ⊘10am-5pm mid-Mar–Sep) Straddling the banks of the River Eamont, on the foundations of the old Roman fort of Brocavum, Brougham Castle (pronounced 'broom') was begun in the early 13th century by local notable Robert de Vieuxpoint, and reinforced by the Clifford family as a defensive stronghold against Scottish raids. You can clamber up to the top of Vieuxpoint's striking central keep for fabulous views over the Eden countryside, and there are Roman tombstones on display in the castle grounds.

On your way back to town, it's worth detouring via the 14th-century mansion of **Brougham Hall**, which houses a craft centre, chocolate shop, tearoom and smokehouse.

Nearby is a Stone Age earthwork known as **King Arthur's Round Table**. The standing stones that marked the spot have long since disappeared, although you can still make out the monument's central plateau and encircling ditch; the site was clearly connected with a second, much larger henge at **Mayburgh**, a few hundred metres to the west.

Penrith

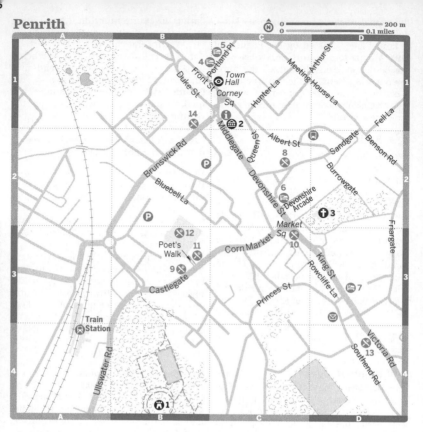

🛏 Sleeping

Penrith's best B&Bs are side by side along Portland Pl, although there's a second cluster of more downmarket places along Victoria Rd.

Lounge HOTEL ££

(☏01768-866395; www.theloungehotelandbar.co .uk; King St; s £55, d £90-95; ☏) Penrith's newest and funkiest place to stay is this snazzy number on King St, just a couple of minutes from the market square. Inside it's clean and pleasantly contemporary: cream and cappuccino tones in the smallish rooms, lively pattern prints and funky furniture in the downstairs bistro-bar. There's a three-bedroom apartment for longer stays.

Brooklands B&B ££

(☏01768-863395; www.brooklandsguesthouse .com; 2 Portland Pl; s £38, d £75-85; ☏) The town's most elegant B&B is this Victorian redbrick on Portland Pl. Rich furnishings and posh

extras (such as White Company toiletries, fridges and chocs on the tea tray) keep it a cut above the crowd.

Brandelhow B&B ££

(☏01768-864470; www.brandelhowguesthouse.co .uk; 1 Portland Pl; s £35, d & tw £70; ☏) Bang next door to Brooklands, things are more staid at this friendly, family-run guesthouse. Nothing remarkable about the rooms, but the little treats make it worth considering – such as the sit-down welcome tea accompanied by Bootle Gingerbread or Lanie's Expedition Flapjack.

George Hotel HOTEL ££

(☏01768-862696; www.lakedistricthotels.net /georgehotel; d £108-180; ☏☏) You won't find a better location in Penrith than the one belonging to this scarlet-bricked stalwart right on the market square. Once the town's main coaching inn, it's now mainly frequented by business travellers – expect efficient service

Penrith

◎ **Sights**

and corporate rooms in creams, taupes and beiges, plus a rather quaint bar and country restaurant.

Hornby Hall   HOTEL **££**
(☎01768-891114; www.hornbyhall.co.uk; Brougham; d £80-100; 🅿) Aspiring aristocrats should head for this amber-stone manorhouse, 3 miles south of Penrith in Brougham. The five sunny rooms overlook the manicured grounds; two are reached via a Hogwarts-esque spiral staircase, and breakfast is served in the 16th-century dining hall with its original stone hearth and Victorian range. Dinner is available at £20/30 for two/three courses.

✖ Eating

Penrith's **farmers market** fills Market Sq on the third Tuesday of every month from 9.30am to 2pm. There are large branches of Morrisons and Co-Op supermarkets near the town centre for self-caterers.

TOP CHOICE ⟩ Yanwath Gate Inn   PUB **£££**
(☎01768-862886; Yanwath; mains £16-19) Gastropub gorgeousness is the order of the day at the Yat, 2 miles south of town. It's been named Cumbria's Top Dining Pub three times by the *Good Pub Guide,* and the grub puts many of the county's gastronomic restaurants to shame: wild venison, saltmarsh lamb, Brougham Hall chicken and crispy pork belly, chased down by Cumbrian cheeses and beers from three local breweries.

No 15   CAFE **££**
(15 Victoria Rd; lunches £6-10) Our tip for lunch is this groovy cafe-gallery, with blackboard specials of tempting pies, salads and wraps accompanied by first-rate coffee and freshly mixed smoothies. Look out for the art and photography exhibitions in the annexe, and late-night music sessions.

JJ Graham   DELI **£**
(www.jjgraham.co.uk; 6-7 Market Sq) This historic grocer's shop is a treat for picnic supplies. Wicker baskets are filled with warm crusty bread, glass chiller cabinets are crammed with cheeses and cold cuts, and assorted cakes and biscuits are stacked up on the counter tops. You'll even find bottled beers from Cumbria's top breweries.

INLAND CUMBRIA PENRITH & THE EDEN VALLEY

WORTH A TRIP

LONG MEG & HER DAUGHTERS

The third-largest prehistoric stone circle in England, Long Meg and Her Daughters stands in the centre of a rolling field near the village of Little Salkeld, 6 miles northeast of Penrith. It's thought that the circle would have originally contained up to 77 uprights; today only around 27 are still standing in their original places, while many more have toppled over or been shifted over the course of the centuries.

Local legend maintains that the circle was once a coven of witches, zapped into stone by a local wizard. The circle is also said to be uncountable (if anyone manages twice the spell will be lifted) and a terrible fate awaits anyone who disturbs the stones. Just outside the circle stands Long Meg herself, a 12ft red sandstone pillar decorated with faint spiral traces; another local legend says that the stone would run with blood if it were ever damaged.

The circle is situated along a minor road three-quarters of a mile north of Little Salkeld, just off the A686. Follow the signs to the 'Druid's Circle'.

DON'T MISS

BAKED TO PERFECTION

There are two renowned bakeries around Penrith.

The **Watermill** (☑01768-881523; www.organicmill.co.uk) in Little Salkeld is one of the last remaining mills in England powered in the time-honoured fashion using two overshot waterwheels. You can see the wheels in action year-round on a **self-guided mill tour** (£2 for 1st person, £1 for extra people), or if one of the bakers is free they'll show you around in person. There's also a tearoom where you can pick up organic breads, cakes and other goodies. Courses in bread making, milling, baking and oven making are offered regularly throughout the year.

Meanwhile, the 100%-organic **Village Bakery** (www.village-bakery.com) in Melmerby is renowned for its sourdoughs, Russian ryes, French country loaves and granary breads, not to mention an irresistible selection of lemon drizzle cakes and dark chocolate tortes.

Magic Bean   BISTRO ££
(☑01768-867474; Poet's Walk; mains £6-14; ☻lunch & dinner Mon-Sat) A rather curious restaurant tucked away along a little alleyway. During the day it's a fairly traditional cafe serving light lunches and afternoon teas, but after dark it spices things up with a range of spicy Indian dishes.

Grants of Castlegate   BISTRO ££
(☑01768-895444; Castlegate; mains £8.95-14.95; ☻lunch & dinner Wed-Sun) Glossy split-level bistro on Castlegate, plundering global flavours for its catch-all menu – expect everything from stir-fries and chicken breast to risotto and ravioli. It's bright and modern, and popular with Penrith's wine-bar crowd, but the food's fairly ordinary.

Toffee Shop   SWEETS
(www.thetoffeeshop.co.uk) This traditional confectioner has been making creamy toffees and tasty fudges for nearly 100 years.

Cranstons   BUTCHER
(www.cranstons.net; Ullswater Rd) Established in 1914, this well-regarded butcher produces award-winning Cumberland sausages, hams and bacons. It has its own large food hall just outside the town centre.

ℹ Information

Branches of Lloyds, HSBC and Barclays are on Market Sq.
Penrith Library (☑01768-242100; St Andrew's Churchyard; internet per ½hr £1; ☻10am-7pm Mon & Tue, to 1pm Wed, to 5pm Thu & Fri, to 4pm Sat & Sun)
Tourist office (☑01768-867466; pen.tic @eden.gov.uk; Middlegate; ☻9.30am-5pm Mon-Sat, 1-4.45pm Sun)

ℹ Getting There & Around

Bike Hire

Arragon's Cycle Centre (☑01768-890344; www.arragons.com; Brunswick Rd; ☻9am-5.30pm Mon-Sat)
Cycle Active (☑01768-840400; www.cycle active.co.uk) Near Brougham Hall.

Bus

The bus station is northeast of the centre, off Sandgate.
104 (45 minutes, hourly Monday to Saturday, nine on Sunday) Penrith to Carlisle.
X4/X5 (hourly Monday to Saturday, six on Sunday) Travels via Rheged, Keswick and Cockermouth en route to the Cumbrian Coast.

Train

Penrith has frequent connections to Carlisle (£5.70, 15 minutes, hourly) and Lancaster (£13.70, 50 to 60 minutes, hourly).

AROUND PENRITH

Rheged

Cunningly disguised as a Lakeland hill 2 miles west of Penrith, **Rheged** (www.rheged .com; ☻10am-6pm) houses a large-screen Imax cinema and an exhibition on the history and geology of Cumbria, as well as a retail hall selling Cumbrian goods from handmade paper to chocolate and chutneys.

The cinema offers a regularly changing line-up of around six films, shown on a loop throughout the day. A new flick starts hourly; one film costs £6.50/4.80 per adult/child, with each extra film costing £3.50/2.20.

The frequent X4/X5 bus between Penrith and Workington stops at the centre.

Eden Ostrich World

Near the village of Langwathby, this rather odd **animal park** (www.ostrich-world.com; adult/2-15yr £6.25/5.65; ⊙10am-5pm Easter-Oct, to 4pm Wed-Sun Nov-Easter) is a mix of working farm and exotic zoo. Among its oddball attractions, you can watch sheep being milked, pet a zebroid (a cross between a zebra and a Shetland pony) and view the resident flock of ratites (a family of flightless birds that includes the ostrich). It's bound to be a big hit with the kids, and there are outdoor and indoor play areas for when they get bored.

Hutton-in-the-Forest

Owned by the Inglewood family since 1605, this truly magnificent **stately home** (www .hutton-in-the-forest.co.uk; adult/7 16yr £8.50/3, gardens only £5/free; ⊙house 12.30-4pm Wed, Thu & Sun mid-Apr-Oct, gardens 11am-5pm Sun-Fri Apr-Oct) was built in several stages spanning six centuries. It began life in around 1350 as a fortified pele tower, and successive generations of owners added and expanded to the architectural mix. It's still owned by the second Lord Inglewood, an ex-barrister, Euro MP and current hereditary peer in the House of Lords.

Highlights include the delicate Renaissance facade and the grand neo-Gothic South Front, complete with castellations and arched windows. The twin towers were both added during the Victorian era, including the southeast tower, designed by noted architect Anthony Salvin (who built a number of churches around the Lake District, remodelled Muncaster and Greystoke Castles and also built the house on Derwent Isle on Derwentwater). Formal gardens surround the house, filled with clipped topiary, three landscaped lakes and a 17th-century dovecote.

Inside the house is even more impressive. Among the rooms on display are a lavishly furnished drawing room, an elegant library and a surprisingly domestic great hall, bedecked with coats-of-arms, antlers and armour. Look out for the famous 17th-century Cupid staircase, featuring carved depictions of the winged cherub surrounded by acanthus leaves.

The house is 6 miles northwest of Penrith.

Appleby-in-Westmorland

Tucked in an ox-bow curve of the River Eden, the sweet market town of Appleby was once the second-most important in the Eden Valley, and until the formation of the new district of Cumbria in 1974 served as Westmorland's county town.

It's a sleepy, charming slice of old England, with traditional butchers, village shops and tearooms dotted along its central street, Boroughgate, which slices through the town to the sandstone facade of **St Lawrence's Church** and the **Cloisters**, a pleasant covered arcade built by Robert Smirke (who also designed Lowther Castle).

The town's most famous resident was the redoubtable Lady Anne Clifford, a local aristocrat and part-time philanthropist who devoted much of her life to restoring neglected estates, churches and castles. One of her pet projects was the Norman keep of **Appleby**

DON'T MISS

GREYSTOKE CYCLE CAFE

For long-distance bikers on the C2C route, this eccentric **cafe** (☑017684-83984; www .greystokecyclecafe.co.uk; ⊙noon-6pm Fri, 10am-6pm Sat Easter-Sep, plus 10am-6pm 2nd Sun of month) in the village of Greystoke has become an essential stop. It has a lovely tearoom serving hot meals, drinks and afternoon teas, and also has a dedicated Cyclists Barn stocked with inner tubes, puncture repair kits and other bike spares. But it's worth a visit even if you're not cycling: the cafe runs a programme of 'quirky workshops' throughout the year, encompassing everything from bike-maintenance to willowcraft, greenwood spoon-carving, water divination, weaving and drystone walling. You can even learn the basics of blacksmithing and silversmithing. See the website for the latest schedule.

The cafe is 5 miles east of Penrith on the B5288.

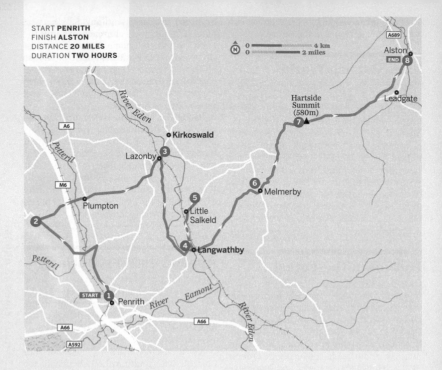

Driving Tour
Road to the Pennines

❯ The Automobile Association (AA) has dubbed the road trip from Penrith to Alston along the A686 one of Britain's top 10 drives, and with good reason.

Begin by picking up some supplies for the journey at JJ Graham in ① **Penrith**. Head northwest from town on the A6, and follow the signs to the country manor of ② **Hutton-in-the-Forest**, renowned for its ostentatious architecture and beautifully landscaped estate.

Follow the minor road to Plumpton, continue on the B6413 via ③ **Lazonby**, and turn south onto the B6412 to Great Salkeld. Follow signs onto the A686 to Langwathby, where you can stop in to see the curious menagerie at ④ **Eden Ostrich World**, or make a detour to the stone circle of ⑤ **Long Meg and Her Daughters** near Little Salkeld.

Either way, continue on the A686 through Melmerby, where you can make a memorable lunch stop at the ⑥ **Village Bakery**, famous for its breads and cakes.

Once you've fuelled up, begin the long, looping climb on the A686 up to ⑦ **Hartside Summit** (580m/1904ft), one of the most spectacularly sited road passes anywhere in England.

The switchbacking road makes for lively driving, and the views open up as you climb up the side of the ridge. At the top of the pass you'll be able to take a break at a car park and small roadside cafe. The panorama from here is quite staggering, stretching across the valley all the way to the distant Lakeland fells – see if you can spot the tops of Helvellyn, Great Gable and Skiddaw way, way out to the west.

Keep following the A686 as it trundles along a narrow ridge road, passing through the bracken-covered fields, plunging dales and austere countryside so characteristic of the Pennines. Eventually you'll wind up in England's highest market town at ⑧ **Alston**, where you can take an optional ride aboard the steam trains of the South Tynedale Railway.

Castle (closed to the public), which stands at Boroughgate's southern end and served for several centuries as the family seat of the Clifford family.

Appleby's other claim to fame is its historic **horse fair**, which has been held since 1685 and still attracts a colourful pageant of painted gypsy wagons to the town's streets every June.

🛏 Sleeping & Eating

Tufton Arms   HOTEL ££

(☎017683-51593; www.tuftonarmshotel.co.uk; Market Sq, Appleby; s £59-113, d £97-212; ℗) First a 16th-century coaching inn, then a Victorian house, now a spiffing town hotel. All the rooms are different: plaster engravings and chandeliers meet muted paints and bespoke wallpapers in some, while others are the picture of restrained *Homes & Gardens* sophistication. It's dead in the centre of Appleby, and the classy bistro (mains £10.95 to £21.95) turns out the town's best food.

Marton House   B&B ££

(☎017683-61502; www.martonhousecumbria.co.uk; Long Marton; s/d £50/75; ℗) Just a few rooms at this russet-coloured manor house in the village of Long Marton, but they're beauties: huge, relaxing and rural-cosy, with period interests ranging from original hearths to vintage baths. The house is grandly ringed by gardens, and breakfast is served in an orangery on summer mornings.

ℹ Getting There & Away

Appleby sits on the Settle-Carlisle Railway line: see p172 for fares and times. The most useful bus is the 563 from Penrith (30 minutes, six to eight Monday to Saturday).

Alston

POP 2227

Surrounded by the bleak hilltops of the Pennines, isolated Alston's main claim to fame is its elevation: at 305m above sea level, it is the highest market town in England (although it no longer has a market).

It is also famous among steam enthusiasts thanks to the diminutive **South Tynedale Railway** (☎01434-381696, talking timetable 01434-382828; www.strps.org.uk; adult/3-15yr return £6/3; ☉Apr-Oct), which puffs the hilly country between Alston and Kirkhaugh, along a route that originally operated from 1852 to 1976. The return trip aboard a steam

or diesel locomotive takes an hour, with around five daily trains in midsummer.

Opposite the station is the **Hub Heritage Museum** (☎01434-382272; donations welcome; ☉11am-4pm on railway days), which houses a display of antique cars, old farming implements, period posters and sepia photos in a vintage railway-goods shed.

Alston's library and **tourist office** (☎01434-382244; alston.tic@eden.gov.uk; Town Hall, Front St; ☉10am-5pm Mon-Sat, to 4pm Sun) are in the Town Hall, at the foot of Alston's steep cobbled main street.

🛏 Sleeping & Eating

Yew Tree Chapel   B&B ££

(☎01434-382525; www.yewtreechapel.co.uk; Slaggyford; s £45, d £70; ℗) Quirky B&B in a converted church, with the original organ and stained-glass windows still in place. The decor is boho-chic, and there's fresh bread, cinnamon toast and gourmet muesli for brekkie. It's in Slaggyford, 3 miles north of Alston.

Lowbyer Manor   B&B ££

(☎01434-381230; www.lowbyer.com; Alston; s £33, d £66-90) This simple B&B is the best option in Alston proper, worth a look for its sweetly homespun decor (all the quilts were sewn by the owner's relatives). The house is looking a touch tired in spots, but it's handy for the steam train – the station's only a stroll away.

WORTH A TRIP

NENTHEAD MINES

Over 40 miles of subterranean tunnels wind their way through the **Nenthead Mines** (☎01434-382037; www.npht.com; visit with mine tour £7/3, otherwise by donation), sunk between the 17th and 19th centuries to extract the rich deposits of lead, zinc and other minerals buried beneath the Pennines rock. A one-hour guided tour takes in some of the gloomy mine workings; you'll need something warm to wear and sturdy shoes, as it's just 10°C underground. The tour visits several deep shafts and explains some of its powerhouse machinery; elsewhere you can visit the remains of an old smelt works and waterwheel complex, or try your hand at a spot of metal panning.

INLAND CUMBRIA ALSTON

Lovelady Shield
HOTEL £££

(☏0871 288 1345; www.lovelady.co.uk; Nenthead Rd, Alston; d £100-175; ℙ) Definitely not everyone's cup of tea, but this flouncy country house just outside Alston is the place if you're a fan of *Homes & Gardens* interiors. It sits in its own private grounds and has views over the River Nent.

Alston YHA
HOSTEL £

(☏0870 770 5668; The Firs; dm £11.95; ⊙Easter-Oct) Basic hostel with three dorms overlooking the South Tyne Valley. It's popular with walkers and cyclists on the Sea to Sea Cycle Route (C2C), so book ahead.

ⓘ Getting There & Away

The handiest bus is the 680, which runs from Nenthead to Carlisle via Alston four times daily Monday to Saturday.

KENDAL

POP 28,398

Locally known as the 'Auld Grey Town' thanks to the grey limestone and slate used in its buildings, Kendal occupies a hallowed place in the hearts of many hill walkers thanks to its sweet and powerfully pepperminty treat, Kendal mintcake.

This calorific energy bar was concocted by accident by a local confectioner in the mid-19th century, and it's been a staple item in British rucksacks ever since (even making it to the top of Everest during Edmund Hillary and Tenzing Norgay's landmark ascent in 1953).

Kendal amounts to more than its mintcake, though: it's also an ideal gateway to the southern Lakes, with some intriguing galleries and an excellent arts centre to explore, and the national park's eastern border just 10 miles to the west.

⊙ Sights & Activities

Old Town
HISTORIC SITE

The heart of old Kendal centres on the streets of Stricklandgate and Highgate. The town developed into a prosperous market town following the granting of its charter in 1189. It was especially known for its trade in cloth and wool – 'Kendal green' is mentioned in Shakespeare's *Henry IV*, and the town's motto is *Pannus Mini Panis*, meaning 'wool is my bread'.

The town centre's buildings were laid out in a distinctive grid of regimented plots, linked by 'yards' which would have been used for activities such as tanning, dying, weaving and so on. There are around 150 yards in all, many of which still bear the names of their original owners (look out for Dr Manning's Yard on the right-hand side as you walk up Highgate).

During the Industrial Revolution Kendal became an industrial hub for everything from shoe and carpet manufacture to snuff making, and the river would have clattered with the sound of mills, looms and assorted machinery.

FREE Kendal Museum
MUSEUM

(www.kendalmuseum.org.uk; Station Rd; ⊙10.30am-5.30pm Wed-Sat) Housed in a former wool warehouse, Kendal's town museum was founded in 1796 by a local natural-history enthusiast, William Todhunter.

It's a typically fascinating mix of Victorian ephemera. Its echoey halls contain everything from Roman coins to Egyptian scarabs, medieval coin hoards and model boats, while the Natural History Gallery is crammed with a spooky menagerie of stuffed animals, including a great bustard, a flamingo bagged in 1860 and a polar bear that once belonged to the Earl of Lonsdale. There's also a large collection of rare rocks and minerals, based almost entirely on the enormous collection amassed by John Hamer, a local potholer and amateur mineralogist.

Alfred Wainwright, of *Pictorial Guide* fame, was honorary curator from 1945 to 1974. His former office has been reconstructed inside the museum, with some of the author's original drawings and a collection of his belongings (including his rucksack, walking jacket, spectacles and well-chewed pipe).

Entry is currently free, although charges may have been introduced by the time you read this.

Abbot Hall Art Gallery
GALLERY

(www.abbothall.org.uk; adult/under 18yr £6/free; ⊙10.30am-5pm Mon-Sat Apr-Oct, to 4pm Mon-Sat Nov-Mar) This art gallery is housed in a lovely Georgian villa and displays one of the northwest's best collections of 18th- and 19th-century art. It's especially strong on portraiture and Lakeland landscapes. Look out in the beautifully restored rooms for works by Constable, Varley and Turner, as well as portraits by John Ruskin and local boy George Romney, born in Dalton-

ALFRED WAINWRIGHT

Few names are more famous in Lakeland than that of Alfred Wainwright (known to his followers as AW). Born in Blackburn in 1907, Wainwright was an accountant by trade, but he became besotted with the fells following a chance climb up Orrest Head in 1930.

Fell walking quickly developed into a passion for AW. He devoted every spare weekend to travelling to the Lakes in order to tackle a new fell, or rehike an old one from a different route, especially following his move to the Kendal Treasurer's office in 1941.

Initially for his own amusement, he began to document his walks through detailed journals, hand-drawn maps and painstakingly accurate pen-and-ink drawings. The more he walked, however, the more Wainwright became dissatisfied with the existing guidebooks, which gave little indication of the geological quirks of each individual fell. So it was, in 1952, that he conceived his great project: to climb all the major Lakeland fells and record his favourite routes, noting down his own thoughts, experiences and philosophical musings along the way.

Having divided the area into seven sections according to the Ordnance Survey maps, and factoring in the time taken up by his daytime job as Borough Treasurer, he reckoned it would take 13 years to complete, averaging roughly one handwritten page per day. His routine was nearly always identical: he would rise early, travel to the Lakes by bus, climb all day, treat himself to a fish-and-chip supper, and then spend the following week writing up his notes, and drawing illustrations from photographs he had taken on the hills.

Initially, Wainwright had only vague intentions of collecting the work into a book, but it soon became apparent that he was creating something unique: part walking guide, part illustrated artwork and part philosophical memoir.

Encouraged by his friend Henry Marshall (Kendal's chief librarian), Wainwright finally published his first volume, *The Eastern Fells*, in 1955. It was an overnight success and led to six subsequent books. The last volume, *The Western Fells*, was completed in 1966, precisely on time for the schedule that Wainwright had set himself 13 years earlier.

The original guides were followed by further books, including *Pennine Way Companion* and *A Coast to Coast Walk* (a long-distance route that he devised in 1973). Well over two million books have now been sold, but despite their enormous success, the books were never intended as a money-making scheme: Wainwright gave away most of his profits to animal charities.

Wainwright died in 1991, and as requested in his will, his ashes were scattered near the shores of Innominate Tarn on Haystacks, his favourite mountain. The guides have recently been updated by Wainwright's walking disciple, Chris Jesty, but even so many people still prefer to carry the original volumes with them on their hikes.

For more information, contact the **Wainwright Society** (www.wainwright.org), which keeps the official register of all its members to have completed all 214 Wainwright summits.

in-Furness in 1734, and a key figure in the 'Kendal School'.

Museum of Lakeland Life   MUSEUM
(www.lakelandmuseum.org.uk; adult/child £5/ 3.50; ◎10.30am-5pm Mon-Sat Apr-Oct, to 4pm Mon-Sat Nov-Mar) Directly opposite Abbot Hall, this museum re-creates various scenes from Lakeland activity during the 18th and 19th centuries, including spinning, mining, weaving and bobbin making. There's also a reconstruction of the study of Arthur Ransome, author of *Swallows and Amazons*.

FREE **Kendal Castle**   RUIN
On the eastern bank of the River Kent stand the ruins of Kendal Castle, first constructed during the 13th century and later occupied by several baronial dynasties, including the Parr family (although local claims stating that Catherine Parr, sixth wife of Henry VIII, was born at the castle are probably more fiction than fact). Only a couple of solitary turrets of this once-powerful stronghold now remain, but the plateau offers fine views over town and countryside.

Kendal

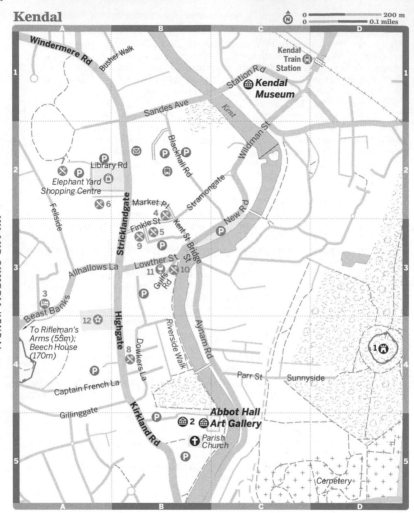

INLAND CUMBRIA KENDAL

From the town centre, follow Aynam Rd onto Parr St to get to the castle.

Holmescales ACTIVITY CENTRE
(📞01539-722147; www.holmescales.com) This centre near Kendal offers paintballing, quad-biking, archery, shooting and amphibious 'Argo Cats'. It also has special 'Secret Agent' days, during which you can learn how to stalk like an assassin and, erm, drive a tank.

Treks and Trails OUTDOORS
(📞01539-567477; www.treksandtrails.co.uk; Kendal) One-day navigation courses. Basic course £125, advanced £165.

🎊 Festivals & Events

Kendal Mintfest ARTS
Jugglers, acrobats and musicians hit Kendal for this street arts festival in early September.

Kendal Mountain Festival OUTDOORS FESTIVAL
(www.mountainfest.co.uk) Annual mountain-themed celebration encompassing books, film and live talks in November.

🛏 Sleeping

Beech House B&B ££
(📞01539-720385; www.beechhouse-kendal.co.uk; 40 Greenside; s £60-75, d £80-100; 🅿🛜) A

Kendal

supremely elegant B&B, set back from the town centre up the steep hill of Beast Banks. It's lodged inside a lovely Georgian house and has a really inviting line-up of rooms: some have velvet sofas and posh cushions, others roll-top baths and his-and-hers sinks. The overall feel is rather refined and upmarket, and the breakfast is about the best in Kendal. There's a small car park next to the house.

Hillside B&B ££
(📞01539-722836; www.hillside-kendal.co.uk; 4 Beast Banks; s £35-41, d £66-82; 📶) If Beech House is full, then this small and welcoming B&B on the steepest section of Beast Banks is a good reserve. The standard rooms are plainly furnished but good value: the superior room is a bit snazzier and looks out over Kendal. Parking is on-street; the owners can lend you a permit for the duration of your stay.

Heaves Hotel GUESTHOUSE ££
(📞01539-560396; www.heaveshotel.com; Heaves; s £48-58, d £75-85; 🅿) For country-house digs head 4 miles south of Kendal along the A591 to this stately mansion, owned by the same family for the last century. It's a rambling

place with oodles of Georgian finery: stately staircases, corniced hallways, and cracking views of green grounds. The Gandy Room's the top pick.

🍴 Eating

Kendal's **farmers market** is one of the county's best, and is held in Market Pl on the final Friday of every month from 9.30am to 3.30pm. There are also large branches of Booths and Marks & Spencer just off the main street.

New Moon BRITISH ££
(📞01539-729254; 129 Highgate; 2-course lunch £8.95, mains £9.95-16.95; ⊙lunch & dinner Tue-Sat) Kendal's best food is served at the fresh and modern New Moon, which takes the best of Lakeland produce and gives it a zippy Mediterranean spin – roast duck breast in a five-spice and honey marinade, pork with Parma ham, hake with a pesto crust. The two-course Early Supper menu, served before 7pm, is great value at £9.95. Book ahead.

 Wheatsheaf PUB ££
(📞01539-568254; www.thewheatsheafbrigsteer.co.uk; mains £13.75-16.95; ⊙lunch & dinner) It's a couple of miles west of Kendal in teeny Brigsteer, but this distinguished village pub is a must-visit. It was originally a favourite haunt of the local hunt, but it's now justifiably vaunted for its food, with a menu that dabbles in polished dishes such as pan-roasted duck breast in plum jus, or roast spring chicken with fondant potato and pancetta. The restaurant's been newly redone in a mix of shiny oak, stone and original beams, but the old bar still has lashing of country character. It's essential to book for Sunday lunch.

Waterside Wholefoods CAFE £
(Kent View, Waterside; lunches £4-10; ⊙8.30am-4.30pm Mon-Sat; 🌱) Kendal's veggies hang out en masse at this heart-warmingly cosy riverside cafe, a longstanding staple for chunky doorstep sandwiches, fresh soups, wholemeal wraps and naughty-but-nice cakes.

Grain Store BISTRO ££
(pizzas £6.50-9, mains £9-16.50; ⊙from 10am Mon-Sat) For a quick pre-film meal or a plate of something hot to go with your pint, the Brewery Arts Centre's restaurant is a great bet. It's especially strong on stonebaked

DON'T MISS

LOW SIZERGH BARN

Near Sizergh Castle, this fantastic local **food shop** (www.lowsizerghbarn.co.uk; ⊙shop 9am-5.30pm, tearoom 9.30am-5.30pm) is the place when you want to be sure your goodies are 100% food-mile free. Nearly everything in the shop is sourced from the Lakeland area, from homemade chutneys to farm-reared hams and Cumbrian puddings (look out for the award-winning flapjacks from Kendal Jacksmiths and organic wines from Mansergh Hall).

Once you've stocked up your picnic basket, you could plump for a cuppa in the tearoom, follow the farm trail or watch the cows being milked at 1.15pm (the action's beamed live to TV screens). If you've ever wondered what life down on the farm is really like, this is the place to find out.

pizzas: you can choose to eat in the dining room or order in the Vats Bar next door.

1657 Chocolate House　　　　CAFE £
(54 Branthwaite) Chocoholics can sink into cocoa-fuelled ecstasy at this über-frilly cafe, where waitresses in starched bonnets dish up 18 sorts of hot chocolate including almondy Old Noll's Potion, violet-infused Queen's Corsage or bitter-choc Dungeon. Handmade chocolates and umpteen mintcake varieties are sold in the cellar.

Staff of Life　　　　　　　BAKERY £
(www.artisanbreadmakers.co.uk; 27 Finkle St) Hidden away down the squeezeguts alleyway of Finkle St, this renowned bakery makes some of Cumbria's finest artisan breads. Master baker Simon Thomas looks after the breads, while partner Julie takes care of the cakes, and if you fancy picking up some tips, you could always attend one of their regular bread-making courses, held on Sundays for £90 per person.

Baba Ganoush　　　　　　　DELI £
(27 Finkle St) Just across the street from Staff of Life, this smart deli-cafe is a great place to pick up a takeaway sandwich or soup for lunch, and there's usually at least one daily hot choice too. Chiller cabinets are filled with olives, hummus and other deli treats.

Drinking

Burgundy's Wine Bar　　　PUB, WINE BAR
(19 Lowther St; ⊙closed Mon) Don't be put off by the wine bar tag – this is one of Kendal's cosiest places for a drink, whether you're after a quality pinot noir or just a pint of ale.

Rifleman's Arms　　　　　　　　　PUB
(4-6 Greenside) Cracking locals' pub with plenty of ales on tap and regular folk-music nights throughout the week. It's on Greenside, where John Cunliffe (author of Postman Pat) once lived, although sadly the post office which inspired the stories is long gone.

☆ Entertainment

Brewery Arts Centre　　　THEATRE, CINEMA
(☎01539-725133; Highgate; www.breweryarts.co.uk) Excellent arts complex with two cinemas, gallery space, cafe and a theatre hosting dance, performance and live music.

❶ Information

Kendal no longer has a tourist office.

Branches of HSBC, Barclays, Lloyds and NatWest line Highgate and Stricklandgate.

Library (☎01539-773520; 75 Stricklandgate; internet per ½hr £1; ⊙9.30am-7pm Mon & Wed, 9.30am-5pm Tue & Fri, 9.30am-noon Thu, 9.30am-3.30pm Sat, noon-4pm Sun; 🖥)

❶ Getting There & Around

Bus

Useful buses from Kendal:

555/556 Lakeslink (hourly Monday to Saturday, 10 on Sunday), Leaves Kendal en route to Windermere (30 minutes), Ambleside (40 minutes) and Grasmere (1¼ hours), or Lancaster (one hour) in the opposite direction.

505 Kendal to Coniston (one hour) via Windermere, Ambleside and Hawkshead.

X35 Travels south to Grange before returning via Haverthwaite Station, Ulverston and Barrow (hourly Monday to Saturday, four on Sunday).

Train

Kendal is on the main line from Oxenholme, 2 miles south of town. Regular trains run to Windermere (£3.80, 15 minutes, hourly).

AROUND KENDAL

Three and a half miles south of Kendal along the A591, the impressive **Sizergh Castle** (NT; ☎01539-560070; sizergh@nationaltrust.org.uk;

adult/child £7.65/3.90, gardens only £5/2.55; ⊙gardens 11am-5pm daily mid-Mar–Oct, 11am-4pm Nov & Dec, castle noon-5pm Sun-Thu mid-Mar–Nov) is the feudal seat of the Strickland family. The castle is renowned for its pele tower and for the lavish wood panelling on display in the Great Hall. There's a daily guided tour at noon (booking essential), otherwise you can wander around at will after 1pm.

Two miles further south along the A6 is **Levens Hall** (www.levenshall.co.uk; house & gardens adult/child £11.50/5, gardens only £8.50/4; ⊙gardens 10am-5pm, house noon-4.30pm Sun-Thu mid-Mar–mid-Oct), another Elizabethan manor built around a mid-13th-century pele tower. Fine Jacobean furniture is on display throughout the house, but the real draw is the 17th-century topiary garden, a surreal riot of pyramids, swirls, curls, pom-poms and peacocks. Rather peculiarly, it holds a chilli festival in August.

The 555/556 bus runs past the castle gates.

Understand the
Lake District

population per sq km

LAKE DISTRICT   CARLISLE   UK

 ≈ 24 people

The Lake District Today

Sixty Years On

In 2011, the Lake District celebrated its 60th birthday as a national park, and while it certainly isn't without its detractors, there can be little doubt that national park status has had a broadly positive effect on the long-term health of the area: preventing development, prohibiting industrial expansion, preserving the environment and promoting the region as a tourist destination.

Over 15 million people now flock to the Lake District every year, contributing nearly £1 billion into the region's economy. While the cash is certainly welcome, tourism isn't without its downsides. Spiralling visitor numbers and thousands of extra boots on the fells have inevitably had consequences for the fragile Lakeland environment. Nearly nine out of every 10 visitors arrive by car, bringing traffic, noise, tailbacks and air pollution. And in many rural areas, local villages have found themselves swamped by holiday cottages and second homes, pushing up house prices and preventing locals from getting onto the housing ladder.

» Area: 2292 sq km/885 sq miles

» Number of visitors per year: 15 million

» Highest point: Scafell Pike (978m/3210ft)

» Number of listed buildings: 1740

The Changing Landscape

While tourism in the Lake District is booming, other industries are finding it increasingly tough to make ends meet. The fallout from the outbreak of foot-and-mouth disease in 2001, which led to the enforced slaughter of hundreds of thousands of sheep and cattle and forced many farmers to the wall, raised serious fears for the survival of this age-old industry. Hill farming is more than just an industry in the Lake District – it's a way of life, and for many people the survival of farming is inextricably linked to the long-term welfare of the national park.

Many farmers have diversified in an effort to balance the books, embracing everything from cheese making and farm holidays to camping

Best Books

Memoirs of a Fell Wanderer (Alfred Wainwright) Recollections of a life spent among the fells.
Swallows and Amazons (Arthur Ransome) Relive your childhood in Ransome's classic tales.
Grasmere Journals (Dorothy Wordsworth) Wordsworth's

sister documents her life in the Lake District.
Unruly Times (AS Byatt) Highly readable account of Coleridge and Wordsworth's relationship.
A Walk Around the Lakes (Hunter Davies) Comic travelogue by Cumbria-born writer.

Best Poetry

Collected Poems (William Wordsworth)
Lyrical Ballads (Wordsworth & Coleridge)
Selected Poems 1940–1982 (Norman Nicholson)

and of the Lake District (%)

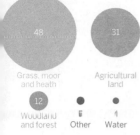

48 Grass, moor and heath

31 Agricultural land

12 Woodland and forest

● Other

● Water

if the Lake District were 100 people

30 would work in tourism
28 would work in business
23 would work in the public sector
19 would be employed elsewhere

barns and even ostrich rearing. Others have embraced the opportunity provided by environmental conservation schemes, restoring drystone walls, renovating farm buildings, replanting hedgerows and converting areas of their land to marshland and meadow.

Uncertain Skies

The issue of environmental stewardship was brought into sharp focus by the floods of 2009. Some of the heaviest rainfall ever recorded in Britain swept across Cumbria, inundating many towns and villages and causing billions of pounds of damage. It was a stark reminder of the imminent and all too real dangers posed by climate change.

In a bold move to begin to address these pressing environmental issues, the NPA has recently established the first-ever 'carbon budget' imposed by a UK national park. Schemes to promote public transport, support local producers and encourage environmentally friendly tourism are hopefully a sign of things to come. Similarly, projects to protect the critically endangered red squirrel and return areas of the countryside to unmanaged wilderness (most obviously around Ennerdale) all bode well for the future.

While there are signs that many Lakeland habitats are returning to rude health – symbolised by the return of the ospreys to Bassenthwaite Lake and golden eagles to Haweswater – there's another deeply contentious environmental issue looming on the horizon. The controversial nuclear reprocessing facility at Sellafield is set to be decommissioned over the next decade, raising the thorny question of whether or not to replace it with a new-generation facility.

As always, there are arguments for and against – some economic, some environmental, some emotional – but this is one argument that is likely to rumble on and on.

» Percentage of dwellings used as holiday or second homes: 15%

» Percentage of visitors arriving by car: 89%

» Ratio of grey to red squirrels: 66:1

Best Films & TV

Miss Potter An affectionate biopic of the children's writer, starring Renée Zellweger and partly filmed in the Lakes.
Withnail & I Cult British classic following two out-of-work actors on a disastrous Lakeland holiday.

Wainwright's Walks BBC series in which Julia Bradbury tackles some of AW's favourite hikes.
The Lakes Jimmy McGovern drama set in a Lake District hotel.
Wainwright Country Jovial presenter Fred Talbot explores lesser-known Wainwright walks.

5 Highest Peaks

» **Scafell Pike** 978m (3210ft)
» **Scafell** 964m (3162ft)
» **Helvellyn** 950m (3114ft)
» **Skiddaw** 931m (3053ft)
» **Great End** 910m (2986ft)

History

It's almost impossible to take a trip around this corner of England without stumbling across reminders of bygone days, from eerie stone circles and ruined forts to medieval abbeys and crenellated castles. Cumbria has a long and turbulent history stretching back over seven millennia, and you'll have a much deeper understanding of the region if you take the time to delve into its ancient past.

Ancient People

Until the end of the last ice age much of the Lake District was covered by glaciers. When the ice-sheets began to melt, the area was slowly settled by hunter-gatherer tribes. Small flints and arrowheads dating from as early as 7000 BC have been found on the Cumbrian coast, including Cartmel, St Bees and the Isle of Walney.

By around 5000 BC, humans were well established, clearing forest and setting up arable farms and cattle enclosures. They began to fashion tools and weapons using Lakeland stone, and developed trade links across Britain and Ireland.

Around the same time, Neolithic people began to construct many stone circles, barrows, dolmens and standing stones, most notably the Castlerigg Stone Circle, near Keswick (believed to have been erected c 3500 BC). Other well-known circles, including Long Meg and her Daughters near Penrith, and Swinside (Sunkenkirk) near Broughton-in-Furness, were built around 1500 BC, possibly on the foundations of earlier sites.

Opinion is divided on the purpose these circles served; some scholars think they served as celestial clocks to mark the changing seasons, while others believe they were used as trading sites, religious centres or public monuments, with each stone perhaps commemorating a great warrior or fallen chieftain.

TIMELINE	5000–1500 BC	500 BC	AD 43
	Neolithic settlements are established across Cumbria. Tribes develop early forms of agriculture, animal husbandry and tool manufacture, and many stone circles, barrows and burial tombs are built across the region.	Celts move into Cumbria from southern areas of Britain, establishing a string of defensive hill forts in important strategic sites. Disparate tribes are united under the Brigantes.	Romans invade mainland Britain and begin to push north towards Cumbria. The British governor Petilius Cerialis commands northern armies against the Brigantes and builds his first timber fort in AD 72.

THE LANGDALE AXE FACTORY

High up on the scree slopes beneath Pike O' Stickle and Harrison Stickle in Great Langdale is one of the largest Neolithic axe factories in Britain. The area has rich deposits of a form of greenstone, a hard form of volcanic stone which can be worked to a fine, sharp edge. Early craftsmen selected their stones carefully, shaped them roughly on the fellside, then spent many hours honing and polishing them: hundreds of 'reject' heads still litter the quarry site.

It seems to have been a lucrative trade: around 27% of all the Neolithic axes discovered in Britain are thought to have originated from Langdale, with examples found as far afield as Ireland and Cornwall.

Celts & Romans

Around 500 BC, Celtic tribes established a string of protective hill forts across Cumbria, such as the one at Carrock Fell. The key tribes included the Carvetii, who mainly occupied the Eden Valley, and the Setantii, who had their stronghold in Lancashire and southern Cumbria. Both were eventually subsumed into the Brigantes tribe, which had taken control of most of northern England by the 1st century AD.

In AD 43, the Romans invaded England and within a matter of decades had either conquered or subsumed the main Celtic tribes. The Romans constructed strategic forts at Ambleside (known to the Romans as Galava), Hardknott (Mediobogdum) and Ravenglass (Glannaventa). True to form, they also built roads to facilitate the transport of troops and supplies; one old route across the Ullswater fells is still known as 'High Street', a hangover from the days of the Roman occupation. Carlisle, known to the Romans as Luguvalium, became a key administrative centre.

The region's most notable Roman monument is undoubtedly the Vallum Aelium, known to us as Hadrian's Wall. Stretching for 73 miles from Bowness-on-Solway to Wallsend on the River Tyne, it was built to protect the 'civilised' south of Roman Britannica from the lawless wilds of Scotland. Initially the western section was turf, later reinforced in stone. It's still possible to visit ruined garrison forts at Birdoswald and Vindolanda.

The Dark Ages

By the early 5th century, the Roman empire was crumbling. In AD 410 the last legion was withdrawn, leaving northern Britain once again to its Celtic chieftains. Remnants of this brief Celtic revival survive in various

Cumbrian Castles
» Carlisle Castle
» Sizergh Castle
» Muncaster Castle
» Penrith Castle
» Appleby Castle

The name of Coel Hen, one of Cumbria's early Celtic kings, is thought to be commemorated in the popular British nursery rhyme, *Old King Cole*.

122	573	875	945
Emperor Hadrian visits Britain and orders the construction of a great wall stretching across the north of England between Bowness-on-Solway and the Tyne River. The wall is mostly completed within six years.	St Kentigern (or St Mungo) undertakes the first recorded Christian mission in Cumbria, probably preaching in the village of Caldbeck and several other areas.	The Danish Viking chief, Halfdan, razes Carlisle to the ground. It remains in ruins for the next 200 years. Norse Vikings establish communities and farmsteads, especially around Langdale.	King Dunmail is defeated by Saxon forces under King Edmund. The county of Cumberland is mentioned for the first time in a document ceding the county to Malcolm of Scotland.

place names (Derwent, Blencathra), and most notably in the county's modern-day name of Cumbria (which derives from the Celts' name for themselves, *Cymry*).

Among the most powerful kingdoms was Rheged, centring on the Eden Valley, which was subsequently annexed by the more powerful kingdom of Northumbria. The native Cumbric dialect gradually gave way to Anglo-Saxon, which was increasingly gaining ground as the 'national' language.

Norse Vikings also began to settle in the area around this time: their influence can still be heard in dialect words such as *force* (waterfall), *ghyll* (ravine), *beck* (stream), *thwaite* (settlement) and *fell* (mountain).

Troubled Times

In 945 AD the last traces of the original Cumbrian tribes were wiped out when the warlord Dunmail was annihilated by the Saxon king, Edmund, who granted control over Cumbria to Malcolm, heir to the Scottish throne. This decision sowed the seeds for several centuries of ongoing conflict between the Scots and English.

More often than not these conflicts were played out along the fractious Anglo–Scottish border, especially around the strategically important centre of Carlisle, which received its first stone castle and city walls in 1122 during the reign of Henry I.

The early Middle Ages saw the foundation of many important religious houses in Cumbria, notably the grand abbey at Furness, built in 1127. Cumbrian monks were responsible for many developments, including the practice of sheep and dairy farming, coppicing (for timber and charcoal), cheese production and wool making – not to mention that most important of Cumbrian pastimes, beer brewing.

Sporadic conflicts and cross-border raids were common, especially following the Scottish victory over the English at the Battle of Bannockburn in 1314.

Rival families of 'Border Reivers' indulged in a bloodthirsty campaign of violence, looting and pillaging, earning the area around Carlisle the ominous nickname of the 'Debatable Lands'.

To defend themselves against the Reivers, many aristocratic families protected their houses with fortified pele towers, examples of which can still be seen at Muncaster Castle, Sizergh Castle and Levens Hall.

A Nation Divided

A brief interlude of calm followed the coronation of James I as the first joint ruler of Scotland and England in 1603, but the region was plunged into yet more conflict during the Civil War. Broadly, the neighbouring

---

Fletcher Christian, the rebellious leader of the mutiny on the *Bounty*, was born in Cockermouth in 1764. His brother subsequently worked at Hawkshead Grammar School and may have taught young John and William Wordsworth.

Find out whether you have Reiver relatives in *The Reivers: the Story of the Border Reivers*, by Alistair Moffat, a romping historical read with plenty of family vendettas and blood-curdling raids to sink your teeth into.

1315	1537	1745	1799
Fresh from his victory at the Battle of Bannockburn, Robert the Bruce lays siege to Carlisle Castle, but is forced to withdraw when the city's commandant, Andrew de Harcla, refuses to surrender.	Following Henry VIII's order to dissolve the monasteries of England, Furness Abbey is forced to surrender its land and wealth to the Crown. The abbey is ransacked and dismantled.	Start of the Jacobite uprisings under the Scottish pretender to the English crown, Bonnie Prince Charlie. The Jacobite rebellion is overthrown the following year at the Battle of Culloden.	The year after the publication of *Lyrical Ballads*, Wordsworth moves into Dove Cottage, near Grasmere, with his sister Dorothy, joined later by Mary, whom he marries in 1802.

regions of Cumberland and Westmorland declared for the king, while the Scots sided with the Parliamentarians.

The region witnessed several bloody battles, and Carlisle became the site of an infamously gruelling siege when the 700-strong Royalist garrison was starved into submission by the Roundhead commander General Lesley.

The prospect of peace heralded by the Act of Union in 1707, which brought Scotland and England under one flag for the first time, proved to be equally short-lived. The Scottish-born pretender to the throne, Charles Edward Stuart (popularly known as Bonnie Prince Charlie), led a series of Jacobite uprisings against the rule of George II, including yet another siege at Carlisle Castle.

The Romantics

During the late 18th century the Lake District found itself at the centre of another revolution. The groundbreaking artists and poets of the Romantic movement drew inspiration from the majestic local scenery, exploring ideas of natural beauty and the 'sublime' in their poetry and paintings.

Hadrian's Wall: an Historic Landscape, published by the National Trust, provides a comprehensive overview of the history of one of the greatest engineering projects ever attempted in England.

HISTORY THE ROMANTICS

THE BORDER REIVERS

During the early Middle Ages, the Anglo–Scottish border was a pretty anarchic place, and the Border Reivers weren't shy of taking advantage of the lack of law and order.

These marauding bands of raiders came from around 70 families or close-knit clans, based on both sides of the border. Clans showed little allegiance to nationality: Scottish Reivers were just as likely to plunder from their own countrymen as from their English neighbours.

The Reivers usually attacked within a day's ride north or south of the border. They chose their targets carefully, favouring places without royal or aristocratic protection, especially those which were unlikely to put up a fight (abbeys and priories were particularly popular).

The Reivers favoured striking hard and fast, mounted on stout moor ponies bred for their strength and endurance. Raiding parties could be anywhere from a dozen to a hundred strong – there are even a few accounts of bands that numbered into their thousands.

Winter was the key season for raiding, when the long nights gave the Reivers the maximum time to do their dirty work. They plundered anything and everything, from crops, cereals and horses to money, jewellery and expensive ornaments. Some goods were kept, while others were sold or bartered for weapons, armour and raiding equipment.

Reiving died out from around the middle of the 18th century, but Reiver family names are still widespread across the Scottish borders, Northumberland and Cumbria: you can see a list of the most common at www.landsbeyondthewall.co.uk/names.html.

The reivers also contributed a number of words to the English language, including 'blackmail' and, of course, 'bereaved'

EOIN CLARKE/LONELY PLANET IMAGES ©

» The grave of William Wordsworth, Grasmere

1850	1902
William Wordsworth dies at home in Rydal Mount aged 80, and is buried in the churchyard of St Oswald's Church in Grasmere alongside his children Dora, Catherine and Thomas.	The National Trust makes its first purchase of land in the Lake District at Brandelhow Woods on Derwent Water, laying the foundations for the future protection of the Lakeland landscape.

The key figure of the Lakeland Romantics was the poet William Wordsworth, who was born in Cockermouth in 1770, and lived most of his life in the region, surrounded by a loose circle of writers including Robert Southey and Samuel Taylor Coleridge. Together they laid down the blueprint for the Romantic movement through a string of landmark poems, celebrating the wonders, mysteries and spiritual consolations of the natural world. Wordsworth's houses in Grasmere and the nearby Wordsworth Museum are among the best places to explore the Lake District's literary heritage.

The Age of Industry

As England's industrial machine gathered steam in the early 19th century, the abundant natural resources of the Lakes proved an irresistible draw. Quarrying and mining exploded across Cumbria; farming, manufacturing and agriculture became increasingly organised and mechanised; the region's coastal ports around Workington, Maryport and Whitehaven bustled with ships bound for the far-flung corners of the British Empire; and factories and mills sprang up to feed the nation's growing need for manufactured goods (you can still visit a 'bobbin' factory near Windermere).

The railway finally reached the Lakes in 1847, when a branch line connected Kendal with Windermere (despite vehement opposition from Wordsworth and many others). Other railways followed, including lines from Penrith to Cockermouth, Ravenglass to Eskdale and around the Cumbrian Coast, bringing with them another phenomenon that was to have a lasting effect on the area's future: tourism.

The Advent of Tourism

Flush with the wealth provided by Britain's growing industrial power, Victorian and Edwardian tourists flocked in huge numbers to admire the Lakeland scenery. Local towns mushroomed to cater for the booming tourist trade, especially in popular resorts such as Grange-over-Sands, Bowness-on-Windermere and Keswick.

Charabancs ferried passengers around the area, stopping off at a series of viewpoints, where visitors were encouraged to admire the landscape backwards using a mirrored device (known as a 'Claude glass', after the 17th-century French landscape painter Claude Lorrain) in order to 'frame' the view.

More-energetic types set out to explore the high fells in the company of local guides, while a gaggle of adventurous gents tackled the cliffs and peaks, starting the long tradition of rock climbing in the Lakes.

The Lake District also became a favourite rural retreat for Britain's industrial elite, who built many lavish mansions across the countryside –

Historic Houses

» Dalemain
» Holker Hall
» Levens Hall
» Blackwell House
» Hutton-in-the-Forest

Religious Buildings

» Furness Abbey
» Shap Abbey
» Carlisle Cathedral
» Cartmel Priory
» St Olaf's Church, Wasdale

1931	1943	1951	1956
The Youth Hostelling Association (YHA) purchases its very first hostel at Thorney How in Grasmere, one of more than 20 established in the Lake District.	Beatrix Potter dies, bequeathing a huge area of land to the National Trust.	The Lake District becomes one of the UK's first four national parks. By the end of the decade a further six areas have also received national park status.	The UK's first commercial nuclear power station opens at Windscale and is ravaged by fire the following year. The same year, the Queen makes her first visit to the national park.

many of which are now either big hotels or tourist attractions (such as Blackwell House, Storrs Hall and Brockhole).

A National Park Is Born

Not everyone was content to watch the Lakeland scenery being reduced to a glorified leisure park, however. A growing band of campaigners began to speak out against industrial expansion, calling for the protection of the area's natural environment.

One of the most vociferous campaigners was the critic, philosopher and polymath John Ruskin, who became a passionate advocate for the importance of environmental conservation. The environmental torch was later picked up by Beatrix Potter, who set up home in the Lake District in the early 1900s, and used the proceeds from her books to purchase houses, farmsteads and large areas of land in order to protect them from development.

THE LOWTHERS

It's difficult to imagine the spectacular power once wielded by the Lowthers, the aristocratic dynasty that has been lording it over eastern Cumbria for the last 800 years. There's been a Lowther in Cumbria since at least the 13th century, and they've been an almost permanent fixture in English upper-crust society ever since, serving as peers, MPs, earls, barons, sheriffs, courtiers, generals, parliamentary advisers and feudal landowners.

Perhaps the most notorious family member is Sir James Lowther (1736–1802), later the 1st Earl of Lonsdale, who became one of the richest men in 18th-century England thanks to his inheritance of three vast fortunes (including the Lowther estate, the entire town of Whitehaven and a cash sum equivalent to a quarter of total British exports at the time).

Despite his unimaginably huge fortune, he was notoriously unpopular, with a reputation for meanness, arrogance, cruelty and licentiousness (explaining his decidedly unflattering nicknames of Wicked Jimmy, the Bad Earl, the Gloomy Earl and Jimmy Grasp-All).

Lowther was married twice and had a string of local mistresses; in his scurrilous memoir, *Reminiscences of the Lake Poets,* Thomas de Quincey relates the dubious legend that the earl kept one of his young conquests embalmed in a glass-topped coffin at Lowther Castle.

Necrophiliac tendencies aside, the earl was certainly tight-fisted; William Wordsworth's father, John, served as his steward and estate manager for more than 20 years, but was still owed more than £4000 by the time Sir James died in 1802. The debt was eventually settled by the earl's heir, William Lowther, and paid to the surviving Wordsworth children; legend has it that when the Bad Earl was buried in 1802, the ground shook so violently the vicar almost fell into the grave.

Their family estate is currently the focus of a major restoration project: see p147 to find out more.

1974

Cumberland, Westmorland and parts of northern Lancashire are incorporated into the new county of Cumbria, despite widespread opposition.

2001

Foot-and-mouth disease devastates farms across the UK; Cumbria is one of the worst affected areas. Ospreys return to Bassenthwaite Lake.

PAUL HOBSON/FLPA/IMAGEBROKER ©

» Osprey in flight

Windermere and
Bowness were
the second areas
of England to be
supplied with
electric street
lighting. Power
was initially
supplied by a
hydro-electric
generator at
Troutbeck Bridge.

Her efforts were supported by the National Trust, which had been founded in 1895 by three Victorian philanthropists – Octavia Hill, Robert Hunter and Canon Hardwicke Rawnsley. In 1902, the trio raised enough funds to buy the 108-acre Brandelhow estate on the west shore of Derwentwater, the first ever property purchase made by the National Trust on the behalf of the nation. Following Beatrix Potter's death in 1943, she bequeathed more than 4000 acres of land and property to the Trust, which remains one of the largest single bequests in the organisation's history.

With more than half a century of environmental stewardship already behind it, it was inevitable that the Lake District became one of the UK's first national parks in 1951, along with the Peak District, Snowdonia and Dartmoor.

20th-Century Controversies

Without doubt the most controversial issue since the foundation of the national park was the decision to site the UK's first commercial nuclear power station at Windscale (now known as Sellafield) on the Cumbrian Coast in 1956 – a decision that became even more controversial when the station witnessed the world's first ever radiation leak the following year, caused by a major fire in one of the reactors.

It's a subject that still stirs passionate debate more than 50 years on, not least as the site is currently being considered as one of the locations for the new generation of nuclear power stations due to be constructed across the UK over the next decade. Almost as controversial was the decision to join the historic counties of Cumberland, Westmorland and part of northern Lancashire into the new county of Cumbria in 1974, despite strong opposition to the plans among many local communities.

The construction
of a 470m-wide
dam at the lake
of Haweswater
submerged the
village of Mardale
in the 1930s.
During periods
of dry weather
some of the
drowned build-
ings occasionally
reappear above
the surface.

Recent History

While tourism has boomed, other traditional industries such as manufacturing, timber, agriculture and, most importantly, hill farming, have endured a long, slow decline. Catastrophic outbreaks of mad cow disease (BSE) in the late 1990s and foot-and-mouth in 2001 forced many already-struggling farmers out of business.

Park authorities and local residents have generally managed to coexist fairly peacefully, but not every initiative (local and national) receives a warm welcome. Heated debates of recent years have concerned the imposition of speed limits on the major lakes, the ban on hunting with hounds, the development of new reservoirs and the strategy of opening up the countryside to ramblers as part of the Right to Roam Act.

More recently, the serious floods of 2009 that swept through the town of Cockermouth and the Cumbrian Coast have focused attention on the growing threat posed by climate change to the fragile Lakeland landscape.

2000–05	2005	2009	2011
The Countryside and Rights of Way (CRoW) Act is passed in 2000, opening up new areas of state and privately-owned land to the public over the next five years.	Damaging storms sweep across Cumbria and the northwest. Carlisle is swamped by the worst floods in living memory. Many other areas of the county are also affected.	Yet more catastrophic floods hit Cumbria, especially the market town of Cockermouth, which receives some of the heaviest rain ever recorded in Britain.	The YHA announces a highly controversial decision to close several historic hostels around the Lake District in an effort to cut costs, including its first ever property at Thorney Howe.

The Lake District's Natural Environment

Geology

Around four million years ago, great ice sheets and glaciers covered much of northern Europe, etching out the distinctive shapes of the Lakeland fells and valleys such as Borrowdale and Buttermere, Langdale and Wasdale. When the ice began to retreat between 15,000 and 10,000 years ago, glacial meltwater became trapped in the valleys, forming the great lakes for which the Lake District is famous.

Each of the major mountain ranges is composed of different rock forms. The oldest is the Skiddaw Group, formed on an ancient seabed around 500 million years ago, which was later raised up above the ocean floor by volcanic action. This range is mainly confined to the northern fells, including Skiddaw and Blencathra.

Next oldest is the Borrowdale Group, made up of hard volcanic rock that's very resistant to erosion. As a result, it's where you'll find the Lake District's highest mountains, including Scafell, Helvellyn and the Langdale Pikes.

Youngest of all is the Windermere Group, made up of softer sandstones and siltstones that are more erosion-prone, giving rise to the gentler scenery of southern Lakeland.

Landscape & Habitats

While the rolling fields and green hills are many people's ideal vision of the English countryside, they're actually not a natural environment: centuries of hill farming, land management, quarrying and agriculture have left an indelible mark on the landscape. Without them, the fells and valleys would quickly revert back to a more 'natural' habitat of scrub, heath, moor and low-level woodland.

Life at the top of the fells is tough: high winds, heavy rain and cold temperatures mean that only the hardiest plants can survive here (mainly heather, bogweed and sphagnum moss). Life gets easier lower down the fells, with heath giving way to areas of bracken, fern and grasses, followed by fields, pastures and meadows nearer the valley floor. One of the rarest habitats is the 'limestone pavement' (such as Whitbarrow Scar, near Windermere), which supports many rare species of wildflowers, butterflies and insects.

Peat bogs are another important habitat – one of the largest is at Foulshaw Moss, near Witherslack, east of Windermere. Towards the Cumbrian coast, the salt marshes around Morecambe Bay are

GREAT FREEZE

The surface of Windermere has frozen solid four times in the last 150 years: in 1864, 1946 and 1963, as well as the great freeze of 1895, when the lake remained frozen for six straight weeks.

good places to see marine plants such as scurvy grass, thrift and sea lavender.

The Lake District is home to large areas of native woodland, rich in broadleaf species such as sessile oak, beech, rowan, yew and hazel. There are also several large conifer plantations (notably at Grizedale, Whinlatter, Thirlmere and Dodd Wood, near Bassenthwaite), most of which are managed by the Forestry Commission. These plantations are controversial as they are mostly composed of non-native species such as pine and fir, although in some areas (notably the Ennerdale Valley) the park authorities are actively aiming to 'rewild' the landscape in an effort to support a wider variety of wildlife and to provide greater biodiversity.

Local writer and photographer Bill Birkett has published a series of lavish photographic books detailing a year in the life of several Lakeland valleys, including Borrowdale, Langdale and the Duddon Valley.

Plants & Flowers

Plentiful rainfall means the Lake District has a huge range of plants and flowers. In spring and summer, the hedgerows, woodlands and meadows are thick with grasses and colourful wildflowers, including primroses, pennyworts, wood sorrel, dogwort, ox-eye daisies, bluebells and wood anemones. Butterfly orchids are one of the loveliest Lake District flowers, but you'll have to keep your eyes peeled to spot them.

The Lake District's most famous bloom is unquestionably the daffodil, an unofficial symbol of the park ever since it was immortalised in Wordsworth's most famous poem. You can still see the daffodils that inspired him along the shores of Ullswater in Gowbarrow Park every spring, although recently there have been fears that the native species *(Narcissus pseudonarcissus)* is under increasing threat from larger and more robust cultivars.

The landscaped gardens of many of the Lake District's country estates were largely planted during the Victorian era, when plant-hunters were bringing a whole range of exotic new plants from the far reaches of the British empire. Species such as rhododendron, camellias, hydrangeas and magnolias flourished in the cool, damp valleys, particularly at gardens such as Holehird, Brockhole and Brantwood.

Top Lake District Gardens

» Holehird
» Holker Hall
» Greythwaite Hall
» Stagshaw
» Brantwood

RED SQUIRRELS

Cumbria and the Lake District is one of the last bastions for the critically endangered red squirrel. This bushy-tailed tree-dweller famously starred in one of Beatrix Potter's classic tales, *The Tale of Squirrel Nutkin,* and was once widespread in Britain, but had suffered a massive decline by the turn of the 20th century – down from around 2.5 million to just 140,000 today.

The main threat to the red squirrel's survival is their own transatlantic cousin, the grey squirrel, which was introduced from North America in the late 19th century as a pet. The introduction had a devastating effect on the smaller, more reticent reds, who soon found themselves bullied off their territories and eaten out of house and home.

The greys also carry a much more serious threat – the 'squirrel pox' virus. Most greys have an inbuilt resistance, but the disease is lethal to the reds and accounts for much of the decline in the red squirrel population over the last century.

The vast majority of the UK's remaining red squirrels live in Scotland, with just 20,000 in England and fewer than 1000 in Cumbria. Recent programmes to establish 'buffer zones' to protect key red squirrel habitats against incursion by the greys have caused considerable controversy, since the only way to effectively ensure the reds' survival is to trap and cull any greys that enter their habitat.

Red populations are carefully monitored, and people are encouraged to report any sighting to the **Red Squirrel Hotline** (☏0845 347 9375) or online at www.saveour squirrels.org.uk.

SHEEP IN THE LAKE DISTRICT

Few creatures sum up the Lake District better than the sheep. In total there are some two million sheep in Cumbria, outnumbering the resident human population by about 50 to one. There are several breeds to look out for, including the Swaledale and the Rough Fell, but the most distinctive breed is the Herdwick, distinguished by its thick grey-black fleece and chalk-white face.

The breed is thought to have been introduced to the area by Norse settlers around the 10th century, and was a favourite of Beatrix Potter's, who established her own Herdwick flock in the 1920s and '30s. It's less valued for its fleece than for its hardy nature: it's happy to live out on the fells in all weathers, and its coat is much more rain-resistant than most breeds. Its free-ranging nature and foraged diet also lends the meat a distinctive gamey flavour that's rapidly gaining favour among the county's chefs.

Lakeland sheep flocks are also unique in the way they're managed. Most flocks are left to range free on the fells, but each has its own specific 'heaf' or territory, passed down the generations from ewe to lamb. The 2001 foot-and-mouth outbreak led to the compulsory culling of around a quarter of Cumbria's Herdwicks, jeopardising not only the long-term livelihoods of many hill farmers but also the inherited heaf boundaries; those farmers who stayed on the land had to 'heft' their new flocks by hand.

Sheep displays form a major part of country shows in the Lake District: the most important Herdwick meet is the Eskdale Show (p102), held every year on the last Saturday in September.

Animals

Along with the ever-present sheep and cattle, the Cumbrian fell pony is another common sight on the hilltops. This hardy little horse generally reaches between 13 and 14 hands high, and is thought to be descended from the pack ponies introduced to Cumbria during the Roman occupation. It was later employed for ploughing, harvesting and 'snigging' (transporting felled timber), and before the advent of roads was the traditional Cumbrian form of transport.

The Lake District's other furry inhabitants include badgers, foxes, rabbits and voles, as well as a sizeable population of red deer, and smaller herds of fallow and roe deer. Look out too for weasels, stoats and otters, which are slowly re-establishing themselves along the riverbanks.

The hedgerows and fields are also good places to spot moths, butterflies and dragonflies. Some of the more unusual butterfly species you might spy include the mountain ringlet, the purple hairstreak, the painted lady, the northern brown argus, the holly blue, but you'll have to be lucky to spy the super-rare marsh fritillary – once common across the whole of England, but now endangered thanks to the drainage of natural marshland.

Common frogs, newts and toads are widespread, and the county supports two of England's largest colonies of the endangered natterjack toad (at Drigg and Sandscale Haws).

The lakes also support several rare species of fish, including the Arctic char; the schelly, a whitefish found only in Ullswater, Haweswater and Brotherswater; and the highly endangered vendace, found only in Derwentwater and Bassenthwaite Lake. More common species to be found are the rainbow and brown trout, the pike and even wild Atlantic salmon.

Bird Life

More than 200 species of bird frequent the Lake District, ranging from the diminutive wood warbler to the elegant whooper swan, which winters in considerable numbers around Elterwater.

Local naturalist Peter Wilde runs a fascinating website at www cumbria-wildlife .org.uk, detailing all his favourite Cumbrian wildlife, with details of where, when and how you can see them.

Best Places for Bird Spotting

» Bassenthwaite Lake
» Tarn Hows
» St Bees Head
» Solway Coast
» Hodbarrow RSPB reserve

THE LAKE DISTRICT'S NATURAL ENVIRONMENT ANIMALS

The best place for bird spotting is along the coast, especially around Morecambe Bay and the Solway Coast, where you might spot pink-footed geese, scaup, wigeon, grey and golden plovers; and the well-known bird reserve at St Bees Head, which supports populations of guillemots, kittiwakes, razorbills, shearwaters and even a few breeding pairs of puffins.

After decades of decline, many birds of prey are also making a slow but steady comeback – especially peregrine falcons, honey buzzards, hen harriers, merlins and goshawks. Even more excitingly, since 2001, Bassenthwaite Lake has been the summertime home for the only breeding pair of ospreys this side of the Scottish border, while Haweswater supports England's only resident golden eagles.

Environmental Conservation

Two of the great English environmental movements – the National Parks and the National Trust – can both trace their roots to the Lake District in the mid- to late 19th century.

Ever the trailblazer, Wordsworth was the first to ponder the concept of a national park in his 1810 *Guide to the Lakes,* in which he famously described the Lake District as a 'sort of national property in which every man has a right and interest who has an eye to perceive and a heart to enjoy'. Inspired by the poet's passionate defence of the Lakeland landscape, clergyman campaigner Canon Hardwicke Rawnsley joined forces with Octavia Hill and Robert Hunter to form the National Trust in 1895.

Thus by the time the government finally bowed to popular pressure and formed the UK's first batch of national parks in 1951, there was already a strong tradition of environmental campaigning in the county. Predated only by the Peak District, the Lake District was (and still is) the largest national park in England, covering a total area of 885 sq miles.

Unlike many other countries, Britain's national parks are protected landscapes rather than strict nature reserves. Domestic building, commercial activity, agriculture and certain heavy industries (such as timber felling and quarrying) are all allowed within the park's boundaries, but strict planning rules and environmental regulations ensure that all development is carefully managed.

In addition to the national park itself, Cumbria also boasts more Sites of Special Scientific Interest (SSSIs) than any other English county, a testament to the area's rich biodiversity and varied habitats. The Royal Society for the Protection of Birds (RSPB) also operates five reserves: Hodbarrow, St Bees, Campfield Marsh, Haweswater and Geltsdale.

Literary Lakes

The Romantics

Key Concerns

During the late 18th and early 19th centuries, Romanticism spanned many art forms, but it was in poetry and painting where its influence was most keenly felt. In a post-Enlightenment world struggling to come to terms with the loss of many long-held notions – aristocratic monarchy, organised religion, divine order – Romantic artists increasingly turned towards the natural world in search of inspiration.

Their work was underpinned by a constant quest for the 'sublime': moments of transcendent perfection which could be directly experienced in the real world. The power of nature to inspire the unconscious mind, whether through a perfect landscape, a sudden storm or a brilliant sunset, was one of the key Romantic preoccupations – so it's hardly surprising that many of them felt such an intimate kinship with the Lake District's grand vistas of craggy fells, babbling rivers and dramatic skies.

The Arrival of the Romantics

Poet Thomas Gray was the first to visit in 1767, followed by writer Thomas West, who penned the first official *Guide to the Lakes* in 1778. But it was William Wordsworth's decision to return to his boyhood county of Cumberland in 1799 that heralded the true beginning of the Romantic movement in the Lake District.

Accompanied by his sister Dorothy, Wordsworth moved into the tiny house at Dove Cottage in Grasmere in 1799. He was followed soon afterwards by two of his closest friends and contemporaries, Samuel Taylor Coleridge (with whom he had published a groundbreaking collection, *Lyrical Ballads*, the year before) and Poet Laureate Robert Southey (who was also Coleridge's brother-in-law – the two men had married sisters Edith and Sarah Fricker in 1795 and 1800). Later they were also joined by the opium-eating essayist Thomas de Quincey, who produced a fascinating account of the period in his rather catty memoir *Recollections of the Lake Poets*.

The Lake Poets

Collectively, Wordsworth, Coleridge and Southey became known as the Lake Poets (a soubriquet that was often used rather disparagingly in reviews as a shorthand for their 'provincial' preoccupations). The three men produced a prodigious output of poems, pamphlets and literary essays during their time together in the Lake District; it's estimated that Wordsworth alone wrote over 70,000 lines of poetry, almost double the output of any other English poet.

Wordsworth's most celebrated doctrines are his notions of 'emotion recollected in tranquillity' and 'spots of time' – vivid moments of

You can still see a desk where the young William Wordsworth etched his name at the Hawkshead Grammar School, which he attended from 1779 to 1787.

AS Byatt's *Unruly Times* is a fascinating account of the often stormy relationship between Wordsworth and Coleridge, as well as a good introduction to the Romantic movement.

experience that continue to provide inspiration long after the experience itself has faded. Famously, he seems to have preferred composing on the move, rather than sitting down in his study: de Quincey later estimated that Wordsworth walked between 175,000 and 180,000 miles during his lifetime.

Lakeland locations are littered throughout his work. He penned poems on everything from yew trees and derelict abbeys to faithful fox terriers, and even managed an entire book of sonnets on the delights of the Duddon Valley – but it's undoubtedly his lyrical ode to daffodils ('I wandered lonely as a cloud...') that remains his best-known work. You can still visit the daffodils which inspired him on the shores of Ullswater at Gowbarrow Park, now owned by the National Trust.

Intriguingly he even found time to pen his own *Guide to the Lakes* in 1810, but later regretted it for encouraging tourism and spoiling the peace and quiet.

> Linda Lear's *Beatrix Potter: the Extraordinary Life of a Victorian Genius* is one of the best Potter biographies, tracing the author's life from her first Lakeland visit through to her years as an environmental campaigner and sheep breeder.

Sites to Visit

Wordsworth's boyhood home in Cockermouth, as well as his houses at Rydal Mount and Dove Cottage, are open to the public. The latter is linked to the excellent Wordsworth Museum, which holds one of the UK's most important collections of Romantic manuscripts and artefacts. You can also visit the graves of the Wordsworth family beneath the ancient yew trees of St Oswald's Churchyard in Grasmere, and stay at Greta Hall in Keswick, which was rented by both Southey and Coleridge during their time in the Lakes.

Children's Literature

Beatrix Potter

By far the most famous children's writer connected with the Lake District is Beatrix Potter, who first visited the area on a childhood holiday aged 16, and immediately fell in love with the pastoral landscape of fields, woodlands, lakes and tarns.

She gained many of the ideas for her books while exploring the surrounding countryside, and later swapped her gentrified Kensington lifestyle entirely for the more down-to-earth life of a Herdwick sheep breeder and hill farmer.

Her charming tales of mischievous bunnies and flustered puddleducks are brimming over with Lakeland scenery; fans will be able to spot countless locations from her books, especially around her cottage of Hill Top in Near Sawrey.

Though best known for her children's tales, she was also a keen naturalist and a talented wildlife painter. The Beatrix Potter Gallery in Hawkshead and the Armitt Museum in Ambleside both have fine examples of her watercolours, depicting everything from fungi to delicate wildflowers.

> **Literary Locations**
> » Dove Cottage, Grasmere
> » Rydal Mount, near Grasmere
> » Hill Top, Near Sawrey
> » Wordsworth House, Cockermouth
> » Beatrix Potter Gallery, Hawkshead

Arthur Ransome

Born in Leeds, Arthur Ransome went to school in Windermere and learned to sail on Coniston Water, a passion that remained with him throughout his life. After working as a journalist in London (covering, among other things, the Russian Revolution), he subsequently moved to the Winster Valley and Haverthwaite, where he wrote many of the *Swallows and Amazons* series, the majority of which are set in a fictionalised version of the Lake District.

The books follow the adventures of the Walker and Blackett children, who Ransome based on the children of his close friend Ernest Altounyan: Taqui, Susan, Mavis, Roger and Brigit. Among their many

SWALLOWS AND AMAZONS LOCATIONS

» **Wild Cat Island** is mainly modelled on Peel Island on Coniston Water.

» The mountain of **Kanchenjunga** is probably the Old Man of Coniston.

» **Cormorant Island** is most likely to be Silver Holme Island on Windermere.

» **Holly Howe Farm** is based on Bank Ground Farm in Coniston.

» The **Peak of Darien** is probably the viewpoint of Friars Crag on Derwentwater.

» The town of **Rio** is clearly modelled on Bowness-on-Windermere.

» **Captain Flint's houseboat** is thought to be an amalgam of the steam yacht *Gondola* and another boat, the *Esperance* (now owned by the Windermere Steamboat Museum).

adventures – half real, half imaginary – the children discover secret islands, conquer mountains and dig for buried treasure, and Ransome made extensive use of the Lakeland scenery while writing the stories.

It can be quite hard to pin down the locations from the stories, as Ransome tended to jumble his influences together in the final books. We've detailed a few of the main ones in the Swallows and Amazons Locations box.

A section of the Museum of Lakeland Life in Kendal contains a reconstruction of Ransome's writing room, and you can take special Swallows and Amazons tours on Coniston Water. Both Arthur and his wife Eugenia are buried in Rusland churchyard.

John Cunliffe

The sleepy Kentmere Valley, east of Windermere, provided the model for the humpbacked hills and up-and-down valleys of John Cunliffe's classic BBC TV series *Postman Pat*. Accompanied by his long-suffering black-and-white cat, Jess, Pat's adventures in and around the valley of Greendale have been a staple feature on British screens since the early 1980s, but he was recently promoted to the local sorting office in Pencaster, a decision which caused howls of protest among long-standing fans.

Postman Pat (www.postmanpat.com) isn't just a British phenomenon. In Israel he's known as Dai Ha'davar, in the Faroe Islands he's called Pedda Post, and in Iran he goes by the name of Pat-e Postchi.

Contemporary Writers

Melvyn Bragg

The extravagantly quiffed broadcaster, academic and man of letters Melvyn Bragg was born in Wigton in 1939 and has set several of his novels in Cumbria, including 'The Cumbrian Trilogy' (*The Hired Man, A Place in England* and *Kingdom Come*) and the critically acclaimed *Soldier's Return*.

He also wrote *The Maid of Buttermere*, based on the tale of Mary Robinson and the notorious bigamist John Hatfield – see p134.

Hunter Davies

Cumbrian writer Hunter Davies has turned his attention to everything from travel writing to biography over the years. His funny and affectionate memoir of his journey along Hadrian's Wall, *A Walk Along the Wall*, was followed by further travel memoirs including *A Walk Around the Lakes* (detailing a trip around the Lake District) and *A Walk Along the Tracks* (exploring some of Britain's disused railways).

More recently, his authorised biography of Alfred Wainwright was written with the cooperation of AW's second wife, Betty, who died in August 2008.

Norman Nicholson

Poet Norman Nicholson lived for over 70 years in the coastal town of Millom, between 1914 and his death in 1987. Nicholson was known for his simple, direct poetic style, and his work echoes with the sights, sounds and voices of the Cumbrian Coast. Much of his work deals with heavy industry, especially the iron mining for which the Millom area was once well known.

Exhibits on Nicholson's work can be seen at the folk museum in Millom, and a stained-glass window in St George's Church is dedicated to the poet.

Alfred Wainwright

By far the best-known, best-loved and possibly most-read Lakeland author is the inveterate fell walker, cartographer and author Alfred Wainwright, the man behind the landmark seven-volume guidebook series *The Pictorial Guides to the Lakeland Fells*.

The first guide was published in 1955, and over 55 years later they've sold well over a million copies, making them the bestselling Lake District guidebooks by a long chalk, not to mention some of the most reliable.

Though born in Blackburn, Wainwright enjoyed a lifelong love for the Lake District, and eventually managed to realise his dream of moving here when he was appointed to the Borough Treasurer's department in Kendal in 1941.

There are many locations linked with the writer: you can see a reconstruction of his office in Kendal Museum, view a plaque dedicated to him in the village church in Buttermere and, of course, visit his last resting place near the top of Haystacks.

Walking the fells with a Wainwright is a long-standing Lakeland tradition, and these days the guides have even gone digital. Check out *Wainwright: The Podcasts* for eight classic walks.

Food & Drink

Where to Eat & Drink

Pubs & Inns

If you like nothing better than warming your feet by a crackling fire with a pint of ale in your hand, then you're in luck. Country pubs have been a staple feature of the Lakeland landscape for centuries, and they're still by far the best place to get a real flavour for local life.

Many have remained reassuringly untouched by the march of modern progress, with hefty beams, slate floors and well-worn decor still very much in evidence, while others have reinvented themselves as chic, sleek gastropubs where the food is every bit as important as the drink. All pubs serve a selection of lagers and soft drinks, as well as lots of local ales. The wine choice is usually more limited.

Food standards vary. some pubs mainly stick to safe, traditional dishes such as pies, steaks and Cumberland sausage, while others make a real virtue of their food.

Restaurants

There's a restaurant to suit every taste and budget in the Lake District. You'll find at least one decent place to eat in all the major towns; we've picked out the very best places in this book with the top choice symbol. While most places are reasonably priced (under £16 for a main dish), there are also some very lavish establishments where you'll pay substantially more – especially some of the well-known country house restaurants.

If fine dining's your thing, there are five restaurants which currently have a Michelin star: three in Windermere (Gilpin Lodge, Holbeck Ghyll and Miller Howe), one in Ullswater (Sharrow Bay) and one in Cartmel (L'Enclume). The latter is run by renowned chef Simon Rogan, who's often touted as the Lake District's answer to Heston Blumenthal; his flagship restaurant regularly features in the UK's top-10 lists and graces all the major foodie guides.

Cafes & Teashops

Afternoon tea is an essential post-hike ritual for many walkers, and there's nearly always a convenient teashop nearby. In general, most Cumbrian teashops and cafes feel fairly traditional (think pine furniture, potted plants and china teapots) and serve the usual range of sandwiches, soups and homemade cakes.

Bakeries

There are some fantastic artisan bakeries dotted around the Lakes, producing a huge range of breads, pastries and cakes. Bryson's in Keswick is one of the best for local specialities such as Cumbrian fruitcake (a traditional rich fruitcake, sometimes laced with booze) and

Best Dining Pubs

» Punchbowl Inn, Crosthwaite

» Brown Horse, Winster

» Pheasant Inn, Bassenthwaite

» Wheatsheaf, Brigsteer

» George & Dragon, Clifton

» Drunken Duck, Barngates

Borrowdale teabread (a loaf-shaped cake filled with sultanas, raisins and currants). Other bakeries of note:

Millstones Watch breads being made at this Bootle bakery.

More? (Staveley) Especially good for cakes and pastries; in Staveley.

Staff of Life Well-known bread maker with a tiny shop in Kendal.

Village Bakery One of the best bakeries in the Lakes, particularly known for its organic breads. In Melmerby.

Watermill Award-winning organic bakery near Penrith.

Regional Specialities

Meat

Unsurprisingly for one of the nation's farming heartlands, meat features heavily in many dishes, whether it's roasted, grilled or wrapped up in pastry and baked in a pie.

Cumbria's oldest and hardiest breed of sheep, the Herdwick, is renowned for its richly flavoured mutton, an essential ingredient in tatie hotpot (a casserole of mutton, potatoes, onions and winter vegetables).

Another staple is the Cumberland sausage, stuffed with herbs and coarsely chopped pork, and sold in a long ring-shaped coil. Spicy and heavily seasoned, it's more reminiscent of a German wurst than an English sausage; some people believe it was first brought to Cumbria by German miners in the 16th century.

Locally reared beef, ham, bacon, sausages and pork are all of high quality, and the region has some renowned butchers, including Higginsons in Grange-over-Sands and Woodall's of Waberthwaite.

Saltmarsh lamb raised on the tidal grasses along the Cumbrian coastline is another delicacy, while local pig breeder Peter Gott has also received national recognition for his rare-breed pork and wild boar, produced organically at Sillfield Farm near Kendal.

Fish

The Lake District is one of the few places which supports Arctic char, a rare member of the salmon family. Windermere char is the one you're most likely to see on menus, either pied, potted or served whole.

Brown and rainbow trout are farmed by several fisheries, including Esthwaite, Bessy Beck and Hayeswater, while Morecambe Bay is famous for its cockles and shrimps (traditionally served potted in butter and eaten on toast).

Seafood is also excellent, and is increasingly sourced sustainably from local fishing fleets around Morecambe Bay and the Cumbrian coastline.

Artisan Food (www.artisan -food.com) is the leading online bible for foodies, with restaurant reviews, features on local producers and all the latest news on the county's dining scene.

Top Food & Farm Shops

» Low Sizergh Barn, near Kendal

» Holker Food Hall, near Cartmel

» Taste! Food Hall, Rheged, near Penrith

» JJ Graham, Penrith

» Hawkshead Relishes, Hawkshead

LAKE DISTRICT MICROBREWERIES

» **Barngates Brewery** (Hawkshead) In-house brewery at the Drunken Duck Inn. Try the Cracker, Tag Lag or Chester's Strong and Ugly.

» **Bitter End** (Cockermouth) The smallest brewery in Cumbria. Cockermouth Pride is always on tap, supplemented by seasonal ales.

» **Coniston Brewery** (Coniston) Home of the original Bluebird Bitter (now available in a pale XB variety) as well as the rich, red Old Man Ale.

» **Great Gable Brewing Company** (Wasdale Head) Lots of choice at the Wasdale Head Inn. All the ales are named after local peaks – try pale, malty Wry'Nose or the hoppy Great Gable.

» **Hawkshead Brewery** (Staveley) One of the original and best microbreweries, with a classic hoppy bitter, red and gold ales, and the dark, fruity Brodie's Prime.

LAKELAND CHEESE

Cheese-making in the Lake District has come on greatly in recent years. Strong, mature cheddars are still the mainstay, although there's an increasing range of specialist cheeses thanks to small-scale suppliers such as **Cartmel Cheeses** (www.cartmelcheeses.co.uk) and **Church Mouse Cheeses** (www.churchmousecheeses.com) in Kirkby Lonsdale.

There are several local cheese makers who are well worth seeking out:

» **Appleby Creamery** (www.applebycreamery.com) Specialist maker that has won several national awards for its blues, cheddars and bries.

» **Thornby Moor Dairy** (www.thornbymoordairy.co.uk; near Carlisle) Handmade cheeses including ewe's, oak-smoked and unpasteurised. The classics are Allerdale (matured goat's cheese) and Cumberland Farmhouse (cheddar-style, made from cow's milk).

» **Wardhall Dairy** (www.wardhalldairy.co.uk; Wigton) Produces a varied range of artisan cheeses and butters, including Arkleby (a Camembert-style cheese), Wardhall Blue (a blue goat's cheese) and Bobbin (goat's cheese wrapped in chestnut leaves).

» **Wasdale Cheese** (www.campingbarns.co.uk/cheese.html) Unpasteurised ewe's- and cow's-milk cheeses, produced in tiny quantities at a small dairy in Murt, Wasdale.

Puddings, Desserts & Cakes

Cumbria's most famous sweet treat is undoubtedly Kendal mintcake, the calorific sugar bar that sustained several landmark British expeditions including Shackleton's Antarctic expedition in 1914 and Edmund Hillary and Tenzing Norgay's trek to the top of Everest in 1953. The real McCoy is a slab of hard sugar flavoured with peppermint oil, but these days you can also buy buttermint, rum butter and chocolate-covered versions.

Almost as famous is Grasmere gingerbread – half crumbly biscuit, half sticky cake – invented by enterprising young baker Sarah Nelson in the mid-1850s and produced to a top-secret recipe. The tiny shop in Grasmere is still the only place to buy it direct (although these days you can also shop online).

Sticky toffee pudding, an indulgent sponge pudding flavoured with hot toffee sauce, is a very common sight on dessert menus, but connoisseurs wouldn't think of buying anywhere other than the Cartmel Village Shop.

Two other sweet specialities hint at the county's rum-running connections – Cumberland Rum Nicky, a latticed tart filled with butter, dates, rum, spices and sugar; and Rum Butter, a fine accompaniment to mince pies and Christmas pudding.

Lastly, Scoop produces handmade ice creams from its base in Staveley, while some of the UK's best toffee and fudge is made by the Toffee Shop in Penrith.

> Kendal mintcake was discovered by accident at Joseph Wiper's confectioners in 1869 when a pan of ingredients for making glacier mints was mistakenly left to burn on a stove.

Drinks

Like much of England, Cumbria's tipple of choice is undoubtedly ale – preferably pumped warm from the barrel. The main name is Jennings, a large family-run enterprise based in Cockermouth, which owns or supplies many local pubs with its range of beers and bitters.

There are also a growing number of microbreweries which produce their own ranges of boutique beers; see the boxed text, for some of the best, including the ever-popular Bitter End in Cockermouth.

Farrer's (www.farrerscoffee.co.uk) is a well-known coffee and tea merchant based in Penrith, and supplies many hotels and cafes around the Lake District.

> The Made in Cumbria website (www.madein cumbria.co.uk) lists local producers and farmers markets in the Lake District, as well as handy recommendations on arts, crafts and culture.

VEGETARIANS & VEGANS

Vegetarians are fairly well catered for: most restaurants offer at least a few veggie options on their menus, although the choice is sometimes quite limited.

For a more extensive choice, there are two excellent vegetarian restaurants to seek out: the excellent Quince & Medlar in Cockermouth, and the equally upmarket Fellini's in Ambleside, whose owners also run a vegetarian B&B near Hawkshead.

Cookery Courses

Looking to polish up your knife skills or master the art of the perfect choux bun? Then why not take some tips from some of Cumbria's top chefs?

Cumbria on a Plate (☎01900-881356; www.cumbriaonaplate.co.uk) Annette Gibbons' 'Food Safaris' include a visit to local farms and producers coupled with a slap-up feed (£120). Themed cookery demos are also available.

Food & Company (☎01697-478634; www.foodandcompany.co.uk; Wigton) Cookery school run by two sisters in the stately surroundings of Mirehouse on Bassenthwaite Lake, with a wide range of cookery demos and hands-on workshops. Prices start from £45.

L'Enclume (☎01539-536362; www.lenclume.co.uk; Cartmel) Book in for a course at Simon Rogan's stellar restaurant and your dinner parties will never be the same again. The day course costs £279 – but it's not everyday you get lessons from a Michelin-starred maestro.

Lucy Cooks (☎015394-32288; www.lucycooks.co.uk; Mill Yard, Staveley) Varied cookery courses run by well-known Ambleside chef Lucy Nicholson. Foundation courses cover the basics, or you can learn how to bake bread, shuck oysters or design the perfect dinner party. Day courses £100 to £150, half-days £40 to £70.

Good Taste (☎017687-72112; www.simplygoodtaste.co.uk/cookery-school) Local chef Peter Sidwell runs themed cookery days. Some focus on skills (such as bread making and butchery), while others cover regional cuisines. Courses cost £100 to £125 per day including lunch.

Watermill (☎01768-881523; www.organicmill.com; Little Salkeld, Penrith) Bread baking, children's cookery and vegetarian food are all covered in the programmes at this award-winning bakery. Day courses cost £55.

Farmers Markets

» Brampton (last Sunday of month)

» Carlisle (first Friday of month)

» Cockermouth (first Thursday of month)

» Kendal (last Friday of month)

» Keswick (2nd Thursday of month)

» Ulverston (3rd Saturday of month)

Survival Guide

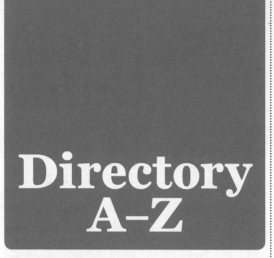

Directory A–Z

Accommodation

Whether it's country houses, boutique hotels, bargain B&Bs or idyllic campsites, the Lake District has some-where to stay to suit all tastes (and budgets). In comparison to many other areas of England, however, prices are relatively high – especially in the peak season from June to August, when space and prices are at a premium.

There are a couple of accommodation-rating schemes that provide a rough (if generic) guide to standards – Visit Britain uses a one to five rosette rating, while the AA uses a one- to five-star rating. Both schemes concentrate more on facilities than on subjective impressions.

The **regional tourist board** (☎0845 450 1199; www.golakes.co.uk) is a useful place to start your search, and will arrange bookings for a £3 fee.

B&Bs & Guesthouses

The B&B is a longstanding British institution, but things have come on in leaps and bounds in recent years. Gone are the days of night-time curfews, Stalinesque landladies and saggy mattresses – some of the B&Bs in this book give the top-end hotels a serious run for their money.

» Most B&Bs offer en suite or private bathrooms, although some may still offer shared facilities for a lower price than a standard room.

» B&B prices are often quoted per person rather than per room. Rates always include breakfast unless otherwise indicated.

» Single rooms are becoming increasingly scarce – often you'll have to take a double room and pay a single supplement (generally around 75% of the double room rate).

» Most places offer simple tea and coffee making facilities in guest rooms; very few offer room service.

» Many B&Bs don't accept credit or debit cards. Those that do will sometimes add a transaction charge to your bill to cover bank fees.

Camping

For many people camping out is an essential part of the Lake District experience. There are some great locations to choose from, ranging from simple farm sites to family-friendly resorts. Facilities vary widely: some places offer little more than a field, cold-water tap and toilet block, while others have their own farm shops, laundry and onsite cafes.

» Some sites are geared solely towards caravans and motor homes, while others are tents only. Check ahead to make sure the site will suit your needs.

» Most sites charge separately for different facilities (eg your chosen pitch, the number of people in your party, whether you're parking a vehicle etc).

» Some sites have electric hook-ups for campervans and caravans.

» Many sites have started to offer timber 'camping pods', which provide a bit more cover than canvas tents.

» Check-out time is usually 11am, although policies vary at each campsite.

» Not all places accept credit cards, so check before you arrive.

Camping Barns

For campers who prefer something sturdier than a nylon flysheet, camping barns can be a good option. The general rule is to imagine you're camping, but under a 'stone tent'; basic facilities generally include sleeping platforms, cold running water and a flush toilet, although some also offer cooking equipment, hot water, showers and a log fire. You'll need your own sleeping bag and other camping gear.

Lakeland Camping Barns (www.lakelandcamping barns.co.uk) has useful listings of camping barns across the Lake District.

Hostels

The **YHA** (Youth Hostel Association; ☑0870 770 8868; www.yha.org.uk) operates most of the hostels in the Lake District – although the recent decision to sell off some of the less profitable ones (including Helvellyn, Kendal and the YHA's first-ever property at Thorney Howe in Grasmere) has not gone down well. Many of the Lakeland hostels are a long way from the drab, pre-fab buildings you may be used to elsewhere, and range from miners' cottages to converted mansions.

As well as the YHA hostels, there are good independent hostels in Grasmere, Windermere and Ambleside. The **YMCA** (☑015395-31743; www.ymca.org.uk) has its main outdoors centre at Lakeside on Windermere, although it's mainly used by activity holidays and school groups.

» YHA membership offers a discount of up to £3 on standard rates. It currently costs £15.95 for adults, £9.95 for under-26s or £22.95 for two adults and their dependents.

» The YHA hostels in the Lake District are often booked solid during weekends and holidays, so plan ahead.

» Prices operate on a sliding scale according to the season and how busy the hostel is. Book early for the best rates.

» Dorms are the norm, although hostels are increasingly offering private rooms to attract couples and families. Most have shared bathrooms and showers, as well as a communal kitchen for guests' use.

» Some hostels offer breakfast, generally in addition to the room price.

» Duvets, sheets and towels are usually provided. Sleeping bags are not allowed in YHA hostels to prevent the transmission of bed bugs.

Hotels

The Lake District has some wonderful country hotels, but they rarely come cheap. The boundary between top-end B&Bs and hotels can sometimes be blurry: the difference generally comes down to the level of service (eg 24hr concierge, room service) and the range of facilities (gyms, in-house restaurants, swimming pools).

Research hotels carefully to make sure you know what you're getting: some Lakeland hotels are strictly traditional, while others are aimed at the boutique market.

» Prices range from around £120 per night up to £300 or more.

» Hotel room prices are nearly always quoted per person, and often don't include breakfast.

» Rates fluctuate wildly according to the season – you'll often be able to find discounts of up to 50% by booking out of season.

Pubs & Inns

Pubs have been a feature of the Lakeland scenery for centuries (inns were often whitewashed to make them stand out to passing travellers). While a few flagship inns have gone down the gastropub route, many pubs have remained pretty traditional in feel, complete with slate flagstones, wood panelling and open fires.

Pubs generally charge similar room prices to B&Bs; count on £60 to £90 for a double.

Rental Cottages

Staying in B&Bs can be expensive, especially if you're travelling as a family. Consequently many people decide to rent a holiday home. There are many rental properties in the Lakes – so many, in fact, that they've become a serious problem for many villages, where self-caterers often outnumber residents by a considerable margin in the summer months.

There's no doubt, however, that renting a cottage is one of the most cost-effective

---

NATIONAL TRUST CAMPSITE BOOKINGS

The NT's four Lake District campsites at Low Wray, Wasdale, Great Langdale and Howthwaite have recently started to accept bookings, much to the delight of regular campers.

For all bookings, contact the **Bookings Coordinator** (☑015394-63862; campsite.bookings@nationaltrust.org.uk; ☺1-5pm Mon-Fri) or book online through the **NT Campsites Website** (www.ntlakescampsites.org.uk). Pitches can be reserved up to 24 hours before your stay for periods of two nights or longer. There's an online booking fee of £5, or £7.50 for telephone and email bookings.

You can also keep up to speed with the latest info such as weather conditions, campsite availability and special announcements via their **Twitter account** (http://twitter.com/NTLakescamping).

THE LAKE DISTRICT'S TOP CAMPSITES FOR...

» **Wild views**: Wasdale Head NT Campsite, Wasdale (p109)

» **Families**: Fisherground Farm, Eskdale (p102)

» **Walkers**: Great Langdale NT Campsite, Langdale (p81)

» **Woodland camping**: Bowkerstead Farm, Grizedale (p94)

» **Quiet nights**: Seatoller Farm, Borrowdale (p132)

» **Lakeside camping**: Waterside House, Ullswater (p141)

» **Isolation**: Turner Hall Farm, Duddon Valley (p105)

» **Ecofriendliness**: Quiet Site, Ullswater (p145)

» **Luxury camping**: Full Circle, near Grasmere (p75)

» **Sleeping in a tipi**: Low Wray NT Campsite, near Ambleside (p62)

ways to visit the region, although facilities and standards vary widely and some properties can be plonked miles away from the nearest village, so it's worth thoroughly researching the surrounding area beforehand.

Major rental companies:

Coppermines & Lakes Cottages (☎015394-41765; www.coppermines.co.uk) Mainly in the Coniston area.

Cumbrian Cottages (☎01228-599960; www.cumbrian-cottages.co.uk) Offers more than 900 properties, including deluxe, pet-friendly and family-specific choices.

Heart of the Lakes (☎015394-32321; www.heartofthelakes.co.uk) Good selection in the Central Lakes, with a smaller range in Keswick and Ullswater.

Keswick Cottages (☎017687-78555; www.keswickcottages.co.uk) Unsurprisingly specialises in Keswick, Braithwaite and the Newlands Valley.

Lakeland Cottage Company (☎015395-76065; www.lakelandcottages.co.uk) Windermere, Ambleside, Keswick, Ullswater, Borrowdale and the western Lakes.

Lakelovers (☎015394-88855; www.lakelovers.co.uk) Good-quality accommodation mainly based around the southern Lakes, with a mix of period and modern choices.

Lakes Cottage Holidays (☎01768-774060, ☎015394-48081; www.lakescottageholiday.co.uk) Offers a mix of traditional and quirky properties.

National Trust Cottages (☎0844 800 2070; www.nationaltrustcottages.co.uk) A limited selection of National Trust properties.

Wheelwrights (☎015394-37635; www.wheelwrights.com) Loads of choices around Ambleside, Grasmere and the Langdale Valleys.

Windermere Lake Holidays (☎015394-43415; www.lakewindermere.net) Waterfront apartments and even a few houseboats available for rent.

Business Hours

Throughout this book, we haven't listed opening hours unless they vary significantly from the times listed here.

Banks 9am to 4 or 5pm Monday to Friday, 9am to 12.30pm Saturday and closed on Sundays.

Museums & Sights Museums and attractions are usually open seven days a week virtually the whole year. Smaller places operate shorter hours and close at least one day a week (usually Sunday). Some of the smaller attractions have reduced opening hours or close completely in winter.

Post Offices 9am to 5.30pm Monday to Friday, 9am to 12.30pm Saturday (main branches to 5pm). Closed on Sundays.

Pubs Generally 11am to 11pm, though city pubs sometimes open to midnight or 1pm on Friday and Saturday. Some country pubs close from 3pm to 6pm.

Restaurants Most restaurants are closed at least one day a week, usually Sunday or Monday. Some are open all day, while others only serve either lunch or dinner.

ACCOMMODATION PRICE RANGES

Throughout this book, we've used the following price ranges for our accommodation reviews. Unless otherwise indicated, quoted rates are for a double room with private bathroom in peak season, so cheaper rates may be available in the shoulder months.

PRICE RANGE	SYMBOL	BUDGET
Budget	£	< £60
Midrange	££	£60-120
Top end	£££	>£120

Climate

Lake District

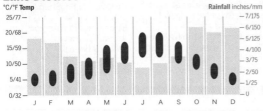

Lunch is usually served from noon to 3pm, dinner from 7pm to 10pm.

Shops & Supermarkets 9am to 5.30pm Monday to Saturday, 10am to 4pm Sunday.

PRICE RANGE	SYMBOL	BUDGET
Budget	£	<£8
Mid-range	££	£8-16
Top End	£££	>£16

Electricity

230V/50Hz

Food

For information on eating out in the Lake District, see our special Food chapter on p207. Throughout this book, we've used the following price ranges for all our reviews, based on the cost of a main meal not including drinks.

Gay & Lesbian Travellers

The Lake District isn't renowned for its gay scene, but you're unlikely to run into much hostility. There's a small gay scene in Carlisle, and gay pub at the **Steam Packet Inn** (☎01900 62186; Stanley St) in Workington.

For more advice, consult www.gaycumbria.com and www.iknow-lakedistrict.co.uk/information/gay_friendly.htm.

Health

Availability & Cost Of Health Care

Health care is readily available and free at the point of delivery for UK citizens. For minor ailments pharmacists dispense advice and over-the-counter medication.

For general advice contact the 24-hour helpline **NHS Direct** (☎0845 46 47; www.nhsdirect.nhs.uk).

Hospitals

Cumbria's main hospitals:
Cumberland Infirmary (☎01228-523444; Newtown Rd, Carlisle)

Furness General Hospital (☎01229-870870; Dalton Lane, Barrow-in-Furness)
Westmorland General (☎015397-32288; Burton Rd, Kendal)

Insurance

» If you're an EU citizen, get an EHIC (European Health Insurance Card) from doctor's surgeries and post offices or apply online. This will cover you for most medical care, but not for non-emergencies or emergency repatriation.

» Non-EU citizens should ask about reciprocal healthcare arrangements before travelling, or take out appropriate travel insurance covering healthcare costs and emergency repatriation.

» Find out in advance if your insurance will make payments directly to providers or reimburse you later

Environmental Hazards
HEAT EXHAUSTION

Heat exhaustion occurs following excessive fluid loss with inadequate replacement of fluids and salt. Symptoms include headache, dizziness and tiredness. Dehydration is already happening by the time you feel thirsty. To treat heat exhaustion, replace lost fluids by drinking water and/or fruit juice, and cool the body with cold water and fans. Treat salt loss with salty fluids such as soup or Bovril, or add a little more table salt to foods than usual.

HYPOTHERMIA

The high fells are exposed and prone to sudden extremes of weather. Always carry waterproof garments, warm layers and a reflective survival blanket. Hypothermia is a possibility if you are exposed to extremes of wind or cold: initial symptoms include shivering, loss of judgment and clumsiness, followed by apathy, confusion and coma. Prevent further heat loss by seeking shelter, warm clothing, hot sweet drinks and shared bodily warmth, and seek medical help immediately.

INSECTS & PARASITES

Ticks are carried by sheep and cattle and can be found in many grassy or wooded areas. Some ticks carry Lyme Disease, which can be a serious illness if left untreated, and may appear as an expanding, reddish rash up to 30 days after the initial bite. There are influenza-like symptoms with mild headaches and aching muscles and joints. If you have been bitten by a tick and experience any of these symptoms, see a doctor.

To avoid being bitten, wear long-sleeved shirts and long trousers tucked into socks. At the end of the day check yourself carefully, especially around the groin and armpits. If you find a tick remove it by grasping it firmly with tweezers, as close to the skin as possible, and pulling directly up. Don't burn it off or crush it, as this encourages the tick to regurgitate into your bloodstream. If this happens, or the tick's head remains in your skin, seek medical attention.

SUNBURN

Sunburn is possible even on a cloudy day. Cover up, use suncream of an appropriate SPF rating for your skin, and wear a hat. If you get burnt, treat the affected area with an aloe vera or calamine lotion and stay out of the sun.

WATER

Tap water quality in Britain is high and you should have no problem drinking it, but don't drink from any streams, lakes, tarns or ponds in the countryside – you can't be sure what's in the water, or what it's flowed through. If you're camping, make sure any water taps are labelled safe to drink, as some are intended only for animal use.

Heritage Organisations

If you're doing a lot of sight-seeing (especially historic houses and gardens), membership of the **National Trust** (NT; www.nationaltrust .org.uk) is a really worthwhile investment.

Standard prices are £50.50/83.50/23.50 per adult/couple/child per year. Family membership costs £55.50 for one adult and their children, or £88.50 for two adults and their children. Membership also grants free parking in the Trust's car parks, which is almost worth the membership price on its own in the Lake District.

US visitors who belong to the **Royal Oak Foundation** (www.royal-oak.org) qualify for free entry to NT properties.

English Heritage (EH; www.english-heritage.org.uk) owns a more limited range of properties, including Carlisle Castle, Shap Abbey, Lanercost Priory and Birdoswald Roman Fort. Annual membership costs £46/80 per adult/couple. Under 19s and students can join for £34.50, and over 60s for £33.50/54.50 per person/couple.

Insurance

A decent travel insurance policy is always a worthwhile investment.

» Check the policy for cover on common problems such as travel hold-ups, luggage loss, theft and flight delays.

» It's worth checking the rules on natural disasters and 'force majeure' events. Flooding and extreme

HIKING MAPS

» If you're planning on anything other than a low-level ramble in the Lake District, a good-quality map is not a luxury, it's a necessity.

» Relatively few paths are waymarked, and often signs at junctions only indicate public bridleways rather than specific trails.

» Packing a compass (and knowing how to use it) is an absolute must.

» Don't try and rely on your mobile phone to navigate – the maps simply aren't detailed enough, and reception can be notoriously patchy on the fells.

» If you're tackling a well-known walk, it's worth looking out for specific route guides in local tourist offices and bookshops, such as the ones published by Altos.

Two companies produce detailed maps suitable for hiking, cycling and general exploring:

» **Ordnance Survey** (OS; www.ordnancesurvey.co.uk) The traditionalist's choice is this orange-jacketed 1:25,000 *Explorer* series. The highly detailed maps (OL4 to OL7) cover the key Lake District areas; standard and waterproof versions are available.

» **Harvey** (www.harveymaps.co.uk) There are six maps (*North, East, Central, Southeast, Southwest* and *West*) is this 1:25,000 *Superwalker* series. Although they sacrifice some of the finer landscape detail for clarity, they're arguably easier to use when you're on the trail. They're also (theoretically) waterproof and tear proof.

weather are rare, but certainly not unprecedented in Cumbria.

» You won't need a specific clause in your policy to cover you for rescue on the fells (mountain rescue in England is a voluntary service funded by charitable donations), but you will need appropriate medical cover in case you need hospital treatment or emergency repatriation.

» Worldwide travel insurance is available at www.lonely planet.com/travel_services. You can buy, extend and claim online anytime – even if you're already on the road.

Internet Access

Many hotels, B&Bs, restaurants and cafes in Cumbria will offer wi-fi access (usually, but not always, free of charge). Throughout this book, we have used the 🛜 symbol to indicate wi-fi access, and the @ symbol to indicate a public computer.

There are relatively few internet cafes in Cumbria, although a number of town libraries offer internet access at public terminals.

Legal Matters

Key legal matters to be aware of:

» Possession and resale of drugs is illegal. Hard drugs such as cocaine, heroin and ecstasy incur stiff penalties, usually a large fine and/or imprisonment.

» Drink-driving is a serious offence. See p225 for speed-limits and other road rules.

Public Holidays

Nearly all banks and businesses close for official public holidays, although many tourist attractions stay open to take advantage of the holiday trade.

WEATHER

The Lake District's weather is infamously unpredictable. While it's always worth checking the latest forecast (especially before you set out on a hike), you should be prepared for all eventualities – rain-gear and proper waterproof boots are indispensable.

The **Lake District Weatherline** (📞 0870 055 0575; www.lake-district.gov.uk/weatherline) provides a five-day forecast courtesy of the National Park Authority (NPA), while the **Mountain Weather Information Service** (www.mwis.org.uk) provides a downloadable forecast for the Lake District and Britain's other mountain parks.

The **Met Office** (www.met-office.gov.uk) provides tailored forecasts for specific areas; you can search by region or input a town or postcode, and get predictions for weather, wind, rainfall, cloud, pressure, temperature and UV risk.

New Year's Day 1 January
Easter Good Friday and Easter Sunday, Mar/Apr
May Day First Monday in May
Spring Bank Holiday Last Monday in May
Summer Bank Holiday Last Monday in August
Christmas Day 25 December
Boxing Day 26 December

Other busy times to look out for are the main school holidays and week-long half-term breaks, when traffic jams and crowds are always at their worst. The dates vary every year, but are generally:

Christmas Mid-December to early January
Easter Week before and week after Easter
Summer Mid-July to early September

Tourist Information

The main regional tourist board for the Lake District is **Go Lakes** (www.golakes.co.uk), while there's comprehensive county-wide information available from **Visit Cumbria** (www.visitcumbria.com). There are tourist offices dotted all over the national park; we've

listed all the relevant offices in the appropriate chapters. Useful websites:

Historic Carlisle (📞 01228-625600; www.historic-carlisle .org.uk) Carlisle and Hadrian's Wall country.

I Know Lake District (www.iknow-lakedistrict.co.uk) Mainly accommodation listings.

Keswick (www.keswick.org) Keswick-specific site run by local tourism association.

Lake District National Park Authority (📞 01539 724555; www.lake-district.gov .uk) Online portal for the NPA.

Lake District Peninsulas (📞 01229-580742; www.lake -district-peninsulas.co.uk) Info on the southern coastal area around Coniston, Cartmel, Grange, Ulverston and Barrow.

Lonely Planet (www.lonely planet.com/england/cumbria -and-the-lakes/lake-district) Planning advice, author recommendations, traveller reviews and insider tips.

South Lakeland (www .southlakeland.gov.uk) Council-run website covering the southeastern area between Kendal and Windermere.

Visit Eden (www.eden.gov.uk /tourism) Eden Valley and

INTERNATIONAL VISITORS

Entering the Region

» European Economic Area (EEA) citizens don't need a visa to visit or work in the UK.

» Citizens of Australia, New Zealand, Canada and the US do not need a visa either, but are prohibited from working during their stay.

» Other passport holders should visit www.ukvisas.gov.uk or contact the local British embassy.

» The gateway towns to the Lakes are Carlisle, Windermere, Kendal and Penrith. All have frequent train connections across the UK and are near the M6 motorway.

Money

Notes and coins from England and Scotland are legal tender in Cumbria. Notes are divided into £50, £20, £10 and £5 denominations. Coins are available in £2, £1, 50p, 20p, 10p, 5p, 2p and 1p denominations.

» Credit and debit cards are widely accepted, with the exception of American Express.

» 'Chip & PIN', where you enter a PIN rather than signing a receipt, is now universal.

» Most larger post offices offer currency exchange (usually commission free). Exchange rates at banks are less favourable and often incur a commission charge.

» Travellers cheques are a rarity in England. Most banks will cash them for a fee.

» Tipping at cafes and restaurants is not compulsory, but it's usual to add 10% to 15% to the bill. Taxi drivers will expect around 10%.

» Bargaining is common at flea markets and jumble sales, but rare in shops.

Post

Postal services are handled by the Royal Mail, which provides services through local post offices. British post-boxes are painted bright red.

» There are two main services: First Class generally guarantees domestic delivery for the next working day, while Second Class can take two or more days to arrive.

» International mail (including postcards) is best sent via First Class Airmail.

» For the latest prices, visit www.royalmail.com.

Practicalities

» Road distances are generally in miles but shorter distances are often measured in metres, while heights are usually given in feet and inches.

» Weights in shops and markets are usually given in pounds and ounces (although the equivalent in kilograms and grams is nearly always quoted).

» Petrol stations quote prices for both gallons and litres. Most other liquids are sold in litres or half-litres, except milk and beer – available in pints.

» The TV system in Britain is PAL. The entire country will have switched over to a digital-only signal by 2012.

Telephone

Many public phones no longer take small change; you'll need to use a credit or debit card, or a pre-paid phonecard.

» The minimum call charge from public phones is currently 40p. For the operator dial ☎100, and for directory enquiries dial ☎118-118.

» UK mobile phones use GSM 900/1800, which is compatible with Europe and Australia, but often not with Japan or the US.

» To avoid roaming charges, invest in a temporary pay-as-you-go SIM card (around £20 to £30) from newsagents or mobile phone shops.

Time

Britain uses GMT (Greenwich Mean Time). If you're here during British Summer Time from late March to late October, clocks are one hour ahead of GMT.

Penrith area information, run by the Eden District council.

Western Lake District (☎01900-818741; www.western-lakedistrict.co.uk) Specific advice for the western national park.

Travellers with Disabilities

As in much of England, access for people with disabilities isn't always as good as it should be. Most attractions have made a concerted effort to facilitate entry for wheelchair users, and to provide facilities for people with sight and hearing difficulties, but in many places the nature of the building or activity inherently limits what can be achieved. The best advice is to phone ahead and ask what the specific operator thinks they'll be able to do (at least that way you'll save a wasted journey).

» Modern developments are legally required to offer wheelchair access, but the same rules don't apply to older buildings.

» Local tourist offices often have lists of disabled-friendly accommodation.

» There's a searchable directory of wheelchair-friendly accommodation at www.iknow-lakedistrict.co.uk/information/disabled_access.htm.

» The **Lake District NPA** (☎01539 724555; www.lake-district.gov.uk) has 21 specific 'Miles Without Stiles' routes that have been 'road tested' for buggy pushers and wheelchair users: see www.lake-district.gov.uk/index/enjoying.

» The visitor centre at Brockhole has good disabled access – push-wheelchairs are available inside the house, with electric ones for use in the gardens, and there's a 'Brockmobile' electric bus to transport visitors from the car park.

» Most local buses and coaches aren't set up to accommodate wheelchairs.

» Most modern trains have at least one carriage that is wheelchair-accessible, although the same can't be said for heritage railways.

National sources of information:

All Go Here (www.allgohere.com) Hotels and businesses certified as disabled-friendly.

Disability UK (www.disabilityuk.com) Huge online directory for travellers with disabilities.

Volunteering

Volunteering has a long and distinguished heritage in the Lake District, and there are plenty of schemes that allow you to get involved in looking after the unique Lakeland landscape in a hands-on way.

Cumbria Wildlife Trust (☎01539-816300; www.cumbriawildlifetrust.org.uk) Conservation charity that runs programs in wildlife monitoring, tree planting, scrub clearance and boardwalk building.

Fix the Fells (☎015394-34633; www.fixthefells.co.uk) An ambitious project to repair hundreds of miles of damaged footpaths in the Lake District, run in conjunction with the National Trust. Group volunteer programs are offered at High Wray Basecamp, with shorter individual programs sometimes available.

Friends of the Lake District (☎01539 720788; www.fld.org.uk) Community-based charity that runs volunteer conservation days practically every week of the year. Brush up your skills in bracken control, hedge laying and woodland management.

National Park Authority Volunteer Scheme (☎01539-724555; www.lake-district.gov.uk) Official conservation programs run by the National Park, including wildlife surveys, litter clearing, tree replanting and footpath repair.

National Trust Working Holidays (☎0844 800 3099, www.nationaltrust.org.uk/workingholidays) The NT organises regular working holidays in the Lake District offering opportunities for everything from scrub clearing to drystone walling. Places are limited so you'll need to apply well ahead.

Transcript

GETTING THERE & AWAY

Air

Cumbria doesn't have its own airport, but there are several within a couple of hours' travel. The most useful is **Manchester Airport** (MAN; www.manchesterairport .co.uk), which has its own train station offering direct connections to Carlisle, and Windermere and Kendal via Oxenholme. Other regional airports close by include Blackpool, Glasgow, Liverpool and Newcastle.

For further information, head to shop.lonelyplanet .com to purchase a downloadable PDF of the Manchester, Liverpool & the Northwest chapter from Lonely Planet's *England* guide.

Booking online in advance gets the cheapest tickets. Standard anytime train fares from Manchester Airport:

DESTINATION	SINGLE (£)	DURATION (HOURS)
Barrow-in-Furness	31.10	2½
Carlisle	45.50	2¼
Kendal	32.30	2
Windermere	35.50	2¼

Land
Bicycle

Several long-distance cycling routes run through Cumbria. For information on cycling paths throughout the UK, the best resource is **Sustrans** (www.sustrans.org.uk), which publishes detailed guides and trail maps to most major routes. You can order them direct through Sustrans' **online shop** (www.sustrans shop.co.uk).

Cycle Routes (www .cycle-routes.org) is another useful online resource for long-distance bike routes in the UK.

For information on taking your bike on public transport, see the boxed text, p222.

C2C (Sea-to-Sea; www.c2c -guide.co.uk) 147-mile route developed by Sustrans, connecting Whitehaven on the west coast with Sunderland on the east. It's England's most popular long-distance cycle route, with nearly half the length using off-road paths or disused railways.

Cumbria Way (www.cumbria waycycleroute.co.uk) Two- or three-day route, running for between 72 and 80 miles, depending on the exact route. It starts in Ulverston, runs through Elterwater, Grasmere, Keswick, Bassenthwaite and Hesket Newmarket and ends in Carlisle.

Hadrian's Cycleway (www .cycle-routes.org/hadrians cycleway) 174 miles from

---

CLIMATE CHANGE & TRAVEL

Every form of transport that relies on carbon-based fuel generates CO_2, the main cause of human-induced climate change. Modern travel is dependent on aeroplanes, which might use less fuel per kilometre per person than most cars but travel much greater distances. The altitude at which aircraft emit gases (including CO_2) and particles also contributes to their climate change impact. Many websites offer 'carbon calculators' that allow people to estimate the carbon emissions generated by their journey and, for those who wish to do so, to offset the impact of the greenhouse gases emitted with contributions to portfolios of climate-friendly initiatives throughout the world. Lonely Planet offsets the carbon footprint of all staff and author travel.

SHUTTLE BUSES & BAGGAGE COURIERS

If you're doing a long-distance hike or bike ride, you'll be faced with the problem of what to do with your gear. Thankfully, there are several companies that offer a door-to-door baggage courier service between hotels, B&Bs and campsites. Prices vary according to the route, but generally start at around £6 to £8 per 20kg bag.
Brigantes (☎01729-830463; www.brigantes englishwalks.com)
Coast-to-Coast Packhorse (☎017683-71777; www.cumbria.com /packhorse)
Sherpa Van (☎0871 520 0124; www.sherpavan.com)

Ravenglass to South Shields, via Carlisle, Brampton and the Pennines, mostly following NCN72.
Reivers Route (reivers-route .co.uk) 172 miles: Tynemouth to Cockermouth, Workington and Whitehaven, taking in fine sections of the Northumbrian and Cumbrian countryside. Often used as a return route for cyclists on the C2C.
W2W (Walney-to-Wear; www .cyclingw2w.info) Complementary route to the C2C, starting at Walney Island on the coast, and circling through Barrow, Ulverston, Grange, Kendal and Kirkby Stephen. The route terminates in either Sunderland (153 miles) or Whitby (172 miles).

Bus & Coach
National Express (www .nationalexpress.com) runs one coach per day up and down the M6, connecting London Victoria Coach Station with

Windermere via Preston (the NX570 service). From Windermere, the bus continues to Ambleside, Grasmere and Keswick.
» There are usually also four direct coaches a day to Carlisle from cities including Manchester, Birmingham, Edinburgh and Glasgow.
» If you want to travel direct to Windermere from these cities, you need to connect in Preston with the daily NX570 coach from London.
» As always, early booking and travelling off-peak gets the cheapest fares.

Standard fares and journey times to/from Windermere:

DESTI-NATION	SINGLE FARE (£)	DUR-ATION (HR)
Birmingham	32.70	4¾
Lancaster	10.70	1¼
London Victoria	33.80	8
Manchester	21.60	3¾
Preston	11.50	2

Standard fares and journey times to/from Carlisle:

DESTI-NATION	SINGLE FARE (£)	DUR-ATION (HR)
Birmingham	38.90	5½ to 6½
Edinburgh	18.10	3½
Glasgow	18.10	2
London	34.80	8
Manchester	24.90	3¼

Car & Motorcycle
The M6 cuts through the east side of Cumbria, passing close to the Lake District's three gateway towns: Kendal (southbound take junction 39 onto the A6, northbound take junction 36 onto the A590), Penrith (junction 40) and Carlisle (follow junction 43 for the city centre).
» Count on a journey of five hours from London, 1½ hours from Manchester or Liverpool,

and two hours from Glasgow or Edinburgh.
» Allow extra time for traffic, especially during the peak season in July and August and Bank Holiday weekends.
» BBC Radio Cumbria and other local stations carry regular traffic reports that detail accidents and traffic black spots.

Train
The only direct train service to the Lake District is to Windermere, which is the terminus for the branch railway line from Staveley, Kendal and Oxenholme. From Oxenholme, there are connections at least hourly along the main West Coast line between London Euston, Carlisle and Scotland.
There are also two useful coastal lines: the Furness Railway from Lancaster to Barrow-in-Furness, and the Cumbrian Coast Line from Barrow north to Ravenglass, Whitehaven, Maryport and Carlisle.
The three main operators:
First Transpennine Express (www.tpexpress.co .uk) Runs a direct route from Manchester Airport to Manchester city centre, Preston, Lancaster, Oxenholme, Penrith and Carlisle en route to Edinburgh or Glasgow. Also runs the Furness Railway from Lancaster to Carnforth, Arnside, Grange-over-Sands and Ulverston, terminating at Barrow-in-Furness.
Northern Rail (www.northern rail.org) Regional services across northern England, including the Tyne Valley line (sometimes referred to as the Hadrian's Wall line) between Newcastle-upon-Tyne and Carlisle, the Settle-Carlisle Railway (see p172) and the Cumbrian Coast line.
Virgin Trains (www.virgin trains.co.uk) Operates most intercity services between the south and Scotland.

Sample off-peak fares to/from Windermere:

DESTI-NATION	SINGLE FARE (£)	DUR-ATION (HR)
Birmingham	63	2¾
Edinburgh	51	2½-3
Glasgow	45	2¼
Kendal	4	¼
Lancaster	11.90	¾
London	86.80	3¼
Manchester	19.90	1½-2
Preston	15	1

Sample fares and times to/from Carlisle:

DESTI-NATION	SINGLE FARE (£)	DUR-ATION
Edinburgh	22.90	1½
Glasgow	23.50	1¼
Kendal	11.50	1¼
Lancaster	26	¾
London	96.30	3½
Manchester	47	2
Whitehaven	9	1¼

Classes

Most intercity trains have 1st- and 2nd-class carriages; paying the premium entitles you to more legroom, comfier seats and usually a dining car or buffet. On certain weekend trains you might be able to upgrade to 'weekend 1st' for between £10 and £20, either at the station or from the conductor. Note that advance tickets don't qualify for the weekend 1st upgrade; it's only available to off-peak or anytime ticket holders.

Tickets & Railcards

For timetables, fares and travel details, contact **National Rail Enquiries** (☎08457 484950; www.national rail.co.uk) or the **Trainline** (☎0870 010 1296; www.the trainline.com).

» Travelling off-peak and booking in advance gets substantial discounts on standard anytime fares.

» There are three ticket categories – advance and off-peak tickets are the cheapest, but are valid only on the date and time specified on the ticket. Anytime tickets are more expensive but allow travel on any train on any date.

» If you're booking a return, check the price for two single tickets – it often works out cheaper.

» Railcards entitle you to one-third off standard fares and are available for under 25s, families, over 60s, disabled travellers and HM Forces members.

Rail Passes

Rail Rover tickets are worth considering if you're visiting the Lakes along with other areas of northern England. These tickets are valid from 8.45am Monday to Friday, and anytime on Saturday and Sunday on any of northern England's train services. They must be purchased in advance direct from train stations or Northern Rail.

North West Rover (adult/child £60/30) Allows four days' travel in eight throughout Northwest England. A seven-day Rover costs £74/37.

North Country Rover (adult/child £76/38) Covers coast-to-coast travel anywhere north of Leeds/Preston and south of Carlisle/Newcastle. Four days' travel in eight.

Walking

Long-distance trails that wind their way across the Cumbrian fells include the following:

Allerdale Ramble 54 miles via Borrowdale, Keswick, Skiddaw, Cockermouth and the Solway Firth.

Coast-to-Coast Walk (www.coast2coast.co.uk) 190 miles from St Bees Head on the Cumbrian Coast to Robin Hood's Bay, near Whitby in North Yorkshire.

Cumbria Way (www.the cumbriaway.info) 70 miles from Ulverston to Carlisle.

BIKES ON PUBLIC TRANSPORT

Transporting your bike on public transport is possible, but you'll need to plan ahead.

» **Northern Rail trains** can carry two bikes. Reservations aren't available; spaces are allocated on a first-come, first-served basis.

» **Virgin trains** can usually carry four bikes. You'll need to make a reservation on the bookings line (☎08719 774 222) or at the station when you buy your ticket.

» **First Transpennine trains** can usually carry two bikes. Reserve at the station or by phoning ☎0845 600 1674.

» **The 505 bus** from Windermere to Coniston has a rack with space for two bikes. Phone ☎01539-722143 to make a reservation, You'll need to say which bus you're catching and where. Bikes can be loaded at Windermere Station, Ambleside, Hawkshead and Coniston.

» **The AD 122 bus** will take two bikes on the bus if there's room. Call ☎01434-322022 to book a spot.

» **Boats** Ullswater 'Steamers', Windermere Cruise Boats and the Coniston Launch will all carry bikes for free when space is available.

Dales Way (www.dalesway.org
.uk) 80 miles from Bowness-
on-Windermere to Ilkley in
Yorkshire, traversing riverside
paths and disused railways.
Cumbria Coastal Way 150
miles from Silverdale to the
Scottish border.

GETTING AROUND

For general information, fares
and timetables on public
transport, contact **Traveline**
(☎0871 200 22 33; www.traveline
northeast.info).

Bicycle

Cycling is becoming an
increasingly popular way to
visit Cumbria and the Lake
District – but you're not
going to get away without
tackling some hills.

Bike-hire shops and
equipment suppliers are
readily available throughout
the region, and the excellent
website run by **Cycling
Cumbria** (www.cyclingcumbria
.co.uk) is packed with route
suggestions and general
cycling advice.

Boat

Windermere, Derwentwater,
Ullswater and Coniston all
have cruise boats which stop
at various jetties around the
lake. Most allow you to hop
off at one jetty and walk to
the next one. See the
relevant chapters for details.

In addition to its cruise
boats, Windermere also has
a ferry service that carries
cars, motorcycles, caravans
and pedestrians (you can
even take your horse if
there's room). It runs year-
round across the lake from a
jetty just south of Bowness
to Ferry House on the lake's
western shore. Note that
queues can be hideously
long, especially in summer
and on busy bank holidays.

» Row boats and motor
boats are available for hire on
most of the larger lakes.

» Some also have boating
marinas offering yachting or
windsurfing.
» There are strict speed
restrictions on all lakes
within the national park,
so powerboating and
waterskiing are not permitted.

Bus

The main bus operator in
Cumbria is **Stagecoach**
(www.stagecoachbus.com),
which runs a fairly good
bus network between the
main towns and villages –
although services are much
patchier once you get out
into the countryside.
» Most routes offer full
services from around Easter
to October, with a drastically
reduced winter timetable.
» Throughout this book,
we've given details for
summer bus timetables
only unless otherwise
indicated.
» Stagecoach publishes a
free booklet, *The Cumbria &
Lakesrider*, which contains
full timetables for its routes
and is available from tourist
offices.

» Download timetables from
Stagecoach (www.stagecoach
bus.com/northwest/timetables
.php) and **Cumbria County
Council** (www.cumbria.gov.uk
/roads-transport).

Bus Routes

Perhaps the most useful
service is the **555
(Lakeslink)** – quite possibly
the only bus service in
England to have had a book
written about it (*55 555
Walks* by Robert Swain).
The service runs between
Lancaster and Keswick via
nearly all the main Lakeland
towns, including Staveley,
Windermere, Troutbeck,
Ambleside and Grasmere; a
couple of daily buses run on
to Carlisle via Wigton (when
the bus changes number to
the 554).

Other useful bus numbers:
505 (Coniston Rambler)
Links Kendal, Windermere,
Ambleside and Coniston.
599 (Lakesrider) Open-top
bus between Bowness and
Grasmere.
X4/X5 (Trans Cumbrian)
Penrith to Workington via
Troutbeck, Keswick and
Cockermouth.
77 (Honister Rambler)
From Keswick to Buttermere
and Honister Pass.
78 (Borrowdale Rambler)
Keswick to Borrowdale
Valley.

Bus Passes

There are several bus passes
available for individual areas
of Cumbria, mainly useful if
you're only travelling within a
limited area.

Otherwise, you might as
well buy the **North West
Explorer** (adult/child/senior
£9.75/6.50/6) pass, which
gives unlimited travel on
all buses in Cumbria and
Lancashire. A family pass
covering two adults and
three children costs £19.50.
You can buy the ticket from
the driver or from bus station
ticket offices.
Carlisle Dayrider (adult
£2.60) Unlimited travel in
Carlisle.

THE CROSS-LAKES EXPERIENCE

To help cut down on summer traffic jams, the **Cross-Lakes Experience** (⊘mid-Mar–Oct) is an integrated transport service which allows you to cross from Windermere to Coniston without needing to get behind the wheel.

Windermere cruise boats operate from Bowness to Ferry House, from where the Mountain Goat minibus travels to Hill Top and Hawkshead. From Hawkshead, you can catch the X30 bus to Moor Top, Grizedale and Haverthwaite, or catch the 505 bus to High Cross, Hawkshead Hill and Coniston Water, then take a cruise boat across the lake.

The route operates up to 10 times daily from Bowness to Coniston (roughly hourly from 10am to 5pm). The only drawback is that the buses get very crowded in summer, and if they're full you'll have to wait for the next one (as you can't prebook). Cyclists should note there's only space for five bikes on the minibuses.

Current prices for a one-way fare from Bowness are as follows. Discounts are also available for return fares.

DESTINATION	ADULT	CHILD (4-15YR)	FAMILY (2 ADULTS, 3 CHILDREN)
Ferry House	£2.50	£1.50	£7.25
Hill Top	£5.25	£3.00	£14.80
Hawkshead	£6.20	£3.40	£17.50
Coniston (incl boat)	£11.00	£6.05	£30.70

For info and timetables, contact **Mountain Goat** (☑015394-45161; www.mountain-goat .com; Victoria Rd, Windermere) or ask at any tourist office.

Central Lakes Dayrider (adult/child/family £6.50/5/13) Covers Bowness, Ambleside, Grasmere, Langdale and Coniston; includes the 599, 505 and 516.

Honister/Borrowdale Dayrider (adult/child £6.50/4.75) Valid on buses 77/77A, 79 and 86 in the Borrowdale and Buttermere valleys.

Ruskin Explorer (adult/child £16.40/7.50) Includes travel on the 505, a cruise on the Coniston Launch and entry to Brantwood.

Car & Motorcycle

More than 90% of visitors end up travelling to the Lake District by car, and while it's undoubtedly convenient to have your own wheels, you might end up rueing the decision once you've spent a few days negotiating the summertime snarl-ups.

If you do bring your own car, it's worth thinking about leaving it parked at wherever you're staying and travelling around by bus.

Driving-tour itineraries are described in all On the Road chapters.

Hire

Expect to pay between £30 and £50 per day for a small- to medium-sized car, or between £220 and £250 a week. You'll find rental offices for most of the big firms in Carlisle.

For something more memorable, **Lakes & Dales** (☑01768-879091; www.lakes anddales.co.uk) hires classic soft-top cars, including Austin Healeys, Morgans and Triumphs, while **Rainbow Camper Hire** (☑017687-80413; www.vwcamperhire.net; Keswick) lets you live out the hippie dream with its vintage VW camper vans.

Parking

Parking in the Lakes can be a pain. On busy summer mornings practically all the major car parks (especially the ones near well-known trailheads) are bumper-to-bumper by around 9am.

» Expect to pay around £2 to £3 for an hour's stay, and anything upwards of £5 to £8 for all-day stays.

» Make sure there are no valuables on display in your car, and if you want to be extra careful, you might consider removing your car stereo.

» National Trust members can park at NT car parks for free (assuming there's a space).

» To park on the street in many Cumbrian towns, you need a timed parking disc (available from shops, tourist offices, post offices and some B&Bs).

» Parking is limited to one or two hours. Turn the disc dial to your arrival time, put it on your dashboard, and make sure you don't overstay the allotted time.

Road Rules

All EU (and most other international) driving licences are valid in England for up to 12 months, but if you're bringing your car from overseas you will require (at least) third-party insurance.

The legal blood-alcohol limit is 80mg per 100ml (0.08%), and if you're caught over the limit you could face a heavy fine and/ or prosecution.

Key road rules:

» drive on the left
» always wear seatbelts
» wear crash helmets on motorcycles
» give way to the right at junctions and roundabouts
» use the left-hand lane unless overtaking
» don't use mobile phones or other devices while at the wheel
» children up to three years old must always travel in an appropriate child seat.

Unless otherwise indicated, speed limits are as follows:

» 30mph in towns and built-up areas
» 60mph on main roads and single carriageways
» 70mph on dual carriageways and motorways.

Hitching

Hitching is possible, although you might find yourself facing some lengthy waits – British drivers are much less likely to stop to pick up hitchers than they once were. Travellers (especially solo females) should understand that they're taking a small but potentially serious risk, and we don't recommend it.

If you decide to go by thumb, remember that hitching on British motorways is illegal – so you'll have to try your luck at service stations or dual carriageway lay-bys.

Taxi

Taxis can be a useful way of covering short distances, especially if you're in a small group, but if you're travelling any further than 10 miles or so, it quickly starts to become an expensive option. Unlike in the cities, you won't usually be able to flag down a cab in Cumbria; you'll either have to find a taxi rank (such as the ones at most train stations), or contact a local cab company.

Tours

If you've got a limited time to spend in the park, taking an organised tour can be a great way of cramming in the sights. Most are conducted in small minibuses or coaches, but they pack a lot in, so there won't be much time for dawdling.

There's usually a minimum person limit. Admission charges to sights aren't always included – ask before you book.

Lake District Tours (☑015395 52106; www .lakedistricttours.co.uk) Small family-run operator with options including a Beatrix Potter Tour (adult/child £33.50/10.50) and a photography tour (£51/38) to scenic viewpoints such as Ashness Bridge, Castlerigg Stone Circle and Thirlmere.

Lakes Supertours (☑015394-42751; www.lakes -supertours.co.uk) Full-day minibus trips, including a Potter and Wordsworth tour (adult/child £32/21) and a western lakes trip (adult/ child £34/22) including Hardknott Pass and Duddon Valley.

Mountain Goat (☑015394-45161; www.mountain-goat .com) One of the oldest operators. Options include a full-day Ten Lakes Tour (adult/child £36/26), a full-day Wrynose and Hardknott trip (£36/26), and a half-day Potter tour (£26/21) to Tarn Hows, Hawkshead and Yewdale.

Touchstone Tours (☑017687-79599; www .touchstonetours.co.uk) Another reliable minibus operator, operating similar trips to Mountain Goat.

Train

Apart from the Kendal to Windermere branch line and the vintage railway services, only the Cumbrian Coast is accessible by train.

FIVE SCENIC TRAIN TRIPS

» **Settle–Carlisle Railway** (p172) One of the great railway classics, traversing 72 miles of track, 20 viaducts and 14 tunnels scattered across the Yorkshire Dales and eastern Cumbria.

» **South Tynedale Railway** (p181) Wonderful cross-country railway that cuts through the bleakly beautiful landscapes of the North Pennines.

» **Lakeside and Haverthwaite Railway** (p53) Vintage steam service from Haverthwaite to Lakeside on the shores of Windermere.

» **Ravenglass and Eskdale Railway** (p100) Originally built to ferry iron ore, and now arguably the ultimate toy train set.

» **Threlkeld Mining Museum** (p117) Catch a rattling transport train into one of the largest and oldest Lakeland quarries.

There are a couple of rail passes for specific lines; otherwise, the Lakes Day Ranger (see the boxed text, p223) offers the best value.

Cumbria Round Robin (adult/child/family £26/13/17.15) Valid for a circular trip in either direction between Carlisle, Oxenholme, Lancaster, Grange-over-Sands, Barrow-in-Furness, Whitehaven and Carlisle.

Cumbrian Coast Day Ranger (adult/child/family £17/8.50/11.20) Buys a day's travel between all stations along the Cumbrian Coast line.

Glossary

beck – river or stream, from Old Norse *bekkr*

butty – slang for sandwich

char – type of fish found in some Cumbrian lakes, related to the salmon

cob rustic building material, usually made from compacted earth, clay and straw

copse – small area of woodland

crag outcrop of rock, derived from the Celtic word *creic*, meaning rock

Cumberland sausage – traditional Cumbrian coiled sausage made of pork

dale – valley, from Old Norse *dalr*

damson – a soft fruit related to the plum, used to make jams, chutneys and gin

drystone wall a traditional form of wall built without the use of mortar

fell – mountain, from Old Norse *fjall*

force – waterfall, from Old Norse *fors*

ghyll – ravine, from Old Norse *gil*

grange – old dialect word for farm

gurn – to pull a face

heaf – sheep's territory, customarily passed down from ewe to lamb

Herdwick – native Lakeland sheep, distinguished by its black fleece and white face

la'al – Cumbrian word for little, as in La'al Ratty

mere – a pond or lake

mintcake – hard Cumbrian sweet made of boiled sugar, traditionally made in Kendal

motte-and-bailey – early form of castle, usually consisting of a keep or fort on a raised hill

Roundhead – alternative word for Parliamentarian during the English Civil War

scree – broken rock and gravel found on steep mountain sides

tallow – animal fat, used to make candles

tarn – mountain lake

tatie – potato

thwaite – Old Norse word for clearing

vendace – endangered species of whitefish native to the Lake District and parts of Scotland

behind the scenes

SEND US YOUR FEEDBACK

We love to hear from travellers – your comments keep us on our toes and help make our books better. Our well-travelled team reads every word on what you loved or loathed about this book. Although we cannot reply individually to postal submissions, we always guarantee that your feedback goes straight to the appropriate authors, in time for the next edition. Each person who sends us information is thanked in the next edition – and the most useful submissions are rewarded with a free book.

Visit **lonelyplanet.com/contact** to submit your updates and suggestions or to ask for help. Our award-winning website also features inspirational travel stories, news and discussions.

Note: We may edit, reproduce and incorporate your comments in Lonely Planet products such as guidebooks, websites and digital products, so let us know if you don't want your comments reproduced or your name acknowledged. For a copy of our privacy policy visit lonelyplanet.com/privacy.

OUR READERS

Many thanks to the travellers who used the last edition and wrote to us with helpful hints, useful advice and interesting anecdotes:

B Marje Beckett **N** Kate Nicholson **W** Lorayne Woodend

AUTHOR THANKS

Oliver Berry

A big thanks to everyone who helped me on this book, especially the dedicated park workers, tourist office staff, publicans, brewers, jam-makers, chefs, hikers, bikers and volunteers whom I met along the way. Back home, thanks to Susie, Mo and Gracie, to TSP, and to the Hobo for constant companionship on the road. Thanks to my twin CEs Glenn van der Knijff and Katie O'Connell, to the map-makers and editors in Melbourne, and anyone else I've criminally overlooked here.

ACKNOWLEDGMENTS

Climate map data adapted from Peel MC, Finlayson BL & McMahon TA (2007) 'Updated World Map of the Köppen-Geiger Climate Classification', *Hydrology and Earth System Sciences*, 11, 163344.

Cover photograph: Small boat at dawn by Wastwater, Cumbria. George Kavanagh/ Getty ©. Many of the images in this guide are available for licensing from Lonely Planet Images: www.lonelyplanetimages.com.

THIS BOOK

This 2nd edition of Lonely Planet's *Lake District* guidebook was researched and written by Oliver Berry. The previous edition was also written by Oliver Berry. This guidebook was commissioned in Lonely Planet's London office, laid out by Cambridge Publishing Management, UK, and produced by the following:

Commissioning Editors Katie O'Connell, Glenn van der Knijff

Coordinating Editors Catherine Burch, Andrea Dobbin

Coordinating Cartographer Jacqueline Nguyen

Coordinating Layout Designer Paul Queripel

Managing Editors Helen Christinis, Brigitte Ellemor

Senior Editor Susan Paterson

Managing Cartographers Adrian Persoglia, Amanda Sierp

Managing Layout Designer Jane Hart

Assisting Editors Justin Flynn, Chris Girdler, Kathryn Glendenning, Ceinwen Sinclair

Assisting Cartographers Ildiko Bogdanovits, Jennifer Johnston, Jolyon Philcox

Cover Research Naomi Parker

Internal Image Research Aude Vauconsant

Indexer Amanda Jones

Thanks to Ryan Evans, Trent Paton, Gerard Walker

index

how to use this book

These symbols will help you find the listings you want:

- ⊙ Sights
- 🏄 Beaches
- 🏃 Activities
- 🎓 Courses
- 👉 Tours
- 🎊 Festivals & Events
- 🛏 Sleeping
- 🍴 Eating
- 🍷 Drinking
- ☆ Entertainment
- 🛍 Shopping
- ℹ Information/Transport

These symbols give you the vital information for each listing:

- 📞 Telephone Numbers
- ⊙ Opening Hours
- Ⓟ Parking
- ⊜ Nonsmoking
- ❄ Air-Conditioning
- @ Internet Access
- 📶 Wi-Fi Access
- 🏊 Swimming Pool
- 🥗 Vegetarian Selection
- 📋 English-Language Menu
- 👪 Family-Friendly
- 🐾 Pet-Friendly
- 🚌 Bus
- ⛴ Ferry
- Ⓜ Metro
- Ⓢ Subway
- ⊖ London Tube
- 🚊 Tram
- 🚉 Train

Reviews are organised by author preference.

Map Legend

Sights
- 🏖 Beach
- 🛕 Buddhist
- 🏰 Castle
- ✝ Christian
- 🕉 Hindu
- ☪ Islamic
- ✡ Jewish
- ⓞ Monument
- 🏛 Museum/Gallery
- 🏚 Ruin
- 🍇 Winery/Vineyard
- 🐾 Zoo
- ⊙ Other Sight

Activities, Courses & Tours
- 🤿 Diving/Snorkelling
- 🛶 Canoeing/Kayaking
- 🎿 Skiing
- 🏄 Surfing
- 🏊 Swimming/Pool
- 🚶 Walking
- 🏄 Windsurfing
- ⊕ Other Activity/Course/Tour

Sleeping
- 🛏 Sleeping
- ⛺ Camping

Eating
- ✖ Eating

Drinking
- ☕ Drinking
- ☕ Cafe

Entertainment
- ☆ Entertainment

Shopping
- 🛍 Shopping

Information
- ✉ Post Office
- ℹ Tourist Information

Transport
- ✈ Airport
- ⊗ Border Crossing
- 🚌 Bus
- ⊕ Cable Car/Funicular
- 🚲 Cycling
- ⛴ Ferry
- Ⓜ Metro
- 🚝 Monorail
- Ⓟ Parking
- Ⓢ S-Bahn
- 🚕 Taxi
- 🚉 Train/Railway
- 🚊 Tram
- ⊖ Tube Station
- Ⓤ U-Bahn
- • Other Transport

Routes
- Tollway
- Freeway
- Primary
- Secondary
- Tertiary
- Lane
- Unsealed Road
- Plaza/Mall
- Steps
- ⊨ ⊐ Tunnel
- Pedestrian Overpass
- Walking Tour
- Walking Tour Detour
- Path

Boundaries
- — ·· International
- State/Province
- — – Disputed
- Regional/Suburb
- Marine Park
- Cliff
- Wall

Population
- 🔴 Capital (National)
- ◉ Capital (State/Province)
- ● City/Large Town
- ● Town/Village

Geographic
- 🏠 Hut/Shelter
- 🗼 Lighthouse
- 👁 Lookout
- ▲ Mountain/Volcano
- 🌴 Oasis
- 🌳 Park
-)(Pass
- 🏕 Picnic Area
- 💧 Waterfall

Hydrography
- River/Creek
- Intermittent River
- Swamp/Mangrove
- Reef
- Canal
- Water
- Dry/Salt/Intermittent Lake
- Glacier

Areas
- Beach/Desert
- + + + Cemetery (Christian)
- × × × Cemetery (Other)
- Park/Forest
- Sportsground
- Sight (Building)
- Top Sight (Building)

OUR STORY

A beat-up old car, a few dollars in the pocket and a sense of adventure. In 1972 that's all Tony and Maureen Wheeler needed for the trip of a lifetime – across Europe and Asia overland to Australia. It took several months, and at the end – broke but inspired – they sat at their kitchen table writing and stapling together their first travel guide, *Across Asia on the Cheap*. Within a week they'd sold 1500 copies. Lonely Planet was born.

Today, Lonely Planet has offices in Melbourne, London and Oakland, with more than 600 staff and writers. We share Tony's belief that 'a great guidebook should do three things: inform, educate and amuse'.

OUR WRITERS

Oliver Berry

Oliver's trekked through many of the world's mountain ranges, but he still finds himself returning to the fells of the Lake District year after year. He hasn't quite managed to conquer all the Wainwrights just yet, but he's well on his way, and managed to bag a few more while researching this book. He's written regularly for Lonely Planet on many guidebooks, including recent editions of *Devon, Cornwall & Southwest England* and *Great Britain*. He also writes regularly for several publications including *Lonely Planet Magazine*. When he's not out on the road or up a mountain, he can probably be found on the beaches of his home county in Cornwall, UK. You can see his latest work at www.oliverberry.com.

Read more about Oliver at:
lonelyplanet.com/members/oliverberry

Published by Lonely Planet Publications Pty Ltd
ABN 36 005 607 983
2nd edition – March 2012
ISBN 978 1 74179 739 8
© Lonely Planet 2012 Photographs © as indicated 2012
10 9 8 7 6 5 4 3 2 1
Printed in China